AF553852

FACETS OF INDIAN CULTURE

Facets of Indian Culture

Papers Presented in the International Conference
The Growth and Development of Indian Culture

edited by

NALINI RAO

ADITYA PRAKASHAN, NEW DELHI
and
S.R. RAO MEMORIAL FOUNDATION FOR INDIAN
ARCHAEOLOGY, ART AND CULTURE

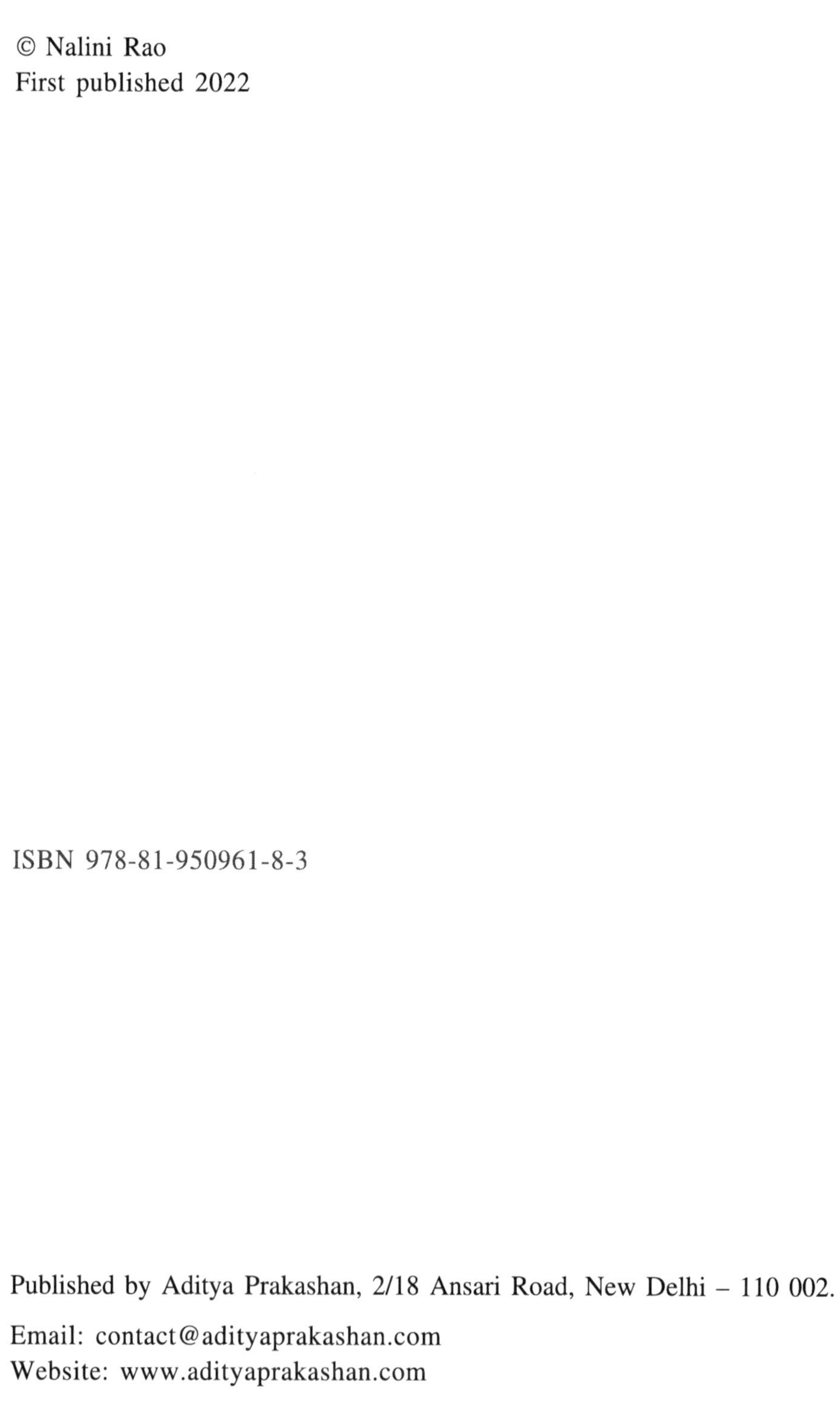

First published 2022

ISBN 978-81-950961-8-3

Published by Aditya Prakashan, 2/18 Ansari Road, New Delhi – 110 002.

Email: contact@adityaprakashan.com
Website: www.adityaprakashan.com

Printed at Thomson Press (India) Ltd.

Contents

II. Philosophy, Religion and Texts

III. History and Ideas

Preface

Dr. S.R. Rao Memorial Foundation for Indian Archaeology, Art and Culture held an International Conference on The Growth and Development of Indian Culture: Historical and Literary Perspectives (Prehistoric Period–12th C CE) 29th June–1st July 2018. Bengaluru, India. Academic Sessions took place at Executive Development Center, Institute of Hotel Management, SJP Campus, Bengaluru. www.srraofoundation.org

Some of the papers have been incorporated here although there were many more that were read by scholars in their respective areas of expertise. The Conference Committee had received 81 abstracts among which 72 were accepted. A total of 67 papers were read by scholars in (53 in English, and 14 papers in Kannada) by 72 participants (some having two participants). Discussions by 19 chairs of various sessions were stimulating. An addition of about 31 outside scholars (i.e., non-participants) attended on June 30 and about 12 outside scholars on July 1. Among the 67 presenters, 14 were from abroad. The Sessions were divided into Indian Archaeology, Language and Literature, Ancient Texts and Concepts, Ideas and Practices, Science and Heritage, Indian Art and Society, Text Books in USA and Interpretations, Art, Crafts and Society, Ancient Goddesses, Buddhism and Jainism, Archaeology and Science, Philosophy and Religion, historical methodology, Indian Archaeology and History, Discourse on Women and Indian History, Indian Art and Visual Culture. A unique aspect of the International conference was the session in Kannada in which eminent Kannada scholars chaired the sessions.

The keynote address was delivered by Dr. Arvind Jamkhedkar on the The Concept and Development of Temples and Chaityagrihas of South and Southeast Asia during the inauguration. The S.R. Rao Foundation Annual Memorial Lecture was delivered by Dr. Mani on Excavations at Kunal. S.N. Sridhar, from SUNY was the moderator for the whole day. The inauguration was held at the Mythic Society and an exhibition on Indian Archaeology was curated by Dr. K.P. Poonacha. In addition, an art exhibition on Rabindranath Tagore was installed by Indira Gandhi Center for the Arts, and a cultural program was the final highlight. The Conference was a big success and the participants presented excellent papers. Some of the statements made by participants: "I would like to thank you for the most wonderful conference." "The two day paper presentations in S.R. Rao international conference was an eye opener as to the interest people have in varied subjects and the passion with which they pursue them. For me it was an exhilarating and enlightening experience. I was also awed and nervous to be presenting my paper in front of such erudite scholars on such a prestigious platform."

Some other remarks by participants "Thank you very much for the opening you have given to many of us who are just budding researchers. The conference has given me the incentive and encouragement to strive towards excellence in my chosen field." "I could not thank all of you in the Foundation personally. Please do accept and pass on to everyone else......, my sincere thanks you for the opportunity to present my work, as well as for all the hard labor that has gone into making the event a success. Particularly so, when it is a very small group of people." "The conference had an overwhelming success. Hearty congratulations to your tremendous efforts."

Acknowledgements

The Board Members of the Dr. S.R. Rao Memorial Foundation for Indian Archaeology, Art and Culture are grateful to the Co-sponsors for their immense help in making the conference a success. It is particularly grateful to Indian Council of Historical Research, and National Museum Institute, New Delhi, for their generous financial help. The Mythic Society was the host for the inaugural event and the foundation is indebted to the organization for its assistance in various ways. Other organizations that we would like to thank are Soka University of America (CA, USA), Dharma Civilization Foundation, (USA), and Taksha Institute (USA) and IGNCA that organized the Art Exhibition on the works of Rabindranath Tagore.

We are thankful to the following scholars who read excellent papers in the conference: S. Kalyanraman, Arjun Rao, S.N. Sridhar, Bharat Gupt, Alka Pande, Anupama Jayasimha, Swaminathan Venkararaman, Gomadi Gowda, Namrata Rathore Mohanta, Dessislava Vendova, Vinay Kumar, Udaya Kumar, Sridhar Melkote, Durga T.K., Diya Mukherjee, Tiatoshi Jamir, Chandra R., Suvrata Vinod, Rekha Rao, Garima Kaushik, Gautam Jantakal, Sanket Purnanand, Hari D. Kandadai and Hema DK., Naval Krishna, Sarvamangala, Mohak Gosavi. Papers in Kannada were read by Devarakonda Reddy on Restoration of Lakshmeshwara Temple Complex, Venkateshaiah on Restoration and Conservation of Ancient Monuments, Anitha H.C on Tanjore Paintings, Aruna K.R. on Prakrit and Apabhrahmsha Literature in 10th C, G.V. Kallapura on Mayamata, Krishna Murthy on a Unique Buddhist Chaitya Complex at Rajaghatta, Dr. Nalini Venkatesh on Rattamatha of Arhaddasa, V. Sandhya on Chavundraya's Lokoparam, K.B. Shivatarak on Recent Excavations in Karnataka, Srikantam Nagendra Shastsry on Musical Terminologies in Kannada Poetry, S.V. Sujatha on Female characters in Adipurana of Pampa, Parimala Chittor on Manasollasa of Someshwara, M.N. Prabhakar on Karnataka Architecture. The Foundation is appreciative of

Nalini Venkatesh and Meena Rao for their efforts to put together the papers in Kannada. The Foundation is grateful to Aditya for publishing this book.

Finally, but not the least, I express my gratitude to all the Board Members of the Foundation: Dr. K.P. Poonacha, Vice Chairman; Dr. Choodamani Nandagopal, Secretary; Dr. Sundara Adiga, Head of Advisory Board, S. Gopal Rao, Managing Trustee; Meena Rao, Treasurer for their dedication and service.

Nalini Rao
Chairperson, S.R. Rao Memorial Foundation

Introduction

Facets of Indian Culture is a compendium of research papers read at the International Conference on The Growth and Development of Indian Culture: Dr. S.R. Rao Memorial Foundation for Indian Archaeology, Art and Culture http://www.srraofoundation.org/international-conference.html. The aim of the conference was to bring together researchers and scholars from abroad and within India, to exchange and share their recent research findings and to stimulate discussion about the interactive growth and development of Indian culture from early times to twelfth century CE. Its principal objective is to trace the trajectories of its development and the dynamic interplay of various forces such as intellectual ideas, historical events, economic influences and artistic representations.

The theme of the conference pertained to the interaction between various cultural traditions and local influences that have inspired the growth of Indian culture, and its self-definition. Scholars have agreed that over centuries, ancient and early medieval Indian culture has been re-framed and re-interpreted which has posed challenges to scholars to re-discover on the basis of historical evidences its complex system of traditions, networks, and organizations. The ancient history of communities in India is particularly challenging, and the leadership of historians, archaeologists, and literary scholars can help in providing insight into their tangible and intangible heritage. A multi-disciplinary approach in the conference provided new insights into ideas and practices that have stimulated its growth and development as a cultural process and a way of life.

Facets of Indian Culture does not include all the papers read, but provides a glimpse at the quality and rigor of research by the scholars. They have been divided into four overlapping sections: Archaeology and Science, Philosophy and Texts, History and Ideas, Arts and Historical Method. The papers have not been edited either for uniformity of diacritics, notes or references and the content has not been changed.

Dr. S.R. Rao Memorial Foundation for Indian Archaeology, Art and Culture

www.srraofoundation.org

The Memorial Foundation is a non-political, public educational and charitable Trust inspired by the vision of Dr. S.R. Rao, archaeologist and emeritus scientist, whose mission was to promote the study and research of archaeology, history, art and culture of India. The goals of the Foundation have arisen out of a concern for the neglect of cultural values in the education of the future generation and the loss of interest in India's past heritage. The Foundation aims to promote dissemination of historical/cultural knowledge by the production of books, videos, interactive websites on archaeological sites, educational programs for schools, and on-site workshops. It hopes to provide an authentic interpretation of indigenous Indian culture by incorporating scientific research and an accurate re-interpretation of Indian history, philosophy, archaeology and art. Finally, the Foundation aims to support other governmental organizations for preservation of archaeological sites.

The S.R. Rao Memorial Foundation for Indian Archaeology, Art and Culture has been active since 2014 and has published books and organized seminars. The Nehru Memorial Museum and Library has housed some of Dr. Rao's original documents. A Memorial Foundation Lecture has been instituted by the Foundation and the First Memorial Lecture was delivered by Dr. Bisht on Indian Archaeology in New Delhi, 2014. Memorial lectures have been delivered by Dr. Dhavlikar (2015), Dr. A.V. Narasimha Murthy (2016) and Dr. A. Sundara (2017). A Colloquium on Heritage Tourism and Historical Preservation was held on 25th July, 2015 which discussed the challenges of Heritage Tourism in India. The Foundation has been carrying on the legacy of Dr. S.R. Rao and hopes to serve the cause of education and an authentic interpretation of Indian history cultural heritage with the help of all interested scholars, students and public.

I. Archaeology and Science

Buddhism in Karnataka: Excavations at Sannati and Kanaganahalli

K.P. Poonacha

Abstract

The archaeological excavations conducted at Kanaganahalli in the Gulbarga District in Karnataka, between 1991–1999 has revealed the existence of a large Buddhist settlement that existed during the Hinayana phase of Buddhism in 1st C BCE and flourished till the Mahayana priod of 3rd C CE. The discovery of the major rock edicts of Mauryan emperor Aśoka establishes that this region was part of the Mauryan empire during the time of Aśoka and it appears that a urban settlement had been in place prior to the influence of Buddhism. I contend that people in this region of Karnataka accepted Buddhist creed even during the pre-Aśokan times which got accentuated after Aśoka became a follower of this creed. This paper briefly examines the architectural remains, as well as few sculptures, particularly the royal ones, and throws light on the spread of Buddhism and its importance.

The archaeological vestiges in the early historic sites are usually identified with "well laid brick built cities, fortification using mud and burnt bricks, coinage, intense trade and commerce, writing (from 3rd Century BCE onwards) and literature."[1] During this period it is well known that Asoka is said to have enlarged and constructed 84000[2] Buddhist Stupas all over his kingdom. A large number of Buddhist sites have been reported from Andhra Pradesh and to a lesser extent in the remaining states of Karnataka, Tamilnadu and Kerala. Excavations conducted in some important early historic sites associated with

[1] A. Ghosh (ed.), *An Encyclpaedia of Indian Archaeology* (ed.), New Delhi, 1989, vol.I, p.131.

[2] E. Hultzsch, *Inscriptions of Aśoka, C II*, vol.I, New Delhi, 1991, Indian reprint, p.xiii.

Buddhism in Karnataka viz., Brahmagiri,[3] Banavasi,[4] Vadagaon-Madhavpur[5] and Sannati[6] have revealed cultural artefacts attributed to the Maurya, Chutu and Satavahana levels datable to 3rd C BCE to 3rd century CE. Buddhism declined in Karnataka from 4th century CE onwards and sporadic Buddhist remains are reported from Haigunda (4–5th C CE),[7] Rajaghatta (5th C CE),[8] Aihole (6th C CE),[9] Dambal (10th C CE).[10] For a short-period Tantric Vajrayana Buddhism flourished in some pockets such as Kadri (10–11th C CE)[11] in the coastal belt of Karnataka and subsequently vanished from the scene. The previous and the present field works at sites such as Sannati (Ranamandala) Hurasagundgi, and Kanaganahalli (in the Bhima valley) have provided significant information pertaining to the general cultural ramifications in the area. Sannati (Latl 6°49'40"N; Long 76°54'30"E), attracted the attention of scholars ever since Kapatral Krishna Rao[12] reported the important archaeological vestiges in 1954. Later Seshadri[13] (1965), Desai[14] (1968), Nagaraja Rao[15] (1978 & 1985), Sarma[16] (1989), Paddayya[17] (1991) reported on art, numismatics, epigraphy and prehistory aspects of the site. However the chance discovery of the major rock edicts XII, XIV

[3] R.E.M. Wheeler, "Brahmagiri and Chandravalli: Megalithic and other cultures", *Ancient India*, no.4, Delhi, 1948.

[4] A.V. Narasimha Murthy & others, *Excavations At Banavasi*, Mysore, 1997, pp.71–77.

[5] A. Sundara, Two Thousand year old Town and its Architecture in Vadagaon Madhavpur in M.S. Nagaraja Rao (ed.), Madhu, Delhi, 1990.

[6] M. Seshadri, Buddhist Monuments at Sannati, *Quarterly Journal of Mythic Society* (QJMS), vol.LV–I, nos.1–4, Bangalore, 1965, pp.35–37.

[7] A. Sundara, "Ittichina Kelavu Puratatva Sodhagalu" (Kannada), *Karnataka Bharati*, vol.8, no.2, Dharwar, 1981, pp.13–14.

[8] A Buddhist site recently excavated by Mysore university.

[9] Nagaraju, S., Vestiges of Buddhist Art, in *MARG* (Heritage of Karnataka), ed. by Sarayu Doshi, Bombay, 1982, pp.25–34.

[10] Ibid., p.33.

[11] Ibid., pp.30–32.

[12] Kapatral Krishna Rao, Sri Chandala Parameswari, *Karnataka Samskrutiya Samshodane* (a collection of articles), Usha Sahitya Male, Mysore, 1970, pp.257–261.

[13] M. Seshadri, op. cit., pp.35–36.

[14] P.B. Desai, A New Buddhist Center, in *The Journal of Karnataka University— Social Sciences*, vol.IV, pp.3–8.

[15] M.S. Nagaraja Rao, *Progress of Archaeology in Karnataka*, 1956–1972, Mysore, 1978, pp.29, 35–36.

[16] Sarma, I.K., R.V. Siva Sarma and J. Varaprasada Rao, Rock Edicts of Aśōka from Sannati, Chitapur Taluk, Gulbarga District (Karnataka), in *Indian Museum Bulletin*, New Delhi, 1989, pp.7–15.

[17] Paddayya, K., Early Historical Localities and a Mesolithic site at Sannathi, in A.V.N. Murthy and I.K. Sarma (eds), *Sri Rāmachandrikā, Prof. Oruganti Ramachandriya Festschrift*, vol.I, Delhi 1993, pp.1–10.

and separate rock edicts I & II (partially available) of Mauryan emperor Aśoka (Fig.1) in the precincts of Chandralamba[18] temple located at the

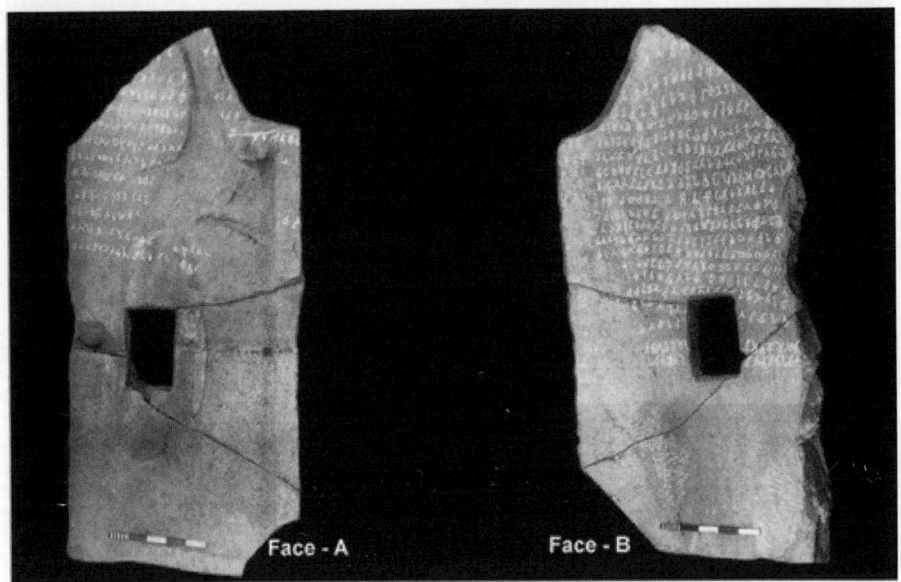

Fig.1. Remains of Major Rock-Edicts of Aśoka.

outskirts of Sannati village firmly established the fact that Sannati was part of the Mauryan empire during the time of Aśoka and it appears that already a urban settlement had been in place. I contend that people in this region of Karnataka accepted Buddhist creed even during the pre-Aśokan times which got accentuated after Aśoka became a follower of this creed. There appears to have been brisk trade activity involving iron, gold, lapidary between the traders of Mauryan and Andhra-Karnataka region particularly in the lower Krishna and in the Tungabhadra valley. This paper briefly examines the architectural remains, as well as few sculptures, particularly the royal ones, and throws light on the spread of Buddhism and its importance.[19]

The excavations carried out by the Directorate of Archaeology and Museums, Mysore, in the southwest corner of the Raṇamaṇḍala[20] area attest the intense structural activity of early historic period in this site. The place-name "Kanaganahalli", literally meaning the 'village of Kanaka', appears to have direct association with Kanakamuni—one of

[18] Kapatral Krishna Rao, Sri Chandala Parameswari, *Karnataka Samskrutiya Samshodane* (a collection of articles), Usha Sahitya Male, Mysore, 1970, pp.257–261.

[19] K.P. Poonacha, *Excavations at Kananganahalli (Sannati)*, ASI, New Delhi, 2011.

[20] A. Sundara, Excavations at Sannati, 1986–1987, *Puratattva*, no.17, 1987, p.226.

the *Mānushi* Buddhas. It is interesting to note that the Nigali Sagar[21] pillar inscription of Emperor Aka records that *Dēvanāmpiya Piyadasi* (Aśoka) enlarged the *stūpa* of the *Buddha Kōnākamāna* to twice its original size in his 14th regnal year. And when he revisited the site after his 20th year of coronation he erected an inscribed pillar specifically in honour of Konagamuni, the former Buddha. An inscription at Bhārhut refers to him as *Bhagavatō Konigamēna* and there is also a depiction of him in the form of a totemic tree, personal-*Bōdhi* tree (*Udumbara—Ficus glomerata*) in sculptural art in the circular medallion of the ninth pillar (*tabha*) in the southeastern quadrant.

There are at least two epigraphical references to Kanakamuni within the Sannati area. One of these found at Sannati, begins with an invocation to Lord Kanakamuni as *Jayati Bhagavam Kanakasa* (Line 1). The other, found in the *stūpa* site itself, is engraved on a mutilated seated image of Lord Buddha and reads—*Sidham bhagavā samasabudho Konāgamuni*. This form of Buddha is known as Konāgamāna and Konigamēna by the southern Buddhists and as Kanakamuni, and Konakamuni etc., by the northern ones.[22] In the light of the above, in the etymological context, the retention of letter *ga* in the toponym Kanaganahalli is noteworthy and the present nomenclature of the village therefore appears to be a derivative after Kanakamuni. It is pertinent to note here that the hamlet Kanaganahalli was the north-eastern suburb of greater Sannati, at the nucleus of which the Mauryas and the Sātavāhanas had their fortified township, presently identified as Raṇamaṇḍala, the periphery of which was dotted with many *stūpas* and monasteries at north, northeast and east respectively at Anegutti, Benagutti, Kanaganahalli and Hurasgundgi.

Excavations at Kanaganahalli

Prior excavations had been conducted here, but in between 1996–1998 & 2006–2007 regular horizontal excavation was taken up in the *stūpa* mound with the objectives of (i) exposing the overall structural complex along with the accessory units in their extant plan and elevations, (ii) understanding the different structural phases in a chronological framework along with the construction methodology adopted, and (iii) to correlate the already known epigraphical, numismatic and cultural material from the explorations and excavations in the fortified township of *Raṇamaṇḍala* and other localities of greater Sannati. The excavation

[21] E. Hultzsch, op.cit., p.165.

[22] A. Cunningham, op.cit., p.132.

carried out in the trenches, each of 10 m square covering the entire mound and its periphery has laid bare a systematically and meticulously built *stūpa* complex. At the centre of the site is a much-disturbed structure of the *mahāchaitya* (*stūpa*) (Fig.2), which is surrounded by

Fig.2. Excavated *stūpa* at Kanaganahalli (Sannati).

10 small and big brick and limestone veneered votive *stūpas,* square platforms for the worship of *Buddhapādas* and a large brick-built monastery, rectangular on plan, along the northern periphery of the complex.

The main *stūpa* is oriented at about 15° northwest from the true north-south axis. The extant damaged *stūpa* built in limestone standing to a height of nearly 3 m has in its composition, a completely disturbed dome, part of upper drum with its massive sculptured veneering supported by collars at base, an upper non-functional circumambulatory passage, a base (*vēdikā*), a 3.25 m wide circumambulatory passage—all enclosed by a 2.50 m tall railing pierced with entrances at north, south, east and west and entrance door sill, moonstone (*chandraśilā*) complete the composition. Four disturbed *āyaka* platforms abutting the lower drum, at cardinal directions opposite to the entrances, a feature commonly seen in the *stūpa* architecture of the lower Krishna valley, have also been exposed. However the placing of colossal statues of standing Buddha on separate pedestals veneered with cornices along the periphery with sculptured friezes depicting the great events in the life of the Lord Buddha on the southern and western *āyaka* platforms is a unique feature of the site. A rare aspect and a deviation from the well-known contemporary Buddhist centres in lower Krishna valley, is the positioning of as many as eight *Mānushi* Buddhas over the circumambulatory passage against unsculpted lower drum panels in the intra-cardinal directions of the *stūpa*. However, one of the seated Buddha sculpture was accommodated on the eastern *āyaka* platform in addition to the four *āyaka* pillars positioned on it. Another important feature is the location of an image of *Yaksha* outside the railing, to the left of moonstone at north, south and west. The bowls of offering, cut in stone, probably placed over the head of these *Yaksha* images (*pushpavāhakās*) were also found nearby. Other remains include a circular votive stupas and a monastery complex and a stump of a pillar, recalling a Mauryan stupa.

Structural Remains

The extant *stūpa* measures roughly 26 m in diameter and 94.30 m at the railings, 74.35 m at the lower drum and nearly 68.14 m at the upper drum, in circumference respectively. Structurally, the existing remains of the *stūpa* at the top reveal, bottom portions of broken veneered slabs of the upper drum each held *in situ* by a semi circular collar resting upon a ledge of about 75 cm in width, provided at the top of the 1.20 m high lower drum and constitutes the upper circumambulatory passage. An *āyaka* platform measuring approximately 3.60 m in length and 1.25 m in width, abuts the lower drum. Around the lower drum a 3.75 m wide circumambulatory passage is provided. This passage is enclosed by a decorated railing of 1.95 m in height above the ground and the exterior face of each railing is composed of 4 lotus medallions and probably crowned by an *ushṇīsha* evident from tenons on the top of railings. Each railing is held by 4 cross bars adroned with lotus medallions. In the cardinal directions, corresponding to each *āyaka*, the railing takes an outward right-angle position to a distance of nearly 3 m. In between the distal uprights of the railing an entrance sill decorated with lotus medallions is provided which is preceded by a semicircular moonstone. The railing is slightly above the floor of the circumambulatory passage. Evidences of *Yaksha* sculptures bearing flower-bowls (*pushpavāhakā)* are encountered nearer to these entrances except the eastern entrance and thus completing the structural composition. The *āyaka* platforms appears to have been introduced by extending the brick veneering by a meter in the four cardinal directions as part of the second phase of constructional activity of the *stūpa*. This structural activity appears to be of the Phase–II, Period–II of construction since already an inner drum built in dressed limestone slabs of lesser dimensions (Period–I) has been exposed during the course of excavation. The limestone construction of the lower drum of the *stūpa* was enlarged further by encasing with brick veneering of 90 cm width which in turn was further veneered with 1.20 m high ornate and non-ornate limestone panels over which a sculptured cornice to hold the panels was hoisted which also incidentally formed part of the narrow upper circumambulatory passage.

The excavated *stūpa* was profusely decorated at the drum levels with sculptured slabs of limestone. The lower drum was also veneered with sculptured as well as plain slabs. Theme-wise, the sculpted slabs depict *chaitya* worship, *dharmachakra* adoration, panels of Muchilinda Nāga, *vṛiksha-chaitya*, *Nāga-bandha-chaitya*, depictions of popular monasteries of contemporary times, episodes like gift of Jētavana by Anāthapiṇḍika to Lord Buddha and *stūpas* with reliquaries. The lower drum slabs treated with sculptures measure 1.65 m in height, 1.22 m in width, 12–15 cm in thickness and have an upper border of 12.5 cm and a rough undressed portion of 35 cm at the bottom respectively. The sculptured portion measures 1.04 × 1.09 m. As in the upper drum slabs, in these too, the sculptor has provided an offset between the *pattikās* at front towards right measuring 35 cm and nearly 4 cm at left of the panel and induces a slight semi-circular curve in the left corner to interlock and articulate it with the immediate next panel. Non-ornate lower drum slabs were used as the backdrop, when the seated Buddha sculptures were introduced, at a later date, at the intra-cardinal directions of the *stūpa*.

The narrow passage or ledge intervening the lower and upper drum also served as cornices above the lower drum. Mentioned as *puphagahaṇi* (*pushpagrāhṇikā*—flower receptacle) in the inscriptions, these cornices are interesting architectural members which have functionally a dual purpose of (1) holding the top of the ornate/non-ornate *vēdikā* panels *in situ* and (2) to function as pseudo-upper circumambulatory passage. Each cornice member measures nearly 75 cm in length, 57.2 cm in width and has a total height of nearly 30 cm out of which a ridge of semi-hexagonal section measuring 5–6 cm in height is provided at the periphery. The peripheral chamfered facet of the ridge measuring 4 cm in width contains donatory inscriptions. The top facet of the ridge measures 5 cm and the inner facet measures 4 cm. These cornice members underneath, at the periphery, have a curved groove of nearly 6–8 cm into which the top of the lower drum slabs fits.

Each upper drum slab measures 3.30 m in height with a variable width of 1.15 to 1.30 m and an average thickness of 15 cm. The panel is divided into three registers separated by two horizontal borders (*paṭṭikā*) of 13 cm width. The first and second registers, from the top, each measuring 1.03 m in height with a border of 15 cm separating them, are sculpted in low relief to a depth of nearly 4 cm out of the total thickness of 15 cm of the entire slab. The median border is of a row of geese with lotus stalks held in their beaks (*hamsa-paṭṭikā*). Depending upon the orientation and location of the panel to be articulated, a pilaster with addorsed animal motifs is sculptured either to the left or right side of the panel. There are two panels each having pilasters on both sides and without any pilasters.

The border of 13 cm between second and third register is used for inscribing, to label the subject, name of doner or theme depicted in the panel. The lower most register measures 36.5 cm in height and depicts the three-barred railing. The border of 13 cm above this register is used for inscribing, to label the subject, name of donee or theme depicted in the panel. Below the railing panel, is a dressed unsculpted portion of nearly 26–30 cm, followed by an undressed portion of nearly 21 cm. This undressed portion is usually covered and held by a collar. The bottom edge of the massive panel is provided with 2–3 semicircular notches for manoeuvring to the desired place and safe handling at the time of construction.The pattern followed for narration on upper drum slabs is usually from the top of the panel to the bottom. Depending upon the subject, the composition of characters is seen.

Sculptures on the Stūpa

Themes depicted in these panels resolve into three categories: (i) episodes narrating the events of the life of the Master, (ii) select Jātaka stories and, (iii) portrait sculptures of Maurya, Sātavāhana rulers and other kings. The upper drum is crowned by friezes of animals, which act as a collar before the hemispherical dome rises. Generally, these slabs measure 55–57 × 90–110 × 14–16 cm in their height, width and thickness respectively. The dome of the *stūpa* is completely destroyed and as such the elevational features will have to be inferred by meticulously collating the available scattered material and circumstantial evidences. The dome slabs on an average, measure 56 cm in length, 35 cm in width and nearly 10 cm in thickness. Interestingly some of the dome slabs contain label inscription. Since many devotees, from laymen to monks and royalty, contributed for the construction of the *chaitya,* they were boldly inscribed.

The *harmikā* is lost. However, the available architectural members retrieved during the excavations show that the *harmikā* had an austere railing pattern. The finding of mutilated massive circular fragments of the umbrellas (*chhatras*) indicate that at the centre of the *harmikā*, the central shaft of the *chhatradaṇḍa* was inserted and the three umbrellas (*chhatras*) were hoisted with the larger umbrellas at the bottom and the smaller disc at the top. There are also squarish sockets nearer to the periphery, perhaps for suspending garlands and festoons. The cone at the under surface in some, is treated with lotus petals opening outwards from centre to the periphery.

After decorating the lower drum and *āyaka* platforms with ornate and non-ornate veneering slabs the pavement slabs of the circumambulatory passage have been laid. During the course of excavation, an earlier circumambulatory passage of irregular shaped thin limestone slabs was encountered at a depth of 40 cm laid parallel to the offset of the lower drum indicating the existence of an early phase of construction. This is further buttressed from the fact that almost all the uprights of the present railing rest over this earlier circumambulatory passage and some of the uprights of the first phase of construction are reused as supports at the bottom of the present railing. It is interesting to note that in the fifth phase of Period–II of construction and expansion, the architects have introduced as many as ten seated images of Buddha in the *stūpa*. Of these, while eight were located on the floor of circumambulatory passage one each was placed right on the northern and eastern *āyaka* platforms. During the course of excavation, except for the sculpture of Buddha retrieved from the northwest, rest were displaced and greatly mutilated due to the impact of the collapse of massive architectural units of superstructure. These sculptures were the exclusive contributions of sculptors and devotees hailing from *Vakāmṭaka Vishaya* (Vidarbha region of the present Maharashtra) as evident from the inscriptions found on the pedestals. As per the inscriptions these represent the eight *Mānushi* Buddhas. In the cardinal directions entrance sills are fashioned out of a monolithic block of limestone measuring 2.80 m in length, 1.37 m in width and 23 cm in thickness. Beyond the sill, in the cardinal direction, a huge monolithic slab fashioned into a semicircular moonstone is positioned.

Yaksha on the northern side was found lying slightly away from the entrance is mutilated and dislodged from its original position at the entrance facing west. However, features such as the grinning face, wide open eyes, heavy *sanghāti* tucked behind and a necklace are clearly discernible. Inspite of mutilations, the extant torso and head of this

Yaksha appear to closely resemble the much-famed Pītalkhōra *Yaksha*. At the southern side only the feet of the *yaksha* figure along with part of the pedestal measuring 50 cm in length, 40 cm in width and about 30 cm in height have been found. The *stūpa* was provided with a decorated railing, 94 m in circumference. In its heyday, the railing pillars or uprights (*tabha*) stood to a height of 2.55 m including the undressed bottom,each pillar is connected with four row of cross bars (*sūchi*) and a decorated coping (*ushṇīsha*) The four row cross bars (*sūchi*) appears to be a early feature. Depending upon the space between the mortices and the interspace between the two uprights, the size of the *sūchi* or crossbars varies. The crossbars are fashioned out of rectangular limestone slabs with elliptical cross-section so as to fit into the mortice. The exterior surface of the circular medallions are decorated with a variety of lotus floral designs as in the case of the uprights.

As many as 36 donatory inscriptions have been noticed on the inner face of the uprights, of which 14 have been found towards northwest. They range from a simple single line record of 1st–2nd century AD characters to a long three-lined inscription written lengthwise on the corner upright of western *āyaka* mentioning the donations made by a certain Sātvāhana Sramaṇa of Utarahakona during the fifth regnal year of Vasismṭhiputra Siri Sātakarṇi. Interestingly, all the inscriptions are engraved neatly and deeply almost at the eye level along the inner face.

Thus, in a nutshell, the *Mahāchaitya* represents the features of the *hinayāna* phase in its formative phase of Period I and up to phase four of Period II and suddenly transforms into a prolific *mahāyāna* site in the subsequent phase V. In its structural composition, it exhibited an austerely plain dome topped by a fairly tall umbrella within a *harmikā* resting over a sculptured upper drum which in turn rested on a circular decorated lower drum intervened by a narrow upper circumambulatory passage. *Āyaka* platforms abutting the lower drum in the cardinal directions accommodated images of Buddha, *Buddhapādas* and *āyaka* pillars and a paved circumambulatory passage, enclosed by an ornate railing.

From the excavations at Kanaganahalli, an unfathomable wealth of details pertaining to *stūpa* architecture have been laid bare. This *stūpa* is extensively embellished throughout its architectural composition, save the dome, and offers a wider perspective into the vividity of aesthetic composition, freshness in approach in a *hīnayāna* frame of Buddhism in the beginning and M*ahāyāna* depictions of a slightly later period. The sculptural depictions of the *stūpa* reflect in its first four phases the themes of Buddha worship in the form of ornate, non-ornate *stūpa*, *jātaka* tales of the previous birth of the Lord and narratives from the life of Buddha all in the *Hīnayana* symbolic forms, interspersed with the portraits of kings like Aśoka, Udayana, Māndhāta, Sōmarāta, Mahāgōvinda, Chhimukha Sātavāhana, Sātakarṇi, Mātalaka, Sundara Sātakarṇi and Puḷumāvi, etc., are at the lower drum and at upper drum.

Lower drum (Vēdikā)

The ornate *vēdikā* slabs reflect a systematic development of Kanaganahalli art with certain stylistic features of their own supported by the palaeography of the inscriptions noticed on them. Sometimes the themes and art forms of *stūpa* embellishment from Bhārhut, Sānchi, Pītalkhōra and the Deccan have also been introduced here with suitable modifications. We see a gradual metamorphosis from the cruder depictions, especially of human figures and other art motifs. This gradual change is because of the successive re-articulation that was being carried throughout in the 2nd and 3rd phases of Period–II which is equally applicable to the upper drum slabs as well. Interestingly, the aritists of one phase have assiduously followed the previous stylistic traits in the treatment of the subject as also the embellishment patterns to arrive at a homogenous rendering in the entire *stūpa*.

The articulation of the lower drum slabs and their workmanship (excluding those that were dismantled and reset or those that were replaced during renovations in the second phase) are exclusively of the first phase of the early Śātavāhana manifestations. Here the *Hīnayāna* themes revolve around the worship of the Buddha in different forms of lion, *vajrāsana* with *pāda*, horse, *stūpa*, *dharmachakra* in railing, *vṛiksha chaitya*, *buddhapāda* and *triratna*.

Theme wise, spread over the first three phases, these decorated lower drum slabs resolve into the following groups. 1. Dharmachakra depictions; 2. Stūpa and worship of relics: a) Simple plain stūpa, b) Ashṭabhāga stūpa of Rāmagrāma, c) Stūpa of relics (Dhātu chaityas), d) Evolved type stūpa (of lower Krishna valley), e) Crest relic worship (Sudhamālaya), f) Bōdhi tree-Vṛiksha Chaitya or Bōdhi maṇḍa) Worship of Vajrāsana; 3. Monastic complexes: a) Jētavana, b) Monastery; 4. Nāgas; 5. Yakshi-śri; 6. Wheel of life—Bhavachakra.

The artist in phase I and II while articulating the lower drum veneerings, has utilised a sculptured cornice referred to as pushpagahani in the inscriptions. He has used ingeniously, various decorative elements like triratna, swastika, nandipāda, stūpa models, pūrna-kalaśas, animated moving animals like beaked winged lion, buffalo, horse, deer, stag, elephant, bull, bird and human head all within a framework of garlands and railing designs. The usage of different types of floral designs at the tabha imitations is astonishing and reflects a freshness in the great skill of the artists in minute filigree work recalling the expertise of a jewel maker or an ivory carver. The narrow top ridge of these pushpagrāhis bears inscriptions and also the frontal face of some bear square and circular perforations to drain off the water. These get replaced by sculptured narrative cornices rendering the life of Buddha during the phase–III of expansion of the stūpa at āyaka platforms.

There are reliefs on the upper drum slabs: In the first and second phase of early sculptural activity of embellishing, the artists of the stūpa had an elaborate unhindered canvas for expressing their skill in carving with intense fervor (Fig.3). The themes opted by them include the

Fig.3. Birth of Buddha (upper drum slab).

previous birth (Jātaka) tales of the Lord, the major events of his life, themes associated with post mahāparinirvāṇa towards the spread of Buddhism, the people associated with such a righteous act and lastly the portraits of the Sātavāhana rulers who directly or indirectly participated in the cause of the stūpa in a total area of narration running into approximately 94.4 sqm. The men and women depicted in Kanaganahalli sculptural art fall into the category of (1) celestials,

(2) royal personalities, (3) noblemen and traders, (4) servants attending the royalty and noblemen, (5) monks and (6) common man.

Jātaka tales

The depictions of the Jātaka tales at Kanaganahalli range from monoscenic to polyscenic. The Jātakas of Hamsa, Śuka, Nalapāna (Jātakam Jāgarakhasa) and Sonakīya (Chāmpēyya) are monoscenic and are narrated in a single register capturing the climax of the scene following the idiom of Bhārhut. The polyscenic depictions range from 4–6 scenes in equal number of registers and depending upon the major events of the story are composed, giving importance to the continuity of narration following the Sānchi and Amarāvati idiom. It is also to be noted that such depictions reflected upon Buddhist religion, contemporary life, art-traditions, beliefs and practices. The Jātakas, rendered in 17 registers of 10 panels, are: 1. Velāmiya, 2. Vēssantara, 3. Hamsa & Śuka, 4. Chhaddanta, 5. Jagarakha (Nalapāna Jataka), 6. Aridamiya, 7. Māndhāta-Rāya Chakavati Satrajano, 8. Story of King Udayana, 9 Story of Devi Sāmivati, 10. Sonakiya & Champeyya, 11. Sudasomiya (Sutasoma) Sajiniya—preamble to Sutasōma, 12. Vidura Paṇḍita. These Jātaka stories get interrupted by panels delineating historical events, events from the life of Buddha, portraits of royal personalities and other themes. The life story of the Master from the birth of the lord as Bōdhisattva down to the mahāparinirvāṇa are graphically captured in as many as 32 registers of 16 panels adorning the upper drum.

The role of Aśoka towards the cause and propagation of the Dharma is too well known to be elaborated here. However, since he appears as one of the major depictions here certain events that were part of his endeavours like commissioning the emissaries far and wide is also projected here. As per the Ceylonese chronicle Mahāvamśa, the third Buddhist Council (Mahā-sanghīti) was held in c. 250 BC, at Pātaliputra under his patronage, under the chairmanship of Moggaliputta Tissa (Upagupta in the northern texts). After the council, several missionaries headed by teachers of repute were dispatched to propagate Dharma to different regions. Amongst them five missionaries Mūlakadēva, Sahadēva, Kassapagōtta and Majjhima (Madhyma) were dispatched to the Himalayan (Himavat) region under the leadership of Dundubhissara (Dundubhīsvara). All these teachers are depicted in as many as six registers of three panels respectively followed by the panel of Mauryan king Aśoka. Incidentally, all these panels were the gifts of a gahapati Tondaka during the 16th regnal year of Chhimukha Sātavāhana.

Kings and other historical personages

This *stūpa* site has brought to light duly labelled portrait relief sculptures of royal personalities. Amongst them the rulers of the *Mahājanapadas* like Mahāgōvinda, the king of Magadha is depicted. Even Udayana, is depicted here with labelled inscription. The famous Mauryan monarch Aśōka is depicted at two places in the upper drum along with label inscription besides getting depicted in association with the worship of Rāmagrāma *stūpa* at the lower drum without any inscription to affirm this.

Amongst the Sātavāhana rulers, right from the founder of the dynasty Chhimukha Sātavāhana, down to Puḷumāvi under whose period this veneering of the great *chaitya* appears to have been completed, are found depicted including Sātakarṇi, Mātalaka and Sundara Sātakarṇi. Apart from the above kings, sculpted head of Yajña Sātakarṇi found near one of the accessory structures adds to the gallery of the Sātavāhana rulers depicted here. Thus, apart from the depiction of the Aśōka, for the first time, reliefs of more rulers of the Sātavāhana dynasty occur here after the famous statue gallery at Naneghat. Other than the above, the legendary king of Varanasi elevated to the status of a Bōdhisattva frequently appearing as the ruler of the place in the *Jātaka* tales also gets depicted here as *Bōdhisatō Kasirāya*. Interestingly reliefs of some of the main characters of the *Jātaka* tales are depicted prominently such as Prince Arindama etc.

Aśōka's endaevours in the spread of Buddhism is well known. This interesting panel depicts the sculptural representation of King Aśoka appropriately located succeeding the panel of the procession of *ārya Kassapagōta* and his entourage to emphasise that he was instrumental in augmenting the third Buddhist Council at Pātalīputra under Tissa and after the Council the earlier referred teachers proceeded towards the spread of Dharma.

The upper register of the panel in its top border is inscribed *Rāya Asoko* (Fig.4). The panel has a royal figure—Aśoka along with his queen flanked by two female *chauri* bearers and a female *chhatra* or umbrella bearer. The composition of the panel is very elegant and the king stands majestically in *dvibhanga* with his face turned slightly towards left as if in conversation with the queen. His right hand with heavy bracelets of pearls is kept akimbo and a *kēyūra* adorns the upper arm. He wears an elaborately decked turban held by fan shaped frontal knot. He wears, heavy ear ornaments and a *vaksha-hāra.* While most of the royal figures or other portraits of noblemen and celestials in other panels do not wear

Fig.4. Mauryan Emperor Aśoka.

yajñōpavīta, Aśoka is shown with *yajñōpavīta*. He wears a *pītāmbara* held by a laced *uttarīya* tied in a knot to the left at his waist and an extra large part of the *pītāmbara* shown in the form of slender lines reaching upto the ankle of his and his queen jointly flow down all along the left leg. The *chhatradhāriṇi* surprisingly has an elaborate hair dress, a *chuḍāmaṇi*, heavy anklet and short but heavy *chāmara*. At the left top corner, a *chauri*-bearer with an elaborate fan like hairdress and decorated with *karṇa kuṇḍala* is shown holding the short handle of the *chauri*. The queen, to his left, looks at him adoringly with pride. She stands in *tribhanga* and is playing with her ear ornament in her right hand. A string of pearls as *vakshahāra,* an ornate *kēyūra* in left hand and different wristlets for both the hands are the other ornaments. She has a *kaṭi-bandha* with a fastening hook at the waist over the *pītāmbara* and has unusually heavy multi-coiled anklet. The queen is attended upon by a *chauri*-bearer with moderate hairstyle, *kēyūra*, wristlets, ear ornaments and heavy anklets. Even the drapery lines and a girdle at the waist are well sculpted. She holds a short handled heavy *chāmara*.

The image of Standing Buddha on the āyaka platform at south, is one of the finest sculptures of standing Buddha erected over a separate lotus pedestal, unique to this place. Easily, it is the best specimen from Karnataka, for its composition, plasticity, expression and execution. Be it the dakshiṇāvarta curl gently rising to form the low ushnīsha at top or the elongated well delineated ear lobes reflecting a mahāpurusha, or the gentle folds of the long heavy drapery covering the Lord, the benign smile, with wide open eyes as if beckoning the devotees with an assurance of benevolence—this is an unsurpassed creation of Vākāṭaka-vishaya sculptors. The lotus pedestal, which accommodated the above standing Buddha image, is circular in shape. There are two inscriptions of two lines each inscribed on the lotus pedestal. A certain, Najika, son of Venu upādhyāya and maternal grandson of Aśvabhūti upādhyāya carved the image.

It is interesting to note that in the fifth phase of Period–II of construction and expansion, as many as ten seated images of Buddha were added in the stūpa. Of these, while eight were located on the floor of circumambulatory passage one each was placed right on the northern and eastern āyaka platforms. During the course of excavation, except for the sculpture of Buddha retrieved from the northwest, rest were displaced and greatly mutilated due to the impact of the collapse of massive architectural units of superstructure. These sculptures were the exclusive contributions of sculptors and devotees hailing from Vakāṭaka Vishaya (Vidarbha region of the present Maharashtra) as evident from the inscriptions found on the pedestals.

All are carved in round and some retain the cortex of the original stone formations on their back side. These seated images of the Buddha kept over the āyaka platform at north and east and in the intracardinal directions in the pradakshiṇāpatha have been placed by using the non-ornate vēdikā slabs as the backdrop. The respective pedestal inscriptions inform that they are Mānushī Buddha representations such as Vipaśyin, Śikhi, Viśvabhū, Krakuchchaṇḍa, Kāśyapa, Śākyamuni-Siddhārta, Kanakamuni and Maitreya (Anāgata). The sculpture of Śākyamuni is repeated. It is interesting to note in this connection that the Manushi Buddhas appear for the first time in sculptural art in the Hīnayāna context at Bhārhut. The names of only six of the eight Buddhas are engraved along with their corresponding Bōdhi trees or the totemic trees (Bhagavatō Vipassinō Bōdhi etc). The next representation of the eight Mānushī Buddhas in their fully developed Mahāyāna theological concept appears only at the Mahā Stūpa at Kanaganahalli. The iconic figures of these Buddhas, duly identified with label inscriptions appear to have been positioned as per standard canonical injunctions. The epigraphs on the pedestals also indicate that all these images were contributions of persons hailing from Vākāmṭaka Vishaya and were executed by a group of sculptors who belonged to the same family and the same school of art accounting for the striking similarities. The Mānushī Buddhas also appear in the Mathura school of art during the times of Huvishka—a contemporary king of Yajña Śri Sātakarṇi. At Sanchi, in the niches of the cardinal directions of Stūpa–I, four of the Dhyāni Buddhas are introduced during the Gupta period.

As part of expansion of the stūpa, it is already envisaged that the āyaka platforms of the second phase were enlarged and adorned with the Buddhapādas (Fig.5). In accordance with the sectarian principles of

Fig.5. Buddhapada.

hinayānanism Buddha is not depicted in human form at this site also. His presence is indicated only by a symbol. Excavations have yielded as many as twelve complete Buddhapāda slabs amongst which nine are inscribed. The more ornate and inscribed ones were positioned over the āyaka platforms or on the flower receptacles (pushpagrahiṇis) opposite to the entrances prior to the installation of the images of Buddha. Stylistically, the Buddhapādas at the site could be grouped into two categories. The ornate and inscribed ones which are positioned over the āyaka platforms could be ascribed between 1st C BCE and 1st C CE, while the non-ornate ones could be ascribed to mid–1st to early 2nd century CE.

Inscriptions from the excavated *Maha Stūpa*, Kanaganahalli

The excavation has brought to light a wealth of epigraphical records. More than 250 inscriptions written in *Brāhmi* script and *Prākrit* language are discovered ranging from a five-lettered donatory label inscription to an eleven line epigraph. Sometimes the inscription is continued onto the neighboring architectural unit if it is the donation of the same individual as in case of the inscription issued in the 16th (regnal) year of Chchimukha Sātavāhana by *gahapati* Matisēka (Mahiseka) Toṇda of *Tokhisa* family found on four *mēdhi* slabs. Sometimes two different records are sculpted on the same architectural unit as in case of lower drum slab. These records have valuable bearing on the architectural, historical and cultural connotations of the Sātavāhana period.

The inscriptions are found on various architectural members of the *stūpa* and accessory structures viz., Railing, flower receptacles, slabs paved in the pseudo-*pradakshiṇā-patha,* on the pedastals of sculptures of Buddha,drum and dome slabs. Period-wise the epigraphs of the place can be classified into those assignable to the pre-Christian and early Christian era, and those assignable between 2nd century AD to 3rd century AD. Ranging in date from 1st century BC to 1st century AD, these are essentially associated with the early Sātavāhana phase of the structural/ ornamentation activities in the stūpa complex. From the point of view of religion, the thematic delineations associated with these inscriptions have a pronounced Hīnayāna affinity. Palaeographically these records show a preference to linearity, shallowness and narrow characters or letterings with varied size depending upon the surface or architectural units they are engraved, the height at which they are engraved and so on. Records assignable to the 2nd century AD to 3rd century AD: are These are associated with the middle and late phase of the structural embellishment in the stūpa complex and the thematic delineations associated with the records show a gradual preference to the Mahāyāna ideologies. It is interesting to note that the latest records in this group especially those engraved on the Buddha pedestals and

Buddhapādas indicate the supremacy of Mahāyana Chētiyavādins in the site.

Palaeographically, these records show a preference to neatly and deeply engraved smaller letters with ornamental serifs and vowel indicators with artistic curves. Consonant conjunct forms and precursors of distinct nail headed variety of the succeeding period also appear. Yet another feature noteworthy is perfect parallel arrangement of lines and interspacing of words. Even the donatory inscriptions tend to become longer with the names of the patron king, mentioning of his regnal year along with the season, months/fortnight and the day.

Inscriptions belonging to the late 3rd Century AD (250 AD) (Buddha pedestals)/or late Mahayāna phase on the pedestals of The sculptures of the Buddha present the latest stage of evolution in the script. Mentioning of many names of the Sātavāhana rulers is a striking feature of the inscriptions, though in a different context. As many as eight names of the Sātavāhana monarchs are mentioned in the inscriptions. The most significant aspect however is the appearance of the name of Mauryan emperor Aśōka. Simuka, Siri Sātakarni, Sundara Sātakarni, Mātalaka, Siva Siri Pulumāvi, Gautamiputra Sātakarni, Vasistiputra Siri Sātakarni, Yajñaśri Sātakarni, and Māthariputra Pulumāvi are some of the names of Satavahana rulers appearing in these records.

Inscriptions also throw light on the geographical divisions and place names. Kanaganahalli *stūpa* forming part of the suburb of the greater Sannati was very much in contact with the well known contemporary Buddhist centres on the one hand and leading trade centres on the other as it is located on one of the trade routes of the ancient Dakshiṇāpatha connecting Pātaliputra and Banavāsi via Paithan and Vidiśa. It had contacts especially with the major trade centres like Isila and Kupana (Koppal) in the far south, Dhānyaṭataka (Amarāvati) and Kōtura on the northwest and east, Vakataka Vishaya and Ujjain in the central and further western India. Obviously, the names of these places figure prominently in the epigraphs.

Inspite of the fact that the sculptural delineations in the early phase has a strong *Hīnayana* affinity and in the second phase the emphasis is laid on the *Mahāyāna s*chism of Buddhism and the existence a monastic complex (*Bōtika* [*Bodhikā*?] *vihāra*) at Kanaganahalli, the epigraphs do not refer to any specific sect of Buddhism like *Thēravāda, Mahisāsaka* etc. A number of terms referring to the hierarchy of the monks and teachers like *thēra, āchāriya, dhamakadhika, pavayita, bhayata, bhiku* and *samana* with their disciples are mentioned by name. But, the specific sect to which they belonged to is conspicuous by its absence.

Only two references to *sutatikas* (*Sūtrāntikas*—proficient in *sūtras*) occur. However, the sculptural depictions of Kāshypa, Dudhubisara (Dundubhisvara) and others who were deputed by the Mauryan Emperor Aśōka for the spread of Buddhism in the Himalayan region and scant references to Haimavata sect in the form of *Himalāya dhama sisēhi* (disciples of Himalayadhama) suggests the religious sect at Kanaganahalli could be of Haimāvata. The absence of mention of any specific sect here is akin to Bharhut and Sanchi epigraphs and unlike that of Amaravati in the northeast and Karla, Bhaja, Kanheri, Nasik etc., in northwestern Deccan.

References

1. A. Ghosh (ed.), An *Encyclpaedia of Indian Archaeology* (ed.), New Delhi, 1989, vol.I, p.131.
2. E. Hultzsch, *Inscriptions of Aśoka*, *CII*, vol.I, New Delhi, 1991, Indian reprint, p.xiii.
3. A. Cunningham, *The Stupa of Bharhut: A Buddhist Monument*, Varanasi, 1962, p.127.
4. R.E.M. Wheeler, "Brahmagiri and Chandravalli: Megalithic and other cultures", *Ancient India*, no.4, Delhi, 1948.
5. A.V. Narasimha Murthy & others, *Excavations At Banavasi*, Mysore, 1997, pp.71–77.
6. A. Sundara, *Two Thousand year old Town and its Architecture in Vadagaon Madhavpur in M.S. Nagaraja Rao* (ed.), Madhu, Delhi, 1990.
7. M. Seshadri, Buddhist Monuments at Sannati, *Quarterly Journal of Mythic Society* (QJMS), vol.LV–I, nos.1–4, Bangalore, 1965, pp.35–37.
8. A. Sundara, "Ittichina Kelavu Puratatva Sodhagalu" (Kannada), *Karnataka Bharati*, vol.8, no.2, Dharwar, 1981, pp.13–14.
9. A Buddhist site recently excavated by Mysore university.
10. Nagaraju, S., Vestiges of Buddhist Art, in *MARG (Heritage of Karnataka)*, ed. by Sarayu Doshi, Bombay, 1982, pp.25–34.
11. Ibid., p.33.
12. Ibid., pp.30–32.
13. Kapatral Krishna Rao, Sri Chandala Parameswari, *Karnataka Samskrutiya Samshodane* (a collection of articles), Usha Sahitya Male, Mysore, 1970, pp.257–261.
14. M. Seshadri, op. cit., pp.35–36.
15. P.B. Desai, A New Buddhist Center, in *The Journal of Karnataka University—Social Sciences*, Vol.IV, pp.3–8.
16. M.S. Nagaraja Rao, *Progress of Archaeology in Karnataka,* 1956–1972, Mysore, 1978, pp.29, 35–36.
17. Sarma, I.K., R.V. Siva Sarma and J. Varaprasada Rao, Rock Edicts of Aśōka from Sannati, Chitapur Taluk, Gulbarga District (Karnataka), in *Indian Museum Bulletin*, New Delhi, 1989, pp.7–15.

18. Paddayya, K., Early Historical Localities and a Mesolithic site at Sannathi, in A.V.N. Murthy and I.K. Sarma (eds.), *Sri Rāmachandrikā*, *Prof. Oruganti Ramachandriya Festschrift*, vol.I, Delhi, 1993, pp.1–10.
19. Sarma, I.K., R.V. Siva Sarma and J. Varaprasada Rao, op.cit.
20. E. Hultzsch, op.cit., pp.xiii–xvii.
21. A. Sundara, Exacavations at Sannati, 1986–1987, *Puratattva*, no.17, 1987, pp.226.
22. E. Hultzsch, op.cit., p.165.
23. A. Cunningham, op.cit., p.132.
24. A.M. Shastri, "Satavahana Statue Gallery at Naneghat", paper presented at the World Archaeology Congress, New Delhi, 1995.
25. Sir John Marshall and Alfred Foucher, *The Monuments of Sanchi*, vol.II, Delhi, 1982.
26. M. Seshadri, op.cit., pp.35–36.
27. G.S. Gai, *Annual report on Indian Epigraphy* 1965–1967 (reprint), New Delhi, 1989.
29. M.S. Nagaraja Rao, Brahmi Inscriptions and their bearings on the great Stūpa at Sannati in F.M. Asher and G.S. Gai (ed.), *Indian Epigraphy*, New Delhi, 1985, pp.41–45.
30. Sarma, I.K., R.V. Siva Sarma and J. Varaprasada Rao, op. cit., pp.7–15.
31. *Indian Archaeology*—A Review (1991–1992), New Delhi, pp.45–66.
32. I.K. Sarma and J. Varaprasada Rao, *Early Brahmi inscriptions from Sannati*, New Delhi, 1993.
33. J.R. Howell, *Excavations at Sannati*, New Delhi, 1986–1989, pl.XXI–XXVII.
34. *Indian Archaeology*—A Review, 1997–1998, pp.77–93.
35. J.R. Howell, *Excavations at Sannathi*—1986–1989, New Delhi (Memoir of A.S.I. no.93), 1995, pp.44–68.
36. Mitra Debala, *Buddhist Monuments*, Sahitya Samsad, Calcutta, 1980, p.190.
37. Devaraj D.V. and Talwar H.T., *Interim Report on the Excavations at Sannati*, 1993–1995, Directorate of Archaeology and Museums, 1996, pp.9–17.
38. *Indian Archaeology*—A Review; 1990–1991 to 1992–1993.
39. Debala Mitra, op.cit., p.23.

—x—

Advantages and Challenges in Identifying Heritage Sites Using Historical Records and Geospatial Tools: Malaprabha River Basin as a Case Study

Kuili Suganya and *M.B. Rajani*

Abstract

Malaprabha River valley in Bagalkot district of Karnataka has protected monuments in 45 settlements, whereas hundreds of historical sites and settlements in the basin spanning approx. 11,549 sq km are recorded in literature published in the past, but most of their locations are undocumented, uncertain or unknown. The present study is an attempt to geotag (identify geographical coordinates) historical sites in Malaprabha river valley mentioned in historical records and to visualize them geospatially. This paper will discuss the methods and challenges in geo-tagging sites mentioned in the historical records and will point at prospects of using Remote Sensing to correlate the location of known/ documented sites with the geographical setting for identification of unknown and undocumented sites.

Introduction

Geospatial data of Indian archaeological monuments and sites are available only if they are protected by government departments or a well-known location geotagged in web portals like google maps and BHUVAN. Though digital technologies and location services are well-developed, and despite efforts by people and the government organizations, the availability of geospatial data of heritage sites and monuments remains a challenge.[1] Many of these sites are reported in literature published in the last 150 years (in antiquarian report and gazetteers), but information of their locations are not readily available

[1] IDHS, 2017.

which is required for conducting geospatial analysis on a specific site or group of sites belonging to larger landscape. In the absence of such a database, these sites and monuments are vulnerable to damage and destruction.[2] This paper uses Malaprabha river valley (known as the "Cradle of Hindu Temple Architecture")[3] located in Bagalkot district of Northern Karnataka as a case study to illustrate the challenges and advantages of extracting information about geographical locations from non-spatial data[4] about heritage sites and monuments found in published literature.

Malaprabha valley contains a variety of archaeological remains both rock-cut and freestanding built architecture. Bagalkot and Belgaum districts through which the river Malaprabha flows houses approximately 135 monuments in 45 settlements that are protected by Archaeological Survey of India (ASI)[5]—of which 57 monuments are in Aihole and 11 monuments each in Badami and Pattadakal. About 75 monuments in the districts of Bagalkot and Belgaum are protected by the Department of Archaeology, Museums and Heritage, Karnataka.[6] Pattadakal is a World Heritage Site (WHS) whereas Aihole, Badami and Nagaral are in the tentative list since 2015.[7] Under the Heritage City Development and Augmentation Yojana (HRIDAY) scheme, heritage assets in and around Badami have been listed and an area of 40 sq km around Badami has been delineated as heritage zone (this delineation includes Sidalapadi, Mahakuta, Nagaral and Banashankari).[8]

Geographical Information Systems (GIS) is being increasingly used in the studies of archaeological landscape and accurately geo-tagged data of heritage sites are the primary data that is necessary for spatial analysis. Geo-tagging involves attributing geographical coordinates to photos, videos, audio clipping, narrative or text associated with a location. In today's world we widely use location services—if we want the nearest restaurant, ATM or bank, etc, we search and find them on Google maps—and take such information for granted. This information is available on Google map because they have been geotagged by respective businesses to help people easily find what they are looking

[2] Gupta, Das, Chittirai Balan, Kumar & Rajani, 2017.

[3] https://whc.unesco.org/en/tentativelists/5972/ (accessed on 09 June 2018).

[4] data which does not contain precise geo-coordinates.

[5] http://asi.nic.in/alphabetical-list-of-monuments-karnataka-dharwad/ (accessed on 09 June 2018).

[6] http://asi.nic.in/protected-monuments-in-karnataka/ and http://www.karnatakaarchaeology.gov.in/department/monuments/belgaum-division/ (accessed on 09 June 2018).

[7] https://whc.unesco.org/en/tentativelists/5972/ (accessed on 09 June 2018).

[8] http://hridayindia.in/downloads/chp/CHP_for_Badami.pdf (accessed on 09 June 2018).

for. Digital geo-tagging information about a location enables one to navigate to the location using GPS or other satellite navigation services on personal mobile phones. Therefore latest technologies have made it possible for common man who has a smartphone to navigate to a site using digital location. If such location information of every historical site is documented and made available, it will firstly raise awareness about the site and also act as a deterrent to activities that can cause damage to the sites.

In an archaeologically important area as Malaprabha valley which houses many heritage assets, locations of only a few seem to be known; these are recognized and protected sites whose locations can be found in the heritage spatial database. This paper aims at identifying unprotected monuments, sites and settlements of historical importance within the Malaprabha river valley by listing them, geo-tagging, geo-spatially documenting and analyzing their spread. Geo-tagging involves finding the geo-coordinates of the monuments and heritage sites mentioned in literary records. This information is generally found as part of a narrative/inventory/gazetteers/exploration reports which in most instances do not include geographical coordinates. Once geotagged this data is visualized in the geospatial platform in co-relation with multiple spatially co-registered data like remote sensing images[9] and geo-referenced old maps.[10] Here in this study the literary records consulted for listing sites are Gazetteers, British records, Epigraphical records and published research. In the following sections, we first describe the study area, then explain the methodology, further we list the different kinds of challenges in identifying, inventorying and geo-tagging sites, then we discuss the geographical patterns of the river valley and finally points at prospects of using remote sensing to correlate the location of known/ documented sites with the geomorphological setting to identify unknown and undocumented sites through predictive modelling.

Study Area

Malaprabha river has its origin in the Western Ghats or Sahyadri mountain range near a village called Kankumbi (760 m altitude) in the state of Karnataka and joins Krishna at Kudalasangama (500 m altitude) covering a distance of about 350 km. This monsoon fed river is a right bank tributary to river Krishna and has Bennihalla, Hirehalla and

---

[9] Like Multispectral images, False colour images and Digital Elevation Models (DEM).

[10] Geo-referencing is a method by which the geo-coordinates of known locations are registered to a published old map and brought in to geo-spatial platform.

Tuparihalla[11] as its major tributaries. This river flows through the geological formations of Granitic gneiss and lower Kaladgi (limestone, quartzite and Shale). Lower Kaladgi geological formation is located between the Granitic Gneiss to its south, Dharwar craton to its west and Deccan trap to its north.[12] This river has a higher gradient when flowing over lower Kaladgi formation and has a lower gradient while traversing the Granitic gneiss and along the boundary of Kaladgi and Granitic gneiss formations.[13] To the north of this river basin is Ghataprabha basin (a tributary to river Krishna) and to the south is the Tungabhadra basin. Upper reaches of Malaprabha river up to Khanapur receives an average rainfall of 2000 mm (sub-humid climatic zone) and downstream from Khanapur and beyond Bailhongal area becomes a rain-shadow region by receiving an average rainfall of 600 mm (semi-arid climatic zone).[14] The vegetation of western part of the basin up to Bailhongal is an intermix of deciduous and evergreen forest and transits into dry-deciduous vegetation with shrubby, drought-resistant species with spines and thorns. Red soil is found at the foothills whereas, south and east of the basin has rich black soil.[15]

This valley has been inhabited since pre-historic times[16] and there are several historical built forms seemingly organized in the context of water features (like tanks, step-wells and on the riverfront). Badami an ancient Chalukyan settlement known for its cave architecture has several of its historical buildings around a tank that are protected on its east by a sandstone ridge, other Chalukyan sites at Aihole and Pattadakal are located on the banks of river Malaprabha. Similarly, temples at Mahakuta and Banashankari are located in the context of step-wells. Some fortifications dot the landscape, which was constructed between the 17th and 18th century CE during the regime of Bahamanis, Nizams of Hyderabad and Maratha rulers. This river has its catchment in the *taluks* (sub-district) of Badami, Bagalkot, Belgaum, Dharwad, Gadag, Gokak, Hubli, Hungund, Khustagi, Kundgol, Nargund, Navalgund, Parasgad, Ron, Ramdurg, Sampgaon, Saundatti and Shiggaon—covering 18 taluks spread across Bagalkot, Belgaum, Dharwad and Gadag

[11] http://wgbis.ces.iisc.ernet.in/energy/water/paper/ETR129/sec1.html (accessed on 09 June 2018).

[12] Joshi R.V., 1955.

[13] *ibid.*

[14] *ibid.*, Purandara, Varadarajan & Venkatesh, 2008.

[15] Joshi R.V., 1955.

[16] *ibid.*, Pappu & Deo, 1994.

districts of Karnataka.[17] The study area covers the entire Malaprabha river basin encompassing above-mentioned taluks in the districts of Bagalkot, Belgaum, Dharwad and Gadag districts of Karnataka thus covering a larger landscape area of 11,549 sq km.[18]

Methodology

The main objective was to carry out (a) geospatial listing of monuments and sites found in the Malaprabha river basin which have been discovered and listed in the sources like Gazetteers,[19] British records,[20] Epigraphical records and other published works, (b) geo-tagging of the sites and bringing them into the geospatial platform by identifying their geographical coordinates using Indian geoportal BHUVAN (BH)[21] and Google Earth (GE) and (c) geospatially visualize them to find patterns that exist in the larger landscape. The listing was restricted to the extents of Malaprabha river basin and the following explains first the listing of pre-historic sites and then moves on to the listing of ancient sites. The method used for this study for listing out historical sites would aid in future studies which aim to understand man-land relationship where the geographical and geomorphological setting is considered to significantly influence the settlement location.

Two main categories of pre-historic sites from the published works are listed in this study: Palaeolithic and Megalithic sites in the Malaprabha region. Palaeolithic sites are listed mainly through the works by Pappu and Sushama Deo,[22] Joshi,[23] Ravi Korisettar & Petraglia.[24] Megalithic remains are identified through the presence of megalithic built structures, burials and surface-remains as found and discussed by Sundara.[25] These publications have listed geographical coordinates (latitude and longitude) to the accuracy of degree and minutes of the arc but without the accuracy of seconds—which present an error up to 2 km. To obtain the exact location of the site, satellite images from BH and GE

[17] Prior to the formation of Karnataka State in 1956, the districts mentioned above were under the administration division of Bombay Karnataka, the southern division of Bombay State.

[18] http://nihroorkee.gov.in/rbis/basin%20maps/Krishna/malaprabha.htm (accessed on 09 June 2018).

[19] Gazetteers of Bombay Karnataka, Mysore State and Karnataka State.

[20] Antiquarian remains report.

[21] https://bhuvan-app1.nrsc.gov.in/bhuvan2d/bhuvan/bhuvan2d.php (accessed on 09 June 2018).

[22] Pappu & Deo, 1994.

[23] Joshi R.V., 1955.

[24] Korisettar & Petraglia, 1993.

[25] Sundara, 1975.

were helpful. Besides, Indian geoportal BH provides administration boundaries which help narrow down the search area.

Reports of Antiquarian remains were compiled by Robert Sewell, Henry Cousens and Jas. Burgess (in the late 19th century) for Bombay and Madras Presidency.[26] These lists of antiquarian remains are categorized taluk-wise for every "*zilla*" (district) of the time and do not include a detailed recording of native states (eg. Ramdurg State which falls within the study area) that were not part of the territory under British jurisdiction. These reports lists the locations of settlement and monuments with their geo-coordinates to the accuracy of degree and minutes of the arc but not seconds, which makes the geo-tagging task challenging especially when most of the sites may not be existing in the same condition at present. Gazetteers referred for this study included a chapter titled "Places of interest" which lists sites of historical importance.[27] They are usually listed under the administrative boundaries (*taluk* and district) of the time. Except for Imperial Gazetteer of India 1909, the rest do not provide geographical coordinates. Reviewing these sources helped in listing out many sites that were not included in the other sources. The book of inscriptions of the Chalukyas of Badami, edited by Shrinivas V. Padigar lists the names of sites that have inscription and also names of places mentioned in the inscriptions.[28] This book was used for listing places of antiquity from epigraphical sources; in this book, the location of sites are identified with the name of settlement along with the *taluk* and district they belonged then, without mentioning the geographical coordinates.

Challenges in geo-tagging identified sites

Assimilating a list of sites from various literary sources was not as simple a task as it seemed at first. One faces several challenges as we scrutinized each of the literary sources mentioned above for listing and geo-tagging the historic settlements and monuments. The primary challenge was that the administrative boundaries (*taluk* and district) of the study area have changed over time. Hence one needs to examine old maps and records in correlation with the current administrative boundaries to identify the location of the site correctly. Also, we found

[26] Burgess, 1885; Cousens, 1897; Sewell, 1882.

[27] Campbell, Gazetteer of the Bombay Presidency Volume XXI Belgaum, 1884a; Campbell, Gazetteer of the Bombay Presidency Volume XXII Dharwar, 1884b; Campbell, Gazetteer of the Bombay Presidency Volume XXIII Bijapur, 1884c; Enthoven & Edwardes, 1909; Palande, 1959; Sathyan, 1966; Kamat, 1987; Parthasarathy, 2002; Jeelani, 2006.

[28] Padigar, 2010.

multiple settlements with the same name and multiple spellings; this indeed made the task of listing more difficult. Furthermore geotagging of settlements using the published geo-coordinates sometimes was with printing error and as mentioned earlier the co-ordinates not having the accuracy of seconds of arc created additional complexity. Finally, these literary sources with its challenges mentioned above had its advantages —as some sources as part of the narrative mention features that are large enough to be identified on satellite imagery (for instance a fort wall), which can be used as a clue for visually identifying the location using BH and GE.

Our study area is covered under the erstwhile administrative boundaries of Bombay Presidency as *zillas* of Belgaum, Dharwad and Kaladgi. Presently the new Bagalkot district where many of the sites mentioned in the antiquarian report fall under are carved out of the erstwhile Bijapur district.[29] Similarly, the sites of Kaladgi *zilla* of Bombay Presidency was with Bijapur district until 1997 and later attached to Bagalkot district. Hence it was important to cross verify the settlements between the current and pre-independence administrative boundaries when the data was from a pre-independence literary source. Though these district's limits have remained more or less the same, the area which were under native states, like the Ramdurg, Shirahatti, Savanur Jhagirs were not extensively dealt with in the antiquarian remains report. The reports of antiquarian remains of Madras and Hyderabad provinces were also examined so we do not miss out on any sites.[30]

Identification of the location of sites with similar names was even more challenging. For instance, there are: (a) sites with a similar name, different *taluk* and same district (Eg. Avaradi and Kittur are found both in Ramdurg and Sampgaon *taluk* of Belgaum district), (b) more than one site with the similar name within the same *taluk* (eg. Naghral of Badami *taluk* of Bagalkot district), (c) sites with a similar name—in a different district (eg. Amargol—Dharwad and Gadag district, Hallur—Bagalkot and Belgaum district, Hebbali—Bagalkot and Dharwad district, Hosur—Gadag, Belgaum and Bagalkot district and Itagi—Belgaum and Gadag, (d) sites with similar-sounding names/spelling (like Hungund/Hunagunda in Hungund *taluk* in Belgaum district versus Hungund/Hungundi in Ron *taluk* in Gadag district) can easily be mistaken to be the same site if one is not alert about the geo-coordinates or the *taluk*

[29] Jeelani, 2006.
[30] Sewell, 1882; Yusuf, 1953.

mentioned in the literature (e) The name of the sites mentioned in the 1884 gazetteer has changed over time (eg. Degamve is currently Degaon of Sampgaon taluk of Belgaum district) (f) some sites have different names in published literature from that on maps (eg. Megundikolla of literature is locally called as Torgal Tanda).

The other main challenge was, the Antiquarian report of 1885, marked some sites as "uninhabited" or "ruined" but it also mentions such sites having built heritages features (like temples, tanks and inscriptions).[31] These are not marked in recent SOI maps or any geo-portals like GE and BH. Identifying such locations and cross verifying the same with the old record was a challenge (eg. Talwarkop, Akkargal, Arasibidi and Bhavihal). Sometimes the geo-coordinates given in published reports can be wrong (for eg. Arasibidi) due to printing errors or due to details (such as seconds of the arc) missing, this poses a further challenge. Finally, in the case of Arasibidi, the location could be identified using the information from a blog,[32] a published paper and on-ground validation.[33] The similarity in names can pose further difficulty (Eg. Bavihal in Sampgoan *taluk* of Belgaum district can easily be mistaken for this lost, unprotected and uninhabited site of Bhavihal of Dharwad *taluk*, Dharwad district). Talwarkop is yet to be identified.

Due to the lack of precision in the geo-coordinates available for sites in published reports (only degrees minutes and no seconds of an arc) causing displacement for up to 2 km, the geoportals had to be explored spatially to exactly pin the correct location by cross verifying with the Indian geoportal BH for its accuracy and authenticity of the administrative boundaries and locations. Where geo-coordinates of the site was not mentioned, identification had to be done by positioning based on the distance and direction from the nearest location, *taluk* and district described in the listing and cross verified with Survey of India Maps (SOI) and BH geoportal.

Fort walls and enclosure walls are features that are easily identifiable on satellite imagery. In old records, forts are often not mentioned as a prime feature but as an ancillary to an associated feature. For example in the antiquarian remains report of Bombay Presidency para 178 lists four temples and seven inscription stones in Naregal village of Ron *taluk*. Here inscription number three is said to be located "in front of the

---

[31] Burgess, 1885.

[32] https://karnatakatravel.blogspot.com/2013/04/arshibidu-temples.html (accessed on 09 June 2018).

[33] Details are presented in the paper Suganya, 2020.

temple of Hanumanta to the west of the fort".[34] This led to analysing the landscape using geospatial data and techniques explained in detail in the next section) for identification of fort sites. These forts were cross verified with a blog[35] where the author of the blog has been regularly visiting ruins in Karnataka and recording the remains through his writings and photographs.

Geospatial visualization

The site names and metadata (like geo-coordinates, sub-district and district names) were tabulated in an excel spreadsheet. This was saved in CSV format and imported into geospatial software to create a vector layer in KML format. The KML file was then used on GE and BH for visualization. About 106 prehistoric sites, 176 historic settlements and 45 fortification sites have been geotagged (refer to Fig.1). Among them, 176 settlements, about 25 sites are derived from the transcribed version of inscriptions of Chalukyas.[36] The listed 176 settlements are identified based on the following attributes; (a) Settlements having one or more historical remains mainly sacred built forms (b) The name of the settlement where the inscription was found, however, the antiquarian report does not mention of an ancient built form (c) Settlements that are mentioned in inscriptions and not listed in Gazetteers and antiquarian remains report.

As the geotagging process was carried out with the help of geoportals BH and GE, certain distinctive settlement patterns emerged between the settlement location and its geographical setting. These patterns that exist are listed as

a. settlements were located at the foothill along with a water feature and fortification at the summit (Santageri, Kelur, Belur) (Fig.2b),
b. the settlements were located at the foothill along with a water feature and a fortification located on a flat summit (Gajendragad, Kodtgeri, Kelur),
c. Ancient sacred built forms located in a narrow valley along with a spring (Shabari Kolla, Mahakuta, Hale Mahakuta, Siddana Kolla, Megundikolla),
d. Settlements with a water feature located within a C-shaped curvature of a hill range (Badami, Hooli, Guledgudda) (Fig.2b),
e. Settlements along the water divide of the river basin and around first-order stream (Nagavi, Hosur, Gadag, Naregal).

---

[34] Burgess, 1885.

[35] https://karnatakatravel.blogspot.in/ (accessed on 09 June 2018).

[36] Padigar, 2010.

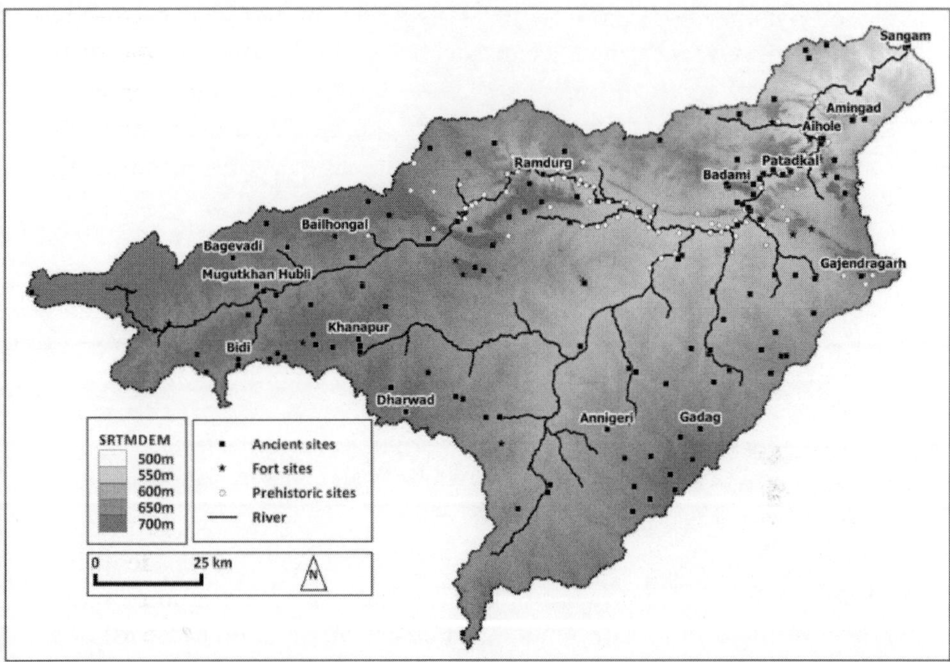

Fig.1. Digital Elevation Model (DEM) of Malaprabha river basin with the ancient, fortifications and prehistoric sites marked. SRTM DEM downloaded from USGS website 2014.

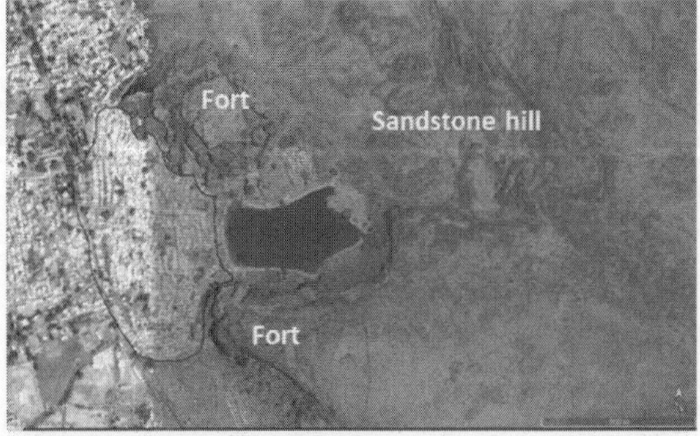

(2a) Badami and its environs

Fig.2(a). Google Earth image of Badami settlement located edging a water feature and the C-shaped hill.

(2b) Kelur and its Environs

Fig.2(b). Google Earth image of the Kelur settlement at the foothill having a water feature and a fortification at its summit.

Regional level visualization of the settlement-location in a geospatial interface resulted in certain unique settlement distribution patterns:

I. The palaeolithic sites were found mainly along the Malaprabha river with few sites along Benihalla and Hirehalla—the right bank tributaries of river Malaprabha.

II. Megalithic sites were found along the Malaprabha river valley, but mostly closer to foothills and at locations where the river is closer to the hills.

III. Settlements geotagged based on historical built remains were located either along Malaprabha river valley spreading along the course of the river or at the water divide of the river basin. Few of these settlements are found along the major tributaries of Malaprabha.

IV. Fewer settlements were found in the centre of the basin. Most of the fortifications are located on top of a hill, whereas few are located along the slopes. There are also fortified palaces located in the plains amidst settlements which are locally called as Desai Vadae.

This method of listing the sites recorded in historical texts and carrying out geospatial visualization and categorization of the settlement typology with reference to the geographical features aided in identifying many fortifications which were sometimes not mentioned in the records used for this study. Fortifications located at the summit of the hillocks at Chiknal, Dammur, Gudur, Guledgudda, Halsiddeswara, Hooli, Kelur,

Kodgeri and Santageri were identified based on the geographical patterns as a hillock, flat summit, settlement and water features that emerged as the geo-tagging was being carried out. These identified fortification sites are known to local people and those interested in the history[37] of the area. These observations on the geological patterns and settlement location need further detailed analysis and are subject for future investigations to throw light on to why certain locations were chosen for the settlements in the past and comprehend the significance of local geology, topography and geomorphology on the site selection processes.

Future prospects

The geospatial inventory of heritage sites created as part of this study is a geospatial data set that would aid in understanding settlement formation by pointing towards understanding reasons for site selection and its geographical setting in the archaeological landscape. This can assist studies that require comparison of site location with the geographical setting to map and analyze past man-land relationships. Such studies which focus on understanding the man-land relationship has been carried out for a specific period between identified sites and its geomorphic settings.[38] Geospatial tools and analysis can aid in site selection processes by enabling visualization that shows a synoptic view of all connected features in the landscape. Based on this dataset and the results from geospatial analysis—archaeological explorations can be carried out to identify potential archaeological sites by integrating data on geology, climate, vegetation and other data sets along with remote sensing images and brought in to the geospatial platform for carrying out predictive modelling. This geospatial study of heritage sites and geo-tagging did throw light into the few basic site preferences (like a water source, settlement, hillock) that probably would have dictated the choice for a habitation site. Thus such task would benefit the scholarship, experts in the field and the government for purposes of planning cultural heritage conservation and management.

Acknowledgements

This research has been conducted as part of a project funded by the Department if Science and Technology under the consortium Indian Heritage in Digital Space.

---

[37] blog 'Journeys across Karnataka'.

[38] Pappu & Deo, 1994.

References

1. Burgess, J., 1885, *List of the Antiquarian Remains in the Bombay Presidency*, Bombay: Archaeological Survey of Western India.
2. Campbell, J.M., 1884a, *Gazetteer of the Bombay Presidency Volume XXI Belgaum* (Vol.21), Bombay: Government Central Press.
3. Campbell, J.M., 1884b, *Gazetteer of the Bombay Presidency Volume XXII Dharwar* (Vol.22), Bombay: Government Central Press.
4. Campbell, J.M., 1884c, *Gazetteer of the Bombay Presidency Volume XXIII Bijapur* (Vol.23), Bombay: Government Central Press.
5. Cousens, H., 1897, *Revised list of the Antiquarian Remains in the Bombay Presidency* (Vol.8), Bombay: Archaeological Survey of India.
6. Enthoven, R.E. and Edwardes, S.M., 1909, *Imperial Gazetteer of India Provincial Series Vol.II,* Calcutta: Superintendent of Government Printing.
7. Gupta, E., Das, S., Chittirai Balan, K.S., Kumar, V. and Rajani, M., 2017, November 25, The need for an Archaeological database (R. Navalgund and R. Korisettar, eds.), *Current Science, 113*(10), 1961–1973.
8. IDHS, I.H., 2017, January 09, *Interdisciplinary Cyber-Physical Systems (ICPS)*, Retrieved April 19, 2019, from the Department of Science and Technology: http://www.dst.gov.in/indian-heritage-digital-space-research
9. Jeelani, S., 2006, *Gazetteer of India, Karnataka State Gazetteer*, Bijapur District (Bagalkot District included), Bangalore: Government of Karnataka.
10. Joshi, R.V., 1955, *Pleistocene Studies in the Malaprabha Basin*, Poona—Dharwar: Deccan College and Karnataka University.
11. Joshi, S., 1985, *Defence Architecture in Early Karnataka*, Delhi: Sundeep Prakashan.
12. Kamat, S.U., 1987, *Karnataka State Gazetteer, Belgaum District*, Bangalore: Government Press.
13. Korisettar, R. and Petraglia, M. 1993, Explorations in the Malaprabha Valley, Karnataka, *Man and Environment, XVIII*(1), 43–48.
14. Padigar, S.V., 2010, *Inscriptions of the Calukyas of Bādāmi* (c.543–757 AD). Bangalore, Karnataka, India: Indian Council of Historical Research, Southern Regional Centre.
15. Palande, M.R., 1959, *Gazetteer of Bombay State: Dharwar District* (revised edition) Volume XXII, Bombay: Government Printing Publication and Stationery.
16. Pappu, S.R. and Deo, S.G., 1994, *Man—Land Relationships during palaeolithic Times in the Kaladgi Basin, Karnataka.* Pune: Deccan College Post-Graduate and Research Institute.
17. Parthasarathy, T., 2002, *Gazetteer of India Karnataka State: Dharwad District* (revised edition including Gadag and Haveri districts), Bangalore: Government of Karnataka.
18. Purandara, B.K., Varadarajan, N. and Venkatesh, B., 2008, August, Simultaneous transport of water and solutes under transient unsaturated flow conditions—A case study, *Journal of Earth System Science*, 117(4), 477–487.

19. Sathyan, B.N., 1966, *Mysore State Gazetteer Bijapur District*, Bangalore: Government Press of Printing Stationery and Publications.
20. Sewell, R., 1882, *List of the Antiquarian Remains in the Presidency of Madras Volume I* (Vol.1), Madras: Archaeological Survey of Southern India.
21. Suganya K., 2020, Challenges in Geospatial Documentation of Unprotected Built Heritage Sites in India, *Current Science*, 118(6), pp.877–882.
22. Sundara, A., 1975, *The Early Chamber Tombs of South India, A study of the Iron Age Megalithic Monuments of North Karnataka*, Delhi: University Publishers (India).
23. Yusuf, S., 1953, *Antiquarian Remains in Hyderabad State*, Hyderabad: Archaeological Department, Government of Hyderabad.

Websites

1. www.whc.unesco.org/en/tentativelists/5972/ (accessed on 09 June 2018).
2. www.asi.nic.in/alphabetical-list-of-monuments-karnataka-dharwad/ (accessed on 09 June 2018).
3. www.asi.nic.in/protected-monuments-in-karnataka/ (accessed on 09 June 2018).
4. www.www.karnatakaarchaeology.gov.in/department/monuments/belgaum-division/ (accessed on 09 June 2018).
5. www.whc.unesco.org/en/tentativelists/5972/ (accessed on 09 June 2018).
6. www.hridayindia.in/downloads/chp/CHP_for_Badami.pdf (accessed on 09 June 2018).
7. www.wgbis.ces.iisc.ernet.in/energy/water/paper/ETR129/sec1.html (accessed on 09 June 2018).
8. www.nihroorkee.gov.in/rbis/basin%20maps/Krishna/malaprabha.htm (accessed on 09 June 2018).
9. www.karnatakatravel.blogspot.com/2013/04/arshibidu-temples.html (accessed on 09 June 2018).
10. https://bhuvan-app1.nrsc.gov.in/bhuvan2d/bhuvan/bhuvan2d.php (accessed on 09 June 2018).
11. http://www.dst.gov.in/indian-heritage-digital-space-research [Accessed 19 April 2019].

— x —

Palimbothra to Patna: Reconstructing the Ancient Landscape using Geospatial analysis

Sonia Das and *M.B. Rajani*

Abstract

In the past the city of Patna, in Bihar, India, was known by several other names including Pushapura, Kusumapura and Pataliputra. Starting from the records made by the Greek Ambassador Megasthenes (3rd century CE) and Chinese pilgrim Faxian (5th century CE) to later colonial explorers, all have mentioned the cultural and political importance of Patna across several centuries. We have conducted a regional survey of the area using remote sensing to enhance our understanding of features mentioned by Megasthenes, Faxian and Xuanzang and also clarify the reason for the differences in opinion of Buchanan when compared with Cunningham and his successors. This study will identify features as mentioned by Buchanan and Cunningham, and finally will report the extent of fort wall and other archaeological features identifiable using remote sensing.

Introduction

The city of Patna, in Bihar, India, was known by several names including Pushapura, Kusumapura and Pataliputra. Records made by Megasthenes (3rd century CE) and Faxian (5th century CE) to later colonial explorers have mentioned the cultural and political importance of Patna across several centuries. Megasthenes, who visited the city Palimbothra (identified as Pataliputra) during Chandragupta Maurya's reign (3rd to 2nd century CE), left a detailed written description of a fort with towers and royal gates surrounded by a moat. Buchanan conducted a survey in the early 19th century, but was unable to find any resemblance between the modern city of Patna and Megasthenes's Palimbothra. Subsequent excavations by Cunningham (1861), Beglar (1872), Waddell (1895), Spooner (1913) and others (KPJRI, 1951–

1955) have claimed to support this correspondence, for instance by identifying Mauryan pillars at Kumhrar in southeast Patna.

The debate around identification of Palimbothra as described by Megasthenes dominated the nineteenth century Indian Archaeology triggered by Major James Rennell's map[1] of 1788 marking Patna as a fort, which resulted in associating Patna with Palimbothra. Buchanan did a survey and made a detailed plan of the city which had a fort on the north eastern side. Unlike his visits to sites like Nalanda (Buchanan 1922:266), in Patna Buchanan does not mark or observe any archaeological mounds. Later Cunningham in his report gives a map of Panch Pahari area in Patna (Cunningham 1871: plate 41). This area is not covered in the map referred to by Buchanan. Megasthenes has recorded that Palimbothra was at confluence of Ganges and Erannaboas. Erranaboas was later identified as river Sone (Mc Crindle 1877; Cunningham 1871:154). This led scholars to believe that Patna could be ancient Palimbothra. Sone is believed to have changed its course and now it joins river Ganga 30 km (approx.) west of Patna. Buchanan refers to a fort wall (also marked in the map) in dilapidated condition and Cunningham refers to an area fortified by Sher Shah Suri (Cunningham 1871:156). Both these seem to be the same. This fort was built by Feroz Jung Khan in 1042 (Buchanan 1922:179). The mounds at Kumrhar, in the southwest of the fortified area, mentioned by Cunningham were excavated and Mauryan pillars were found. In this study we have identified the extent of fort wall observed and mapped by Buchanan. Further by comparing the shape and extent mentioned by Megasthenes we propose that it is possible that the ancient city of Palimbothra maintained the shape as what Buchanan surveyed in 19th century. We have tried to explore remote sensing and associated geospatial technologies together with available old maps and historical records, to contextualise Patna. These tools and its relevance to landscape archaeology have been established. In this study, the use of remote sensing and Geographic Information System (GIS) enables us to compare land use patterns across different time periods and also visualize and geographically contextualise the city in the current state.

A Spatial Comparison of Buchanan's and Megasthenes Description of Patna

When Buchanan visited Patna in 1812, he was conducting a topographical and statistical survey where he was recording dimensions

[1] https://www.lib.umich.edu/online-exhibits/exhibits/show/india-maps/item/5140?exhibit=136&page=1193 (Accessed on 05 Mar 2020).

of settlements, trade, practices, occupation and population among other things. He found it difficult to demarcate the boundary of the settlement of Patna. In his survey record he mentions “To exclude what is without the walls would reduce its dimensions to a trifle, while the suburbs are built in a very straggling ill-defined manner.”(Buchanan 1922:173). The plan in Buchanan’s record made by a native assistant (Buchanan 1922) demarcates a walled area, roads, temples and important landmarks. Old survey maps have been used to find and demarcate archaeological features through geospatial analysis in sites like Chitradurga (Nalini and Rajani 2012:387) and Srirangapatna (Gupta et al. 2017:1057) in Karnataka and Nalanda in Bihar (Rajani 2016; Rajani and Das 2018). Similar method of analysing old map was undertaken in this study towards examining the Buchanan’s plan for Patna. However, this plan proved to be very challenging to georeference as it is not to-scale, annotations are in Persian (hence identifying place was purely by shape) and the subsequent land-use/land-cover changes have been so profuse that it was very difficult to identify common ground control points. Hence the features drawn on the plan have been carefully studied. Features such as buildings, road intersections and patterns of land use are visually compared and identified in current satellite data (fig.1 Google earth imagery dated 01 Mar 2016).

The Golghar (Brown 2016:53) which is a dome shaped building used as granary has been identified (see fig.1a). Buchanan in his report

Fig.1(a). Google earth imagery (01 Mar 2016) showing Golghar on the banks of river Ganges.

writes that he demarcates the extent of Patna as 9 miles in length and 2 miles in width. Buchanan writes "The width from the bank of the Ganges is on an average about 2 miles, but some part of the channel of the Ganges, and of the islands opposite to the city, must be also considered as belonging to this jurisdiction, so that on the whole I shall allow it an extent of 20 square miles". The plan has a kind of grid markings on its frame that is after every 10th line there is a cross mark (see fig.1b). We will consider cross marks as a division for further calculations. The length of the city which is 9 miles as mentioned by Buchanan should then be equivalent to 190 lines marked on the plan. Hence by calculation every division comes approximately up to half a mile (0.47 miles).

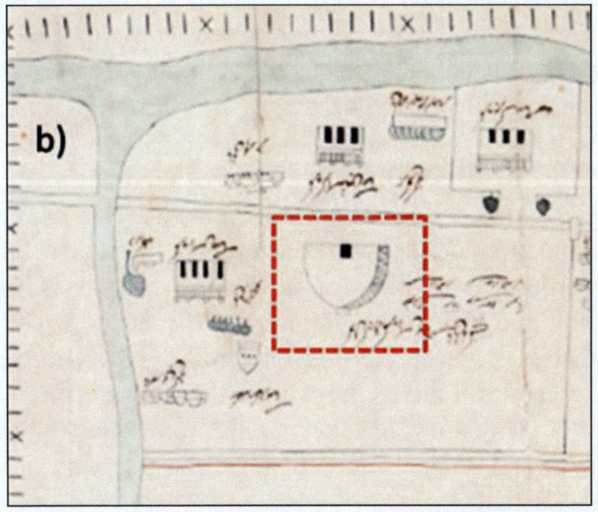

Fig.1(b). Portion of plan of Patna from Buchanan's record (1811–1812) showing Golghar.

Buchanan surveyed area of 20 square miles, with shape of the city as parallelogram; Palimbothra as described by Megasthenes was also in shape of a parallelogram. Megasthenes describes the area as 80 stadia in length and fifteen in breadth in shape of a parallelogram surrounded by wooden palisades (Mc Crindle 1877:66). Both Megasthenes and Buchanan's observation of the site is that it is similar in shape. Megasthenes's perimeter for the city would be approx. 33.8 km and area of 25.5 square Km (Schlingloff 2013:32) and according to Buchanan's survey in 1812, the area would be 20 square miles, which is 51.79 square Km, but this also included width of the river Ganga (refer plan of Patna, Buchanan 1922).

This comparison leads to the question whether it is possible for Palimbothra of (3rd century CE) to maintain the same shape till 19th century. Geographically Patna is situated at the banks of Ganges. It is quite possible that the river must have changed its width around Patna (Swamee and Parkash 2003:213) but it also acts as a natural boundary for the city on the north. On the southern side the city till date is thinly populated and sparsely built as these are low lying areas and gets flooded in the monsoon. Hence it is quite possible for Patna to have maintained the contours. The settlement of Patna seems to follow a linear pattern dictated by the river in the north and a depressed topography to its south which doesn't allow it to spread beyond the narrow band. This seems consistent with the pattern of this city as marked in Buchanan's plan, also visible in recent satellite imagery (fig.2) and probably is the reason for its shape to be compared with "parallelogram" by Magasthenes and Buchanan. It is also possible this strip has been a river island in its geological past with river brading to its north and south.

Tracing the Fort Wall Seen by Buchanan in 1812

The plan by Buchanan records a fort wall whose remnants cannot be traced on ground. Remote sensing in India has been successfully applied to find archaeological features in rural sites such as Nalanda (Rajani 2016), Halebidu and Belur (Rajani and Kasturirangan 2014). These sites are less disturbed by urbanization and thus identifying cropmarks is possible. In case of Patna, the city has been of importance from 3rd century CE. The city has been built and rebuilt and thus it is challenging to find any traces to demarcate the fort wall and find extent of archaeological features.

The fort wall on north eastern side of Buchanan's plan of Patna can be traced on satellite data by analysing road network. Buchanan says "The fort in the north-east corner of the city is now so overrun with modern buildings that its form can be no longer distinguished, nor could I perceive any remains, except some old gates." The inscription on the fort wall attributes its erection to Feroz Jung Khan (Buchanan 1922: 179). Cunningham says that fort was built by Sher Shah Suri. He further supports his argument of Patna being Palimbothra by saying that Sher Shah retained the old city and fort wall (Cunningham 1871). However Cunningham does not give a plan or location of this fort wall.

Major indicator of fort wall's extent is the pattern of road network. In an urban setting roads often preserve the shape and extent of past fort walls (Navalgund and Rajani 2017). The road network as drawn in 1812 map has been geospatially analysed. The other indicator is the existence of temples called Paschim Darwaza (translates to western door). Though there are no structural remains of the fort wall. The reference to Paschim Darwaza is an indicator. This is also supported by the distance calculation. Paschim Darwaza temple is around 5 miles from Golghar which is same as the respective distance calculated on Persian map used by Buchanan dating from1812. By distance calculation from 1812 map and by analysing road network the extent of fort wall has been identified (see fig.2).

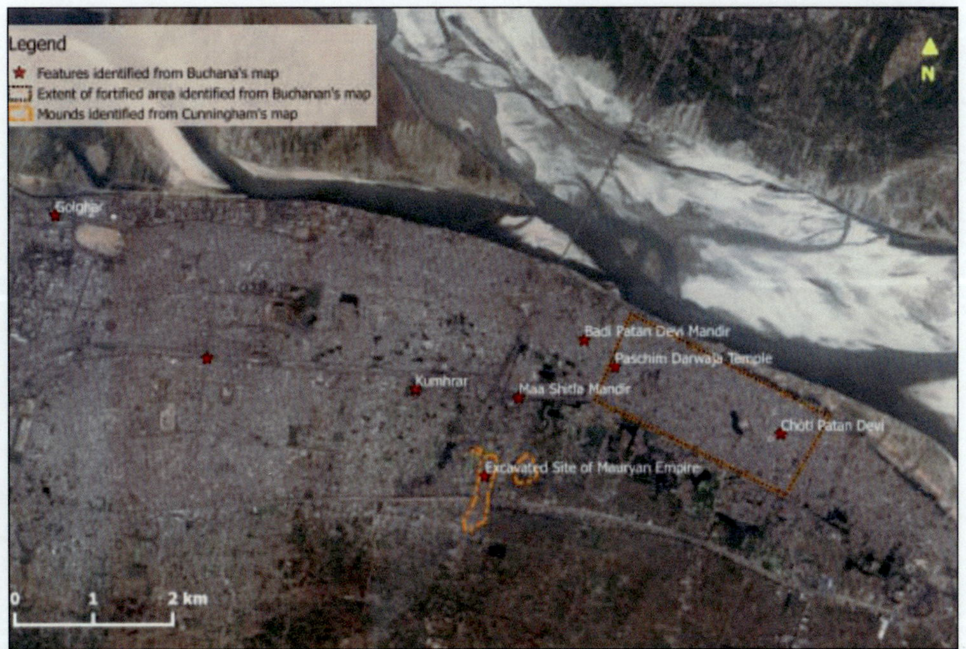

Fig.2. Map showing extent of fort wall and archaeological features in Patna.

Conclusion

This study is a preliminary step towards using satellite data with old maps to demarcate and find the ancient city of Palimbothra or Pataliputra. Due to urbanization and in the absence of structural remains of fort wall, Patna poses a unique challenge. This study shows that even without any structural remains or ruins it is possible to identify the extent of past settlement and fort. The "parallelogram"shape of the city was remarked by both Megasthenes and Buchanan. However, there could be other settlements along the river that could have this shape too. A future direction for this study also could be to do a regional geospatial study along the banks of Ganga to check if there are any other site that match the description of Palimbotra of Megasthenes.

Cartographers, archaeologists and surveyors have done a good amount of work on Patna and this should be continued and supported by adopting scientific tools, such as remote sensing and GIS. We have used old maps and satellite data to trace the site and we see scope for further strengthening of our argument by using historical satellite images from CORONA series of satellites. Declassified Corona data can be analysed to identify more features. CORONA data dates back to 1965 and the chance of identifying archaeological signatures especially in case of an urbanised city like Patna are higher. The excavated wooden palisades have been important findings and it can further enrich our knowledge by dating them. It is possible to date wooden palisades using radiocarbon dating techniques (Sanjurjo-Sánchez 2016). Thus by building on the research of previous scholars and integrating it with new scientific techniques, there is scope for Patna to reveal more interesting archaeological as well as geological information.

Acknowledgements

We thank Dr. Prashant Keshavmurthy for translating parts of the Persian map of Patna dating from 1812. We would like to thank NIAS for institutional support. The fieldwork and remote sensing analysis was carried out with support from SERB project (YSS/2015/000754).

References

1. Brown, Rebecca M., 2005, 'Paṭnā's Golghar and the Transformations of Colonial Discourse', in *Archives of Asian art* 55, no.1 53–63.
2. Cunningham, Alexander, 1871, 'Reports of Tours in the Gangetic Provinces from Badaon to Bihar in 1875–1876 & 1877–1878'' Volume 11, Simla: Printed at the Government Central Press.
3. Francis Buchanan Hamilton, 1922, '*Journal of Francis Buchanan Kept during Survey of Patna and Gaya (1811–1812)*', Journal of the Bihar and Orissa research Society, ed. by V.H. Jackson. https://archive.org/details/in.ernet.dli.2015.263205.
4. Gupta, Ekta, Sonia Das and M.B. Rajani, 2017, 'Archaeological exploration in Srirangapatna and its environ through remote sensing analysis.' Journal of the Indian Society of Remote Sensing 45, no.6, 1057–1063.
5. Mc Crindle, J.W., 1877, '*Ancient India as Described by Megasthenes and Arrian*, Indian Antiquary.' https://archive.org/details/in.gov.ignca.34982.
6. Modi, Jivanji Jamshedji, 1917, 'Ancient Pataliputra: Dr. D.B. Spooner's Recent Excavations at its Site and the Question of the Influence of Ancient Persia upon India', *Asiatic Papers*.

7. Nalini N.S. and M.B. Rajani, 2012, 'Stone Fortress of Chitledroog: Visualizing Old Landscape of Chitradurga by Integrating Spatial Information from Multiple Sources', *Current Science* 103 (4):381–87.
8. Rajani M.B., 2016, 'The Expanse of Archaeological Remains at Nalanda: A Study Using Remote Sensing and GIS', *Archives of Asian Art* 66 (1):1–23. https://doi.org/10.1353/aaa.2016.0010.
9. Rajani M.B. and Sonia Das, 2018, 'Archaeological remains at Nalanda: a spatial comparison of 19th century observations and the protected World Heritage site' in Records, Recoveries, Remnants and Inter-Asian interconnections, ed. by Anjana Sharma , ISEAS—Yusof Ishak Institute.
10. Sanjurjo-Sánchez, Jorge, 2016, 'Dating Historical Buildings: An Update on the Possibilities of Absolute Dating Methods', in *International Journal of Architectural Heritage* 10 (5), Taylor & Francis: 620–35. https://doi.org/10.1080/15583058.2015.1055384.
11. Schlingloff, Dieter, 2013, Fortified Cities of Ancient India: A Comparative Study, London: Anthem Press.
12. Swamee P.K., Parkash B., Thomas J.V. and Singh S., 2003, 'Changes in channel pattern of River Ganga between Mustafabad and Rajmahal, Gangetic Plains since 18th Century' in International journal of Sediment Research, 18(3) 219–231.

— x —

Understanding the Past through Pottery: A Case Study of the Early Medieval Brahmaputra Valley (7th–12th centuries CE)

Preetee Sharma

Abstract

The traditional sources used for writing the history of the Brahmaputra Valley includes primarily a group of 33 inscriptions and chiefly two literary sources; the Kalika Purana and Yogini Tantra. The historical narrative followed is a description of political history centered on dynastic shifts with very few exceptions in the recent past. Hence, to investigate about the socio-economic processes one has to analyse alternate and subaltern sources like the material cultures such as pottery. This is a systematic study of the pottery from five medieval sites of the Brhamaputra Valley, using traditional textual, epigraphical sources to investigate about the socio-economic processes. The excavated pottery from the sites of Ambari, Bhaitbari, Garhdol, Suryapahar and Paglatek has been classified and their distribution pattern has been analysed as well as compared to discover the trends across the sites. This pottery data will eventually be compared with the conventional historical sources for a more critical engagement with the otherwise lesser known history of ancient and early medieval Assam

The study of the pottery from five sites of the Brahmaputra Valley, extends roughly from the period 7th to 12th centuries CE (see fig.1). Out of the five sites, four are located within Assam: Ambari in Kamrup district, Garhdol in Sonitpur district, Paglatek and Suryapahar in Goalpara district, and Bhaitbari located in the West Garo Hill district of Meghalaya. I have attempted to document the distribution pattern and multiple attributes of the pottery of this period and region. I have discussed and analyzed the different aspects of pottery such as fabric, decorative patterns and diagnostic patterns while situating them in spatial as well as temporal contexts. The study has focused on the micro and the

Fig.1. Location of five sites across the Brahmaputra Valley.

macro perspectives of pottery from the Brahmaputra Valley. It is also an attempt to start a dialogue between the archaeological sources and the historical sources of the early medieval period of the region. Overall, this is an attempt at developing a comprehensive understanding of the socio-economic and political processes of the Brahmaputra Valley by studying the pottery from the region. The sites of Ambari, Garhdol and Paglatek have been excavated by the State Directorate of Archaeology Assam. The last season of Ambari excavation was a joint exercise between State Directorate of Archaeology Assam and Archaeological Survey of India. Excavation at Suryapahar has been conducted by the Archaeological Survey of India. Bhaitbari was excavated for a season in 1992 by the Prehistory Branch of ASI, Nagpur. The potteries I have studied have been excavated mostly by the above mentioned state agencies.

The established historical narrative for the region under study in the period between 5th to 12th centuries CE is primarily dynastic in character. The early history of *Pragjyotisha-Kamarupa* or Ancient Assam region till the middle of 4th century CE is vague and confusing,[1] due to a lack of historical sources. The history of Early Assam or

[1] Baruah, 1985:87.

'*Pragjyotisha-Kamarupa*' region from mid 4th century CE has been constructed by the historians chiefly on the basis of epigraphic sources. Though, textual and numismatic sources are also present for the period under study, epigraphs have been the backbone of historical studies done on this period. There are 31 reported inscriptions within 5th to 13th centuries CE period. At three places coins belonging to this period have been found. Among the textual sources the *Kalika Purana* and *Yogini Tantra* which was composed in Assam itself in about 10th century CE and 16th century CE respectively are considered most important.

Among the researches done on the early Assam or the early medieval period one can see that beyond creating a political historical narrative of the region, not much has been attempted. The source mainly used by the historians to write the political history of the Brahmaputra Valley is epigraphs. An attempt to have an alternate reading of this source has been attempted only by a handful. Within Archaeology we can see a massive lacuna in terms of scholarly engagement. Most studies done are art historical in character with emphasis on description rather than analysis. Also a few pottery studies that have been attempted in the region shows a lack of understanding of sub-disciplines such as ethno archaeology. Also, most studies are guided by their quest to establish 'continuity' over long periods of time. And the pottery classifications attempted are very problematic in their generalizations, since they are based on random pottery samples. Thus, the studies have not employed the principles of a systematic pottery classification which is essential to glean out all micro details from this source.

Review of Literature

My review of literature is divided into two parts. The first part covers studies about pottery studies and the second part includes those studies from which are derived the theoretical and methodological ideas related to the study of pottery.

Part 1: A large section of the studies in this section concentrate on Ambari. There is a predominant interest among the scholars on Ambari as it is one of the most extensively excavated sites in the region of north east India. While compared to Ambari the other sites have hardly been given due importance, there are no published studies on pottery in the case of the other sites. The pottery studies on Ambari mostly have done pottery classification on the basis of a single attribute like the color or fabric of the pottery. The works of Sharma, Ashraf and Mahanta[2]

[2] Sharma et al., 2006:45–57.

and Goswami and Roy[3] will fall in this category. Sonowal[4] in contrast to others, who have emphasized more on the South East Asian connections, draws similarity between the Ambari potteries with that of the pottery from the Gangetic plains sites.

Furthermore, some works have made an attempt to understand the excavated pottery through studies on the present potter communities. These ethnographical endeavors can be seen in the works of Sharma, Ashraf and Mahanta[5] and Roy.[6] In all these works, the overarching concern is to trace the continuity from pre historic times to the present times. However, these assumptions are not well substantiated with the evidence. This idea of changelessness and continuity in potting tradition is problematic. It fails to recognize the micro details that are embedded in different regions as well as periods. Since there is a huge time gap, one has to be cautious about suggesting continuity between the ancient past and the present. Similarly, the temporal and spatial changes easily get overlooked in such studies.

Part II: Dales and Kenoyer[7] have provided a systematic classificatory scheme for understanding the Mohenjo Daro pottery which can be used for classifying pottery elsewhere as well. Their contribution to pottery study in the Indian subcontinent is remarkable as it has introduced a classification model very different from the traditional way of pottery classification. Mishra[8] has studied the pottery of the chalcolithic site of Balathal and provides a good example of systematic and scientific pottery study. He has attempted a comprehensive classification of the pottery including decorated wares and a statistical analysis of the data collected on the pottery. Selvakumar[9] in his article discusses the paddle impressed pottery technique and its prevalence across different regions of the Indian sub continent. It has been reported from the Neolithic period till the modern times. But, he points out that the cord impression on Neolithic cord/paddle impressed pottery of the Vidarbha region might have not been a conscious effort but a byproduct of the paddle anvil technique. The studies of Dean Arnold,[10] Prudence Rice,[11] Carla

[3] Goswami and Roy, 1972:22–27.

[4] Sonowal, 2006:83–86.

[5] Sharma et al., 2006:45–57.

[6] Roy, 2006:66–72.

[7] Dales and Kenoyer, 1986.

[8] Mishra, 2008.

[9] Selvakumar, 2014:192–198.

[10] Arnold, 1985.

[11] Rice, 1987.

Sinopoli[12] and Heather Miller[13, 14] provide the basics of any pottery study. These studies have explicated in great detail the theoretical framework involved in pottery classification and analysis. Arnold's study throws light on the paradigmatic shifts within pottery studies through some case studies. Rice has tried including in her work almost all the concepts and issues related to the study of pottery. Sinopoli discusses apart from the different approaches to pottery classification, the relationship between pottery, state processes and social systems. Miller who along with summarizing most of the basic works in pottery study, talks of the technique and the other aspects of pottery making in relation to the social factors.

Analysis

A comparative study of pottery across a historically contiguous geographical zone such as the Brahmaputra valley will entail that there will be a search for common features across the pottery deposits. I found a few commonalities within pottery deposits across the five sites along with certain distinctive traits. The two chief common features observed are kaolin pottery and paddle groove bowl forms. I will be discussing both these aspects below. But, I will begin with a discussion of the pottery distribution pattern of Brahmaputra Valley temporally within the sites and spatially across the valley. Regarding the pattern of distribution of the pottery, in all the five sites the pottery recorded were first sorted into the three broad categories of diagnostic pottery, non-diagnostic pottery or body sherds and decorated pottery. The following table shows the counts and weight in each category within the five sites. The highest quantity is recorded at Ambari followed by Garhdol. In all the sites except Suryapahar the quantity of diagnostic pottery is way higher than the other two categories (see Table 1). This seems to be a reflection of the on field policy followed by the excavating agencies wherein the diagnostic parts of pottery were considered more valuable and stored.

The pottery distribution pattern at Ambari records pottery deposits from layers 1 to 8 (roughly from 7th to 15th centuries CE) with the peak in layer 4 (roughly 11th–12th centuries CE). At Bhaitbari pottery deposits are recorded from layers 1 to 3 (roughly 10th to 13th centuries CE) with peak in layer 3 (roughly 10th–11th centuries CE). The pottery deposits at Garhdol are recorded from layers 1 to 9 (roughly 6th–11th centuries CE) with the peak in distribution recorded in layers 3 and 4 (roughly

[12] Sinopoli, 1991.

[13, 14] Miller, 2007.

Table 1. Counts and weight of Diagnostic, Non Diagnostic and Decorated Pottery across the five sites.

Site	Pottery Category	Counts	Percentage %	Weight (Kg)	Percentage %
AMBARI	Diagnostics Non-diagnostics Decorated	3082 705 496	71.95 16.46 11.58	135.799 20.256 12.811	80.41 11.99 7.58
Total		4283		168.866	
BHAITBARI	Diagnostics Non Diagnostics Decorated	150 131 45	46 40.1 13.8	7.236 1.288 0.341	81.6 14.5 3.84
Total		326		8.865	
GARHDOL	Diagnostics Non Diagnostics Decorated	825 598 278	48.5 35.15 16.34	27.355 17.188 5.149	55.04 34.58 10.36
Total		1701		49.692	
PAGLATEK	Diagnostics Non Diagnostics Decorated	221 73 93	57.10 18.86 24.03	8.591 2.148 2.068	67.07 16.77 16.15
Total		387		12.807	
SURYAPAHAR	Diagnostics Non Diagnostics Decorated Wares	59 96 33	31.3 51.06 17.55	2.090 2.221 0.692	41.7 44.3 13.83
Total		188		5.003	

9th–10th centuries CE). At Paglatek the pottery deposits have been recorded from layer 1 to 3 (roughly 8th to 11th centuries CE) with the peak recorded at layer 1 (roughly 10th–11th centuries CE). The pottery distribution pattern at Suryapahar is recorded from layer 1 to 4 (roughly 7th to 11th centuries CE) with the peak at layer 4 (roughly 7th–8th centuries CE) (see Table 2).

The established historical narrative of the Brahmaputra Valley is basically an account of political or dynastic history. This political history of the successive kings in chronological order has been created primarily through epigraphic sources. Apart from this, there is also the additional information provided by the inscriptions regarding the shift of capital city of the *Pragjyotisha-Kamarupa* empire. I compare this information

Table 2. Pottery distribution across layers in the five sites.

Site	Layer	Count
Ambari	1	299
	2	655
	3	722
	4	1474
	5	224
	6	311
	7	10
	8	104
Bhaitbari	1	93
	2	115
	3	155
Garhdol	1	18
	2	304
	3	567
	4	576
	5	190
	6	143
	7	81
	8	18
	9	5
Paglatek	1	175
	2	156
	3	150
Suryapahar	1	34
	2	44
	3	49
	4	94

with the pottery distribution data I have generated to initiate a dialogue between history and archaeology within this region.

The Ratnapala-Bargaon copper plates of 1035 CE recounts that the coming of the Salastambha dynasty into power in 650 CE led to the shifting of the capital from Kamarupa (present Guwahati city) to Hattapesvara (present Tezpur town). The archaeological site of Garhdol is in the vicinity of modern day Tezpur town. This shift might have affected the structure of the core area of the earlier *Pragjyotisha-Kamarupa* empire. It probably affected peripheral area which was not under direct rule and where legitimacy of the state was relatively weak.[15]

[15] Boruah, 2010:50.

A comparison of pottery distribution pattern at Garhdol with the epigraphic information regarding capital shift is required to understand the actual impact of political developments on the socio-economic processes. At Garhdol the peak in pottery distribution is recorded around roughly 9th–10th centuries CE (see Table 2) where as the shift is recorded in the last decade of 7th century CE. In fact on close observation one can read a gradual build up of the peak from 8th to 9th centuries CE. Thus, it would be safe to assume that political decisions such as a shift of political centers definitely can have an impact on the economy and society. But, this impact on the material culture might not be very drastic but rather of very gradual character.

With the coming of the next dynasty the Palas of Assam into power in 990 CE there was another shift of the political center. This time the capital was shifted from Hattapesvara (present Tezpur town) to Durjaya during the reign of King Ratnapala as mentioned in the Bargaon copper plates which provides a detailed description of the new political center. The Durjaya capital is identified with the present Ujan Bazar—Ambari area of the Guwahati city (Boruah 2010:83). The Ambari archaeological site is nearby. Again towards the end of the 12th century CE during the reign of King Dharmapala the capital was shifted to Kamrupnagara identified with the ruins of North Guwahati (Ibid:83), (see Fig.2).

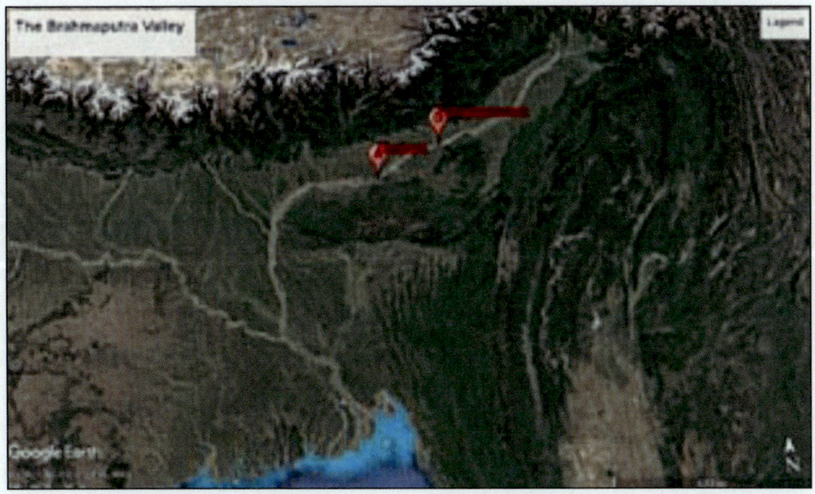

Fig.2. Map showing Location of Hatappesvara and Durjaya.

At Ambari a comparison of the pottery distribution pattern with the capital shift of the 10th century CE gives a slightly different picture to that of Garhdol (see Table 2). The peak at Ambari is recorded in the

11th–12th centuries CE and the shift takes place in the last decade of 10th century CE. It is possible that the region of ancient Guwahati was emerging as an important center which was identified by the ruling authority and it prompted the transfer of capital. Thus, an immediate impact can be read on the pottery distribution pattern at Ambari.

Kaolin Pottery Distribution Pattern

Kaolin clay is white in colour and devoid of ferric content. It is a very fine variety of clay with no inclusions in its natural form. The chemical composition of the kaolin clay is 46.54% SiO_2, 39.50% $A12O_3$ and 13.96% H_2O which is $A12O_3.2SiO_2.2H_2O$ (aluminum silicates with hydrates).[16] In North-East India it is found at Karbi Anglong, Golaghat and Lakhimpur districts of Assam and at Mawphlong of Meghalaya.[17] To make kaolin clay suitable for pottery making potting temper have to be added to make the eventual pottery resilient. The tempering material used in the kaolin pottery of the Brahmaputra Valley is normal red clay or powdered pot sherds which renderes a buff shade to the finished pottery. The normal clay with ferric content when mixed with the kaolin clay made the pots resilient and gave a pinkish hue after firing. Though different pots exhibited different shades as some pots were more reddish-pinkish while others were more on the off white side. To be more precise I also compared the kaolin pot sherd shade with the Munsell soil-color charts. It seems mostly, the kaolin pottery shades were within 7.5R 8/2, 7.5R 8/3 and 10R 8/2 shade range. This variety in shade probably points towards varying contents of temper (clay with ferric content) used in the kaolin clay during clay preparation by the potters.

During pottery classification at these five sites I sorted the pottery into the various categories on the basis of the pottery fabric. Pottery fabric analysis is the study and classification of pottery on the basis of firing technique, pottery inclusions and the function of the clay matrix.[18] To this, I have added another dimension which is distribution pattern as it is an integral part of my study. Here, I will discuss the overall percentage of occurrence of kaolin pottery in each site. I will further discuss the varieties of kaolin fabric observed. At Ambari in overall pottery distribution kaolin pottery records 45.04% of occurrence. Through careful fabric analysis I identified 12 different varieties of

[16] Saikia et al., 2003:93.

[17] Tahir and Ahmed, 1998:179.

[18] Orton et al., 1993:67.

fabric here. Out of which three fabric types are kaolin based fabric: unslipped kaolin fabric, slipped kaolin fabric and oxidised red slipped kaolin fabric. The last fabric type which has never been identified before seems to be a special technique developed by the potters of the region. In this technique, after making a pottery form out of kaolin clay a slip of normal red clay is applied. Incidentally, red slipped kaolin fabric records 24.5% of occurrence within the entire pottery fabric distribution. This fabric has been mostly found with decorations which indicate its preference among potters for depicting decorations. The reason for this seems to be the bi chrome effect created on the red slipped kaolin fabric when stamped or incised, as it perforated the top red layer and exposed the inner pale shade (see fig.3). The percentage of occurrence of red slipped kaolin pottery within decorated pottery at Ambari is 49.71%. In fact among the decorated pottery at Ambari there was a overall preference for kaolin pottery with 64.97% of occurrence.

Fig.3. Red Slipped Kaolin Fabric with bichrome effect).

The kaolin pottery at Bhaitbari is 12.5% in the entire pottery distribution recorded. A total number of four fabric varieties have been observed here. The kaolin pottery recorded includes two fabric types: unslipped kaolin fabric and red slipped kaolin fabric. There is no occurrence of kaolin pottery within the decorated pottery at Bhaitbari. At Garhdol kaolin pottery has recorded a 7.01% of occurrence across the total pottery assemblage. A total number of eight pottery fabric varieties is observed here. Two kaolin fabric types were recorded here: unslipped kaolin fabric and red slipped kaolin fabric. Among the decorated pottery the occurrence of kaolin fabric recorded is 11.49%. Only red slipped kaolin fabric has been observed within the decorated pottery of Garhdol. At Paglatek 13 varieties of pottery fabric has been observed and documented. Among the entire pottery assemblage kaolin pottery records 31.76% of occurrence. Six varieties of kaolin fabric is observed at Paglatek: unslipped coarse kaolin fabric, unslipped kaolin fabric, slipped coarse kaolin fabric slipped kaolin fabric, red slipped kaolin coarse fabric and red slipped kaolin fabric. Among the decorated pottery I recorded three kaolin fabric varieties: slipped coarse kaolin fabric, red slipped coarse kaolin fabric and red slipped kaolin fabric. Among the decorated pottery kaolin pottery records 40.2% of occurrence. The percentage of occurrence of kaolin pottery at Suryapahar is 4.52%. In all total six varieties of pottery fabric is recorded here. Only one variety of kaolin fabric is reported here which is the red slipped variety with 4.52% of occurrence. No kaolin fabric has been observed amongst the decorated pottery.

The presence of kaolin pottery in the Brahmaputra Valley has been cited by quite a few scholars. In fact M.K. Dhavalikar has suggested that kaolin can be called a distinctive marker of the pottery cultures of the region. He further suggests the term 'Ambari Ware'[19] for the kaolin pottery due to its abundant occurrence at Ambari. Through the above discussion I wanted to engage in a critical assessment of the prevalence of kaolin ware in the Brahmaputra Valley. Across the five sites, Ambari records the highest prevalence followed by Paglatek. The lowest prevalence is observed at Suryapahar followed by Garhdol. At both these sites there is no presence of kaolin within the decorated pottery. The red slipped kaolin fabric is an innovative technique used by potters in the region, extremely prevalent. It has been reported in all the five sites. It is interesting to note that though this technique is widely prevalent; there were still certain techniques which probably took time to muster. It is reflected in the high occurrence of coarse kaolin pot sherds at Paglatek.

Paddle Impressed Bowls

The paddle impressed bowls are squat bowls or *handi* forms which are carinated in the middle body and they come in a wide range of rim

[19] Dhavalikar, 1973:137.

patterns. The base is globular in form which is created through the technique of paddle and anvil (see fig.4). This paddle and anvil technique also gives it a distinctive decoration which is seen in the lower body of the bowl. This decoration or groove is replicated on the bowl surface from the paddle, while repeatedly hitting on the pot surface.

Fig.4. Paddle Impressed Bowls.

The paddle impressed decoration seems to be performing a function. Mostly they were observed at the bottom of globular bowls which were short in height with a wide orifice. The decorative patterns usually start from the mid-point of the bowl where it curves towards the bottom. Most probably the function that these patterns adhered to was to provide stability to these pots by reducing the pot's movement when kept on a flat surface, like a floor. Also these decoration types probably helped in providing a good grip on an otherwise smooth and globular surface. While handling these bowl forms which seems slightly on the heavier side especially with contents would definitely require a good grip. Mostly these bowl forms have a high breakage percentage around the neck area. The neck and the carinated section is the weakest part which further comes under pressure if the handling is not careful. This is probably a reason behind rare occurrence of these bowl forms intact with rims.

At Ambari the peak in distribution is clearly recorded in the layers 2 and 3 which roughly correspond to 12th to 14th centuries CE (see table 3).

Table 3. Counts of Paddle Impressed Pottery layer wise at Ambari.

Layer	Counts of Paddle Impressed Sherds at Ambari
1	29
2	62
3	84
4	53
5	6
6	13
8	1

Similarly, at Bhaitbari the peak can be seen in layer 3 which roughly corresponds to 10th–11th centuries CE (see Table 4).

Table 4. Counts of Paddle Impressed Pottery layer wise at Bhaitbari.

Layer	Counts of Paddle Impressed Sherds at Bhaitbari
1	13
2	9
3	23

At Garhdol the peak in distribution is recorded in layer 2 (roughly 11th centuries CE) followed by layer 3 (roughly 10th centuries CE) (see Table 5).

Table 5. Counts of Paddle Impressed Pottery layer wise at Garhdol.

Layer	Counts of Paddle Impressed Sherds at Garhdol
1	18
2	82
3	44
4	28
5	35
6	5
7	10
8	18

At Paglatek the peak in distribution is recorded in layer 1 or roughly 10th–11th centuries CE (see Table 6).

Table 6. Counts of Paddle Impressed Pottery layer wise at Paglatek.

Layer	Counts of Paddle Impressed Sherds at Paglatek
1	40
2	33
3	14

At Suryapahar the peak in distribution is recorded in layer 2 which roughly corresponds to 9th–10th centuries CE (see Table 7).

Table 7. Counts of Paddle Impressed Pottery layer wise at Suryapahar.

Layer	Counts of Paddle Impressed Sherds at Suryapahar
1	3
2	12
3	9

The paddle impressed bowls have widely occurred in the five sites of the present study. In fact there is a sort of homogeneity in the production process of these bowls which indicates their usage for a common purpose. This commonality of function of this vessel form probably made its production process across the valley more or less homogenous in the early medieval Brahmaputra Valley. Though there are a few assertions of localized variations observed at Garhdol, Paglatek and Suryapahar respectively. The hypothesis I would like to forward regarding the purpose is the usage of these bowls probably in rice preparation or cooking. As rice was an integral part of the food economy of the region the material culture like pottery will play an important role in the culinary aspects.

Selvakumar in his article suggests dispersal of the technique of paddle impressed pottery from North East India via Bengal coastal route to southern India.[20] I cannot put an affirmative to this hypothesis but it seems there definitely is a connection between these two regions as reflected in this decoration type. The paddle impressed pottery has been

[20] Selvakumar, 2014:204.

reported in number of other sites in the north east. This further indicates the importance of this bowl type with paddle impressions in the rice based economies of the Indian subcontinent. Though, this will require further investigation before coming to a possible conclusion.

The pottery distribution pattern analysis has been used to understand the historical processes of a lesser known period in the history of Brahmaputra Valley. The early medieval period in the historical writings has mostly focused on the political aspects. One reason cited for this is the paucity of sources. I have used the known historical sources with the sub alternate source of pottery to have a more nuanced understanding of the early medieval period of Assam. The site settlement pattern as reflected in the pottery distribution pattern has been compared with the epigraphic sources. It seems that mere transfer of capital or political centers did not immediately attract human habitation. It seems various factors such as ecology, geography; social and economic factors played an equal role. The dominant political historical understanding of early medieval Assam can be critically evaluated through such engagements with the material cultures of the period. An engagement between both history and archaeology disciplines within the ambit of their methodologies and disciplinary rigor will aid in a holistic understanding of the past.

The five sites of Ambari, Bhaitbari, Garhdol, Paglatek and Suryapahar belonging to the early medieval period has shown a number of similarities across the pottery deposits. Two such similarities are the kaolin pottery and paddle impressed bowls. These two aspects have been discussed in detail at the micro as well macro level. It is interesting to note that within the broad similarities certain distinctiveness exists as represented by the usage pattern of various kaolin fabrics. But, one cannot overlook the fact that the use of kaolin clay as raw material and the paddle impressed bowls are distinctive markers of the pottery tradition practiced at the Brahmaputra Valley. In the historically connected region of Brahmaputra Valley there seems to be networks and linkages existing. The transfer of ideas related to craft practices and movement of people practicing crafts in the early medieval riverine zone of Brahmaputra Valley is represented through these commonalities observed across pottery deposits. It seems such connections and networks transcended the political processes as well as boundaries in the region.

References

1. Ahmed, P. and M. Tahir, 1998, *Geography of North-East India: A Comprehensive Book for Graduation Courses*, Guwahati: Mani Monik Prakash.

2. Arnold, D.E., 1985, *Ceramic Theory and Cultural Process*. Cambridge: Cambridge University Press.
3. Baruah, S.L., 1985, *A Comprehensive History of Assam*. New Delhi: Munshiram Manoharlal.
4. Boruah, N., 2010, *Historical Geography of Early Assam*. Guwahati: DVS Publishers.
5. Dales, G.F. and J.M. Kenoyer, 1986, *Excavations at Mohenjo Daro, Pakistan: The Pottery*, Pennsylvania: Sheridan Press.
6. Dhavalikar, M.K., 1973, 'Archaeology of Gauhati', in *Bulletin Deccan College Research Institute*, Vols.31–32:137–149.
7. Goswami, M.C. and S.K. Roy, 1972, 'A Report on Selected Potsherds from Ambari, Assam', in *Bulletin Department of Anthropology (Guwahati University)*, Vol.1:22–27.
8. Miller, H.M.L., 2007, *Archaeological Approaches to Technology*, London: Academic Press.
9. Misra, A., 2008, *Beyond Pots and Pans: A Study on Chalcolithic Balathal*, New Delhi: Aryan Books International.
10. Orton, C.P. Tyers and A. Vince, 1993, *Pottery in Archaeology*, Cambridge: Cambridge University Press.
11. Rice, P.M., 1987, *Pottery Analysis: A Sourcebook*, Chicago: The University of Chicago Press.
12. Roy, S.K., 2006, 'Religious Institution and Pottery of Assam: An Ethno-archaeological Study', pp.65–72, in *Ambari Archaeological Site: An Interim Report*, ed. by H.N. Dutta. Guwahati: Directorate of Archaeology Assam.
13. Saikia, N.J, D.J. Bharali, P. Sengupta, D. Bordoloi, R.L. Goswamee, P.C. Saikia and P.C. Borthakur, 2003, 'Characterization, beneficiation and utilization of a kaolinite clay from Assam, India', in *Applied Clay Science Journal*, vol.24:93–103.
14. Selvakumar, V., 2014, 'Carved Impressed Paddle, Cord and Fabric Impressions on the Ceramics from Southern and North-eastern India', in *50 Years after Daojali Hading: Emerging Perspectives in the Archaeology of North East India,* ed. by Tiatoshi Jamir and Manjil Hazarika, New Delhi: Research India Press.
15. Sinopoli, C.M., 1991, *Approaches to Archaeological Ceramics*, London: Plenum Press.
16. Sharma, H.C., A.A. Ashraf and H.C. Mahanta, 2006, 'Ceramic Tradition in Brahmaputra Valley, Assam: A Case Study from Ambari, Guwahati', in *Ambari Archaeological Site: An Interim Report*, ed. by H.N. Dutta. Guwahati: Directorate of Archaeology Assam.
17. Sonowal, M., 2006, 'A Brief Report on the Potteries of Ambari Excavation', in *Ambari Archaeological Site: An Interim Report*, ed. by H.N. Dutta. Guwahati: Directorate of Archaeology Assam.

— x —

Buddhist Monastic Settlements in Medieval Bengal (5th–12th C CE): A Spatio-Temporal Study of Raktamrittika and Shribandada Mahavihara in West Bengal

Shatarupa Dutta

Abstract

Various sources suggest that Bengal was once a flourishing Buddhist centre of learning under notable imperial rules of the Mauryan in the early times and later under the Pālas and Senas. This paper will address the archaeological history of early medieval Bengal, roughly between 5th to 12th centuries CE, focusing on the Buddhist influence over the region and the process in which it took its institutionalised loose itinerant body of ascetics to their organisation as a formalised body of monastics settled in monumental monastic complexes and their dynamics with the state. It will look into the state-religion relationship, patronage, the settlement patterns and the socio- economic influences of these monastic establishments.

Archaeological investigations reveal that the region of Bengal, from the beginning of the historical period, has been associated with Hinduism, Jainism, and Buddhism. Various sources suggest that Bengal was once a flourishing Buddhist centre of learning under notable imperial rules of the Mauryan in the early times and later under the Palas and Senas. The travel account of Chinese pilgrim Xuanzang, who visited the land of Bengal during 7th century CE mentions that Lord Buddha visited several parts of Bengal in order to propagate his ideas of Dhamma. Centuries later, the great Mauryan emperor Ashoka traced the route that Buddha journeyed in and built stupas at the sanctified locations.[1] The present study will address the archaeological history of Buddhist Bengal in the early medieval times, roughly from 5th–12th C CE, the Pre-Pala and Pala periods, focusing on possible ways to

[1] Ahir, 2003.

study Buddhist monasteries of this region rather than considering them only as religious institutions. A comprehensive study of different regions in their totality from each of these aspects would contribute to a systematic representation of its macro history. In the broader context, engaging with the process of trans-regional establishment of Buddhist institutions throughout South Asia and even beyond, provides an insight into their involvement and function in the activities of the state.

Bengal had an intensive trade network, both inland and maritime, led to the growth of various urban centres which substantiated the maritime trade from ports like Tamralipti. Early Buddhist and Jaina texts and the Greek and the Chinese accounts refer to the region of Punḍravardhana as the native land of the tribal people called the Punḍras and later as Punḍranagar, as an urban centre.[2] Due to the royal patronage of Asoka,[3] the trade routes connecting Central Asia and the maritime world of the Bay of Bengal came into popularity during the Kushana period (1st–3rd century CE) when Buddhism was patronized by the dynasty and it extended its influence to China and other Asian countries through the silk route.[4] By 7th century onwards, the settlement patterns and the process of urbanisation in Bengal had already begun to take a full-fledged form under the regional powers.[5] However, in contrast to a Brahmanical injunction against sea voyage, Buddhism actively supported voyage because of which the religion travelled to far lands where it rooted deeply amongst the local communities and hence, was able to maintain efficient networks.

The monastic establishments were close to the banks of rivers, such as Chandraketugarh, Rajbadidanga, and Moghalmariand had links with Karnasubarna and Tamralipti. This is based on the account of Xuanzang who directly commuted his journey from the port of Tamralipti to Rajbadidanga in Karnasubarna.[6] Bengal became a part of the foreign trade by sea to distant regions of Sri Lanka and the countries[7] of South East Asia.[8] The nature of the maritime trade involved interaction between craftsmen, artist and religious envoys which further led to exchange of skills, ideas and religious ideologies.[9] To corroborate with the literary sources, in the sites of the Eastern coast of India, the

[2] Majumdar, 1971.
[3] Neelis, 2011.
[4] Liu, 2010:42.
[5] Epigraphia Indica, vol.XXVI:125.
[6] Beal, 1884.
[7] Tripati, 2000.
[8] Ray, 2006:72.
[9] Ray, 1997:16.

archaeological excavations at the coastal areas of Bengal and Odisha have yielded rouletted wares, knobbed wares, Northern black polished wares (NBPW), Chinese ceramics, silver punch-marked coins, Roman coins, Kharoshti scripts and semi-precious stones. Very similar kind of pottery ware was also found from Bali, Bangladesh, Java, Malaysia, Thailand and Vietnam.[10] The Chinese ceramics, rouletted wares and knobbed wares and the Roman coins indicate trade relations with China and Rome. The terracotta seals form Chandraketugarh and Bangarh contains symbols of conch with depiction of marine vessel full of corn and another seal inscribed in mixed Brahmi-Kharoshti script referring to —*Tridesayatra*, the voyage to three countries (ways).[11] During the 4th–5th C CE when the temples of eastern India were still in their initial phase, Buddhist monastic establishments began fortification using the new medium of burnt bricks.[12]

There was not only external involvement, but also there were internal involvements like the adapting cultures and the rituals of other places which transformed many indigenous rituals of the Buddhism.[13] These influences can be seen in the several depictions of the maritime activities on the pillars, panels or structures of the stupas. Currently, placing the process of Bengal's early urbanisation in the broader framework of the urbanisation of other regions, particularly northern regions becomes difficult as each and every region has its own genesis of development based on its geographical and demographical nature and cannot be framed in a fixed time period. Whether a site is urban or not is decided by looking at several factors such as the type of residential buildings, spaces of human interaction, religious institutions, roads and other infrastructures and other community spaces and presence of royal power. The distribution of early medieval sites and the varying contexts of occurrence of material culture at the sites reveal that this micro-region witnessed a fairly detectable early medieval settlement horizon datable on the basis of inscribed sculptures, the temple remains in stone and final dimension of bricks at the structural sites.

[10] Gupta, 2007:25.

[11] Sarma, 1991.

[12] Ray, 2006:72.

[13] Tripati, 2000.

The intermixing of the cultures and rituals were very much evident in the Buddhist settlements are still practised by the people of these areas. Festivals like Bali *yātrā* (voyage to Bali) which is an ancient sea voyage festival dedicated to the safety of the merchants, originally practised in Bali, Java, Malay, Sumatra and Thailand, is still celebrated by the people of Odisha as a social function.

The explorations based on the geographical data provided by an inscription, at the empirical levels, bring forth the archaeological database from a region that already has yielded a number of other clusters of archaeological settlements of the early medieval period and the different categories of artefacts derived from such a study may raise larger issues such as the relevance of specific ranges of artefacts as determinants of—early rural or urban medieval|| settlements. In contrast with the popular image, the early Buddhist monasteries are to be located close to the big settlements for various reasons of safety, accessibility to resources and offerings from the lay communities. The growth of religion in this region was under patronage from the royal sources and merchant guilds that enabled free movement of laymen in the monastic areas.

The 5th–6th century inscription from Malay Peninsula (modern Malaysia) clearly denotes the maritime connections of Bengal which was facilitated from the ports like Tamralipti.[14] But on the more firm grounds, it can be said that Bengal carried a great influence when it came to cultural transmission through missionary activities and of which we come to know from an inscription from Java dated 782 CE, that talks about *Kumāraghośa*, an inhabitant of Gauda who was a guru and who set up an image of *Mañjuśrī* in the temple built by the Javanese king in 8th century CE.[15] Similar activities caused the development of Buddhism in far lands of Java and its neighbouring regions during the Palas period and this close connection between the Palas and South Asian kingdoms explains the artistic similarities in the architectural styles and sculptures that can be witnessed in both the regions. This close connection also caused differences in the script of the regions giving rise to proto-Bengali alphabets in the Bengal region.[16]

Thus Buddhism developed a close connection with the state as well. Rulers supported the philosophical basis of the teachings which gave rise to a symbiotic relationship between these ruling bodies and the sangha and contributed to the integration of the monastic communities into the daily activities of trade and economy. A large part of the Buddhist canonical texts state that certain goods and serviceswere to be prohibited for trade, which implies that inexplicitly all other kinds of trade was allowed. Since, trading becomes an occupation which requires a lot of time, administrating the process, finance and other small

[14] JASP, vol.I.

[15] Acri, 2016:87–101.

[16] Majumdar, 1971:582–583.

problems that may appear every now and then, agricultural activities were much more advisable. But *Aṅguttara nikāya* speaks about the capable merchant who should have the proper knowledge of the good's value and prices and should know from where to buy and where to sell the goods in order to gain the most profit. In fact, one of the disciples of Buddha who by profession was a merchant was famous for his generosity.[17]

The Rajbadidanga mound in the village of Jadupur on the old river bed of Bhagirathi in Murshidabad bore the famous Raktamrittika Mahavihara for which the archaeologists tried to trace the land for many years only to gain the success by a team of archaeologist from Calcutta University led by Dr. S.R. Das in 1962.[18] As suggested by the archaeologists after examining the material culture from the site of Rajbadidanga, the early phase (phase 1) of activities on the mound date back to 3rd–4th C CE, which was the time period when the entire region of the Brahmaputra valley (present day Guwahati, Tezpur), northern part of Bangladesh and some parts of Bihar and West Bengal were consolidated under Kamarupa kingdom, a frontier kingdom of the Guptas that was being ruled by different dynasties having their own capitals.[19] Hence, chronology of the site indicates that it was the Varmans who were in the power when Buddhist influence began as the some of the seals found during the excavation had Buddhist elements (*dharmacakra*) and pointed towards the presence of a monastery. It was later during the excavation of phase 3; a seal was found on which the name of the monastery, i.e., Raktamrittika Mahavihara, was inscribed —*Raktamrittikasangharama*.[20] The name of the monastery,—Raktamrittika literally means red soil or red earth which is justified if one takes a look at the colour of the soil around the entire region of Murshidabad. The presence of lime and oxide of iron makes the soil appear as greyish or reddish and due to the clayish nature of the soil with less amount of laterite; it is still used by the villagers for painting walls and floors which again generates a cooling affect during the summers. The lime-plastered walls and floors of the monastery were also painted with red clay soil which during the excavations came into exposure.

---

[17] Budhhist Studies,—Anathapindika—The Feeder of the Poor, https://www. buddhanet.net/ e-learning/buddhism/disciples11.htm (Accessed January 18, 2018).

[18] Das, 1968.

[19] Sircar, 1990:64.

[20] IAR, 1966–1967:47.

The site produced number of inscribed seals bearing names of individuals such as—*Sri Vanika Varendrasya*,[21] the merchant of Varendra could be explained as a part of keeping a record the names of the donators. Amongst these seals two such inscribed seals are to be highlighted here, one inscribed with Pallava characters dated back to 5th–7th C CE and one with Roman script carrying the letters—OABORRA, probably a name.[22] These two seals can be linked with the Buddhagupta seal from Malay Peninsula scribed in Pallava script and the Roman seal bearing the name of Horae respectively. These seals with—foreign features|| direct towards the frequency of traders or simply outsiders who visited the monastery either merit earnings or passed through while travelling.

The monastic complex is a *Pañcāyatana*[23] complex enclosed by a rectangular wall, squared shaped shrines at the four corners and the main shrine is in the *trīratha* layout[24] with the entrance to the shrine on the northern side.[25] The floors were *surkhi* rammed. According to the structural remains, the site was enumerated into 5 phases where phase 1 was the earliest structure built on the natural soil and phase 2 comprised of the platform built on a thin layer of soil deposition, dating back to 2nd–3rd to 4th–5th C CE, phase 3 and 4 had the platform and circular basements for the *stupas* and walls running over the circular basements belonging to 5th–6th to 9th–10th C CE. The later structures of the enclosing compound wall and lime plastered floors and platforms painted with red clay soil belong to 9th–10th to the 12th–13th C CE. The addition of the enclosure wall around the monastic structure, in the later phase could be an indication of the change in the ritualistic practices, probably the esoteric practices which required enclosed and secretive space. The recovery of two skulls from a wall of phase 3 and foundation wall of a trench,[26] one of which, after examination leads to the conclusion that it belonged to an adult male above the age of 20 who

[21] IAR, 1968–69:43.

[22] *Ibid.*

[23] *Pañcāyatana* is a type of religious architectural style where the main shrine is built on a rectangular plinth with four smaller subsidiary shrines at the four corners, making a total number of five structures.

[24] *Trīratha* is another type of religious architectural style where the main structure has projection on three sides and the entrance from the fourth side.

[25] IAR, 1964–1965.

[26] IAR, 1963–1964 and 1964–1965.

was decapitated for a significant purpose, most likely human sacrifices.[27] This could be explained by the existence of tantric ritualistic practices as the region of Rajbadidanga was familiarly in contact with the Kamarupa region which was an important centre for the Tantric school of Buddhism. Since in Bengal, the appropriation of Hindu Tantra into Buddhist Tantra and a bridge between two was prevalent in the ritualistic form but the distinct ideologies were developed later, by 8th or 9th century, the esoteric practises started influencing the few monastics of Raktamrittika too and since the rituals were performed secretively to avoid banishment from the sangha, the skulls were kept hidden inside chambers inside the walls.

Table1. Cultural assemblages of Rajbadidanga.

Cultural period	Phase and Structural Remains	Material Culture
Period 1: Early (2nd–3rd to 4th–5th century AD)	Phase 1 and 2: Wall built on natural soil, platform built on slit deposition and wall structure	Pottery: Red and black wares, plain and crude Artefacts: Uninscribed seals, hand-modelled terracotta figurines, balls, discs, beads and shells
Period 2: (5th–6th to 9th–10th century AD) chakra, human	Phase 3 and 4: Circular stupa base, staircase like structure, platforms, walls running over stupa bases.	Pottery: Finely polished pot shards, painted pottery fragments. Artefacts: Inscribed seal (including the one with name of the monastery), burnt grains, stucco heads, copper terracotta figurines, balls, discs, beads and shell objects, iron objects, skulls
Period 3: (9th–10th to 12th–13th century AD)	Phase 5 and 6: Wall enclosing the squared structures, plastered floors, circular stūpa bases, platforms with post holes.	Artefacts: Uninscribed seals.

[27] Das, 1971.

The recently excavated archaeological site at Moghalmari, in the district of West Midnapore, West Bengal, India lies on the south-west border of the district and is in close proximity to the neighbouring state, Odisha. Chinese traveller Faxian visited Bengal during 411–412 CE and in his account recorded about 24 monasteries in the region of Tamralipta (present-day in Medinipur district) and another Chinese traveller, Xuanzang had mentioned of an old Buddhist monastery in Bengal, even older than Raktamrittika Mahavihara (Karnasubarna). However, any proofs of existence of a monastery in the region of Tamluk were not found until the discovery at Moghalmari which now the archaeologists and historians assuming might finally bring the age-old mystery to an end as the site is very close to the port of Tamluk which had extensive connections with distant lands from the Mauryan period. Such material evidence might justify this hypothesis, but looking at the descriptions of the Chinese travellers where this Buddhist monastery at Moghalmari have been said to be spread (over a very large area) and the monastic seal confirming the identity of the monastery the scholars are still hopeful of its link with the Chinese. Presently, the whole village of Moghalmari is on the top of a mound, which is presumably part of the monastic site which now locally is called the—*Sakhi śena* or—*Saśi śena*, the mound was rediscovered in 1999 by a local historian Bratindra Nath Mukherjee who was exploring the Buddhist maritime trade centres in the region of Bengal-Odisha coasts. The mounds or the sites in the study area are locally called as *danga, dhip, dhipi*. From the nature of the record, it is apparent that the sites have both buried artefacts in the form of mounds where the gradational activities are noticeable.

Looking at the various phases in which the monastery was built and the kinds of artefacts which belong to different periods of time and not all of them have its origin from outside this region. This clearly indicates towards the long span of the site and the continuous occupation Moghalmari have had. The bronze artefacts, dating back to 5th and 6th C CE, the copper coin probably belonging to the 7th C CE during the rule of King Sasanka of Gauda, the black ware potteries, all of them represents the various types of influence and patrons that the monastery received.

It has been pointed out by the archaeologists that unlike the contemporary popular Buddhist monasteries of India which bore a large number of stucco figures of religious significance, in Moghalmari the stucco art have been used only as decorative pieces on the main stupa.[28]

---

[28] Datta, 2008:30.

For instance, there is a stucco figure of a *mithuna* and Saraswati on the outer wall which has a similarity with the stucco art on the sculpture panels of temple–2 of Nalanda Mahavihara where along with religious images Barahmanical traditions such as of Śiva, Parvati, there are images of Kinnara and Mithuna as well. Susan Huntington justifies the placement of Hindu images in a Buddhist religious monument by stating that—as a part of the *maṇḍalas* in the Vajryana sect of Buddhism, images of Hindu deities are contextualised into Buddhist domain and are placed in the outer ring of the *maṇḍala*, where the temple is considered to be the centre.[29] If this argument is applied to Moghalmari, then it can be presumed that the main *stupa* structure was built in the Vajrayana phase or it due to the change in the ideology, the *stupa* was altered, perhaps added with such arcitectural features that were prevalent in the domain of Vajrayana sect.

On the basis of all the archaeological evidence including palaeography and the nature of the architecture, and style; we can safely place that the construction and growth here happened in two phases. The first was between the 6th and 7th C CE while the second was in the 9th and 10th C CE. The latter has been has been compared with the contemporary Buddhist monasteries at Vikramshila, Nalanda, Paharpur, Mainamati etc. of India and Bangladesh due to its similarities in terms of stucco decoration and decorative bricks.The archaeological excavations have so far given the outcome by which Moghalmari has been established as a significant part of the Buddhist history of Bengal.

It is to be noted that both the monastic establishments at Karnasubarna and Moghalmari were very close to rivers, i.e., Bhagirathi and Subarnarekha River respectively and since; rivers have always been used very frequently in Bengal for various purposes, the locales used it for their daily movements and the monastic people also must have made use of the same route for their movements that enabled them to interact with the lay population.[30] Moreover, the prominence of river or streams in the landscape of Bengal has been reflected in the development of fluvial geomorphology and fluvio-deltaic architecture and as the Tamralipti port area was sustained by the fluvial channel created by Bhagirathi, Hugli and Rupnarayan rivers. It also suggests a flourishing agrarian economy; the granary at Rajbadidanga, indicates towards the possible engagement of the monastic population in the agricultural activities as well. Similarly, for other sites in close proximity to water

---

[29] Huntington, 1984:24.

[30] Chakrabarty, 2001.

Table 2. Cultural assemblages of Moghalmari

Cultural period	Phase and Structural Remains	Material Culture
Period 1: Chalcolithic/ BRW culture(1300–1200 BC)[31]	*Sijua* formation.[32] Early agricultural settlements. No structural remains	Pottery: Painted BRW with patterns and designs Artefacts: Hopscotch, animal bones
Period 2: Early medieval period	Phase 1: Circular brick structures, *triratha* wall structure, stucco panel, circumambulatory path around the sanctum stūpa.	Pottery: Black polished wares, appliqued red wares, decorated shards, buff and grey wares. Artefacts: Buddha image in *bhūmisparśamudrā,* bricks and brickbats, terracotta lamps, terracotta lamps, inscribed seals, iron nails, bronze figures of Buddha, and *Avalokiteśvara.*
Period 3: Late medieval period (9th–12th century AD)	Phase 2: Stupa structures, large cells converted into smaller fragmented cells, extended circumambulatory path.	Pottery: Red and Black wares, Buff wares. Red and Black wares, Buff wares. Artefacts: Brickbats, charcoal, iron ores and objects (nails, pins, bangles etc.), slag, collapsed materials.

bodies, mapping and analysis of soil compositions might give a better insight of the scenario.

Evidence of a large quantity of iron slag and fair amount of iron objects along with charcoal, stones beads, cowries and conch shells implies the existence of craftsmen within the monastery that could either

[31] Datta, 2004:59.

[32] Sijua formation, popularly known as fluvial landforms is a geomorphological process which is formed by running water that sculpts the land surface giving it a new form. It could either be formed by continuous flow of water, as in a river streams or by floods.

mean that the local or non-monastic people had access inside the monastery or the monks themselves were engaged in craftsmanship. The copperplate inscriptions for land grants indicate the importance of these monasteries in the society in regards to its functions. This also suggests the symbiotic relation between the state and the religion at each level. Similar to Nalanda Mahavihara, these monasteries also must have held some political power, at least at the village levels as they contributed to the economy of the society and in the process of urbanisation, such economic bodies have always been in power in one form or other.

All these observations were helpful in understanding the spatio-temporal functionality of these Buddhist monastic settlements of Bengal. The earlier works cover a much broad area in terms of geographical area and time span as well which has provided a generalised idea of the issue. But in recent times, studies have been carried out from different perspectives to have a better understanding of the functioning of religious bodies in the sphere of economy. Especially, in the case of trading networks and urban development of Bengal, only a few prominent sites like Tamluk and Chandraketugarh are thoroughly discussed while the smaller or less explored sites are often kept out of the picture therefore, creating a gap in the historical narratives or missing out on important links. Explorations and such thorough study from different perspectives of the minor sites can yield potential evidence to connect the links and provide a better scenario.

As the present work examines these aspects of Buddhist monasteries of eastern India, focusing on Bengal (West Bengal) out of their religious sphere, for further study a comparison can be drawn between the Buddhist monastic settlements of western and southern India within the same time period. Since, the early medieval period has been theorised as the phase of urban decay taking place all over the Indian subcontinent but at the regional levels, this theory somehow becomes contradictory. The increase in the volume of trading activities must have required improvement and development in the organisations which further must have made a localised establishment to generate a corporate atmosphere between the commercial bodies and the local population. One can infer the valuable services to the people that these monastic institutions from the epigraphical and literary sources connecting them with the archaeological evidence (sailors, skilled monks). Thus, this comprehensive study of the archaeology of medieval Bengal along with the literary sources and geographical data highlights the vast network in the sphere of Indian trade mechanism and cultural development of the region alongside its neighbouring regions.

Reference

1. Acri, Andrea, 2016, *Esoteric Buddhism in mediaeval maritime Asia: Networks of masters, texts, icons*, vol.27, ISEAS–Yusof Ishak Institute.
2. Ahir, Diwan Chand, 2003, *Buddhist Sites and Shrines in India: History, Art and Architecture*, Sri Satguru Publications.
3. Beal, Samuel, 1884, *Buddhist Records of the Western World*, vol.II, London, Trübner.
4. Beal, Samuel, 1957, *Chinese Accounts of India*, vol.I, Kolkata, Susil Gupta Private Limited.
5. Chakravarti, N.P. (ed.), 1952, *Epigraphia Indica*, vol.26, 1941–1942, Delhi.
6. Chakrabarty, D.K., 2001, *Archaeological Geography of the Ganga Plain: The Lower and the Middle Ganga*, Permanent Black.
7. Das, Sudhir Ranjan, 1971, *Archaeological Discoveries from Murśidābād District, West Bengal*, vol.1, Calcutta: Asiatic Society.
8. Datta, Asok, 2008, *Excavations at Moghalmāri*, The Asiatic Society.
9. Datta, Asok, 2004, "Chalcolithic Culture of West Bengal: An Overview", in *Bulletin of the Deccan College Research Institute* 64: pp.59–72.
10. Das, Sudhir Ranjan, 1968, *Rājbāḍīdāṅgā*, 1962 (*Chiruṭī: Jadupur*): *An Interim Report on Excavations at Rājbāḍīdāṅgā and Terracotta Seals and Sealings*, vol.14, Asiatic Society.
11. Gupta, Sunil, 2007, "The Bay of Bengal interaction sphere (1000 BC–AD 500)", in *Bulletin of the Indo-Pacific Prehistory Association 25*: pp.21–30.
12. Huntington, Susan L., 1984, *The Paala-Sena Schools of Sculpture*, vol.10, Brill Archive.
13. Liu, Xinru, 2010, *The Silk Road in world history*, Oxford University Press.
14. Majumdar, R.C., 1971, *History of Ancient Bengal*, Calcutta.
15. Neelis, Jason, 2011, *Early Buddhist Transmission and Trade Networks: Mobility and Exchange within and beyond the Northwestern Borderlands of South Asia*, Brill.
16. Ray, Himanshu Prabha, 2006, "The Archaeology of Bengal: Trading Networks, Cultural Identities", in *Journal of the Economic and Social History of the Orient 49*, no.1: pp.68–95.
17. Ray, Himanshu Prabha, 1997, "The emergence of urban centres in Bengal: implications for the late prehistory of Southeast Asia" in *Bulletin of the indo-Pacific Prehistory Association 16*: pp.43–48.
18. Sarma, I.K., 1991, Rare evidences on Maritime Trade on the Bengal coast of India in *Recent Advances in Marine Archaeology*, ed. by S.R. Rao, Goa: Society for Marine Archaeology, NIO.
19. Sircar, D.C., 1990, "Pragjyotisha-Kamarupa" in *Barpujari, H.K., The Comprehensive History of Assam I*, Guwahati: Publication Board, Assam.
20. Tripathi, Sila, 2000, *Maritime Archaeology: Historical Descriptions of the Kalingas*, Kaveri Books.
21. Budhhist Studies, Anathapindika, The Feeder of the Poor, Accessed January 18, 2018. https://www.buddhanet.net/e-learning/buddhism/disciples11.htm
22. Chakravarti, Adhir, 2006, *Urban Development in Ancient India*, The Asiatic Society.

23. Jha, Amit, 2015, *Viharas in Early Medieval Eastern India*, Lulu.com.
24. Mitra, Debala, 1971, *Buddhist Monuments*, Sahitya Samsad.
25. Mukherjee, Samir K., 1996, "A Note on Some Buddhist Antiquities in Terracotta from West Bengal", in *Journal of Bengal Art 1*.
26. Mukherjee, S. and Mukherjee, T. Tapas, 2014, "Discovery of a Buddhist Monastery at Moghalmāri", in *Paschim Medinipur. Chitrolekha International Magazine on Art and Design*, vol.4, no.1.
27. Pradhan, Atanu and Jana, Santu, 2017, "*Unearthing Bengal's link with Buddhism*", Tapati Publisher.
28. Soren, Sumit, 2012, "In the Footsteps of Hsüan-tsang, in Karnasubarna", in *Chitrolekha International Magazine on Art and Design*, vol.2, no.1.

Anchoring system in Ancient India, with Reference to Gujarat coast, India

A.S. Gaur

Abstract

The Indian coast, with a long history of maritime activities, has been dotted with several ancient ports. The evidence for this exists in port-related structures on the shore and in relics lying in the sea adjacent. Marine archaeological explorations during the last three decades have revealed the existence of ancient jetties at Dwarka, Rupen Bandar, Porbandar and Sultanpur and offshore anchoring points at Bet Dwarka, Miyani, Visawada and Somnath, Kodinar and Ghogha on the Gujarat coast.

Introduction

The archaeological evidences along the Gujarat coast have indicated that, the area was under intense maritime activities dating back to the Harappan period. The coast has been punctuated with several creeks and tidal rivers those provide sheltered harbour. A few coastal sites namely Lothal (Rao, 1979), Ghogha (Gaur, 2010), Padri (Shinde, 1992), Hathab (Pramanik, 2004), Somnath (Sankalia, 1974), Porbandar (Gaur and Sundaresh, 2006), Dwarka (Ansari and Mate, 1966, Rao, 1990, Gaur et al. 2008), Bet Dwarka (Gaur et al 2005) and Nageshwar (Hegde et al., 1990) have been excavated extensively and the remains of maritime activities have been documented. The time bracket for these sites varies from the early Harappan phase to the Medieval period. Archaeological records from the Gulf countries indicate that during the Harappan period traders from the Saurashtra coast plied their boats as far as Oman, UAE and Bahrain and established their colonies. During the historical period Roman traded extensively as large amount of evidence have been recorded from Saurashtra coast. Recent maritime archaeological investigations suggest that Saurashtra coast witnessed tremendous growth in maritime activities as a large number of stone anchors indicating anchoring points have been found at several places.

An ancient Sanskrit text *Arthasastra* (Kangle, 1963) of Kautilya finds the description of a Superintending of Shipping *(Navadhyaksha)* who was in charge of the ocean going ships and strictly enforced the rules framed for the management of ports. He was empowered to destroy pirates and punish those who did not follow the rules. The owner of the ship had to pay taxes before leaving the port, for example. Further, the anonymous author of the *Periplus of the Erythrean Sea* dating back to the 1st CE (Schoff, 1912) has mentioned a chain of ports along the Indian coast. The ancient texts, including the Indian (such as Tamil Sangam literature, Persian literature) and foreign sources (Ptolemy's Geography, Arian's Indica etc.), have also made ample references on the existence of harbours and ports along the Indian coast during the historical and the medieval periods. Further, *Pattana* is a Sanskrit term for the word port, that has been used in various ancient texts, appearing as two types namely *SamudRapattana* i.e. port on the coast of a sea and *Jalapattana* on the bank of a navigable river (Roy, 1994).

In an archaeological context, structures associated with ports and jetties have been discovered along the Mediterranean coast including at Carthage and Thapsus on the Tunisian coast (Muckelroy, 1977), Caesarea on Israel coast (Raban, 1992) etc. The excavation at Ur on the bank of the river Euphrates had revealed a massive brick structure, identified as a harbour (Woolley, 1974), the oldest remnant of any port structure in the world. Similarly, archaeological studies of the oldest known civilization of the Indian subcontinent, namely the Indus Civilization, indicate the existence of the port structures at Lothal (Rao, 1979), and Kuntasi (Dhavalikar et al., 1996). Further, underwater explorations along the Indian coast, during last two decades have yielded a large amount of data on the existence of ancient ports, jetties and anchoring points. In the last case we refer to places where vessels are known to have moored i.e. to sit at anchor offshore. An important artifact for identification of a port and anchoring point is the anchor itself, and usually these are lost having parted from the parent boat through a break in the cable or other accident such as being abandoned due to the sudden onset of storms or being caught on the seabed. These lost anchors are amply found all along the Indian coast.

The present paper then deals with some elements of the underwater archaeology of ports, jetty and anchoring points along the Indian coast with special mention of the Saurashtra coast as an example of the nature of this resource. The important antiquities mentioned include underwater and onshore timber and stone structures and stone anchors recovered during the marine archaeological explorations.

Coastal explorations along the Saurashtra coast

Saurashtra coast has been an important area where maritime archaeological investigations carried out in the first decade of 21st century. The important site include Dwarka, Bet Dwarka, Miyani, Visawada, Kindar Kheda, Porbandar, Mithivirdi, Kodinar, and in the Gulf of Khambhat (Fig.1). A large number of stone anchors found from these sites. The brief description of each site is given below.

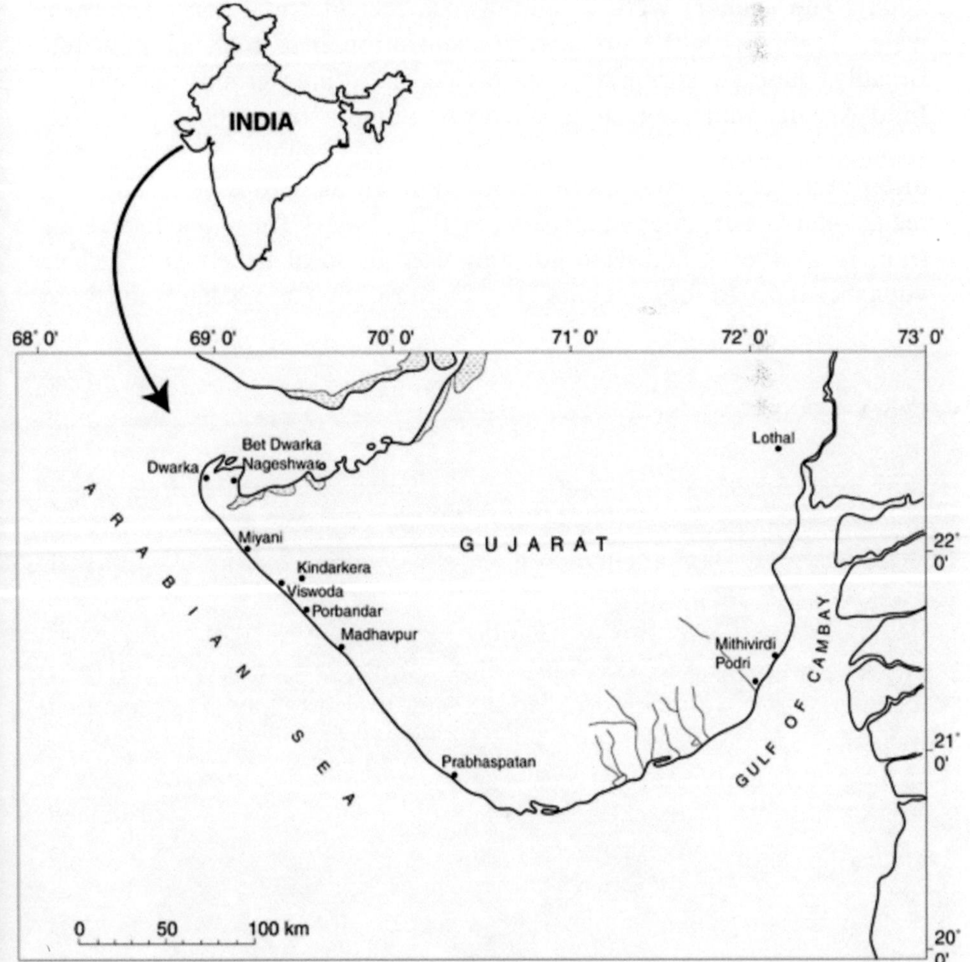

Fig.1.

Dwarka: Maritime archaeological investigations were initiated at Dwarka in 1983 (Rao, 1990) and continued for almost two decades. The extensive diving operations have been undertaken in depths ranging from intertidal zone to water 25 m deep, 1 km off Dwarka. The nearshore underwater topography consists of beach rock formations, covered with dense vegetation. Thick sand deposits, in the small channels, are occasionally noticed. Topography beyond 10 m water depth is sandy with rock boulders and sparse vegetation. A number of artifacts including stone anchors were discovered during offshore explorations in water 3 m and 16 m deep.

Discovery of 125 stone anchors of different shapes and sizes was another important feature of the Dwarka investigations (Gaur et al., 2008). The anchors were noted between the intertidal zone and 16 m water depth, with the greatest concentration in 6 to 8 m of water. Broadly, these anchors have been divided into three groups: composite, Indo-Arabia, and ring stone anchors. Composite anchors are often chiseled out of a thin limestone block and are triangular in shape. They often include an upper circular hole known as a rope hole and two rectangular lower holes referred to as fluke holes. These anchors range from 16 to 496 kg and were probably used by local fishermen for short voyages. Indo-Arabia anchors (Fig.2) were cut from a hard and long

Fig.2.

stone block and are characterized by a tapering upper end pierced with a circular hole and a wider lower end containing two rectangular holes on either face of the block. These anchors are larger than the composite anchors, ranging from 82 to 668 kg, and were used by large vessels undertaking extended voyages such as the Arabian Dhow. Similar anchors have been reported from several port sites of India, Sri Lanka, Arabian coast and east African coast. . Twenty-four ring stone anchors were also located at Dwarka water and they are of various sizes ranging from 20 to 245 kg in weight. Similar ring stone anchors have been reported from Oman waters (Vosmer 1999).

Bet Dwarka: The Island of Bet Dwarka is situated about 30 km north of Dwarka in the entrance of the Gulf of Kachchh. It is famous for its temple dedicated to the Lord Krishna. The Island is a narrow crooked strip of sand and rock about 13 km long. The area is referred to as the Gulf of Barake in the Greek sea guide *Periplus Maris Erythraei* (Schoff 1912), although Ptolemy mentioned Barake as an island in the Gulf of Kanthi, which has been identified as the Gulf of Kachchh (McCrindle 1885). In the seventeenth century BC, the late Harappan people established their settlement on the northwest part of the island (Gaur and Sundaresh 2003). They used rich fish and shellfish resources available around the island as evidenced by a large fishhook and several shell artifacts recovered from the site (Gaur and Sundaresh 2004; Gaur et al., 2005). The scanty habitation deposit suggests that the site was abandoned after a couple of centuries. The southeast coast of the island was again inhabited during the eighth century BC. A vast expansion that followed reached its zenith during the historical and medieval periods. Bet Dwarka continued to be an important center of maritime activity until the emergence of the Okha port in the Okhamandal area in the mid 20th century.

The large quantity of amphorae sherds that were discovered includes examples whose morphology is very similar to Roman amphora types of the fourth through fifth century CE. These ceramic wares were mainly used for exporting wine and olive oil originating in the Roman Empire. As olive oil was in less demand in India and the sherds exhibit a resin coating, it is most probable that the majority of the Indian finds represent wine amphorae (Gaur et al., 2006). A large number of stone anchors representing composite and Indo-Arabia types have been found in 6 to 8 m of water close to the present jetty of Bet Dwarka. The majority of the composite anchors were cut from locally available limestone blocks. Their circular upper hole is often broken whereas the lower two rectangular holes tend to be preserved. The anchors are very similar to those reported from Dwarka and other places in Saurashtra. The Indo-Arabia anchors are predominantly made of a hard rock such as basalt, although some examples are made of hard stone. The stone anchors have been dated to the historical and medieval periods. In addition to the stone anchors, the expeditions also uncovered two 70 kg lead anchors in the vicinity of the amphorae. They are circular in shape with an axial hole and are very similar to ring stone anchors recovered from Dwarka and other places in Saurashtra.

Pindara: The ancient temple site of Pindara is situated on the Northern Saurashtra coast in the Gulf of Kachchh. A huge temple complex (10 by 10 m) is exposed during low tide in Pindara about 300 m from high water line (Gaur and Sundaresh, 2007). A floor area of dressed limestone blocks is well preserved, although the upper works have been destroyed and the stone blocks have been washed or taken away. The temple was dedicated to the Lord *Shiva*, as a *yoni* is present in the sanctum (*Garbhagriha*). The architectural feature of the submerged complex corresponds more or less with the existing temple on the shore of Pindara. The size of the submerged temple must have been contemporary to other surviving temples in the Pindara group of temples that date to the seventh through tenth centuries CE. The archaeological evidence indicates that shoreline has changed significantly during the last 1000 years on the Saurashtra coast.

Miyani: Ancient site of Miyani is situated between Dwarka on the east and Porbandar on the west. This is also famous for ancient temples dating back to the 10th century AD (Sampura, 1968). On the coast of Miyani a temple dedicated to Goddess (locally known as Harshadmata) is situated on a high hill. A vast creek known as Meda creek runs a few kilometers in hinterland area, which has been used as a sheltered harbour for the country craft, particularly fishing vessel. The coastal area is consisted of plain sandy beaches except a high hill over which a temple of Goddess is situated. Underwater explorations have been undertaken about 1 km offshore of Harshad Mata temple. The seabed comprises of sandy channels and rocky outcrops. There is not much vegetation growth noticed. Several places small gravels were also noticed. Sand is comprises of clayey element which makes visibility very poor. Twelve artifacts were discovered from here.

Visawada: Visawada also know as Mul Dwarka is situated about 40 km west of Porbandar and about 20 km east of Miyani. The Hindu pilgrimage center and a temple dedicated to the Lord Krishna, is situated in the middle of the town. A creek (known as Kindari Creek) runs to a long distance at least up to Kindar Kheda (a Harappan town) and perhaps Kindari name derived from this particular ancient town. The western side of the coast is represented by a high cliff while the eastern coast is consisted of sandy beach.

Explorations have been undertaken off Kindari Creek about 500 m from coastline. Seabed topography is consisted of sandy channels and rocky outcrops. At several places small boulders and dense growth of vegetation was observed. Water depth varies between 8 to 5 m, however, archaeological findings were concentrated between 5–6 m water depths. Total 14 stone anchors have been found and they represent by three varieties known as composite, Indo-Arabia and ring stone types.

Somnath: The Prabhasa—Somnath coast forms a straight line revealing a vivid manifestation of marine aeolian and fluvial processes that have resulted in a number of important geomorphic land forms, as the near shore zone is characterized by the formation of recent alluvium deposits, sand bars, mud flats and mangroves swamps. The coastal zone is covered with beaches and littoral sand, oyster beds and sand dunes. The explored area in Somnath water is located at a distance of 400 m south-west of the Somnath temple. The study area is comprised of rocky out crop and sandy patches. During the first season 6 objects, second season yielded 8 objects and present season 2001 yielded 21 ring stones. A large number of ring stones have been recorded off Somnath on the Saurashtra coast. Out of 43 total discovered stone anchors, 80% belong to ring stone category. The water depth varies from 7 m to 15 m. The ring stone noticed in less than 8m water depth and the growth of seaweeds also noticed, however ring stones of deeper depths have a layer of greyish marine growth.

Kodinar (Mul Dwarka): A small coastal village known as Mul Dwarka near Kodinar in the district of Junagad is one of the claimant of the original Dwarka of Mahabharata. The proximity with Junagadh hills on the north and sea on the south the town has been associated with Dwarka (Sankalia, 1966). An ancient temple is situated on a raised land close to the sea. The shrine is dated to the post 10th century AD (Sampura, 1968). A circular structure of about 4 m in height constructed with similar type of dressed limestone blocks as of the temple in situated close to ancient temple. Locally this structure is called as *Diva Dandi* (lighthouse). If this structure has served as lighthouse then this may be the oldest remains of lighthouse on the Saurashtra coast.

The exploration in inter tidal zone yielded a composite stone anchor. The anchor gets exposed during low tide. It is made of sedimentary rock. The anchor has an upper circular hole and lower two holes are square. The upper portion is semicircular and edges are sharp. The thickness of anchor gradually increases from 12 cm at upper end to 20 cm at lower end. The anchor is similar to those reported from Dwarka (Gaur et al., 2008) and Bet Dwarka (Gaur et al., 2005) and dated between the historical and the medieval periods.

The underwater investigations in and around Mul Dwarka (Kodinar) have been of significant in respect of understanding the archaeology of this region. Now the data of underwater explorations from all the three Dwarka on the Saurashtra coast are available and the most common aspects of them is the present of similar type of stone anchors, therefore, the tradition of Dwarka at these places might have been existed at a same time (in the Early Medieval Period). Another common aspect of these sites is the presence of Harappan and late Harappan settlement within close proximity, for example, Nageshwar and Bet Dwarka near Okhamandal Dwarka, Kindar Kheda near Mul Dwarka (Visawada) and Kanjetar and Kaj near Mul Dwarka (Kodinar). All the three Dwarka have ancient temples dated to the 10th–12th century AD. Nonetheless, these sites were ancient busy ports and perhaps temples were served as coastal marker point for navigator and also they worship before embarking on the long voyage.

Mithi Virdi: The small village Mithi Virdi is situated about 30 km south east of Talaja, a *taluka*, headquarter. The village is lying on a raised plateau close to the seashore. A small seasonal river merges with the sea on the western side of the village. Archaeological site is located about a km west of the village in an agriculture field. The area is comprised of reddish soil with small quartz gravel signifying the flow of the river channel from this area.

Five stone anchors are lying in an agricultural land (ground nuts are the important crop of this field) about 1 km north of the seashore. Three anchors are lying together at a distance of 10 m and oriented in the east-west direction. One anchor is in a broken condition. The fourth anchor is laying partially buried north of the other three and oriented in the east west direction.

All the anchors are similar to each other in shape and sizes. The anchors have rectangular cross-sections and trapezoidal longitudinal sections. These have sharp edges and chisel marks on them are clearly noticed. They have been cut from conglomeratic sedimentary grit rock, which is dark brown in colour and small gravel can be noticed. The anchors have only lower two rectangular holes and upper circular hole is absent in all the anchors.

Ghogha: The town of Gogha is located on the mid western coast of the Gulf of Khambhat in Bhavnagar district of Gujarat. A famous Gujarati proverb "*Lankani lari ane Ghoghono var*" (Bride of Lanka and groom of Ghogha) indicates direct overseas relation between Gogha and Sri Lanka in the past (Chaukasi, 1989). The presence of ancient Jaina temples at Gogha dating back to the 10th–11th centuries suggest that this was a religious center also. The earliest Arabic inscription from Gogha dates to 1170 AD (Oza, 1885). During the British period ships up to 1500 tons were laden here (Habib, 1982).

The exploration at Gogha was undertaken during low tide and findings were recorded with still photography and drawing. A large number of stone anchors were recorded between 100 and 200 m distance from the high water line. The majority of the anchors belong to the Indo-Arab type and nearly about 40% anchors are fragmented. Interestingly, the fresh surface of broken part suggests that fragmentation of the anchors took place during the manufacturing stage and not during the anchoring processes. A composite anchor made of lime stone is another noteworthy finds from the site. A few anchors unfinished were also found from Gogha and Hathab. However, these anchors submerge in 5 to 7 m water depth during high tide. Thus, it indicates that big boats were anchoring at this point during high tide. The author of the *Periplus of the Erythrenean* also refers that during low tide boats rest on the seabed.

The exploration in inter tidal zone has also yielded several sherds of the glazed ware in the vicinity of stone anchors. These include a jar with internally and upper half externally glazed and rests of the sherds are glazed only internally. There are three main type of glazed ware i.e. green, blue and brown. These are very similar to the Islamic glazed ware found from various parts of the country (Mohammad, 1985). The medieval period glazed ware at Hastinapur (Lal, 1954–1955) was found in association with coins of Balban (1206–1287 AD). The sherds recovered from the inter-tidal zone of Ghogha are very similar to those reported from another medieval period site at Lashkarshah in Khambhat which have been dated to 14–16th century (Bhan, 2006). Thus the glazed sherds Ghogha may also be dated to the late medieval period.

Hathab: Hathab an early historical site finds mention as *Astacampra* in the Periplus of Erythrenean Sea (Schoff, 1912). On shore excavation yielded rich antiquities of the historical period and maritime contact with the west. It is located about a km in hinterland. The exploration in inter tidal zone of Hathab yielded 2 anchors similar to those of Indo-Arab type and one anchor with a wide groove surrounding in middle of the anchor. This is very similar to those reported from Japan and Chinese waters.

Discussion and Conclusions

The port plays a dominant role in facilitating the sea trade and there were several ports all along the India coast since antiquity. The prerequisite of the selection of any port site include a sheltered place particularly protection from high wind and rough seas, sufficient water depth for sailing the vessel and a suitable anchoring point. Besides structural part of the port, it is also important to keep in mind that the enough products from the hinterland reach to the port and from the port to hinterland. The majority of the ancient ports were situated on the river banks and the back waters. A few Harappan sites including Kuntasi (Dhavalikar et al., 1996), Amra, Lakhawavel and Vasai (Rao, 1991) on the northern Saurashtra coast are located on the banks of tidal rivers where tidal variation is as high as 5 m that helped mariners to reach up to the site during high tide.

The archaeological findings have indicated the existence of several ports, jetties and anchoring points along the west coast of India from the protohistoric period (Ray, 2003) onward. The discovery of a large number of stone structures and anchors at Dwarka suggests that it was a busy port during the historical and the medieval times (Gaur et al., 2004). This is a direct reflection of the practices referred to above. Though there is no remains of an ancient jetty at Bet Dwarka the presence of the stone anchors in inter tidal zone indicate that the high tide was effectively used for beaching the boats. Conversely, the northwest coast of India has jetties in creeks, which are made of limestone blocks while southern side traditional wooden jetties continued to be in use.

The tidal variation and seabed topography played a significant role in construction of jetties. As stated earlier, that the higher tidal variation in Gujarat has been used by the navigators to anchor the boats in inter tidal zone and loading unloading of boat become easier. It has also been confirmed with the discovery of stone anchors from inter tidal zone areas of Dwarka, Bet Dwarka and Armada. The stone anchors are the indicator of the ancient anchoring points and underwater findings have indicated that the preferred anchoring points on the Saurashtra coast falls between 5 and 7 m water depth.

Acknowledgements

I thank Director, CSIR-National Institute of Oceanography, Goa encouragement and for providing facilities during the study and thanks also due to the members of the marine archaeology centre for the help rendered during the field work. Shri. S.B. Chitari prepared line drawings.

References

1. Ansari, Z.D. and Mate, M.S., 1966, *Excavations at Dwarka*, Pune: Deccan College Postgraduate and Research Institute.
2. Chaukasi, U.M., 1989, *Gazetteer of Bhavnagar District* (in Gujarati), Ahmedabad: Government of Gujarat.
3. Dhavalikar, M.K., Raval, M.R. and Chitalwala, Y.M., 1996, *Kuntasi: A Harappan emporium on West Coast*, Pune: Deccan College Post-Graduate Research Institute.
4. Gaur, A.S. and Sundaresh, 2003, Onshore excavation at Bet Dwarka Island, in the Gulf of Kachchh, Gujarat, *Man and Environment* XXVIII(1):57–66.
5. Gaur, A.S. and Sundaresh, 2004, A late Bronze Age Copper Fish-hook from Bet Dwarka, Gujarat: An evidence on the Advance fishing Technology, *Current Science*, 86(4):512–514.
6. Gaur, A.S., Sundaresh and Vardhan P., 2005, Ancient shell Industry at Bet Dwarka, *Current Science* 89(6):941–946.
7. Gaur, A.S. and Sundaresh, 2006, Excavation at Bokhira (Porbandar) on the Southwestern coast of Saurashtra, *Man and Environment*, XXXI (1):33–39.
8. Gaur, A.S., Sundaresh and Sila Tripati, 2004. Dwarka: an ancient harbour. *Current Science*, 86.9:1256–1260.
9. Gaur, A.S., Sundaresh and Vora, K.H., 2005, *Archaeology of Bet Dwarka Island: An Excavation Report*, New Delhi: Aryan Books International.
10. Gaur, A.S., Sundaresh, Sila Tripati, 2006, Evidence for Indo-Roman trade from Bet Dwarka waters, West Coast of India, *International Journal of Nautical Archaeology*, 35.1:117–127.
11. Gaur, A.S. and Sundaresh, 2007, Evidence of Shoreline changes in the Gulf of Kachchh, based on the submerged temple complex at Pindara, *Current Science*, 92.6:733–735.
12. Gaur, A.S. Sundaresh and Vora, K.H., 2008, *Underwater Archaeology of Dwarka and Somnath (1997–2002)*, New Delhi: Aryan Books International.
13. Gaur, A.S., 2010, Gogha: An Indo-Arab trading Post in the Gulf of Khambhat (Cambay), *International Journal of Nautical Archaeology*, 39.1:146–155.
14. Habib, I., 1982, *An Atlas of the Mughal Empire*, Delhi: Oxford University Press.
15. Hegde, K.T.M., Bhan, K.K., Sonawane, V.H., Krishnana, K. Shah, D.R., 1990, *Excavation at Nageswar Gujarat: A Harappan Shell working site on the Gulf of Kutch*, Vadodara: M.S. University of Baroda.
16. Kangle, R.P., 1963, *The Kautilya Arthasastra, Part II, An English Translation with Critical and Explanatory Notes*, Bombay: University of Bombay, later edition, 1972.

17. Lal, B.B., 1954–1955, Excavations at Hastinapura and Other Explorations in Upper Ganga and Sutlej Basins, *Ancient India*, 10–11:5–151.
18. McCrindle, J.W., 1885, *Ancient India as described by Ptolemy* (reprinted in 1985), New Delhi: Today & Tommarrow's Printers and Publishers.ohammed, K.K., 1985, Glazed ware in India, *Puratattva*, 15:105–110.
19. Muckelroy, K., 1977, *Maritime Archaeology*, Cambridge: Cambridge University Press, UK.
20. Oza, V.G., 1885, *Old research collection of Bhavnagar*, Bhavnagar.
21. Pramanik, S., 2004, Hathab: An Early Historic Port on the Gulf of Khambhat. *Journal of Indian Ocean Archaeology*, 1:133–140.
22. Raban, A., 1992, Sabastos: the royal harbour at caesarea Maritima—a short-lived giant. *International Journal of Nautical Archaeology*, 21:111–124.
23. Rao, S.R., 1979, *Lothal-A Harappan Port Town*, Memoir of Archaeological Survey of India, 78, New Delhi: Archaeological Survey of India.
24. Rao, S.R., 1990, Excavation of the legendary city of Dvaraka in the Arabian Sea, *Journal of Marine Archaeology*, 1:59–98.
25. Rao, S.R., 1991, *Dawn and Devolution of the Indus Civilization*, New Delhi: Aditya Prakashan.
26. Ray, H.P., 2003, *The Archaeology of seafaring in ancient South Asia*, Cambridge: Cambridge University press, UK.
27. Roy, U.N., 1994, Dronimukha and Lothal, *The Role of Universities and Research Institutes in Marine Archaeology* (ed. S.R. Rao), Goa: National Institute of Oceanography, pp.33–36.
28. Sampura, K.F., 1968, *The structural temples of Gujarat*, Ahmedabad: Gujarat University.
29. Sankalia, H.D., 1966, Dwarka in Literature and Archaeology, *Excavations at Dwarka* (Ansari and Mate), Pune: Deccan College Postgraduate and Research Institute.
30. Sankalia, H.D., 1974, *Prehistory and Protohistory of India and Pakistan*, Bombay.
31. Schoff, W.H., 1912, *The Periplus of the Erythraean Sea: Travel and Trade in the Indian Ocean by a Merchant of the 1st century*, New York (Reprinted in 1974), New Delhi: Oriental Books Reprint Corporation.
32. Shinde, V., 1992, Padri and the Indus Civilization, *South Asian Studies*, 8:55–66.
33. Vosmer, T., 1999, Maritime Archaeology, Ethnography and History in the Indian Ocean: An Emerging Partnership, in *Archaeology of Seafaring: The Indian Ocean in the Ancient Period* (ed. H.P. Ray), Delhi: Pragati Publication, pp.291–312.

—x—

II. Philosophy, Religion and Texts

Worship of Divine Mother: Philosophy of Srividya and its Spiritual Significance

Yajneshwar S. Shastri

Worship of Divine Mother: philosophical and spiritual Significance of Śrīvidyā

Tantra-śāstra is one of the important branches of Indian thought. Philosophically it represents quintessence of Upaniṣadic philosophy. Spiritually, it is practical scripture of Vedānta. It prescribes the means by which the highest aim of life is fulfilled in an easy way by all, without any discrimination of caste, creed, race and gender. The paper provides a background of the three kinds of Āgamas or Tantras namely, Vaiṣṇava, Śaiva and Śākta. Śāktatantra (from the Śākta denomination) deals with worship of Divine mother and within the Śāktatantra there are three sub-schools: Kaula, Miśra and Samaya. The Samaya group is most important among the Śāktatantra on account of its philosophy and purified method of worship. Furthermore, an understanding is provided of Śrī Vidyā worship—Śrīvidyopāsanā, as a form of worshipping Parabrahman—Supreme Reality as a female entity—Universal Mother, seen by Advaita by Ādi Śaṅkarācārya, along with yantras, meditation. It probes into Śrī Vidyā and its numerous names, such as Śrī Lalitā-Divine beauty, mother of grace, one who sports; Rājarājeśvarī—the eternal empress of all sovereignties, Parābhaṭṭārikā—most imperial majesty or the supreme and sovereign ruler; Kāmeśvarī—the mother of love, goddess of desire; Śrīsundarī—the mother of beauty, Tripurasundarī—the most beautiful in all three worlds, Tripurā, Śrī Mīnākṣī, Śrī Kāmākṣī and Śrī Viśālākṣī. Here, an attempt is made to elucidate the philosophical and spiritual significance of Śrīvidyā through the power of the mantra in the text.

There are three kinds of Āgamas or Tantras namely, Vaiṣṇava, Śaiva and Śākta. Viṣṇu and his consort Lakṣmī are the main deities of Vaiṣṇava Āgamas. Vaiṣṇava Āgamas deal mostly with Qualified Monism, philosophy of devotion, image worship, rules of temple art and architecture, method of worship, worship of Viṣṇu and Tulasī etc. They lay emphasis on devotion and are suited even to the lowest intellectual capacity. More than 108 works with various commentaries belong to this Āgamic tradition show its popularity in olden days. There are 28 Śaiva Āgamas with various commentaries and several independent texts dealing with Śaiva philosophy, method of Śiva worship, temple art and architecture and method of meditation. Philosophically, they preach Śivādvaita, i.e. unity of individual soul with Śiva (Paramātman). They also deal with devotion to Lord Śiva, the process of Yoga and the development of Kuṇḍalinī power.

Śāktatantra has its own history and philosophy. In Śāktatantra, Parāśkti, the force Supreme, the universal Divine Mother (Jagadambā, Śrīmātā) is worshipped as Ultimate Reality. It is one without a second, Absolute Existence, Consciousness and Bliss (saccidānandasvarūpiṇī), similar to Brahman of the Upaniṣads. It propagates Śaktyādvaita i.e. non-duality of Śakti, the unity of individual soul and Śakti, the universal soul. They also talk about path of sādhanā to reach ultimate goal by process of mantra-yoga and Kuṇḍalinī yoga. There are three sub-schools within the Śāktatantra—Kaula, Miśra and Samaya. They have their own independent treatises. The Kaula group has 64 treatises with various commentaries and the Miśra group has 8 treatises with several commentaries.

The Samaya group is most important among the Śāktatantra on account of its exalted Philosophy and purified method of worship. It has Śubhāgamapañcaka and hundreds of independent treatises exploring its philosophy and method of worship. This group of literature points the way to liberation along with the material prosperity. It represents the finest philosophy inherited by the Upaniṣadic literature. It actually represents the quintessence of mysticism which is based on the doctrine of unity of the Individual soul and the Supreme Brahman (Supreme Reality), proclaimed in the oldest Upaniṣads such as "This ātman is Brahman" (ayamātmā brahma—Māṇ.Up.2), "I am the Brahman" (aham brahmāsmi—Br.Upa.I.4.10), "That thou art" (Tattvamasi—Chānd.Up.), and "Pure Consciousness is the Brahman" (Prajñānam Brahma-Aitereya Upa.). This sect of Śāktatantra has touched the keynote of the Advaita Philosophy by accepting the unity of individual soul (jīva) and the Supreme Reality, the Brahman. This Tantra repeatedly states in clear terms that the highest form of yoga-union is the attainment of unity of the individual soul with the Supreme Soul (Aikym jīvātmanorāhuḥ yogam yogaviśāradāḥ-Kulārṇavatantra.ix.31). This Samaya method of Śakti Worship is accepted as the supreme path of realization of Advaita by Ādi Śaṅkarācārya. Its path is purely internal, though, as the first step in the spiritual advancement, it prescribes the external worship of image (vigraha) and diagram (yantra). Internal worship, which consists of inward prayer, deep meditation and solemn contemplation, is considered supreme by the followers of Samaya path.

Śakti worship is not new development in the history of Indian Culture. In this ancient land, for ages the worship of Universal Mother has been prevalent. Worship of Divine Mother was recognized since thousands of years. Divine Mother worship has been traced to the Indus Valley civilization. Śakti cult seems to have prevailed in India at least in circa 3000 BC. The number of hymns written on various goddesses and more than 40 names of goddesses mentioned in the Vedas, indicate a fully articulated form of Śakti worship. The Śakti is specifically referred to in the Ṛgveda with her eight different attributes such as Durga, Kali, Tara etc. Durgāsūkta, Devīsūkta, Śrīsūkta, Rātrisūkta, Uṣassūkta and Prithivīsūkta of the Vedas are clearly indicative of worship of Mother Goddess. The Veda talks about three Goddesses, producer of delight, 'tisro devīr mayobhuvaḥ' (Ṛg.I.I–25 varga. āprī sūktam) The Śvetāśvatara Upaniṣad mentions the One, unborn, red, and white and dark- 'ajām, ekām, lohita-śukla-kṛṣṇām'. There are certain mantras in Ṛgveda and other Vedas which indicate worship of Triangle (Trikoṇa) and Śrīcakra (Ṛg.IV.III.1 varga).

Śrīvidyopāsanā comes under Samaya School of Śāktatantra. Worship of Śrīvidyā is thousands of years old. It is certainly Vaidika, because it is derived from Mantras of Ṛgveda and Atharvaveda (Śrī Lalitātriśati Śāṅkarabhāṣya, Introduction—Y.S. Shastri, p.19). It has a great tradition and antiquity. Śāktatāntric texts mention that Lord Śiva himself has revealed the secrets of Śrīvidyā or Śrī Lalitā. He is the first spiritual teacher of this tradition (Śrīcaryānātho parama Śivo prathamaguruḥ- Nityāṣodaśikārṇavaṭīkā). There are textual evidences that Guru Dattātreya, Hayagrīva, Paraśurāma, Śrī Rāma, Balarāma, Durvāsa, Agastya, Lopāmudrā were great worshippers of Śrīvidyā or Śrī Lalitā. The text Jñānārṇava gives a list of twelve pioneers of Śrīvidyā: Manu, Candra, Kubera, Lopāmudrā, Manmatha, Agastya, Agni, Sūrya, Indra, Skanda, Śiva, and Durvāsa (7.1).

Śrīvidyā is a Universal Mother. She is known by several names in Śāktatāntric texts as Śrī Lalitā—Divine beauty, mother of grace, one who sports; Rājarājeśvarī—the eternal empress of all sovereignties; Parābhaṭṭārikā—most imperial majesty or the supreme and sovereign ruler; Kāmeśvarī—the mother of love, goddess of desire; Śrīsundarī—the mother of beauty, Tripurasundarī—the most beautiful in all three worlds and so on. She is also known as Tripurā, Śrī Mīnākṣī, Śrī Kāmākṣī and Śrī Viśālākṣī.

Śrī Lalitā or Śrī Devī Herself is called Śrīvidyā in Lalitāsahasranāma (Śrīvidyāyai namaḥ—585). Really speaking, the mantra or Sound formula of the Goddess Śrī Lalitā is known as Śrīvidyā. Śrī being a prefix used to denote auspiciousness. Śrīvidyā means the highest knowledge, wisdom, which destroys the ignorance and confers the highest knowledge, by knowing which everything else is known. Therefore, it is known as Brahmavidyā.

Worship of Śrīvidyā is prescribed by the Śāktatantra to obtain worldly prosperity, riches, enjoyment, happiness and ultimately self-realization or liberation. It is said that worldly riches, enjoyment and liberation are at once present for the worshippers of Śrīvidyā (Śrīsundarī sevana tatparāṇām bhuktiśca muktiśca karasthiteva). Lakṣmīdhara in his commentary on Saundaryalaharī states that "where there is excessive enjoyment, there is no possibility of liberation. Similarly, where there is pure desire for liberation, there is no worldly enjoyment. But those who worship the lotus feet of Śrī Lalitā, for them both worldly enjoyment and liberation are in their hands (Yatrāsti bhogo na hi tatra mokṣaḥ, yatrāsti mokṣo nahi tatra bhogaḥ. Śiva-padāmbhojayugārcakānām bhuktiśca muktiśca karasthiteva (Saundaryalaharīṭīkā, p.22).

According to Śāktatantra, the Śakti, the eminent spiritual energy manifests itself as the fifty letters of Sanskrit Alphabet (pañcāśad varṇarūpiṇī). She manifests herself as entire śabdaprapañca—world of words. The vowels (svaras) known as matrices (mātṛkās) are of the nature of Śakti, while the consonants (varṇas) are of the nature of Śiva (Akarādi kṣakārāntā matṛka pīṭharūpiṇah. Kakārādi kṣakārāntāvarṇāstu Śivarūpiṇah. Pañcāśad varṇarūpeṇa śabdākhyam vastu suvrate. Qoted in Śrīlalitātriśatibhāṣya, Intro. p.17). Without vowels, consonants cannot function independently. Even they cannot be pronounced properly. Therefore, it is said that without Śakti, Śiva is just śava, corpse, no name and resting, dwelling place (Vinā śkatyā nāma dhāma navidyāte). He cannot even move. Thus, there is a unity between the two. The union of the two i.e. Svara and vyañjana (vowels and consonants), Śakti and Śiva, is illustrated by the seed-syllables (bījākṣaras) which are involved in the mantras. In fact, the letters themselves are the mantras, which are all derived from the goddess (Te sarve eva mantrāsyuḥ tvamādyā prakṛtiryathā (Mahānirvāṇatantra 5.19).

The letters are called 'varṇas' because they are alive with energy and awareness, reflecting the goddess herself. The fifty letters are collectively known as the goddess Mālinī, with a retinue of fifty-five attendant—deities who are all looked upon as her energies (Śaktis). Here, the differentiation of the vowels as matrices (mātṛkas) and consonants as extended sounds (varṇas) are the fabric out of which all mantras are woven. So, all mantras are form of Śaktis and they are derived from the goddess. In this sense, according to this Śāktatantra, upāsanā of any Mantra is upāsanā of Śakti only.

Thus, Śakta tantric tradition gives importance to Mantra—mystic syllables or seed letters (sound formula) known as bījākṣaras. The words contained in the mantra protect the devotee from bonds of phenomenal existence and from all fears. In other words, vibrations of these letters of sound formula create protective shield around the devotee and bring worldly prosperity and help the devotee to attain self-realization. (Śrī Lalitātriśatibhāṣyam, p.16). These mantras contain unimaginable power, states Paraśurāmakalpasūtra (Mantrāṇām acintya Śaktitā—I.7).

The seed letters are said to be divine and potent and they make for the efficacy of mantra. Even the fire hidden in the fuel is brought out by friction, likewise by the power of the mantra, devotion to the deity facilitates the manifestation of godhead (Yathā kāṣṭhagato vanhiḥ vyajyate mathanādibhiḥ. Tathā mantraprabhāveṇa bhaktyābhivyajyate śivaḥ (Śrīvidyākoṣa, p.9). Merely by reciting these seed letters, the presence of the deity is secured (Śruṇu devi pravakṣyāmi bījānām devarūpatām. Mantroccāraṇamātreṇa devarūpam prajāyate (*ibid.*, p.10). The sound formula is the sound body of the deity. It is the deity itself formulated in articulated sound. This sound body has a remarkable co-relation with the form of the deity that is contemplated in meditation.

Pañcadaśākṣarīmantra (fifteen lettered mantra) is sound formula of Śrī Lalitā or Śrīvidyā. Infact, this sound formula itself is known as Śrīvidyā. (With a secret seed-sound at the end, this Pañcadaśakṣarī becomes ṣodasī, the famous sixteen-lettered mantra.) Pañcadaśākṣarī-mantra is really amplified form of Bālātripurasundarīmantra i.e. aim, klīm, sauḥ. These three seed-sounds of Bālā are amplified, the first to five letters, the second to six letters and the third to four letters to form the fifteen lettered Pañcadaśākṣarīmantra.) Pañcadaśākṣarī, as name suggests, contains 15 letters. There are twelve kinds of Pañcadaśākṣarī-mantra. Among these, the Śrīvidyā worshipped by Kandarpa or Manmatha (Cupid), beginning with letter 'k' known as Kādividyā and Vidyā of Lopāmudrā, beginning with the letter 'ha' known as hādividyā are mostly in practice.

According to Kādividyā tradition, formation of Pañcadaśīmūla-mantra is: ka, e, ī, la, hrīm, ha, sa, ka, ha, la, hrīm, sa, ka, la, hrīm. According to Hādividyā tradition, it is like this: ha, sa, ka, la, hrīm, ha, sa, ka, sa, la, hrīm, sa, ka, la, hrīm. Among these two kinds of sound formula, Kādividyā is most important and earlier to Hādividyā. It is said that in entire Tantrasastra, Śrīvidyā or Pañcadaśākṣarīmantra is the most sacred and important mantra of Śrī Lalitā and there also Kādividyā (Tantreṣu Lalitādevyāḥ tesu mukhyamidam mune. Śrīvidyātu mantrāṇām tatra kādiryathā matā—L.S.). There are three distinct divisions in this Pañcadaśākṣarīmantra which are called kūṭas—peaks. The first Kūṭa is called 'vāgbhavakūṭa' consists of first five letters (i.e. ka, e, ī, la, hrīm. This is the source of sound, the first vibration and represents knowledge). The second is 'Kāmarājakūṭa' consists of six letters (i.e. ha, sa, ka, ha, la, hrīm. This group is king of love, the first desire and represents fulfillment of all desires). The third is 'Śaktikūṭa' consists of remaining four letters (i.e. sa, ka, la, hrīm. This group is the force, the first activity and represents will power). This sound formula is the unity of Śiva and Śakti. In this Sound formula certain letters represent Śiva and certain letters represent Śakti (i.e. Three kakāras, two hakāras are of Śiva and seven letters are of Śakti and three Hrīmkāras used in this formula are indicative of unity of Śiva and Śakti). This sound formula of Śrī Lalitā is so powerful that recitation of this surely brings desired result.

Śrīvidyā mantrasādhanā is said to be the highest of all mantrasādhanā. There is no mantra which is equal to Śrīvidyāmantra. It is called King of all mantras. (a). Śrīvidyā eve mantrāṇām—L.S. pūrvabhāga, 17; (b) Śrīmantrarājasadṛśo yathā mantro na vidyate—L.S. Uttarabhāga, 47. It is said that 'after worshipping various deities, after pursuing various lines of disciplines either in this birth or in previous births, by the dint of such practices, as a result of the grace of those deities, one gains entry into the ' sanctum sanctorum' of Śrīvidyā. After traversing many paths this Royal Road comes into sight. It is also said in the Lalitātriśati-phalaśruti that 'one who has no birth hereafter or one who is Śiva himself, he only receives Vidyā of fifteen letters i.e. pañcadaśākṣarī (yasya no paścimam janma yadi vā śaṅkaraḥsvayam. Tenaiva labhyate vidyā Śrīmat pañcadaśākṣarī—24). Such a meritorious person is initiated to this vidyā.

Significance of this is brought out by texts like Tripurātāpiny-upaniṣad, Yoginīhṛdaya, Jñānārṇva, Vāmakeśvaratantra, Lalitātriśati, Lalitāsahasranāma, Varivasyārahasya, etc. and commentaries on Saundaryalaharī etc.

Tripurātāpanīya Upaniṣad states that Gāyatrī mantra, Jātavedase mantra and Tryambakamantra are connected to Pañcadaśākṣarīmantra of Śrīvidyā. It explains the meaning of Pañcadaśīmantra and describes how each group of Pañcadaśīmantra represents Gāyatrīmantra. Yoginīhṛdayam states that Navārṇamantra of Durgā is nothing but Pañcadaśākṣarīmantra or Śrīvidyā. The significance of Śrīvidyā or Sound formula of Śrī Lalitā is that if you chant this Sound formula (i.e. Pañcadaśākṣarīmantra) you are chanting sound formula of Śiva and Śakti, sacred Gāytrīmantra, Navārṇamantra of Durgā or Caṇḍī, mantra of Jātavedas, Ganeśa mantra and Mantra of Śrī Kṛṣṇa. You are worshipping all in one. She is in the form of all Mantras (Yoginīhṛdaya).

Yoginīhṛdaya gives 6 meanings of Pañcadaśīmantra. Śrī Lalitātriśati gives 300 meanings of Pañcadaśīmantra. That is fully explained by Ādi Śaṅkara in his bhāṣya on it. Bhāskararāya Makhi in his Varivasyārahasya gives 15 meanings of this mantra. Śrī Vīrarāghava Śāstri in his Śrīvidyāmantrabhāṣyam gives 80 different meanings of Pañcadaśīmantra showing relation of this mantra with Vedas, Upaniṣads and Tantraśāstra. Another significance of this mantra is that, there are four kinds of Vidyās viz., (sciences) viz., yajñavidyā—the science of Sacrifice; mahāvidyā—exalted science; guhyavidyā—secret science of mystic syllables and Ātmavidyā—the science of Self or Brahman. The truth is, Śrīvidyā is in all these forms (Yajñavidyā mahāvidyā guhyavidyā ca śobhane. Ātmavidyā ca devī tvam vimuktiphaladayinī. Power of Śrīvidyā, p.16, Ātmavidyā mahāvidyā Śrīvidyā kāmasevitā L.S.—118). Worship of Śrīvidyā or meditation on Śrīvidyā confers supreme knowledge, leads to liberation, a liberation not elsewhere, but here and now, which is the goal of the worshippers of Śrīvidyā. This Śāktatantra declares that by the mere knowledge of Śrīvidyā, all accomplishments result, all desires are fulfilled (Śrīvidyājñānamātreṇa sarvasiddhiḥ prajāyate).

Ways of Worship of Śrī Lalitā

There are three ways of worshipping the Śrīvidyā or Śrī Lalitā viz., Pictorial form or image (Vigrahātmika); Diagrammatic form (Yantrātmikā—Śrī Cakra) and Sacred Sound formula or seed letters (Mantrātmikā—bījākṣaras). Vigrahātmikā worship is the worship of the idol, image or pictorial form of Śrī Lalitā in which She is described as resplendent like newly rising son, three eyed, shining with radiant red clothes, decorated body with various ornaments, having crescent moon on the head, holding in Her four arms weapons like noose, goad, arrow of flowers and sugarcane bow. Each weapons have their own significance (L.S.2–3). Her noose is nothing but Love by which She binds the whole creation. Rāga means attachment. As long as a being is bound to oneself or to others, attached to worldly things, it is noose, pāśa. The moment a being binds him or her to the Divine, he/she is liberated. Anger, wrath, the negative aspect of Love is the goad by which the whole creation is spurred into activity. The sugarcane bow represents mind of a person and five arrows five subtle elements i.e. tanmātras, sound, touch, form, relish and flavor (Rāgasvarūpapāṣādhyā krodhākaraṅkuśojvalā Manorūpekṣukodaṇḍā pañcatanmātrasāyakā—L.S.3–4).

Entire Pañcadaśākṣarīmantra is identified with the image or idol of the Goddess. The first Vāgbhavakūṭa is Her face, the second Kāmarājakūṭa is the portion below Her neck up to the hip and the third Śaktikūṭa is the portion of the body below the hip. Her body-frame is verily three kūṭas, or peaks of the mūlamantra (Lalitāsahasranāma—34–36). Yantrātmikā worship is the worship of Śrīyantra or Śrīcakra (diagrammatic form). Śrīcakra is the visual representation of the same sound formula. The construction of the Śrīcakra follows the symbolism of the three Kūṭas (peaks). Śrīcakra represents entire universe. It also represents human body (Śrī Lalitātriśati—Śāṅkarabhāṣya, Intro. p.24–25). Mantrātmikā worship is recitation of the sacred sound formula (bījamantra) known as 'Pañcadaśākṣarīmantra' (fifteen lettered mantra) or ṣoḍaśākṣarī (sixteen syllable mantra). This kind of worship is purely mental worship.

All these three kinds of worship are the same, because Image or Idol is identified with Śrīvidyā; Śrīcakra is identified with Śrīvidyā and mantra or sound formula is Śrīvidyā itself. We cannot think of Image or Idol or Śrīcakra different from Pañcadaśākṣarīmantra (Its sound formula). Therefore it is said that devotees of Śrīvidyā must comprehend the three-fold symbolism and its hidden import (Saṅketa) while meditating or worshipping Her: (a) the symbolism of the fifteen lettered mantra (mantra-saṅketa); (b) the symbolism of Śrīcakra (Cakra-saṅketa) and (c) the symbolism of worship involving meditation and the recitation of the mystic names (pūja-saṅketa-Yoginīhṛdayatantra—chapters 1–3).

It is also important to note one more thing from the point of view of meditation on Śrīvidyā. When the supreme Goddess subjects Herself to time, She becomes the fifteen divisions of the time factor, known as tithis, which make the waning of the moon. These fifteen digits (Kalās) of the moon form the fifteen lettered Pañcadaśīmantra of the Goddesses. She is the moon in Her fullness i.e. Ṣoḍaśī (sixteen lettered) while the digits are Her aspects. Therefore, it is believed that in external worship (bahiryāga), contemplation of the deity in the disc of the moon on full-moon nights (purṇimā) is very efficacious. In the inner worship (antaryāga) the head center, the thousand-petalled lotus (sahasrāra), is the seat of the mystic moon, the place of the illumined mind. It is described as the ocean of immoral nectar (sudhāsindhu), the great lotus-grove (mahāpadmavana) wherefrom the delight of all existence, the rasa of the union of Śivā and Śakti surges forth. The meditation of the deity in the head-centre, in the thousand-petalled lotus is said to be the highest form of inner worship (Mahāyāga).

In reality, the Ultimate Reality, the Brahman, has no gender. It is neither female nor male, nor nuter (nastrī, napumān, na napumsakaḥ). Śrī Lalitā in reality is pure consciousness. She can be worshipped either in female form or male form or one can just meditate on Her as formless pure consciousness (Strīrūpam vā smared devīm pumrūpam vā vicintayet. Atha vā niṣkalam dhyāyet saccidānandarūpiṇīm). It is mentioned by Ādi Śaṅkara in his Lalitātriśatibhāṣya that Śrī Lalitā can be worshipped also in male form as Lord Kṛṣṇa. Sometimes, She assumes the male form of Śrī Kṛṣṇa and bewitches the whole universe with enchanting magic of the flute. (Kadācid ādyā Lalitā pumrūpā Kṛṣṇa vigrahā. Vamśanādavinodena karoti vivaśm jagat—L.Tri.260).

Philosophy of Śrī Vidyā Worship

Śrī Vidyā worship is a form of worshipping Parabrahman—Supreme Reality as a female entity—Universal Mother. Śrīvidyā is praised by all Upaniṣads (sarvopaniṣd udghuṣṭā. L.S.159). She is known through Vedantic texts (sarvavedāntasamvedyā). She is the gist of all Upaniṣadic texts (Sarvavedāntatāparyabhūmiḥ-Lalitātriśati–43). This Śrī Vidyā sect follows the Upaniṣadic path maintaining that Śakti is the Universal Energy which has brought the universe into existence, which sustains and dissolves the Universe (a. Yato vā imāni bhūtāni jāyante, yena jātāni jīvanti, yat prayantyabhisam viśanti-Tait. Up. Bhṛguvallī–2.b). Layasthiti udbhaveśvarī-Lalitātriśati–34.3); Sṛṣṭi-sthiti-vināśānām śaktibhūte sanātani-Saundaryalaharī, Kavailyāśrama's commentary). Śrīvidyā is called Brahmavidyā, because it removes ignorance of its worshippers and helps them to acquire the knowledge of identity between individual soul and Brahman. It is said that one will receive or initiated to Śrīvidyā only in the final birth, because Śrīvidyā will bestow upon him/her knowledge of Brahman. After that there is no more birth (Carame janmani Śrīvidyopāsako bahvet).

Philosophically speaking Śrīvidyā or Śrīlalitā is a synonym of Brahman of the Vedantic thought (Tripurā parabrahmetyabhidhīyate). The main aim of Śrīvidyā is the realization of Advaita i.e. unity of individual soul and universal soul, unity of Śiva and Śakti. Quite in agreement with the Advaita Vedāntic stand point, Śrīvidyā tradition maintains a dual aspect of universal mother namely saguṇa (having form) and nirguṇa (formless). Texts dealing with Śrīvidyā describes the nature of Śrīvidyā like Upaniṣads describe the Brahman. She is described as indeterminate (nirviśeṣa) as well as determined (saviśeṣa). She is described as Absolute Existence, Absolute Consciousness and Absolute Bliss (saccidānandasvarūpiṇī), in Her Nirguṇa form. She is the mass of consciousness (vijñānaghanarūpiṇī). She is the Reality from which all things originate, sustained and merge in the end (laysthityudbhaveśvarī). She is the inner self of all. She is the highest knowledge (parāsamvid) beyond space and time. She is the ocean of consciousness, in which there is neither rise nor fall. She is non-dual supreme energy. She is self- luminous. She is the only truth and can be realized through direct experience (anubhava).

In Her determinate form, Śrī Lalitā is the most beautiful in all three worlds. She is the supreme deity and all other gods and goddesses are subordinate to Her and offer obeisance to Her. Inspired by Her, Brahmā creates the world, Viṣṇu sustains it and Rudra destroys or withdraws it. She is the moral governess. She is the mother of all and ocean of mercy. She is the bestower of all kinds of riches and happiness (Śrī Lalitātriśati-Śāṅkarabhāṣya, for detailed description, Intro.56–71).

It is important to note that Śrīvidyā tradition lays stress on the dynamic nature of the creative power i.e. Śakti. Though, concept of Goddess Lalitā corresponds to that impersonal Brahman of the Upaniṣads, but it is transformed into a personal divinity that is the omnipotent, omnipresent and omniscient Divine mother, the source, support and end of the entire empirical universe. The supreme transcendental Reality which is nameless and formless conceived through religious imagination becomes Goddess in the qualified form (saguṇa). The formless Lalitā (The Brahman) comes down step by step and assumes the form of a universal Mother. All the paraphernalia for worship are then offered to Her. This concept of the highest as the mother is a special feature of Śāktatantra as a whole and it has its own significance. Mother always nourishes, has a more charitable attitude, easily forgives faults of her children and offers them an opportunity to reform their ways. This attitude of forgiveness and compassion, love and pity are more natural to mother than father. Thus, the formless Lalitā, the supreme Brahman in personified form, becomes the affectionate mother, worshipped in the image or idol or in Śrīcakra. She is conceived as the most high, higher than Sarasvatī, Lakṣmi, higher than Brahmā, Viṣṇu, Īśvara and even Sadāśiva. The worshipper of Śrī Lalitā acquires great learning, becomes exceedingly prosperous and develops charming personality. She fulfills all desires of devotees and confers all sorts of mystic powers to them. The devotee of Śrī Lalitā enjoys all worldly riches and becomes one with Her in the end. Śrī Lalitā grants what is sought for i.e. bestows desired objects (Vāñchitārtha-pradāyinī).

Ādi Śaṅkarācārya commenting on Śrī Lalitātriśati states that it is enough if we worship Śrī Lalitā for long after surrendering to Her with devotion and with determined and focus mind. We need not ask anything. She herself bestows us what is good for us including four goals of life (Cirakālopāsitā sati puruṣārthān aprārthyamānasyāpi svayameva dadāti–260). He even goes one step further and says in Saundaryalaharī (verse 4) that She bestows more than what is sought for (Phalamapi ca vāñchāsamadhikam).

Lalitāopakhyāna of Brahmāṇḍapurāṇa asks us to surrender ourselves completely at Her feet. She will take care of everything of Her devotee (Śaiva tasyāhikam bhāram vahet muktim ca sādhayet. Sadā sannihitā tasya sarvam ca kathayeta sā—Adhyaya 42, verse 69). Just as a cow with profound affection towards her calf, runs after it, wherever it goes, similarly, Divine Mother, Śrī Lalitā will follow Her devotee who has completely surrendered himself or herself at Her feet (Vātsalyasahitā dhenuḥ yathāvatsam anuvrajet. Tathānugacchet sā devī svabhaktam śaraṇāgatam. Adhyaya 42, verse 70).

Ādi Śaṅkarācārya in his Saundaryalaharī beautifully states that if you surrender yourself whole heartedly to Divine Mother then, all your daily activities become worship of Śrī Lalitāmahātripurasundarī. Ordinary talk or prattle is converted into japa (reciting of Her mantra), manual or normal work with hands becomes mudras (gestures, signets), walking or all movements becomes circumambulation (pradakṣiṇā—going around the goddess), eating food and drinking becomes offerings in the holy fire (āhuti), laying down becomes prostrations, (praṇāmas-bowing down). All actions that give comforts, pleasure, happiness become dedication/surrendering to Her. Infact, whatever action is naturally performed is transformed into Her worship (Saundaryalaharī–27).

It is said that this secret knowledge and significance of Śrīvidyā was almost forgotten by the people in the passage of time. The credit of rejuvenating worship of Śrīvidyā goes to Ādi Śaṅkarācārya. It is he who revived sacred worship of Śrī Vidyā and brought out its real philosophy and significance through his remarkable works such as Śrī Lalitātriśati-bhāṣya and Saundaryalaharī. He accepted the worship of Śrīvidyā as the supreme path of realization of Advaita. He initiated his first four disciples into this Śrīvidyā tradition and prescribed worship of Śrīvidyā in all the four centres established by him (Maṭhas). At present, the purified method of worship of Śrīvidyā which is known as Samayamārga shown by Ādi Śaṅkarācārya is considered as the only real path of Śrīvidyā (Sampradāyo hi na anyosti loke Śrī Śaṅkarad bahiḥ).

This Śrīvidyā tradition rejuvenated by Ādi Śaṅkarācārya still continues even today with unflinching devotion and spirit. Lalitāsahasranāma, Lalitātriśati and Khaḍgamālāmantra are very popular among the Upāsakas of Śrī Lalitā (Worshippers of Śrī Vidyā). Even today, on special day of every month of the Hindu calander, Śrī Lalitā is worshipped offering kuṅkuma—vermilian powder or saffron on Image or Idol of Śrī Lalitā or on Śrī Cakra, chanting either Śrī Lalitāsahasranāma (thousand names) or chanting Śrī Lalitātriśati (three hundred names) by the worshippers of Śrī Lalitā.

References

Brahmāṇḍapurāṇa, New Delhi: Rashtriya Sanskrit Sansthan, 2014.

Durgāsaptaśati, New Delhi: Gitapress, Gorakhpur. N.D.

Lalitāsahasranāma with Saubhāgyabhāskara, ed. Pansikar Vasudeva Laksmana Shastri, Bombay: Nirnayasagara Press, 1914.

Nityāṣoḍaśikārṇava, ed. Dviveda Vrjavallbha, Varanasiya, Sanskrit Vishvidyālaya, 1968.

Power of Śrī Vidyā, Ramamurthy N. Nagercoil, CBH Publications, 2013.

Śrī Vidyā—Kośa, S.K. Ramachandra Rao, Delhi: India Books Centre, 2005.

Śrīlalitātriśatībhāṣyam, Ādi Śaṅkarācārya, ed. Y.S. Shastri and Sunanda Shastri, Ahmedabad, Śrīyogi Publications, 2016.

Srīvidyāmantrabhāṣya, K. Veeraraghava Shastri, Chennai, Vavilla Ramashastri and Sons, 1960.

The Ten Great Cosmic Powers, S. Shankaranarayanan, Chennai. Samata Books Pvt. Ltd., 2013.

Tripurātāpanīyopaniṣad—Upanishad Sanchayan, Part 3, Delhi, Chawkhamba. 2014.

Vāmakeśvaratantra—Kashmir Shaiva Tantrik Studies.

Varivasyārahasya, Bhāskararāya, ed. Subramanya Shastri, Madras: Adyar Library, 1947.

Yoginīhṛdayam, Varanasi: Chawkhamba Krishnadas Academy, 2011.

— x —

Cosmology and Psychology of the Rig Veda Following the Lead of Śrī Aurobindo

Debashish Banerji

Abstract

The Rig Veda samhita, accepted as the earliest textual literature of India and the foundational texts of Hinduism, have been relegated to a position of Vedic ritual in Hindu practice and as primitive nature poetry by western Indology. Earlier commentators, such as Sayana, though acknowledging an esoteric meaning for the riks, have not explained them in these terms; and later formulators of Hindu dharma, such as Shankara, though holding Veda as ultimate "evidence" (sabda pramana), look for this in the Upanishads (Vedanta), posited as the "end" and hence the "last word" of the Veda, while ignoring the Rig Veda. Sri Aurobindo (1872–1950) in his book "The Secret of the Veda" proposes a coded symbolism of yoga practice in the hymns and implied mythology of the Veda, founding the earliest cosmology, psychology and teleology of Hinduism. In this talk, I will draw out these ideas, showing the relationship and continuity of Vedic mytho-philosophical ideas in the Upanishads and the Bhagavad Gita.

The earliest wisdom texts of India, and in fact, of the world, are the Veda. *Veda* literally means "knowledge." Textually speaking, there are several ways in which this term is understood—most commonly, it refers to the "four Vedas" (catur veda), the *Rig Veda*, the *Sama Veda*, The *Yajur Veda* and the *Atharva Veda*. Then, there is a larger body of texts, the four *Vedas* plus *Brahmanas, Aranyakas* and *Upanishads*, which are also called Veda. It may seem surprising that the *Upanishads* are included in the Veda, but according to this version, which is commonplace in India, the Upanishads are called *Vedanta*, or end-of-the—Veda, which itself is a historical construction. The *Upanishads* stand in an interesting position vis-à-vis the Veda. They open a hermeneutic gulf, which allows for the distilling of a non-mediated practice from the elite appropriation of the *Veda* by the ritual device of collective control. In doing this they both distance themselves from the Veda and create an intimate relation with it.

On the other hand, asking the western historical question problematizes the singularity of the Veda further. The earliest texts are the *Rig Veda* Samhita, at least 250 years older than the others, which are connected with ritual. The *Rig Vedas* are ten volumes or *mandalas* with invocatory mystic poems to various gods, who seem to personify natural forces. These poems or hymns are called *sukta* and each stanza in them is called a *rik*. Each of the volumes (*maṇḍala*) is attributed to a seer-clan (*rishi-kula*). Seers, called *rishis*, were poets—in fact the common word for poet to this day, *kavih* is used for them. But they were not any poets; they were poets who prepared themselves to become vessels of the Word (*Vak*), a Vedic Goddess who manifest the subjective and objective cosmos by the vibrational and ideational power of her words (RV.1.164, 10.71). This preparation of the rishis was also undertaken through the use of various tools and processes of consciousness, and it is natural to suppose that it is these that find expression in their poems. Indeed, the poems are called mantra, which means a form of words carrying power to convey experiences of a transpersonal nature. Undoubtedly, this was one of the functions of these poems—to cause to awaken the presence and power of the cosmic gods that are invoked, so that we may become like them and be able to contain them all and transcend them.

Each rishi-clan developed presumably their own approach to the goals of the Veda, though it is not clear anymore what these differences were. If the *Rig Veda* is the earliest of the Veda,—it has therefore, in my opinion, a much greater claim to the "authenticity" of the Veda, or what may better be called the truth of the Veda. The *Angirasa* seers are the earliest rishis of the Rig Veda, and have a large number of hymns attributed to them. They are called the forefathers (*pitri*)[1] and given a divine-human status,[2] like avatars, who came with the Idea of the meaning of the cosmos and taught it through two means—an inner and an outer, *yoga* or *kriya*, psychological practice and ritual. Later seers adulate the *Angirasas* as superior even to the gods, as if they were the

[1] "Frequently the seven original Angiras Rishis are described as the human fathers, *pitaro manus. y-ah.*, who discovered the Light, made the sun to shine and ascended to the heaven of the Truth. In some of the hymns of the tenth Mandala they are associated as the Pitris..." (Aurobindo, 1998:159).

[2] "They may have been originally human sages deified by their descendants and in the apotheosis given a divine parentage and a divine function; or they may have been originally demigods, powers of the Light and Flame, who became humanised as the fathers of the race and the discoverers of its wisdom" (Aurobindo, 1998:160).

original arche-poets who released the stolen sun and created the cosmic order with their words (RV.I.71.2, X.79.1), or rather, channeled the order of the creation through the Vedic Word (Aurobindo 1998:168–169).

Returning to the nitty-gritties of the historical question, mainstream dating places the earliest of the books of the Rig Veda, maṇḍalas 2–7, to approximately 1900 BCE–1500 BCE. Two of the remaining three Vedas, the *Yajur Veda* and *Sama Veda*, contain mostly repetitions of the hymns of the *Rig Veda*, along with, in the first case, ritual instructions and in the second, chanting/singing instructions. The fourth Veda, the *Atharva Veda* is believed to be chronologically the last. It contains a number of original hymns mixed in with magic spells of many kinds, which some scholars believe, could be the origin of *tantra* or could have borrowed fromt*Tantra* or could have been co-created with it. All these were composed between 1200–1000 BCE according to academic scholarship. The principal *Upanishads* are believed by academia to have been composed between 7th C BCE and 5th C CE, and Upanishads are still being written.

The hymns in the *Rig Veda* are addressed to gods, many of whom bear a striking resemblance to the Olympian gods of Greece. This is not entirely unexpected, given the shared Indo-European language and culture. But cultures diversify regionally and tie their shared heritage to different concerns. At the same time, the similarities may yield valuable synchronic and diachronic information. We find rituals being offered to these gods, both in Greece and in Vedic India. In Greece, these gods were also invoked in mystery cults which utilized them as animistic and psychospiritual forms of consciousness. This was undoubtedly the case also in India. This line of consideration was extended in modern times through the work of Sri Aurobindo, who approached the texts and hymns as both a scholar and a yogi. In this view, the hymns of the Veda express coded invocations that are part of a cosmology of consciousness that relates through correspondence (the fractal folding of the universe) to the psychology of the individual.

Prior to this, the Vedas attracted the scholarly attention of the West from the 18th century Perhaps the western scholar who is most associated with the Veda is Max Mueller (1823–1900) who read the hymns of the *Rig Veda* as the utterances of a primitive humanity confronted with the enormities of nature—the sun, the wind, the lightning, fire—and responding to these primordial nature forces with wonder and adulation. They projected anthropomorphic divinities onto these forces of nature and thus expressed a glorified nature poetry. Since the early 20th C, the Veda has also been studied as a record of the invasion of the Aryan race; attempting to decipher the geographical locations, cultures encountered and wars fought. Today, the idea of an Aryan Invasion has been put to sleep due to lack of evidence, though the migration into the Indian subcontinent of an Indo-European language speaking people, is thought to be likely. A third scenario (which could be combined with the second) is one of cultural transmission and/or bilingualism.

In India, the most well-known and authoritative commentary on the Veda comes from a 17th C South Indian scholar, named Sayana. This commentary looks upon the Veda mainly as a text for rituals. Prior to Sayana, we find that the Veda is treated as containing knowledge of three kinds. There is knowledge of a ritual kind geared towards worldly success. This kind of knowledge is later called *adhi-bhautika* or worldly knowledge. There is also knowledge of a philosophical and occult nature called *adhi-daivika* or godly knowledge. Finally there is a third level of knowledge called *adhyatmika* or soul knowledge. According to this the Veda contains a Yoga, an approach to spiritual discipline.

Therefore, if we are to consider the Veda as wisdom literature, our first concern should be the decipherment of its cosmology and psychology. Following Sri Aurobindo's lead (1998) we can describe the broad lines of the cosmology thus:

1. Reality is divided into 2 zones or planes in a "vertical" relation—(1) the foundation above (*upari budhnah, rtasya budhnah*) (RV.III.67) or the solar realm of everlasting light; (2) the realm of the alternations of Day and Night, *aho-ratri*, (RV.X.190.2, Atharva Veda VI:128.3) the Two Mothers or Two Sisters, often spoken of as a Wheel.
2. Each of these zones is further divided into three levels. In the "upper zone" these are called the three luminous summits, *trini rochana* (Aurobindo 1998:82). In the lower, they are *prithvi*, *antaraiksha* and *dyaus* (Aurobindo 1998:118); also known as *bhu*, *bhuvar* and *swar*. These are the worlds of Matter, Life and Mind (Ibid.) with which human beings are familiar.
3. These zones are inhabited by beings—in the upper zone, are Aditi and the solar gods, the Adityas (Aurobindo 1998:118, 490–496). In the lower zone, are gods, mortal creatures and demons.
4. This cosmology (which is not a materialist cosmology but a cosmology of consciousness) is folded into each individual being as a psychology. The Veda is remarkable because of this

early coherence of the macrocosm and the microcosm that it presents. In Sri Aurobindo's words:

> "The sons of the Infinite [i.e. the gods] have a twofold birth. They are born above in the Truth as creators of the worlds and guardians of the divine Law; they are born also here in the world itself and in man as cosmic and human powers of the Divine. In the visible world, they are the male and female powers and energies of the universe and it is this external aspect of them... which gives us the external or psycho-physical side of the Aryan worship....But in man himself, the gods are conscious psychological powers" (Aurobindo 1998:493).

5. The mythology of the Veda ties its cosmology and psychology together.

Vedic Mythology

The *Rig Veda* is a collection of mystical poems and making sense of it is like wading through a landscape of dreams. Reality is much more fluid here, not governed by material laws. Beings change form or name or merge into one another. However, once one finds a key to the interpretation, everything begins to fall into place. Some of the hymns are further elaborated in other texts, such as the *Brahmanas* and *Aranyakas*, which may provide keys to the symbolism. Sri Aurobindo provides a valuable key in his text *The Secret of the Veda* (1998). We are lucky to have this, since we can test its ideas against the poems themselves and see how they confirm to his hypothesis.

As we can see from the lines of the cosmology above, the Veda develops its symbolism around the Sun, seen as the Supreme Divine. As such it espouses both a heliocentric and a geocentric theory apropos the relation of the sun and the earth. When looked at from the "upper foundation," we have a heliocentric theory, as might be expected from a realm of everlasting Day. The gods from the realm of Day-and-Night have their origin here and keep their focus on this realm for their support. Hence it is said of Vishnu, seen as the solar deity, *Om tad Vishnu paramam padam sada pashyanti surayah diviva chaksuratatam* (RV.I.22.20). In translation: "Salutations to that Vishnu, whose supreme station the gods behold at all times, like an eye wide-extended in heaven." Since there is no separateness here, all is seen as the distributed Substance of the Sun and in the unobstructed Light of the Sun. It is called That One (*tad ekam*) (eg. RV.III.54.8–9, III.56.2, VII.21, VIII.58.2).

The "lower triple zone" views this same reality in a geocentric manner (Aurobindo 1998:176–178). We, as humans, are born into this experience of discrete appearances and disappearances. The sun rises at dawn and occupies an increasingly central position in the sky, until at noon, it illuminates everything equally. Such a condition brings us closest in experience to the zone of Everlasting Day. However, it begins to "descend" from its summit and disappear in the darkness. Mirroring this cosmic alternation, our human lives move between birth, death and rebirth. Rebirth is not an idea specifically referred to in the Veda, but we may infer it from the idea of the returns of the One.

In terms of the ontology, the Darkness of Night is a gestation of the Sun preparing its rebirth; from this viewpoint, *Ratri* is a Mother (eg. RV. X.127). But, form the viewpoint of the individuals who experience this cosmic ontology, this condition is one of Ignorance, desertion, isolation, error, treachery and unconsciousness. Viewed from this psychological state, the Sun is "stolen" by the "robbers" (*panis*) and hidden in the cave of the demon Hill of Darkness, Vala (eg. RV.I.11.5; RV.II.12.3). The associations and correspondences of gods cause these movements to be repeated in variant tellings. Instead of the Sun, often it is the herds of the Sun that are stolen and hidden, or it may be the dawn goddess, Usha (eg. RV.VII.75). The king of the gods, Indra, who operates from Swar battles against the Panis, Vala and other powers of Darkness and eventually cleaves the Hill of Darkness with his thunderbolt, releasing the cows.[3]

The equation of the solar forces with the cow was one of the figurative correspondences that form a method of Vedic symbology. According to this, a number of material objects of value to the Vedic pastoralists are equated to psychological or cosmic forces. Such an equation aided in the exoteric ritualization of psychological processes, translating its transformative goals to material ones. The cow was undoubtedly one of the most precious possessions of such a society, particularly its milk and its derivatives such as butter, ghee and curds. These were all substances of importance in the Vedic sacrifice, and coded for powers of mental clarity that provided spiritual nourishment. To equate the esoteric and exoteric senses of the cow, the word used for it, *go*, also meant "light."[4] In the symbolic world of the solar gods, their Mother was Aditi, sometimes seen as a Divine Cow (eg. RV.I.153.3), who nourishes all the worlds. The ancient mythos of the Cow as a

[3] "Lord of the thunder, thou didst burst the cave of Vala rich in cows. The Gods came pressing to thy side, and free from terror aided thee. [RV.I.11.15]

[4] Eg. "The cows/rays remove the darkness and extend the light" (RV.VII.79.2).

symbol of the Sun has Indo-European origins, as has the mythos of the release of the Sun from the Cave of Darkness (see RV.I.11.5, II.12.3, X.68.6). In Greek mythology, for example, the Sun God Apollo is a herder with cows, which were stolen by his half-brother Hermes, who hid them in a cave. The myth of the release of the Sun from the cave comes to us also from Japan, where the Shinto Sun goddess, Amaterasu hid herself in the Heavenly-Rock cave to escape the rampage of her brother Susanoo, putting the world in darkness. She was later persuaded to emerge from the cave.

In the Vedic case, however, there is a dead-serious battle involved; and the activities of the gods dramatize the psychology of human experience in its subjection to the forces of annihilation and in its development of means to be victorious. In other words, the cosmic battle is the mirror of the microcosm, where the human being, the Aryan,[5] struggles to find means to survive, both materially and spiritually, through the Night of Ignorance. The primary means it finds is Fire, Agni. Just as the Sun is at the heart of the heliocentric theory, Agni, Fire, is at the heart of the geocentric theory; since the Sun, though transformed and hidden, is present on earth as Fire.[6] The Vedas speak of three kinds of Fire (Agni)—saurya agni (solar fire), vaidyuta agni (electric fire) and jada agni (material fire).[7] These are the three visible forms in which the sun continues to be present in the realm of Day-and-Night. These three forms are represented by the god Surya (Sun) (*suarya agni*) in the "higher firmament," the god Indra (*vaidyuta agni*)[8] in the Swar, and the god Agni (*jada agni*) on Prithvi. In the intermediate vital realm, Antariksha, the solar presence takes a form of invisible energy, the life-force (prana) represented by the God of Wind, Vayu. The psychological symbolism and transformative practice of yoga can be intuited from this and that, in turn, should generate the form of the ritual, since ritual (*kriya*) is nothing but the dramatization of psychological practice (*yoga*). To arrive at the psychological significance, the material manifestations must be translated into their consciousness forms. Agni in consciousness, is the aspiration to freedom, power and enjoyment coded into the

[5] "Arya" is related to the seeker and warrior for truth.

[6] The Force of the Sun is its heat, the Knowledge of the Sun is its Light.

[7] RV.I.164.1 as quoted in Macdonell (1893, 93–94). See also, "According to the experience of ancient yogis, Agni is threefold: (1) ordinary fire, jada Agni; (2) electric fire, vaidyuta Agni; (3) solar fire, saura Agni. Science has only entered upon the first and second of these fires. The fact that the atom is like the solar system could lead it to the knowledge of the third"—Sri Aurobindo in a conversation with Pavitra, as quoted in (Satprem 2008).

[8] Thunder and lightning are manifestations of electricity.

material cosmos and carrying the savor of its lived experience, its ontological quality. This is further present in every will-to-individuation or entity in the cosmos.

At the human stage, Agni has crystallized into the psychic being or soul personality which has arrived at an intensity of knowledge and power where it can discover the real-images of its fulfillment (Nirodbaran, 2001:193–194). To do this, it must find a subjective technology of future-becoming and of self-transformation. It arrives at this through the intensification of Agni within itself and its direction towards the realms of *antariksha, swar* and beyond, to the zone of everlasting Day. From the vital (*antariksha*) worlds, it seeks the intervention of allied cosmic forces, such as Vayu, Rudra and the Maruts, the storm gods, so as to destroy the obstacles in the way with their Power; and form the mental (*swar*), it seeks the help of Indra with his lightnings to show the path in the Darkness. The lightnings of Indra here represent divine intuitions that bring knowledge in the ignorance (Aurobindo, 1998:143–144). These psychological processes of giving shape to the inner aspiration (agni) are aided by the power of the *mantra*, the *Rk* or Vedic hymn as well as other gods and goddesses (Aurobindo, 1998:149–150). It is also aided by the integration around this aspiration of the clarified intelligence and widened thought-mind and its various powers. The inner fire also feeds on blissful enthusiasm (later this will be called *bhakti*; sometimes *utsaha*—in the Veda, it is represented by the god Soma), which intoxicates it and multiplies its energy. Knowledge in the Darkness is the primary prayer of the Vedic seer—s/he lights the Fire of Aspiration and invokes Indra to illuminate the Night with repeated lightnings. S/he calls into service the mental powers, so that they may develop the capacity of receiving Indra's intuitions continuously, a chain of lightnings transforming the normal operations of knowledge. This birth of Indra and his action in the yogi and his intensification through the offering of the prepared mental instruments and the blissful enthusiasm, gives it the power to burst the Hill of Vala and release the Sun or Divine Consciousness in the life of the yogi. From this we can see how logically the greatest number of hymns in the Veda are addressed to Indra and Agni. The preparation of the mental capacities to become intuitive in character is also facilitated through direct invocation to the Sun god in the supreme realm of Gnosis. This is the basis for what is considered today the most sacred Vedic chant, the Gayatri: *Om Tat savitur varenyam bhargo devasya dhimahi dhiyo yonah prachodayat* IRV.X.16.3). (We meditate on the most blessed from of the Sun God, Savitra. May he illumine our intelligence).

The ritual correlates of the process described above can easily be recognized. I quote Dr. Judith Tyberg here, who was a disciple of Sri Aurobindo and an Indologist (1976:pp.180–181):

> [T]he inner sacrifice or the holy action of feeding or quickening the divine immortal spark in man, Agni, the Fire god, will be acted out by kindling the divine fire with the purified and clarified mind, symbolized by the *ghi* and the physical or outer manifestation of the divine in life, symbolized by food or *annam*. Agni thus invoked, calls and invites other gods to share in the fruits of the sacrifice and in turn each brings blessings, or interpreted, [this] means that once the god in man is awakened, it reveals its powers and aspects as the flame of his presence is sustained in life.
>
> Then Indra, god of the Firmament, the Illumined mentality, appears and is represented as constantly struggling and battling with Vritra the Serpent Adversary who covers with his darkness all divine activity and who hides the cows, the rays of truth light in the caves of the Panis or the sense life. Indra is often aided in his fight by Rudra and his hosts of Maruts, the great Destroyer and the storm gods, symbolical of the Breaker of old molds and the powers of will and nervous or vital force. The Ribhus, the Seasons who accompany them are symbolical of the artisans of the god who help one repeat man's divine achievements. Gradually Ushas, the dawn of higher truth comes escorted by the Ashwins, the Horsemen of the Sun, representing swiftness and effectiveness of action in the great journey to Truth and illumination, the Sun.
>
> With the glorious Sun of Truth come his goddesses or aspects: Savitri, Divine Grace which manifests the immortal in the mortal; Mitra, the friend of the gods, the luminous power of love leading to harmony and thought, impulse and action; Varuna, the Vast Expanse, the oceanic wideness and unity of infinite Truth, Aryaman, the chief of the Milky Way, the immortal puissance of clear discerning aspiration leading beyond.
>
> Then follows Rita and Ritachit, Truth in action and Truth-Consciousness with their goddesses of powers: Mahi or Bharati, the Vast Word of greatness of Wisdom that brings us all things out of the Divine source; Ila, goddess of Truth vision or revelation; Saraswati, goddess of streaming Inspiration; Sarama, the hound of heaven, intuition; and Dakshina, goddess of divine Discernment. Soma the god of immortal nectar is the consummation of beatitude, the wine of immortality and divine ecstasy. Thus in the Vedas is portrayed richly the psychological science of the transformation of the human into

the Divine, the mental into the Supramental, the falsehood into the Truth, darkness into Light, mortality into Immortality. There are sufficient hints in the Veda to the effect that this liberation and enlightenment that is being interpreted at the level of individual psychology had a collective and cosmic manifestation also, the vision of a transformed society and a transformed world. There is a myth to this effect too—it is the myth of Martanda (RV.X.72):

Eight are the Sons of Aditi who from her body sprang to life.
With seven she went to meet the Gods; she cast Martanda far away.
So with her Seven Sons Aditi went forth to meet the earlier age. She brought Martanda thitherward to spring to life and die again.

Thus of her eight solar sons, Aditi cast away the eighth, Martanda (literally egg of death) to be born and die. This is the solar Substance subject to the conditions of consciousness that characterize Matter. Whereas the other seven suns belong to the realm of Everlasting Day, Martand belongs to the Realm-of-Day-and-Night, subjectively Birth-and-Death. The materially embodied yogi partakes of this condition. But his job is to use the power of Fire in subjective and objective technologies of transcendence and transformation, so as not only to emerge himself from this condition to that of the Everlasting Day but to revivify the "dead-egg" Sun, Martanda, so that it becomes a solar natural habitat for a transformed humanity.

Equivalents and Allies

We have spoken of a number of correspondences and equivalences in the Veda. To elaborate a little on the more prominent, the solar zone provides many of the more well-known descriptors of Vedic gods and categories. For example, for the Unity Consciousness of the solar zone, it uses the term *Tad Ekam*, That One (eg RV.III.54.8–9, III.56.2, VII.21, VIII.58.2). From this quality and the relation between the absolute solar realm and the relative realm of Day-and-Night, we have the well-known statement in Hinduism: *Ekam sat viprah bahudha badanti* (RV. I.164.92). There is one Truth; the wise speak of it variously. The attributes of this One are given as Satyam, Ritam, Brihad, the Truth, the Right, the Vast (Atharva Veda XII.1.1). Ritam means Right in the sense of the dynamic unfoldment of the Truth in a fashion which keeps everything in balance, which knows what is to be deployed when because All is Itself self-organized through its Knowledge faculty, Supermind.

Out of the One Truth there is, from which proceeds all sense of right, the One which stretches into infinity and to which there is no Outside;

emerges the idea of Duality. Or we may say, in its possibilities of self-experience the idea of Duality is always already present. This 'two-ness' is spoken of in two fundamental ways—cosmologically as Night and Day, *Aho*, day, and *Ratri*, night; and subjectively as the duality of the I—Thou, *Aham*, I, *Sah*, He or That, conjoined and abbreviated to *Hamsa*, which means Swan, a creature that walks on earth, but flies in the sky, on its two wings, I and Thou. The human individual experiences itself always in and through relation. If we look deep enough into reality, we find that it has little meaning other than one of relation. We are here because That which is the One choosing to enjoy itself through relation, became two. The bliss, "Soma" of the self-existent solar Divine (Bhaga) in the One becomes love (Mitra) in the Two and the Many.

Vedic Cosmology and the *Upanishads*

The *Upanishads*, though referred to as "the end of the Veda," distance themselves in important ways from the ritualism and symbology of the Veda. They prefer a more direct philosophical statement and introduce cosmological terms with which we are familiar to this day, due to the interpretations of the Vedantic *acharyas*. We find that the *Upanishads* give explicit terms to some of the divisions of cosmic or transcendental consciousness that the Veda kept hidden or unspoken. Hence, what in the Veda is the solar realm, "the upper foundation," (*upari budhna*) the realm of That One (*Tad Ekam*) is given a name now—Brahman. As a condition of consciousness, it is called *Vidya* (Knowledge) and contrasted with its opposite in the "lower triple realm," *avidya* (Ignorance). The three shining words (Trini Rochana) of the Veda would then be the three qualities of the *Vidya - sat chit* and *ananda*. Similarly the lower realms of *avidya* are divided into three "elements"—*tridhatu*, the lower triple world of Matter, Life and Mind. These three together compose what the Veda calls Prithvi or Earth. Between the *Trini Rochana* and the *Tridhatu*, in the Veda, is a principle known as *Mahar*. This is the solar realm of Gnosis, which the *Upanishads* refer to as *Vijnana* and Sri Aurobindo callls Supermind. He uses this term for lack of any better to denote something that is higher than mind, part of the Knowledge reality but something to which the mind is relative in the sense that the mind emerges from it. Supermind or *Mahar* stands between the causeless, spaceless, timeless, solar realm of the three shining worlds, and our world of mind, life and body in which, reality unfolds through space and time. But this unfoldment through space, time and causation has a meaning to it, and a plot determined by the mediating principle *Mahar*. Mahar as a divine principle is what we commonly call God. The word Brahman, so pervasive in the Upanishads means something quite different in the Veda. It means the Word, and is a synonym for Vak. This is the divine Word. Brahma of the Puranas, who creates by the Word (like the *rishis*) is called, in the *Veda*, the Lord of the Word (*Brahmanaspati*). Out of the totality of infinite ability to express, the divine Word expresses this manifest world through the power of mantra, in an unfoldment.

Variant Myths

The solar mythology of rebirth is not the only myth that is assumed in the hymns of the Veda. But often, other myths are related to the solar one in structure and upon scrutiny, in meaning. Such is the myth of the seven rivers hidden by Vritra, another demon, a Snake-Demon, who is also slain by Indra, so as to release the life-giving waters of the seven rivers. Waters, in Vedic literature, are just a transform of the rays of the Sun. Clouds are solar emanations containing solar power, which is released as nourishing water in the form of rain. A solar god, Parjanya, is responsible for rain. As the solar world is sometimes visioned as Aditi in the form of a Divine Cow, Parjanya is sometimes described as her udder, the lightnings of Indra are her teats and the Rain, her milk. These waters are the modulation of Consciousness forming the ontological foundation of the seven realms we have encountered—3 of the "upper foundation" (*Trini Rochana*), three of the lower (*prithvi, antarisksha, dyaous*), and one of the mid-world of Supramind (*Mahar*). These are called the seven oceans, Saptasindhu and sometimes the seven rivers, *Saptanadya*, or in a more psychological mood, *Saptadheeya*, the seven thoughts. Each of the seven planes of consciousness, is thus seen as an ocean, a vast infinite reality; each of them projecting its own manner of thought, the seven thoughts.

The Solar Gods

We have already encountered the Four Kings (Mitra, Varuna, Aryaman, Bhaga) of the Veda. These are embodiments of the supramental principle Surya or the Sun, also called Savitra and sometimes Surya-Savitra. We saw that the Sun has several other forms, such as Vishnu, Pushan, Parjanya and Martanda. One of its Vedic forms is Yama. Many are familiar with Yama as the God of Death. But etymologically, it is more properly the God of Control. In the Veda, Yama is an aspect of the supramental Sun closely related to the Law of Truth, *Ritam*. We have encountered this sense of Law in the term Ritam, which means Rightness. Yama is the guardian of this law of unfoldment according to which all things proceed. It is this aspect of the guardian of the Law which relates Yama to death. That which cannot abide by the Law of Truth, enters the kingdom of Death; that which follows the law lives in Immortality. This is one of the central secrets of the Veda.

The advent of the Sun God from the Darkness is prepared by a number of solar deities, mostly feminine. In the psychological sense, these are the powers preparing the consciousness to receive the fullness of the Divine. First come the Ashwins, horse riding twins who precede the Dawn. They are physician, healers who bring good tidings of the coming of Dawn. Next comes Ushas, the Dawn goddess, gently illumining the darkness in anticipation of the sun's resplendent chariot lighting up the day. With Ushas comes Savitri. Savitri, derived from Savitra is the daughter of the Sun, the power of Divine Grace. Other female solar powers that are critical to human spiritual progress and divine manifestation are Bharati, Ila, Saraswati, Sarama and Dakshina. Bharati, sometimes referred to as Mahi/Mahin, is the goddesses of Wideness. She widens our mentality, our understandings which are incapable of flexibility or translatability. With the power of Bharati, we see correspondences in all things, and how thoughts may lose their rigidity and become capable of application in many ways. Ila is the goddess of Revelation, who uncovers to the inner vision and understanding the secret significances of all things. Saraswati is the goddess of Inspiration, who opens us to deeper internal knowledge, since indeed, all Knowledge is contained in each of us. By the power of Saraswati, the knower within awakes and brings to the front the knowledge that is hidden. Sarama is the goddess of Intuition. She is figured as a hound because she chases the creatures of the Darkness into their lairs, drawing out their secret motives. This indeed, is the spiritual function of Intuition, going beyond the seen into the unseen. Dakshina is the goddess of Discrimination, a critical faculty, because the power to discriminate directs us within the Darkness. This is the special grace of the goddess Dakshina.

The Powers of Darkness

On the side of Darkness, there is Namuchi (eg. RV), the conscious power of Weakness, which represents lack of sincerity and makes the aspirant fail in his journey. It comes with the voice of temptation that lures us to a life of luxury and ease when there is work to be done. The Panis represent the life of the senses, which carry us away. They make the aspirant give his energies to the pursuit of sensual delights. This is what the Veda refers to as the robbery, the theft. It is the robbery because it is this energy that is meant to support divine illumination. The leader of the Panis is Vala. Vala is represented as a miser just as we are miserly with what we would give to the divine. We hoard it for our ego enjoyment. Vala is also a concealer because it has taken the cows of the divine and shut them in a cave. This is the way in which the Light in us is kept from illumining us. Finally there is Vritra, the Coverer, whom Indra fights. Vritra is the Serpent and the Obscurer; in his coils he hides the seven modaltieis of Knowledge and prevents them from being of use.

Other Ideas

The 10th volume of the Rig Veda (Mandala X) is considered to be the latest of the set and introduces hymns containing new ideas. Two of the most famous of these are the Purusha Sukta (RV.X:90) and the Nasadiya Sukta (RV.X:129). In the Purusha Sukta, the supreme Divine, who was earlier identified with Surya, is referred to as Purusha and hence granted an anthropic, though cosmic and transcendental form. The self-sacrifice of Purusha in the form of a self-dismemberment into four parts, is the theme of this sukta. Each of these parts is a soul-quality (referred to as "color" or varna)—Knowledge, Power, Harmony and Service. These form what are known as the "castes"—Brahmin, Kshatriya, Vaishya and Sudra. As such the hymn does not equate these soul qualities to any humans, but the implication is that Purusha, through his self-sacrifice, generates these four kinds of creatures. Naturally, this hymn has been much derived in our times, due to the cruel inequalities that have become socialized in India in its name. But the hymn merely refers to the fourfold power of divine expression that are integral to Purusha and manifest it through their harmonious action, controlled by the Unity Power and its right distribution (*Ritam*). In Sri Aurobindo's yoga formulation, these fourfold powers of expression are seen in Shakti terms as the four cosmic forms of the Divine Mother—Maheshwari, Mahakali, Mahalakshmi and Mahasaraswati (1999:p.780).

To whom or what does Purusha sacrifice itself? I would say it is the Integral Divine that sacrifices itself to its own power of plurality, so that the Many may independently and together manifest the integral body of Purusha in a collective life. Thus just as Purusha is bound to the creation and its creatures through its sacrifice, the Law of Sacrifice binds the creatures to Purusha. This is the message of the *Purusha Sukta*. Individuals must together manifest the dismembered integrality of Purusha by awakening this integrality within themselves and organizing themselves dynamically through soul-connection. This is equivalent to thinking of the Vedic ritual as a collective sacrifice, the reciprocal dimension of the Purusha's sacrifice. Such growing ensembles could manifest collectively something of the integrality of Purusha, leading to a teleological cosmic vision of a new form of divine manifestation. The 10th Mandala ends appropriately with a hymn for collective reception of the results of the Sacrifice (RV.X.191).[9]

The other famous hymn from the 10th Mandala is the *Nasadiya Sukta*, which has been oft-quoted as a sign of philosophical maturity due to what appears to be its concluding agnostic rhetorical question. Indeed, it is a marked change in the method of language use from other Suktas, which rely heavily on symbolism and coded language. Here, indeed, one encounters the birth of philosophy with its naked intuitions and enigmatic wonder. The hymn talks about the Becoming of Being as a self-birth out of the Mystery beyond Being and non-Being. It ends with the agnostic question, which is more full of wonder than doubt. And it is not rhetorical; it is addressed to the Mystery of Being which is earlier than the Creation but is also the One who has become the Creation. This Sukta inaugurates the power of language use that informs the Upanishads, the language of mystical intuition. Here is A.L. Basham's translation (1954:pp.247–248):

> Then even nothingness was not, nor existence,
> There was no air then, nor the heavens beyond it.
> What covered it? Where was it? In whose keeping?
> Was there then cosmic water, in depths unfathomed?
>
> Then there was neither death nor immortality
> nor was there then the torch of night and day.
> The One breathed windlessly and self-sustaining.
> There was that One then, and there was no other.
>
> At first there was only darkness wrapped in darkness.
> All this was only unillumined water.
> That One which came to be, enclosed in nothing,
> arose at last, born of the power of heat.

---

[9] The symmetry of the starting and ending hymns of the Rig Veda is interesting. These hymns serve as book-ends to what may be called the Adventure of Divine Sacrifice. They begin with a hymn to Agni (I:1), the psychic flame in the individual and the cosmos, that is at the center of the Vedic Sacrifice in its reciprocal version. It ends with a collective hymn for "right" collective distribution and use of the divine powers that result from the Sacrifice (X:191).

In the beginning desire descended on it—
that was the primal seed, born of the mind.
The sages who have searched their hearts with wisdom
know that which is kin to that which is not.

And they have stretched their cord across the void,
and know what was above, and what below.
Seminal powers made fertile mighty forces.
Below was strength, and over it was impulse.

But, after all, who knows, and who can say
Whence it all came, and how creation happened?
The gods themselves are later than creation,
so who knows truly whence it has arisen?

Whence all creation had its origin,
he, whether he fashioned it or whether he did not,
he, who surveys it all from highest heaven,
he knows—or maybe even he does not know.

References

1. Aurobindo, Sri, 1998, *The Secret of the Veda*. Pondicherry: Sri Aurobindo Ashram Trust
2. Aurobindo, Sri, 1999, *The Synthesis of Yoga*. Pondicherry: Sri Aurobindo Ashram Trust
3. Basham, A.L., 1954, *The Wonder that was India.* London: Sidgwick and Jackson.
4. Macdonell, A.A., 1897, *Vedic Mythology*. Strassburg: Verlag Von Karl J. Trubner.
5. Nirodbaran, 2001, *Talks with Sri Aurobindo, Vol I*. Pondicherry: Sri Aurobindo Ashram.
6. Satprem, 2008, *Sri Aurobindo or the Adventure of Consciousness*. Auroville: Mira Aditi.
7. Tyberg, Judith M., 1976, *The Language of the Gods*. Los Angeles: East-West Cultural Center.

— x —

Language of 'Mahā-bhārata Text Narrative for people of Bhārata': A Social outreach of Vedic tradition for social wellness

Venkatakrishna B.V. Sastry

Abstract

There is a critical need to revisit the 'language modeling gaps on 'Saṃskṛtam: the language of Vyāsa's Mahā-bhārata text. This 'Saṃskṛtam Language modeling shift of Mahā-bhārata' is presented in two-timeframes, using the forking reference: '*Mahā-bhārata Tātparya-nirṇaya* (MBT)' a work of ācārya Madhva (circa 1238–1317 CE). The pre MBT language modeling for text narrative of Mahā-bhārata significantly differs from post MBT (Colonial and Oriental) models. At present, the two schools carry unresolved issues of great significance, leading to a disputed position on the 'Message and Social Relevance of Mahā-bhārata'. The future outcome and outreach of Mahā-bhārata studies as a part of Indology in 21st century, depends on the clarity on the perception of relation between Saṃskṛtam as the language of text Mahā-bhārata. This is also an effort to highlight the importance of restoring the broken connection of Yogas and Saṃskṛtam in the current models of Mahā-bhārata studies. This exploration is also perceived as a quest in search of answers to some unresolved issues raised in twentieth century as 'Discovery of India'—'Bharat: Ek Khoj'.[1]

Introduction

There is a critical need to revisit the 'language modeling gaps on 'Saṃskṛtam: the language of Vyāsa's Mahā-bhārata text. This 'Saṃskṛtam Language modeling shift of Mahā-bhārata' is presented in two-timeframes, using the forking reference: '*Mahā-bhārata Tātparya-nirṇaya* (MBT)' a work of ācārya Madhva (circa 1238–1317 CE). The

[1] A 53-episode TV Serial, an Indian historical drama.

pre MBT language modeling for text narrative of Mahā-bhārata significantly differs from post MBT (Colonial and Oriental) models. At present, the two schools carry unresolved issues of great significance, leading to a disputed position on the 'Message and Social Relevance of Mahā-bhārata'. The future outcome and outreach of Mahā-bhārata studies as a part of Indology in 21st century, depends on the clarity on the perception of relation between Saṃskṛtam as the language of text Mahā-bhārata. This is also an effort to highlight the importance of restoring the broken connection of Yogas and Saṃskṛtam in the current models of Mahā-bhārata studies. This exploration is also perceived as a quest in search of answers to some unresolved issues raised in twentieth century as 'Discovery of India'—'Bharat: Ek Khoj'.[2]

In MBT frame, Mahā-bhārata needs to be understood with the keys provided in Śrīmad bhagavad-gītā, considered as the 'heart and soul of Mahā-bhārata'. This is the key to unify the social and spiritual message outreach of Srimad Bhagavad-Gita as the heart of Mahabharata. This entire line of argument is built on one anchor principle: Vedas are Transcendental documents and authority on Sanātana Veda Dharma (= Skt. *Veda-Apauruṣeyatva*). This issue is deeply connected to the language modeling of 'Samskrutham'.

In MBT frame, language model of Saṃskṛtam for Mahā-bhārata is (i) God's language/s ('*Deva-Bhāṣā*') (ii) language related to 'Vedas' (*Veda-Bhāṣā, Mantra-Bhāṣā, Yoga-Bhāṣā*). This modeling of language: Saṃskṛtam is the anchor of '*Yoga-Vedānta: śāstra-sampradāya*' aka mainstream Hinduism. The outcome of this position makes 'Mahā-bhārata a sacred text with 'Śrīmad Bhagavad-gītā' at its heart, a sacred text to build Yoga based spiritual identities'. The language of Mahā-Bhārata-narrative is the language of sacred—ritual and spiritual. Right modeling and understanding of Saṃskṛt language become a *sine qua non* for Mahā-bhārata studies, application and utility by its very design and purpose. Any vitiation or violation of 'Saṃskṛtam Language model' vitiates the purpose, pedagogy and benefit from the text. The integrity of text and language cannot be broken.

The socio-cultural outreach of this model makes Mahā-bhārata a classical text of social and sacred discourse (*Punya-kathā, Hari-Kathā, Vrata-kathā*) at Bhārata for faith-communities. This model of text-context—language unified narrative has shaped India's land, culture and communities for over five millennia. Mahābhārata has served as (i) a

---

[2] A 53-episode TV Serial, an Indian historical drama; First episode date: 29 June 1988; Program creator: Shyam Benegal; Networks: Doordarshan, DD National.

practical utilitarian-text, teaching principles and practices of Sanātana Dharma-Yoga (*Veda-Viniyoga*), (ii) a text for social outreach of Sanātana Dharma by Vedic standards (*Panchamo Veda*), (iii) a text-continuum for consolidation of yoga-teachings across generations (*Yoga-śāstra-paramparaa*), (iv) Make land and language to be sacred objects of worship (*kṣetra, sarasvati*), (v) expand the vision of people to look beyond one life to a bigger scenario of life after life, a generational continuum (*janmāntara, punarjanma*), (vi) See God in human form amidst us (*avatāra*). The MBT model and religion-discourse outreach built around these frames are used for grooming and strengthening the faith-identities of people in sacredness of land, rites of passage and cultural values.

In non-MBT(-Post MBT/Colonial and oriental) models, language: Saṃskṛtam is (a) language of socio-historical human communities ('*Deśa-Manuśya Bhāṣā/ Samāja Bhāṣāa*'), (ii) language of religion-ritual-rites of passage-magic-mystic (*devatā-prarthanā-saṃskāra-yātu-alaukika*) used for framing identities by anchor of history and land. Language is a tool used for social control, oppression and power. (c) a historical heritage resource useful for study of ancient india (*itihāsa-janapada-Bhāṣā*). In non-MBT approach, language is a disposable wrapper holding content that can be ported/poured to any other language-wrap. This approach towards 'language as a disposable wrapper/container over content' leads to the separation of text and the language of text-narrative. In non-MBT perspective, Mahā-bhārata study and research is not dependent or limited by any one language model, much less by 'Saṃskṛtam Language model'; nay Mahā-bhārata studies can be/must be separated (and/or sanitized) from legacy historical Sanskrit[3] language wrapper. The Sanskrit wrapper on Mahā-bhārata should not be allowed to contaminate the content supposed to be delivered by the text! Translation is one sure way to ensure the separation of language and content! Any constraint over Mahā-bhārata text-studies using its legacy language framework with a predefined model, is a conscious introduction of a contaminant for understanding the socio-cultural history of land, people and cultural practices, shaped by Mahā-bhārata. Therefore, academic scholarly work, with due alacrity[4]

[3] Sanskrit is the colonial nomenclature for what traditional schools term as 'Samskrutham'. Vedic Sanskrit is the expression for Chandas part; without any adjective, the term Sanskrit generally refers to the 'bhashaa' part of Paninian Grammar. There is a fuzziness in the use of the term Sanskrit, unless the context makes it otherwise clear. In Mahabharata studies, Sanskrit refers to 'Bhashaa'.

[4] alacrity (noun)—speed and eagerness: promptness in response: cheerful readiness (Source: https://www.merriam-webster.com/dictionary/alacrity).

must guard Mahā-bhārata studies from Saṃskṛt language contamination. The Mahā-bhārata studies can be and must be separated from its legacy historical language wrapper. Thus, non-MBT frames, and many academic research projects built around this construct the land-people-culture-history identities of bhārata differently from the MBT school. Clearly there is a conflict, due to diametrically opposite and divergent positions on Language: Saṃskṛtam modeling in relation to the purpose of Mahā-bhārata text study and outreach.

Conflict identification due to differences in language modeling for Mahābhārata text

The purpose, the declared objective of Mahā-bhārata by its first compiler—narrator, Vyāsa and their followers as understood in Tradition, is 'outreach of Vedic Sanātana Dharma-Yoga practice guidance[5] to everyone in society'. The goal is total wellness, harmonious togetherness for peaceful productivity and prosperity. Keeping this in mind, the design of Mahā-bhārata is deliberately constructed as an evolving text, resonating to the needs of society and communities, inclusively evolving and all the time carrying the stamp of 'Vyāsa authority'. The language of the text serves as a bridge between current society and past. Though Mahā-bhārata is called '*itihasa*', a *kavya*, it stands totally apart from giving any objectivity and priority to detailing of history-lineage of people, land, event-narratives, *de jure*,[6] *de facto*. In order to achieve the stated goals, Saṃskṛt language (standards, methods, systems, rules) must be integral with the text of Mahā-bhārata. The integrity of text and language cannot be broken.

Post MBT (Colonial and Oriental) schools take objection to this approach. The declared objective of Mahā-bhārata, as understood in framework of Indology, linguistics, anthropology, archeology et al., is

[5] The classical opening verse of Mahābhārata reads: *oordhvabbahur viroumyseshah, esha dharmah Sanātanah, dharmaat arthascha kaamascha, sa kimartham na sevyate*:: I shout (*viraumi*) with raised arms (*oordhva-baahu*) to proclaim the eternal message of Sanātana Dharma: Dharma-practice is the root and essence of The Total Wellness, Prosperity (*Artha*) and desire fulfillment (*kaama*), Why dont we all, live in compliance (*sevyate*) and serve to this directive?

[6] [Latin, In law.] Legitimate; lawful, as a Matter of Law. Having complied with all the requirements imposed by law. De jure is commonly paired with de facto, which means "in fact."

A de jure is one that has completely fulfilled the statutory formalities imposed by law.

In comparison, a de facto is one that has acted in Good Faith and would be ordinary but for failure to comply with some technical requirements.

(https://legal-dictionary.thefreedictionary.com/de+jure)

'study of ancient Indian culture, religion, language and communities'—a knowledge on how they lived in the historic past, identification of roots of present practices in religion and culture, the dynamics of shift in modalities and purpose of culture-religion practices and community faith. The goal is to gather verifiable evidence for objectivity of claims that are made by scholars, in contrast to public faith-popular understanding'. For this goal, the design for study-research of Mahā-bhārata cannot be constrained under the locks of 'Language (which is a dynamic variant along the historic timelines and usage-communities. The narrative text element of mystica[7] and magic cannot be accepted as evidence. Mahā-bhārata study and research is not dependent or limited by any one language model, much less by 'Saṃskṛtam Language model'. The social outreach of Mahā-bhārata (academic and scholarly) studies is just limited to identifying the roots of current community identities, cultural practices and faith-practices. The demand to keep the integrity of text and language as a necessary condition for Mahā-bhārata study, research and outreach is unwarranted. The seeds of this line of argument are seen at the processes that triggered the project of ' Critical edition of Mahā-bhārata', more popularly known as BORI project.

Professor M. Winternitz, in 1897, raised this question at the XIth International Congress of Orientalists, held at Paris, where he read a paper drawing attention to the South Indian manuscripts of the Great Epic and concluding with the remark that a critical edition of the Mahā-bhārata was "wanted as the only sound basis for all Mahā-bhārata studies, nay, for all studies connected with the epic literature of India". This demand was pursued through session of congress held in Hamburg (1902), reiterating that a "critical edition of the Mahā-bhārata was a sine qua non for all historical and critical research regarding the Great Epic of India". The outcome of this was Critical edition of Mahā-bhārata project[8] at BORI, Pune and other[9] research projects.

Pandit Nehru's thoughts document this trend in introducing Mahā bhārata, as chapter-section writings in 'Discovery of India'—(select

[7] mystic (noun)—a person who tries to communicate directly with God or other forces controlling the universe. (https://dictionary.cambridge.org/dictionary/english/mystic). (https://www.dictionary.com/browse/mystic)

[8] http://bori.ac.in/mahābhārata_project.html—It was a dream of the General Editors to compile an Epilogue to the Mahābhārata discussing the message of the great book.

[9] The projects are like: History of Dhamraśāstra, Critical edition of Ramayana, Critical edition of Vedic texts and the like. Also see:

http://www.people.fas.harvard.edu/~witzel/canon.pdf

http://www.sophia-project.org/uploads/1/3/9/5/13955288/macdonell_vedas.pdf

passages[10]). These deliberations set the socio-political environment and frame for rest of the projects[11] for exploring (a) the history of Bhārata and (b) Mahā-bhārata connections with 'Veda' on one side and (c) versions of Mahā-bhārata. Pt. Nehru's own thinking and perspectives-position of scholars of orient from BORI gave an academic frame for oriental model of pruning 'traditional-MBT' Mahā-bhārata[12] studies. The 'academic scholars embraced the following perspectives in Mahabharata and Samskruth language studies: (a) 'India as a land of Aryans, the migrating tribes (b) Saṃskṛtam as a branched out language under the 'tower of Babel' anchored theological origin of languages, promulgated as Indo-European linguistics (c) Veda as a historic dated text with layered structure and linear evolution, Rig-veda, onwards (d) taking archeology and physical sciences evidence to date the traditions (e) meddling with 'Vedānga': integrity of 'Saṃskṛt Language traditional model', which split the 'Chandas' and 'Bhāṣā' as two separate historical layers of Saṃskṛt language. (f) Later, the classical Saṃskṛtam-Prakrit relational language modeling also has undergone modifications, the outcome of which is seen in the Prakrit language dictionary[13] project.

Mahabharata—Text-Languages and Evolution of Narratives

Mahā-bhārata resources (textual and other) comes in a plurality of languages: Mainly tagged as Saṃskṛtam, Prakrit's and Dravidian. These multilingual resources are used in Indology studies. Indology is explained as the study of 'history, literature, philosophy and culture of (ancient) India'. The current studies of indology present two distinct linguistic models for three 'ancient languages of Mahā-bhārata texts' and their relations.

---

[10] Reference: http://varunkamboj.typepad.com/files/the-discovery-of-india-1.pdf (Page 107).

[11] Ref: http://bori.ac.in/aioc.html -

[12] The flavors added to Mahābhārata-; Insider of tradition' studies from MBT is an interesting independent topic of separate exploration, more specifically on (a) shift from 'text-plain focus to the 'essence construction (*Tātparya- -nirṇaya*)', (b) acknowledgement in the diversity and interpolations in the text (*grantha-vikshepa*), (c) repositioning of Mahābhārata as a ' Mokṣa-Dharma-Yoga-Śāstra' on the same pedestal of 'Veda-Agama-Kaya' (d) Inclusive accommodation of 'Buddha' in to the 'Vishnu-dashavatāra' listing as 'a delusion-illusion teacher (*moha-ka*) in the form of non-dualistic (*advaita*) and nihilistic (*shoonya vaada*) for the uninitiated trouble makers.

[13] http://bori.ac.in/prakrit_languages.html

Prakrits, called the "Middle Indo-Aryan Languages", true to their name, are the link between the so called "Old Indo-Aryan Languages" i.e. the ancient Indian languages and the "New Indo-Aryan Languages" i.e. modern Indian languages. They were the common parlance of people in their respective ages and a few Prakrits like the Ardhamagadhi, Maharashtri etc. enjoyed the status of preaching language of Jainism.

Historically Mahā-bhārata as a document, evolved across Bhārata, as oral narrative. The first version is called '*Jaya*' (8800 verses: circa 3100 BCE). This has evolved, expanded in an encyclopedic and inclusive way, absorbing local narratives, land history and several facets of cultural heritage of land to emerge in its current form of 100,000 verses (South Indian version/15 to 17th Century), with the title 'Mahā-bhārata'. Traditional schools recognize three 'Saṃskṛtam'—versions of Mahā-bhārata, even though they differ slightly in chapter length and content organization. These are alive in current public memory and in circulation. The editions serve as the relevant text resource to support cultural perceptions, faith, belief in community. The collaborative evidences to support the text are seen in art, architecture, sculpture, religion practices, literature and legends in languages of India. When India, as a nation, uses Mahā-bhārata as the national heritage document, a proper understanding of 'Text- basics' plays a critical role in arriving at conclusions and official presentations. Text-basics cover the modeling of language, content, theme-value construction and pedagogy continuum. The language modeling for the text should cover all the elements of all languages, cultural and religion-context, their inter and intra connections in grammar, vocabulary, usage and end use, connecting purpose and message of text, in the appropriate way it has served the nation and communities.

Mahābhārata Manuscripts: Language Continuum v/s. content—context continuum

The Critical edition of Mahā-bhārata mentions several vulgates of Mahā-bhārata which were available in a distributed way throughout India in several languages and scripts. The Critical edition project refers to the perusal of "235 manuscripts in several brāhmi scripts: Devanāgarī, Bengali, Grantha, Telugu, Malayālam, Nepālī, Śāradā, Maithilī, Kannaīa, and Nandināgarī." The location and scripts of manuscripts indicate that Mahā-bhārata was used throughout the length and breadth of Bhārata. Though scripts were different, the language was 'Saṃskṛtam' and message of mahā-bhārata was same.

The language of Mahā-bhārata text is acknowledged as 'Saṃskṛtam: The 'Bhāṣā' aspect covered in Panini's grammar (circa 700 BCE). This 'model and standard of Saṃskṛt language is a legacy heritage to Mahā-bhārata (3000 BCE) from Rāmāyaṇa (circa 6000 BCE). The language of 'jaya'—(the core version with 8800 verses) Mahā-bhārata (1500 CE up to—encyclopedic version, with one lakh plus verses) uses the same standard and model of language: Saṃskṛtam (Bhāṣā) for the text narrative and outreach. In this long duration, the social, cultural, philosophical scenario at Bhārata has undergone several changes. The rise and march of several prakrits, desi languages with different grammars and scripts in different regions has come in to being. The dynamics of religions and philosophies has changed the footprints of land-sacredness across bhārata. The upgrades in Dharma-śāstra's have been promulgated. With all these changes, going on, Mahā-bhārata stays with the language: saṃskṛtam (Bhāṣā) to continue its outreach of *Dharma Yoga Samskruti* message to society. The Vyāsa- Kathākars keep the text and language of Mahā-bhārata united and alive, sacred and socially accessible. There has been no concept of separation of text from the language of text. Language of text is as sacred as the text itself.

What is Saṃskṛtam Model of Language according to MBT—tradition?

Language: Samskruham (aka Sanskrit) is a continuing language of Vedic traditions. The origin of Saṃskṛtam is rooted in Vedas categorized as *yoga-darshana: sacred vision, mantra, sukta*). The language progresses through Rāmāyaṇa, considered as first work of Saṃskṛt literature *ādi-kavya*. The continuum of language utilization is seen through the passage of Mahā-bhārata in time, as: *hari-kathā, itihasa, panchama veda*. The osmosis of content and language of Mahā-bhārata through the sacred theological literature *Purāṇas* mystical literature of ritual worship—*Agamas, Tantras*, and classical literature *kavya* is a continuous process. According to MBT schools, the Paninian Grammar, generally[14] holds the key to decode the meaning of Saṃskṛt language document. Language of Mahā-bhārata text, by and large conforms to the Paninian rules. The Paninian model of Saṃskṛt language has not been revised or violated in traditional schools, save some exceptional cases. Post MBT colonial schools reject this rigid stand of tradition imposing Panini language model on Vyāsa text-context narrative.

Ācārya Madhva provides a standard formula[15] to position and understand Mahā-bhārata in the same basket of vedas, other sacred works like pancharatra aagama and literary works like ramayana. The entire basket is called *Śāstra*'. This is a technical term from Śrīmad-

---

[14] In some exceptional cases and for some special texts and contexts, some advanced grammars of mystic authority are invoked.

[15] ṛgādayaśca catvāraḥ bhārataṁ pañcarātrakam|mūlarāmāyaṇaṁ caiva śāstramityabhidhīyatē

Bhagavad-Gita[16] (16–24). Anything positioned under the category of Śāstra, is an infallible sacred scriptural authority. The diverse models of texts pooled and placed under this top category talk amongst each other to endorse the outcome. Mahā-bhārata is a Moksha-Śāstra. The language of the text becomes the language of yoga, the language of the sacred, the language of gods, the liberating language. The heart of Mahā-bhārata is Śrīmad-Bhagavad Gita, the Yoga-Śāstra narrated by Supreme Divine Sri Krishna, the Master yogi. This formula locks Mahā-bhārata in the continuum of Vedas[17] and Rāmāyaṇa and fixes Yoga as the heartthrob of Mahā-bhārata. In this frame, Language: Saṃskṛtam (*Chandas and Bhāṣā*) are integrally locked with the text and context of the document. Thus, MBT frame of Indian Classical models endorses the position: language is an integral inseparable part of the content it carries. Therefore, right Saṃskṛt language modeling holds key to the understanding of the utility-application-narrative-practice message of Mahā-bhārata. Scholar of a traditional school does not find any difficulty in applying Paninian grammar rules (Circa 700 BCE) to explain a text of 3000 BCE or 1000 CE!

The importance and continuity of this model of Saṃskṛtam for Mahā-bhārata study on Indian society is noticed in socio-cultural models, professions, socio-religious hierarchies and cultural narratives and norms, religion vocations based on Mahā-bhārata social connectivity to the Vedas. The osmosis of this understanding in Indian society till MBT time frame, has created a 'classical platform' over which the next level of paradigm shift in 17th century in the form of colonial and oriental models of Mahā-bhārata studies need to be studied for evaluation. The current period understanding of Mahā-bhārata studies, presentation and research carries a medley of these paradigm shifts in text, context and language of the Mahā-bhārata from MBT and post MBT schools. The question worth contemplating would be as follows: How should the text and language of Veda Vyāsa-'Mahā-bhārata' be connected in the models used for studies, research and outreach in 21st century, specifically in the discipline of Indology?[18]

---

16 tasmat Śāstram pramanam te, karyakarya-vyavasthitau
jnatva sastra-vidhanoktam, karma kartum iharhasi || (16–24)

17 Vedas are Darshana class texts and use Chandas. Ramayana is Kavya and uses 'Bhāṣā'. Pancharatra is the sacred text which uses Saṃskṛtam as 'Mantra' language of mystica. Śrīmat Bhagavad-gitā is a Yoga Text in Saṃskṛtam, where the technical use of Saṃskṛtam is called 'Vak-Yoga' model.

18 Indology is defined as 'the study of Indian history, literature, philosophy, and culture'. (https://en.oxforddictionaries.com/definition/indology; https://en.wikipedia.org/wiki/Indology).

as a continuum of these shifts? Has the critical edition achieved its professed objective[19] http://bori.ac.in/mahābhārata_project.html—the message of the great book?

Shifts: MBT-Saṃskṛtam Language model in Post MBT (Colonial and Oriental) schools

The MBT model of Saṃskṛt Language—continuum through Mahā-bhārata Texts was challenged and disturbed in colonial period by pioneer scholars of linguistics and Indology. The colonial scholars postulated 'Veda as ancient Indian tribal literature, Aryan panegyrics, chants of religion prayers; Vedic Language as 'historic social, of migrant communities, a language foreign to the soil, spirit and people of Bhārata'. There was nothing divine or sacred in the 'Vedas'! Sanskrit, like other human languages, is historical, society-context based; suffers decay by usage like any other classical language. The language modeling frame carries the hypothesis: All human languages are dynamic and undergo transformations. The text-content cannot be contained by the language wrapper.

The colonial models endorse the position: language is a disposable wrapper over the content; nay a contamination, a hindrance that needs to unpack and peeled off to understand the content it covers. Therefore, any modeling of Saṃskṛt is a hindrance to the understanding of the message of Mahā-bhārata. The pedagogy of Scholar of a traditional school is considered a highly defective, questionable method to understand and interpret texts of different periods, separated by historically long periods. Simply, Paninian grammar rules (Circa 700 BCE) cannot be used to explain a text of 3000 BCE or 1000 CE! This violates the observed phenomenon of 'language dynamics in societies, across several languages'. Saṃskṛt cannot be an exceptional language amidst the rest of human historical languages. Therefore, using Panini frame (700 BCE) to explain Mahā-bhārata of 3000 BCE or 1500 CE vulgate version is pedagogically defective.

The Flash-Clash—Forking point

With this, we have diametrically opposite positions on the relational issue of Text and language of Mahā-bhārata. In 21st century, should we

[19] https://bori.ac.in/mahābhārata_project.html

It was a dream of the General Editors to compile an Epilogue to the Mahābhārata discussing the message of the great book. As a preparatory step for the same a Cultural Index to the Mahābhārata was planned.

go by the position of classical schools or colonial schools over language of Mahā-bhārata?—is the issue to be resolved. The common objective is: Positioning text, Context and Language of Mahā-bhārata in Indology studies. The deeper issue that goes with this debate is 'What is Saṃskṛtam?'—A human historic language subject to all the frailties of usage, like other languages, A sacred eternal cosmic language of Gods which resists all change by caging itself in strict grammar rules to retain its eternal youthfulness? an Artificial language which can generate word-outputs to precisely couch a desired thought expression? How is the language covered by Paninian Grammar unique from rest of the Indian and word languages, especially English?

The shift in 'Saṃskṛtam Language modeling' from classical to colonial/oriental model got prominence in global academic studies in the postcolonial period. According to traditional schools, a proper understanding of the language-modeling of text of Mahā-bhārata is critical in understanding the content, intent, communication and community-culture shaped by this classical sacred text. Misconstruction of language using inappropriate tools and context-positioning will result in miscarriage of the message of text, cultural heritage[20] ancestry, outreach of message[21] of text and mis-project the identities of communities proud of Mahā-bhārata cultural heritage. Missing and messing up with the unity of text—context and language of Mahā-bhārata fails the scholar to understand It's Plan, Purpose and Pedagogy.

Mahā-bhārata—As perceived by People of Bhārata'

Mahā-bhārata is perceived by people of Bhārata in several perspectives. Several descriptive terms associated with Mahā-bhārata help us to understand how people of Bhārata get connected to Mahā-bhārata and put it in to social practice. Sacred narrative for merit (puṇya *kathā*) Fifth Veda (*Panchama Veda*), Narrative of Veda Vyāsa (*Vyāsa-kathā*), The family lineage of Sri Hari (*Hari-(vamsha) Kathā*), Text of Dharma-Yoga Wellness directives (*Dharma-śāstra/Smriti*), Guidance for Liberation—

[20] *Yaadava* 'is one of the major communities of India, who draw their community identity from Sri Krishna; Vahnikula kshatriyas or "Thigalas" of the famous 'Karaga' religious festival in Karnataka connect their identity to Draupadi. Elaborate discussions are provided in Mahābhārata on the social identity in terms of Varna-Jati technicality and nature, social status, professions, duties and paths for spiritual progress.

[21] This shift has made a significant impact on the understanding and social outreach of Mahābhārata. The reference line to explore the impact of 'language-paradigm-shift' is 14th century, where we get the writings of ācārya Madhva, in 'Mahābhārata Tātparya-nirṇaya (MBT)' circa 1238–1317 CE.

Salvation (*Mokṣa Śāstra*), Sacred Past Narrative (*itihaasa*), Encyclopedia of knowledge disciplines (*Vishwa-kosha: yadihasti tadanyatra, tannehasti na tat kvachit, Vyasocchishtam jagat sarvam*), Social Narrative (*Aakhyaanaka*), Meditation Mystica (*Yoga-śāstra*: Gita is heart of Mahā-bhārata).

Mahā-bhārata is regarded as (i) an applied text of utility (Veda-Viniyoga), (ii) an outreach of Sanātana Dharma by Vedic standards (Panchama Veda), and (iii) a consolidation of yoga-teachings of Vedas in an encrypted-symbolic way. Mahā-bhārata predates Jainism and Buddhism. Buddhist and Jataka tales[22] have found entry into the expanding text of Mahā bhārata. There is a Jain version[23] of Mahā bhārata. Sikh sacred texts of 16th century contain Mahā-bhārata incidents listed in Bhai Gurudas[24] vaaran and pauri's. Mahā bhārata, though it looks like a book of 'Vaishnavism', contains equal and balanced accommodation of Saivism and principles of Vedantic Yoga-meditation. The presence of Śrīmad Bhagavad-Gītā as integral part of Mahā-bhārata makes it a work on par with 'Vedas and Yoga's. Mahā-bhārata carries the listing of many holy places related to all major Hindu gods and goddesses.

[22] https://eprints.soas.ac.uk/5568/1/016-S%C3%B6hnen-Thieme.pdf

[23] Jain versions of Mahābhārata can be found in the various Jain texts like Harivamsapurana (the story of Harivamsa) Trisastisalakapurusa Caritra (Hagiography of 63 Illustrious persons), Pandavacaritra (lives of Pandavas) and Pandavapurana (stories of Pandavas). From the earlier canonical literature, Antakrddaaśāh (8th cannon) and Vrisnidasa (upangagama or secondary canon) contain the stories of Neminatha (22nd Tirthankara), Krishna and Balarama.—https://en.wikipedia.org/wiki/Mahābhārata?rdfrom=http%3A%2F%2Fwww. chinabuddhism encyclopedia.com%2Fen%2Findex.php%3Ftitle% 3DMahābhārata%26redirect %3Dno# Jain version

[24] -https://www.searchgurbani.com/bhai-gurdas-vaaran/vaar/10/pauri/8/line/1

It is interesting to note that Sikh sacred texts contain many stories from Ramayana, Mahābhārata, Bhagavata and other popular stories from the public memory. They have become a part of the Sikh sacred texts in since 17th Century. The list of stories covered in Bhai Gurudas vaaran is an interesting reading. The list covers vast range of 'pauri's'—stories from Ramayana, Mahabhārata and Bhagavath. Story of the saints-Dhruv, Prahlad, Bali, the king, Ambaris, King Janak, Harischandar and queen Taramati, Vidur and Duryodhan, Draupadi, Sudama, Jaidev, Namdev, Namdev and Trilochan, Dhanna and brahmin, Beni, Kabir and Ramanand, Sain, The barber, Ravidas, Ahalya and Gautam, Valmiki, Ajamil, The Prostitute, Putana, Demise of krsna at the hands of a hunter. The story of Mahabhārata - Draupadi dragged into open hall is covered in Bhai Gurudas Vaaran—Vaar 10 Pauri 8 of 23. https://www.searchgurbani.com/bhai-gurdas-vaaran/index/vaar/10

Mahā-bhārata mentions names of many historic *janapadas*[25] (kingdoms), saints and sages and people mentioned in Rāmāyaṇa and Vedas. These works are separated in time from Mahā-bhārata by at least a few millennia. The continuity of people identity tag[26] by *janapada* and *gotra* names like 'Bhāratas, Kurus, Panchalas, Madras, Magadhas, Drupadas, Gandharas, Kampilya, Kaikaya, Haihaya, Vashistha, Bharadwaja, Vaishampayana, Vyāsa, Durvasa, Parashurama seen in Mahā-bhārata help to identify a seamless thread of land-people-events history continuum over a long stretch of time. Mahā-bhārata was an oral narrative tradition across all these janapadas of Bhārata. The information unique to the locale and community from many of these janapadas, as observed by the Vyāsa—disciple narrator, was getting added on in an inclusive and slowly expanding text of Mahā bhārata.

Kalhana (c.12th century) of Kashmir was the author of Rajatarangini,[27] a work which provides an account of the history of Kashmir. The rulers of Kashmir are genealogically connected with Mahā-bhārata and Rāmāyaṇa characters. This shows how many historical royal lineages were proud to have a direct lineage link with the characters and events of Mahā bhārata. The cross referencing of history of land events at *janapadas* osmotically flows as oral narratives across Mahā-bhārata text (in to *itivrutta* part) and Purāṇas (in to the *Vamshaanucharita* part).

Mahā-bhārata is a discourse on several aspects of Dynamic Dharma practiced in communities of Bhārata. The criterion to inclusively position a piece of text in the dynamically evolving work of Mahā-bhārata, there needs to be a focus connection. This 'Focus connection and harmony' is 'Hari-Kathā to teach about Dharma-Puruṣa (King, Saint) and Puruṣa-Dharma (Duties and responsibilities). The intention is showing a state and community governed under the guiding principles of Sanātana Dharma. So, the social outcome of Mahā-bhārata is 'Dharma-Prajā-

[25] Mahābhārata in Bhisma parva mentions about 230 janapadas. The land of bhārata had migration of people across janapadas continuously. The names of janapadas continue to be a live memory and a part of temple rituals (-mahasamkalpam part) in bhārata. The concept of 'janpada' is as old as Vedas and Ramayana. The Buddhist and Jain canonical texts refer to the 16 mahajanapadas. The concept of janapada continues through puranas to pre-colonial Indian kingdoms. Every janapada seems to have a sacred place associated with one or other event related to Mahābhārata. The entirety of landscape addressed and covered in Mahābhārata covers the landscape of pre-independence India and at least some parts of South east Asia. The narratives of Mahābhārata in Java is an illustration of this.

[26] The names of several kingdoms occur in the virata parva, and bhisma parva where warriors are described from different locales of Bhārata and beyond.

[27] https://en.wikipedia.org/wiki/Rajatarangini#List_of_kings

Rajya'. While detailing what is 'Mahā-bhārata', it would also be good to be clear on what 'Mahā-bhārata' is NOT! Mahā-bhārata does not fit in to any one specific category tag, except 'Śāstra'! in MBT frame. Therefore, strict positioning of Mahā-bhārata in any one category other than 'Śāstra' would be a short classification and leads to defective understanding of the intent of the text.

Post-colonial construction of Saṃskṛt terms impacting understanding of Mahā-bhārata: Illustrative terms

The colonial scholars preferred the new way of interpreting the Saṃskṛt terms, based on the model of Greek and Latin languages and new pedagogy of philology, comparative linguistics and the like. Where traditional interpretations provided a specific model of interpretation and context specific meaning, the modern researchers exercised their academic freedom to work with different flavors of meaning and context constructions. The outcomes of different methods of interpretation have yielded incongruent outcomes. Due to this discordance in methods, systems, pedagogy and purpose applied to Mahā-bhārata research studies, the modern readers are not getting right keys to unlock the 'soul of Mahā-bhārata' connect to 'Śrīmad bhagavad-gītā'. One can explore the meaning shifts and interpretation perspectives on select terms[28] of Saṃskṛtam, like *shraddhaa, kaama, ashva, varna, dharma, shudra*. These divergences serve as pointers to this discordant position in MBT and Post MBT (Colonial and Oriental) projection.

Thus, we find enough justification and critical need to have a Post 21st century upgrade project to understand Saṃskṛt Language modeling and its impact on 'social outreach of Mahā-bhārata message, its relevance in the study of Indology: 21st Century'. The starting text base can be the last vulgate of tradition referred by MBT schools (as Kumbhakonam, Bombay or Bengal Versions) and 'Critical Edition of Mahā-bhārata from BORI'. The key issue to address would be the

---

[28] Detailing on the primary to tertiary impact due to the meaning shifts of these select Saṃskṛt terms is detailed in several other studies. Shraddhaa is not just faith! Kaama is not gender-sex relation. Ashva is not the animal horse; and ashvamedha is not Horse-sacrifice! Varna is not social order classification on the on the model of caste, race and livelihood-profession. Dharma is not religion, theology orientation, philosophy of exclusive intellectual contemplation. Shudra is not an oppressed member of society, damned by the scriptural sanctions. See: http://www.openthemagazine.com/article/open-conversation/vishwa-adluri-we-have-become-so-used-to-hindu-self-effacement-that-we-now-view-hindus-as-being

http://hunter-cuny.academia.edu/VishwaAdluri

http://indiafacts.org/mahābhārata-modern-scholarship-an-interview-with-dr-vishwa-adluri/

Saṃskṛt Language modeling that is truly needed to understand message of Mahā-bhārata in 21st century.

Wish list: What then could be done Now, in Mahā-bhārata studies for 21st century Indology

The following could be some thoughts, a wishlist, to undertake a fresh initiative for Mahabharata studies:

(A) Indology Appropriate framing, positioning and modeling of Mahā-bhārata.

(B) Tradition Appropriate framing, positioning and modeling of Mahā-bhārata.

(C) Vyāsa appropriateness as the intent of 'The author- compiler-eternal auditor of Mahā-bhārata.

(D) Saṃskṛt—Language appropriate mounting, positioning and modeling where Mahābhārata is Panchama Veda ('Veda- and Language: Saṃskṛtam as Vak-yoga guided by Vedanga Vyakarana).

The goals to accomplish would be:

– Closure of the identified gaps in the current constituted text of BORI edition of Mahā-bhārata

– Deliver the updated 'Mahā-bhārata' revisited, upgraded and aligned to 'Vyāsa Heritage vulgates and oral narrative tradition'.

– Make the 21st century Mahā-bhārata an integrated document for Indology studies to explore Maha-Bhārata National Heritage covering all its traditions and Identity, answering all questions on "History, Past Events, Identity, Culture, Social and Spiritual Unity of traditions from Yoga perspective as presented in Śrīmad Bhagavad-Gita.

– Find new pedagogy system to introduce Mahā-bhārata studies beyond the current four models which miss out proper introduction to 'Saṃskṛtam: the language of Mahā-bhārata'. The four areas of first introduction to Mahā-bhārata that need upgrade are: (i) First readings of Mahā-bhārata at Home for Parent-Children needs[29] (ii) Translation—introduction as classics[30] reading (iii) Review of current academic

[29] Current models of Mahābhārata introduction and explanation are through print and social-visual media like Amar Chitra kathā, Sagar Videos, Regional language films and popular public discourses.

[30] current models needing correction are: Translation writings of 'Mahābhārata as story' presented in English and regional languages, embedded with a bias on Hinduism and translation-limitations of Sanskrit text-terms-concepts translation in portrayal of Dharma as Religion.

published literature[31] (iv) Inter-disciplinary studies[32] based on partial views on Mahā-bhārata. Thus, the pedagogy of critical edition has not presented the total integrated connection of language of text (Saṃskṛtam), context (Mahā-bhārata—as Fifth Veda) and total outreach it has provided to keep the unity of Bhārata as a 'land of Sanātana Dharma-Yoga-puṇya Karma'. The consolidation of Buddhism into the broader plank of Vedic tradition in the MBT model is not fully resolved. Bad modeling of Saṃskṛt has distorted the social outreach of Message of Mahā-bhārata; thus, derailing the MBT-traditional mode of Mahā-bhārata studies at India, prevalent till 15th century CE. The result is distortion in the delivery of message of Mahā-bhārata and Social outreach of Vedic traditions for social Wellness. The distortions in Saṃskṛt language modeling has caused *'Hari (-sacred, spiritual)* to be out of *Hari-kathā'*; Merit *(punya)* out of sacred epic-Scriptures and Prayers *(punya Gita)*. Divinity of the text (veda) and characters are substituted by history and historical persona (*itihasa-kaavya*).

The root shift in post MBT (colonial and oriental) models of Mahā-bhārata research studies, have entertained the 'disconnection of the text and language of Mahā-bhārata' leading to several primary and secondary fall outs. All this has impact on Indology as a discipline which uses Mahā-bhārata as an important resource to portray ancient India that was Bhārata. These issues need to be resolved by addressing the 'Saṃskṛtam Language Modeling' for studies in connection with Mahā-bhārata text and context.

References

1. Kumbakonam Edition of *Mahabharata*—Sriman Mahabharatam, a new edition, mainly based on the Southern Indian Texts, with footnotes and readings. Printed at the Davaji Dadaji's Nirnayasagar Press, Bombay, 1906. Published by T.R. Krishnacharya, proprietor, Madhva Vilas Book Depot, Kumbakonam, printed by R.V. Shedge for the proprietor at the Nirnayasagar Press, 28 Kolbhat Lane, Bombay, 1914.

[31] current resources being: Writings of academic Scholars of orient starting from postcolonial writings in English about Vedic Traditions, Texts and Philosophies, who have reached the point of reading prolegomena to Critical Edition of Mahābhārata and Professor V.S. Suthankars four lectures and early translation- literary narratives of Mahābhārata post 1800 CE, and resources especially at www.sacred-texts.com

[32] Current areas being writings from Scholars of Religion-practices- culture-Anthropology-Indology-Post Modern India studies who get to Mahābhārata through the introductory readings from Gandhi, Nehru, Aurobindo and the backdrop of Bhagavad-gitā, Upanishad philosophies, and the like.

2. Madhvacahrya Mahbharata *Tatparya nirnaya*—with commentaries, ed. Bannanje Govindacharya, Akhila Bharata Madhva Maha MaNnadal Udupi, 1971.
3. Ramachandrashastri Kiṃjavaīekara, *Mahābhāratam* with the Commentary of Nīlakaṇṭha, Citrashala Press, Poona, 1929–36.
4. Chakrabarti, Arindam, and Sibaji Bandyopadhyay, eds. *Mahābhārata*, Now Narration, Aesthetics, Ethics. London, New York and New Delhi: Routledge, 2014.
5. P.V. Kane, *History of Dharmaśāstra*, 5 vols., 2nd ed., Bhandarkar Oriental Research Institute, Poona, 1968–1977.
6. Agarwala, G.C. (ed.), 1979, *Age of Bharata War*, Motilal Banarsidass, Delhi.
7. Majumdar, R.C. (general editor), 1951, *The History and Culture of the Indian People:* (Vol.1) The Vedic Age. London: George Allen & Unwin Ltd.
8. Vaidya, R.V., *A Study of Mahabharat*; A Research, Poona, A.V.G. Prakashan, 1967.
9. James Fitzgerald, 'India's Fifth Veda: the Mahābhārata's Presentation of Itself' in Arvind Sharma and E.J. Brill (eds.), *Essays on the Mahābhārata*, Leiden, 1991.
10. P.K. Gode, '*Nīlakaṇṭha Caturdhara*, the Commentator of the Mahābhārata—His Geneaology and Descendants, Annals of the Bhandarkar Oriental Research Institute 23, 1942, 146–61.
11. Christopher Minkowski, 'On the Success of Nīlakaṇṭha's Mahābhārata Commentary', in F. Squarcini (ed.), *Boundaries, Dynamics and Construction of Traditions in South Asia*. Firenze University Press, Florence, 2005.
12. Rosalind O'Hanlon, 'Letters Home: Banaras Pandits and the Maratha Regions in Early Modern India', *Modern Asian Studies* 44.2, 2010, 201–40.

—×—

Changing Dynamics of the Shrines of Three Female Deities in Varanasi

Namrata Rathore Mahanta

Abstract

The progress of the vedic-brahmanic civilization assimilated into its fold numerous indigenous deities through various innovative methods. Indigenous deities thus assimilated were accorded varying levels of prominence in *Purāṇic* literature. In course of time the validation of the stature of an individual or of a community came to be constructed through practice of rituals prescribed in *Purāṇic* texts. Many indigenous deities with strong human associations as spirits of the dead remained outside the fold of *Purāṇic* literature but continued to have a robust presence in community life through ritual worship. This study focuses on select shrines of three female deities in Varanasi city—*Chaurā Māi*, *Mari Māi* and *Śayari Māta* (*Śayar Mā*). The objective of the study is to trace the impact of changed spatial dynamics of the shrines on the self-perception of the community. The study argues that the new livelihood patterns and infrastructural transformations within the city have challenged the reciprocal relation between the shrine and the community.

Introduction

The Hindu sacred sites present an organic amalgamation of social, economic and ritual based exchanges in a living culture. This complexity is manifested in many forms and is responsible for the concurrent ambivalence, diversity and interconnectedness that forms the external expression of Hindu rites and rituals. As one proceeds, it becomes evident that there are certain common principles at the core which anchor and sustain this colossal diversity in the practice of religion.[1] The idea of the sacred is one such intrinsic principle.

[1] Kosambi, 1956, describes how the prevalent folk rituals were people's attempt to make sense of and reconcile with the forces of nature.

Sacredness is associated not only with the power inherent in the presiding deity but also with the bond created out of regular and repeated acts of consecration carried out by people through worship rituals or *Pūjās*.[2] Even in its simplest form, the Hindu ritual worship involves a complex interdependence between the human and divine. These features are common to the worship of the gods and goddesses in the big temples as well as the local deities worshipped in tiny shrines or under trees in the villages.

While the presence of diverse folk deities, trees, animals, and spirits in the form of *Yakṣa*, *Piśāca*, *Gandharva* and their female counterparts in later-vedic and epic literature are a testimony to their acceptance amongst the people, these are not granted primacy as divinities of any stature in mainstream religious practices. It is in works written by missionaries during the colonial period that subjects such as worship of trees, stones and spirits are given prominence as oriental curiosities from the point of view of an alien culture[3] and recorded as 'Hindu' curiosities.[4]

The local religious sites are seldom the exclusive strongholds of dominant religious groups, or of powerful political dynasties. These are prominent sites of cultural transactions, of economic enterprise, of novel socio-linguistic formulations among many other activities. Situated at the nerve centres of society, these provide vantage points to observe the evolution of present day attitudes of the people, their self perception and their understanding of the changing world around them. Such sites prioritize the body, emotions and feelings of the people. These also grant space and sanction to a range of emotions which are otherwise restrained within more formal worship patterns in the big temples.

The local shrines are dedicated to deities, to a variety of spirits, to trees, to certain men and women who died in extraordinary circumstances. Therefore unlike other gods and goddesses, the local deities cannot be included at the altar alongside family deities. Their worship is conducted at their respective 'sites' only. In absence of historical or literary validation, the collective memory of the people

---

[2] Kosambi, 1962, traces the evolution of mother goddess cult sites from primitive tracks, trade routes and *Jatakas*. An outline of elements of Yakṣa worship found in contemporary Pujā rituals is given by Ananda Coomarswamy, 1971. Asko Parpola (2015) traces it to animisim of early Harappan period.

[3] Bhattacharya, 1996, has discussed at length the different approaches to the religious historiography during colonial period.

[4] Sherring, 1868.

becomes the foremost source for the study of local shrines.[5] The associated oral testimonies become increasingly distant and complex with each passing generation and are also embellished, censored or modified according to the changed circumstances, narrators and audience.

Overview and a note on the choice of method

Studies on Hindu deities that strive to define, characterize, differentiate and categorize are vexed in their attempt when faced with the mutability that pervades the living practice of Hindu religion.[6] The variations in the numerous versions of lists of deities found in ancient literature, conflicting cross references and composite rituals are some of the tangible evidences of this fluidity, and scholars have traced the processes of borrowing, blending and recasting in the evolution of the gods and goddesses of the Hindu pantheon.[7] Literary evidence of similar religious or scholarly engagement with respect to indigenous deities has not been reported so far.

A close study of the evolution and transformation of the goddesses serves to demystify the complex fabric of the Hindu religious practices while revealing the cycles of assimilation and amnesia that had occurred through centuries. The evolution of the mother deities associated with *Skanda*, the dissemination of female principle in the form of *Mūla Prakṛti*, *Ādi Śakti*, *Māhāvidyā*, *Krittikās*, *Matṛkās*, *Yoginis* all point to the dynamic amalgamation of diverse traditions.[8] The *Atharva Veda* abounds in a variety of supra human entities which have the power to grant a variety of magical charms to shield against adversaries, diseases and misfortunes. All of these and more bundled up in an inseparable whole have survived in different forms in the living fabric of society.

The people who worship at the minor shrines that are the subject of this study do not use any kind of text, written or oral; yet they carry with them the memory of an embodied association with the deity. The idea of the deity survives only through the practice of rituals, and rituals are animated in the memory of the living persons who have reinvented these

[5] Early descriptions of village shrines are the ones represented by colonial missionaries during 19th and 20th centuries: Martin (1914), Du Bois (1897), Crooke (1894), Whitehead (1921). Later descriptions of the city of Varanasi by Sukul (1974), Eck (1982) Hertel (1993), Medhananda (2002), Gutschow (2005), Majumdar (2015), Desai (2017) do not make any detailed reference to the local shrines.

[6] Du Bois (1897), Whitehead (1921)

[7] Bhandarkar (1913), Bhattacharya (1999), Kosambi (1962), Hazra (1940).

[8] Chakrabarti (2001) gives a detailed analysis of the transformation of religious processes and the transformation of female deities through the Bengal Purāṇas.

from time to time to accommodate the contemporary reality and have thus kept alive a long hoary tradition in its many colourful forms.[9]

The important question that was faced by this study was to find a method to illustrate this vast range of transformations which could look beyond the creation of categories and binaries of high and low religion, greater and lesser deities and be able to posit such classifications within the larger dynamics of lived reality. This led the study into the realm of the 'modern', a formulation that had gradually descended upon societies through the nineteenth and twentieth centuries, impacted ideas in an unprecedented manner and played an important role in the forging of new identities.

The engagement of religion with the 'modern' created an opportunity to identify new patterns of social identity drawn from a new pattern of religious practices.[10] Within the new practice, the most important constituent of the idea of the 'modern' was its association with the notion of development or 'progress'. When caste did not remain the only ground for assertion of social hierarchy and when upward social mobility could be acquired through economic, educational progress leading to important social and governmental positions and new respectability, the intimate realm of rites and rituals was also impacted and passed through many changes. Its interface with the economic and political manifestation of progress became an important factor. The perception of the twin ideas of 'modernity' and 'progress' swept across the social fabric taking in its spate the most intimate space of the individual—the space of contact with the divine. The urgency to transform, to move from the traditional, intimate, fluid, frame of worship to a more organized, more formal and progressive form became the pursuit of the people and this led to a great transformation in the ritual worship of the local deities.

Collective Memory and Anecdotes

***The Śayari Māta shrine at Kamachhā*:** The *Śayari Māta* shrine is located at the *Kamachhā* crossing. It was earlier known as the *Nimā Māi Caurāha* because of the large *neem* tree which was home to the tree deity *Nimā Māi*. However, *Nimā Māi* is not worshipped anymore and her place is taken by *Śayari Māta* who is addressed as *Śayar Mā* by elderly devotees. There is only a single version of the story of this deity that is narrated by the priest and reiterated by the devotees: Late Sri Baleshwar

[9] The concept of memory and embodied remembrance is drawn from Rao (2014:83–87).

[10] The use of 'practices' to understand cultural change is drawn from Chatterjee (2014) and the operations of 'modernity' from Appadurai (1996).

Prasad, a prominent businessman and had accumulated occult powers through tantric worship of the great goddess. His grandmother Late Smt Jeera Devi also well versed in tantric worship of the great goddess could interact with supernatural powers. Once while she was returning after a holy dip in the Ganges, one such supernatural spirit followed her home and convinced her to establish her shrine. Jeera Devi at once realized that the spirit was none other than the great goddess *Ambā* and promptly established a shrine for the goddess.[11] Regarding the name *Śayari Māta* the priest was convinced that it is one of the many *Purāṇic* names of goddess *Ambe-Gauri.*

***The Śayari Māta Shrine at Sonārpurā*:** The shrine is located on the *Sonarpura* road opposite to the *Kedār Ghāt* entrance. There is only a single version of the story of this deity that is in circulation: Initially there was a *neem* tree that was worshipped by the people of the locality. Then someone kept a consecrated stone there and the people started worshipping it. Later, someone kept a small idol of a goddess. People believed that worship of the deity brought prosperity. When a huge storm tore down the neem tree and the simple shrine, the people decided to build a new shrine. Sri Vijay Kumar Yadav also called Buddhu Sardar (one of the owners of *Ksheer Sagar* Sweet House), Sri Ramdas Chaurasiya (prominent betel leaf merchant) Late Shi Gopalji Gupta (prominent grocery store owner), Late Sri Lakshman Prasad Kannaujia (also called Shastriji) organized the construction of the shrine. Other families also contributed in cash or kind and Gopalji Gupta arranged for morning and evening worship of *Śayari Māta* or *Śayar Mā*.[12] The younger generations of these families maintain a distance from the affairs of the shrine.

The *Mari Māi* Shrine at *Teliya Bāg*: The shrine is located near *Champak* Sweet Mart in the *Teliya Bāg* area at the tri-junction of *Patel Chowk*, *Rājā Bazār*, *Maldahiyā* roads leading to the railway over bridge—*Andhra Pul*. It is partially demolished. There is no priest at this shrine. There are many different versions in the memory of the people regarding the deity and the shrine. In the first narrative *Mari Māi* is one of the forms of the most ancient goddess, the *Devi*. She was there even before the first inhabitants came. No one was there to worship her. When people came and made their houses, they were regularly troubled by a supernatural spirit. A learned man was called from a distant place.

[11] As narrated by Sri Chhotelal, the priest appointed by the family of Late Sri Baleshwar Prasad, residents of Raj Villa, Near Sharda Marbles, Nagwa, Varanasi.

[12] As narrated by Sri Ramdas Chaurasiya, prominent betel leaf merchant and one of the founders of the shrine.

He carried out different rites and through that he came to know that it is the spirit of the *Devi.* He propitiated the *Devi* with rites and rituals and requested her to make her abode under an auspicious tree. Thereafter the goddess was satisfied and decided to stay there. She looks after the well being of the people in the neighbourhood but is ruthless with the evil ones. She once blinded a thief who was trying to escape after stealing many items from the neighbourhood.[13]

In the second narrative too *Mari Māi* is a 'Devi' whose worship was forbidden by a Muslim *'daroga'* (sub-inspector) during British rule. Such was his terror that nobody dared to challenge his order. The Hindu families lived in fear of inciting the wrath of the *Devī.* The women somehow surreptitiously managed to light small lamps. When India became independent in 1947, the owner of Champak Sweet Mart a prominent resident of the area challenged the *'daroga'*. He filed a case in the court challenging the order of the *'daroga'*. Seeing his courage and sentiment, other residents also joined him. The verdict of the court was in favour of the deity and with great fanfare, the owner of *Champak* Sweet Mart built the shrine and the worship of *Mari Māi* was resumed.[14]

In the third narrative *Mari Māi* is an ancient spirit of a low caste woman who must have met with an accidental or untimely death. She haunted this area since ancient times. When the British built the railway over-bridge now known as *Andhra Pul*, the over-bridge area became her favourite haunt and she troubled the people who passed that way. On account of her association with the over-bridge she was called '*Pul ki Mari Māi*'. The prominent families in the area sent for a learned man from Gorakhpur who overpowered the spirit and established her seat at the present location where she is worshipped now. She is the guardian of this area and does not trouble anyone. However she immediately punishes those who try to harm the people of the area.[15]

The *Chaura Māi* Shrine at *Teliyā Bāg*: At walking distance from the *Mari Māi* shrine is the *Teliyā Bāg* circle where the *Chaura Māi* Shrine is located. In sharp contrast to the *Mari Māi* shrine, this shrine is well managed and frequented by devotees throughout the day. The area forms a kind of green circle at the centre of a very busy cross road.

---

[13] Sri Ramchunder Jaiswal (DOB 1928) resident of C–28/77 Teliyabag, his son Sri Shiv Kumar Jaiswal C–28/77 Teliyabag. Sri Bhai Lal Sahu of C–28/78 Teliyabag.

[14] Sri Ramchunder Jaiswal (DOB 1928) resident of C–28/77 Teliyabag, his son Sri Shiv Kumar Jaiswal C–28/77 Teliyabag and Sri Bhai Lal Sahu of C–28/78 Teliyabag. Sri Badri Prasad Chaurasiya, betel leaf merchant whose shop was removed from the shrine by the recent demolition drive.

[15] The anonymous shop attendant at the temple flower shop.

Numerous shrines are located there amidst trees and plants. The central shrine is dedicated to *Chaura Māi* and has a very tall sati mound encased in pure silver covering with intricate designs. The other shrines that surround it are dedicated to *Shiva, Durgā, Shiva-Pārvati, Hanumān*, and *Gaṇpati*. The shrine is surrounded by banners put up by prominent business houses of the area. The complex has a safe enclosure and gates that are locked at night. The people say that the shrine commemorates an extraordinary woman who by the practice of austerities after the death of her husband merged with the divine goddess. Her mortal body turned into a mound of dust and the site became sacred and charged with energy. The temple complex was constructed in parts as and when some devotee's wish was fulfilled by the goddess.

Reconstruction

Kāśhi Khaṇd of the *Skanda Purāṇa* gives a detailed account of the religious sites in Varanasi along with geographical location, architectural features, deities, associated ritual texts, narratives of spiritual realizations. However the smaller shrines that are the subject of the present study are not mentioned in compilations of lists of temples or in maps made by colonial cartographers.[16] The colonial practice of categorization and standardization helped to validate the hierarchy of prominent deities and temples while further obscuring the identity of those lacking in scriptural validation. This, in a way became the impetus for the first step towards the transformation of the local shrines in emulation of the material and spatial dynamics of the major temples. Unlike major temples that were commissioned by the rich and the powerful people at the topmost rung of the social ladder, the local shrines were restructured by the collective effort of common people often belonging to the intermediate castes. As an extension of the newfound identity and economic aspirations of the people, the humble structure of the shrine was replaced by temple like structures of concrete and marble.

The three deities chosen for this study have the maternal marker *Māi/Māta* suffixed to their names. This is the singular feature that is common to the three deities which are otherwise extremely diverse in their attributes. *Chaura Māi* and *Mari Māi* have distinct human linkages. *Chaura Māi* is a female guardian spirit worshipped with no external marker except for a square shaped platform under a prominent tree.

[16] For history of the printed maps of Varanasi see Martin Gaenszle and Jörg Gengnagel (2006).

However *Chaura Māi* shrines often contain a *Sati* mound, the latter being the spirit of an exceptional woman or *Sati* who, because of the strength of her virtues could transcend her mortal self through austerities, and thus merge with the universal female principle. *Mari Māi* is believed to be the irate spirit of a low-caste woman or an unmarried woman, who having died under unnatural circumstances requires unfaltering propitiation, failing which she expresses her malevolent potential to disrupt the welfare of people.[17] *Śāyari Māta* or *Śāyar Mā* is considered to be one of the many manifestations of the great mother goddess. She chooses a worthy individual, reveals her identity and directs the person to establish her shrine. All three are neighbourhood deities worshipped by the people irrespective of caste hierarchy. These are popular with men and women alike and their devotees attribute their welfare and success to the natural benevolence of these deities.

The origin of the three local deities is obscure and devotees typically recall that the "deity has always been there but the shrine was made later". Devotees uniformly narrate that the shrine took its present shape with the collective effort of the neighbourhood. People arrange for the annual feast of the deity just before or after important festivals such as *Śivrātri* or *Dīpāvali*. The *Chaurā Māi* and *Śāyar Mā* shrines are also common meeting points of the men and women of the locality and once or twice a week people gather to sing *bhajans* and *prasād* is arranged by the family that has organized the *bhajan*. The more affluent families of the locality who have left their ancestral home and live in far off places often employ a person to perform ritual worship of the deity on behalf of their family. This person gains importance because of his regular presence at the shrine and soon begins to manage the affairs of the shrine as its part-time priest. In course of time, the narrative that he disseminates becomes the dominant narrative of the deity.

The shrines under discussion are located within the city of Varanasi since the colonial period. During the British period these locations were already prominent: *Teliyā bāg*, *Kamacchā*, and *Kedār* areas were home to the Sampoornanand Sanskrit University, the Beasant Theosophical Society and to the busy pilgrim area around Kedar Ghat respectively. Yet the shrines stood under trees and were not marked by idols or structures of any kind. The idea of the site as sacred was nurtured by people, primarily of the intermediate castes such as *Yadavas, Jaiswals, Chaurasiyas* and *Sonkars*. At a time when caste based occupations were

[17] Unlike Mariamman goddesses of the south, the Mari Māi deities of Varanasi are not directly associated with disease but with a variety of other misfortunes.

slowly losing their structured rigidity and dominance in society, families acquired wealth through trade in sweets, betel leaf, fruits, and vegetables. Opportunity to work for a 'salary' also gave economic strength to people of all castes. The earliest structures or shrines for the deities were made by the people who had met with financial success and attributed it to the grace of the deity. In bits and parts the shrines were built in emulation of temples. As the fortunes of the people rose, the small mound signifying the deity was enlarged, covered with plaster, cloth or metal. Bells were hung, and temple style rituals were performed twice a day. For the people involved it was a marker of their entry to the more elite ranks of the society. With time, the animal offerings were replaced by fruits and sweets. This was often attributed to a vision of the deity who revealed to the devotees her distaste for flesh offerings. As the shrines became larger, depending on the preference of the devotees, other prominent gods and goddesses also came to be enshrined alongside the original deity and attributes of the local deity congealed with those of the canonical gods and goddesses that surrounded them.

Another trajectory that emerged is that of the transformation of the local deity into a *Purāṇic* goddess. In this complex and long drawn process the representative block or mound was overlaid with an image of goddess *Durgā*. The image of Shiva in the form of a linga was also established. The pattern of worship was changed completely to include as a major event the *Shivrātri* festival and the bi-annual *Navrātri* worship of the goddess.

Conclusion

During this study, the idea of sacredness associated with the local shrines emerged as the first direct principle that sustained the initial dynamics of the shrine. However, an exploration of the interconnections between the sacral and the human concerns disclosed efforts of self-assertion in a changing society. A favourable condition for the proliferation of worship of a particular deity at a particular shrine was typically marked by the convergence of three major concepts: the region as the consecrated abode of the deity, the individual's personal association with the region, often during a difficult phase in life and testimonies of other devotees.

The older generation also saw the shrine as proof of their collective strength and will and took great pride in narrating their contribution to the shrine. Majority of the younger respondents were indifferent to the shrines and did not worship there. They were unaffected by the proposed demolition of the shrines and many of them saw it as a positive step to ease out traffic. The infrastructure enhancement activities combined with the fast diminishing neighbourhood affiliation has adversely impacted the shrines. In present times the changing dynamics of the family, the neighbourhood, the way in which economic activity and wealth are perceived have impacted the shrines in different ways. The shrines have begun to lose their neighbourhood devotee base. The congregational nature of the sites is precariously maintained by the elderly people of the neighbourhood many of whom are physically dependent on others to visit the shrine. The old professions and the ways of running businesses have transformed the nature of business transactions that were carried out around the shrines.

The idea of work and leisure is also greatly transformed. The people who used to congregate at these sites are either too old or bedridden. The younger members being too occupied with day to day business prefer to worship the canonical gods and goddesses at home and in their shops. They have moved from the collective to the individual form of worship. Many of them are dismissive of these local deities and consider their worship as mere superstition. The trees and shrines that were a meeting point for small businessmen and devotees are now marked for obliteration to make way for broader roads. With the passing of the elderly devotees, the memory of the shrines, deities and an entire tradition of worship associated with them are likely to be forgotten.

References

1. Appadurai, Arjun, 1996, *Modernity at Large: Cultural Dimensions of Globalization*, Minneapolis and London: University of Minnesota Press.
2. Bhandarkar, R.G., 1913, *Vaisnavism, Saivism and Minor Religious Systems*, Rpt. 2015, New York: Routledge.
3. Bhattacharya, N.N., (1996), *Indian Religious Historiography*, Calcutta: Punthi Pustak.
4. Bhattacharya, N.N., 1999, *The Indian Mother Goddess*, 3rd enlarged edn., New Delhi: Manohar.
5. Chakrabarti, Kunal, 2001, *Religious Processes The Purāṇas and the Making of a Religious Tradition*, New Delhi: Oxford.
6. Chatterjee, Partha, Tapati Guha-Thakurta and Bodhisattva Kar, 2014, *New Cultural Histories of India: Materiality and Practices.* New Delhi: OUP.
7. Coomaraswamy, A.K., 1971, *Yakṣas*, New Delhi: Munshiram Manoharlal.
8. Crooke, W., 1894, *An Introduction to the Popular Religion and Folklore of Northern India*, Allahabad: Government Press, North-western Provinces and Oudh.
9. Desai, Madhuri, 2017, *Banaras Reconstructed: Architecture and Sacred Space in a Hindu Holy City*, University of Washington Press.

10. Dubois, Abbe, 1897, *Hindu Manners Customs and Ceremonies*. https://archive.org/details/in.ernet.dli.2015.211238 Accessed on 30 April 2018, 08:00 hrs.
11. Eck, Diana, L., 1982, *Banaras City of Light*, New York: Alfred A. Knopf.
12. Gaenszle, Martin and Jörg Gengnagel, 2006, *Visualizing Space in Banaras: Images, Maps, and the Practice of Representation*, Wiesbaden: Harrassowitz Verlag.
13. Gutschow, Niels, 2005, *Benares—The Sacred Landscape of Varanasi*, Fellbach: Axel Menges Gmbh.
14. Hazra, R.C., 1940, *Studies in the Puranic Records on Hindu Rites and Customs*. Rpt.2017. Delhi: Motilal Banarasidass.
15. Hertel, Bradley R. and Cynthia Ann Humes, 1993, *Living Banaras: Hindu Religion in Cultural Context*, New York: SUNY Press.
16. Kosambi, D.D., 1956, *An Introduction to the Study of Indian History*, Bombay: Popular Book Depot.
17. Kosambi, D.D., 1962, *Myth and Reality Studies in the Formation of Indian Culture*. https://ia800200.us.archive.org/2/items/MythAndReality/mythandreality.pdf Accessed on 30 April 2018 08:30 hrs.
18. Majumdar, Nandini, 2015, *Banaras: Walks Through India's Sacred City*, New Delhi: Roli Books.
19. Martin, Rev. E. Osborn, 1914, *The Gods of India Brief Description of Their History Character and Worship*, London, Toronto, New York: J.M. Dent & Sons Ltd., E.P. Dutton & Co.
20. Medhananda, 2002, *Varanasi at the Crossroads: A Panoramic View of Early Modern Varanasi And the Story of its Transition*, Kolkata: Ramakrishna Mission, Institute of Culture.
21. Parpola, A., 2015, *The Roots of Hinduism*, New York: OUP.
22. Rao, D. Venkat, 2014, *Cultures of Memory in South Asia Orality, Literacy and the Problem of Inheritance*, New Delhi, Springer.
23. Sherring, M.A., 1868, *Benares The Sacred City of the Hindus*, Rpt. (2016), Varanasi: Pilgrims Publising.
24. Singh, Rana P.B., 2009, *Banaras: Making of India's Heritage City*, Newcastle upon Tyne: Cambridge Scholars Publishing.
25. Sukul, Kuber Nath, 1974, *Varanasi Down the Ages, Np*, Patna
26. Whitehead, H., 1921, *The Village Gods of South India*, 2nd edn., Calcutta: Associated Press; London: Oxford University Press.

— x —

Consciousness From a Philosophical Dogma to a Scientific Phenomenon: Yoga Vasista and Modern Sciences

Sivaram S. and *Rajani Jairam*

Abstract

Consciousness can be defined as the state of awareness of one's existence through sentience, the ability to feel, perceive and experience subjectively. Ancient philosophical text and yoga treatise, Yoga Vasista, has documented in great details about consciousness and elucidated its connection with body and mind and hence on yoga, pranayama and meditation. Recent scientific researches in the context of biology and psychology, have not only substantiated the existence of consciousness but also have helped us better understand how yoga and meditation can positively impact consciousness. Objectives of this paper are (a) to provide an overview on important philosophical and yogic aspects of consciousness as described in Yoga Vasista (b) to present a brief summary on some of the recent scientific and psychological researches on consciousness.

Introduction

Understanding 'consciousness' is one of the important quests that has baffled humankind for a long time now. Discussions on 'consciousness' has traditionally been a subject of debate among philosophers but in the last few decades it has rapidly become an important research pursuit for scientists especially from cognitive, neuro and psychological sciences.[1] Consciousness is either considered from universal (macrocosm) point of view or individual (microcosm) which is defined as the state of awareness of one's existence through sentience, the ability to feel, perceive and experience subjectively. Philosophy primarily looks at

[1] http://www.consciousness.arizona.edu/mission.htm; https://academic.oup.com/nc and https://www.ncbi.nlm.nih.gov/pmc/articles/PMC5641373/

macrocosm in a spiritual context whereas Science primarily looks at microcosm in a physical context. Essentially, macrocosm involves a top-down view whereas microcosm involves a bottom-up view.

Through this research paper, we have tried to bridge the views of macrocosm and microcosm by analyzing how the ancient philosophical dogma on consciousness as envisaged in Yoga Vasishta (YV) is relevant in the context of modern scientific research and to elucidate similarities and differences in their approaches to consciousness. We have chosen YV for this research work as it presents an excellent amalgamation of philosophical thoughts on consciousness and practical yogic techniques such as 'pranava yoga' involving meditation and pranayama that can help in union of microcosm with macrocosm.

YV is an important ancient scripture developed in the format of conversations between Ayodhya King Rama of Ishvaku Dynasty and his guru Rishi Vasishta. YV is considered as an evolved text with primary authorship attributed to Valmiki in BCE and subsequent authorships in 5th CE. YV is also known as Vasista Maha Ramayana and Jnana Vasista and has 'bruhat—large' version with approx. 32000 verses and 'laghu—concise' version with approx. 6000 verses. YV consists of six Prakaranas, namely: Vairagya Prakarana (on dispassion or indifference); Mumukshu Prakarana (on longing for liberation); Utpatti Prakarana (on creation or origin); Sthiti Prakarana (on preservation or existence); Upasanti Prakarana (on dissolution or quiescence); and Nirvana Prakarana (on liberation).

Consciousness from the perspective of Yoga Vasishta

Although there are many views on philosophical approaches to understand consciousness, one of the most important and ancient philosophical expositions on consciousness can be found in Upanishads. Since Upanishadic teachings are ideally delivered one-to-one—directly by an enlightened teacher to an eligible student, hence the element of 'learnings from subjective experiences' is integral to Upanishads. Hence, philosophy of consciousness in the Upanishadic texts align well with the overarching context of this research paper and is counted as an important prelude for understanding the perspectives of Consciousness in Yoga Vasishta. For the purpose of this research paper, we have analyzed Aitareya and Mandukya upanishads to understand the philosophy of consciousness as envisioned in them.

Rig Veda's Aitareya Upanishad concludes "prajñānam brahma" and the most commonly accepted interpretations are "absolute consciousness is Brahman" and "pure and infinite consciousness is Brahman". The term 'brahman' can be considered as the personification of universal consciousness, the macrocosm. While the Aitareya Upanishad personifies macrocosm as Brahman, Atharva Veda's Mandukya Upanishad treats the macrocosm as the yogic state of pure consciousness which is devoid of any content or context and is manifested as silence. With this background of Upanishadic texts, we analyzed YV for its tenets on the philosophical perspectives of consciousness.

Based on the commentaries[2] referenced for this research paper, some importance inferences were drawn and presented here. YV eulogies "Pure Consciousness" as characterized by endless, indivisible and unlimited by space, time and can be known by experience only. YV considers creation as a reflection of consciousness and reflected in itself appears as creation (book 3. chapter 20. verses 40–41). YV recognizes every individual human as consciousness and ultimately the same indivisible, immutable, eternal and infinite Pure Consciousness, and not any physical body (3.14.26). YV conjectures that every individual soul (atman) is the Pure Consciousness (Brahman) in singularity and the ego with its cognition of the objects manifested as duality (2.19.19). YV declares that Consciousness fills the Universe (5.27.2–3).

YV asserts that Brahman is always shining as Pure Consciousness in everyone and everything at all time; is without beginning and end and exists beyond cycles of creation-sustenance-dissolution-recreation (book 6 part 1.49.27). YV further adds that Pure Consciousness is both the unmanifest and manifest and manifestation (creation) began with the vibration of the pure consciousness which was till then in stillness (book 6 part 2.28.10–11).

YV elaborates on the practice of pranava yoga (5.54) and pranayama to help in the process of becoming aware of and to be in perpetual union with Pure Consciousness. YV's book 5 in chapters 78 and 91 explain the techniques of meditation, pranayama and inquiry. This chapter mentions that the objective of yoga and meditation are to establish the reunion of jiva (individual consciousness—microcosm) with the Pure Consciousness (universal consciousness—Brahman or macrocosm). YV explains that pranayama is the method of confining

---

[2] (a) Yoga Vasishta by Valmiki, The original Sanskrit attributed to Sage Valmiki, translated to English by Vihari Lala Mitra (1891), edited by Thomas L. Palotas (2013), Publisher: Handloom Publishing, Shivabalayogi Seva Foundation, Shri Shivabalayogi Maharaj International Trust, Arizona, USA and (b) YOGA VASISHTA SARA, based on a translation made by Swami Sureshananda, 4th edition (2005) Published by V.S. Ramanan, President, Sri Ramanasramam, Tiruvannamalai.

one's consciousness in one's true Self by controlling breath (5.91.21 and 26). Essentially, YV teaches us the importance of yoga, pranayama and meditation that can help us in bridging the microcosm with macrocosm.

Consciousness from the Perspective of Scientific Inquiry

Scientific pursuit to understand consciousness primarily arises from our compelling need to have an understanding on 'conscious state' versus 'unconscious state'. This need is driven by the notion that consciousness is associated with the very identity of us and our relationship with surroundings (external stimuli). Scientific inquiry focuses on brain's neurocognitive and psychological aspects.

Research done by Edelman et al.[1] looks at consciousness as a biological phenomenon—a product of both evolution and development. Through such an approach one can explain selfhood and phenomenal experience biologically in terms of patterns of neural activity. This research also mentions that primary consciousness occurring in animals lack any linguistic capabilities and is an essential process also in humans who possess a higher-order consciousness distinguishable from primary sensorimotor consciousness. Possession of true language with syntax in humans has given rise to higher-order consciousness allowing its possessor to be conscious of being conscious.

New scientific study may explain how brain creates Consciousness —three claustrum neurons seemed connected to most, if not all, of the outer parts of the brain that receive sensory information and drive behavior thus reinforcing Koch's belief that the claustrum,[2] by coordinating inputs and outputs, is involved in the creation of consciousness. Another study observed that burning more calories was linked with greater gray matter volume in key brain areas responsible for memory, learning and cognition.[3] Integrated Information Theory[4] extends the concept of Consciousness to all matter beyond just the living beings—any system's consciousness is determined by its causal properties and is therefore an intrinsic, fundamental property of any physical system.

Scientific study of consciousness from psychological perspective attempts to understand human behavior and the contribution of consciousness on it. According to one study,[5] consciousness evolved as the platform for the volitional control of movement and volition is the sole causal efficacy of consciousness—an important perspective that Psychologists have on Consciousness. This study also explains that Consciousness consists of two integrated aspects—Active—volitional attention and Passive—conscious subjective experience—phenomenal consciousness.

Another research study[6] on consciousness proposes four-dimensional graded consciousness—phenomenal quality—subjective or experiential character, semantic abstractness—referential nature, physiological complexity—bodily mechanisms and functional usefulness—exhibited by conscious information. Psychologists are also trying to understand consciousness and its relationship with experiences in different states[7] such as wakeful, dream, sleep, meditative, drug-induced etc.

Scientific inquiries have so far recorded many observations that link human consciousness directly to the brain activity hence ceases to exist after brain death. Consciousness in humans is linked with one's experiences, memories of such experiences and retrieval at a given time and has a direct relationship to cognitive faculties such as perception, thinking, judgement, language, memory and volition thus dealing with 'individual consciousness i.e., micro consciousness'.

Scientific Inquiry on Consciousness in the Context of Yogic Meditation and Vedic Chanting

For better understanding of consciousness and to find its link with body and mind (physical and mental health), empirical research studies on yoga, pranayama and meditation are important. Such pursuits can potentially provide a rationale on the need for symbiotic relationship of body, mind and consciousness as emphasized in Yoga Vasishta.

Many studies are looking at the positive biological effects of meditation. One such study observed that long hours of repetitive meditation resulted in naturally high production of Dopamine in brain[8]—a biological secret responsible for feeling of deep happiness/bliss in yogis along with less drive towards actions. Dopamine also works as an incentive, naturally urging repetitive meditation. Another study found that meditation's serotonin replenishing effect works[9] to create a utopian chemical environment to produce new brain cells, making one a happier and healthier person. Effect of Vedic chanting (swadhyaya) among the age group of 13–15 on memory (verbal and spatial memories using delayed recall test) and sustained attention (letter and character cancellation tests)[10] was studied at SVYASA and concluded that repetitive chanting improved memory and reduced errors. Another recent study[11] by the Hyderabad campus of BITS Pilani, reveals a "clear improvement in the general cheerfulness and clarity of mind" of students after they chanted mantras. This conclusion was drawn using psychological tests before and after the research. In this study by BITS Pilani, participating students chanted the following five mantras: Gayatri mantra (from Rig Veda), Vishnu Sahasranamam (thousand names of Lord Vishnu), Lalita Sahasranamam (thousand names of Divine Mother), Purusha Suktam (from Rig Veda dedicated to Cosmic Being) and Aditya Hrudayam (invocation to Surya, the sun god). Yoga and meditation practices can positively affect both physical and mental health thus improving the human experience of consciousness through improvement of faculties involved during the chanting.

One study found that through regular exercises such as yoga (burning calories), one can build larger volume of gray matter in key brain areas responsible for memory and cognition thus improving the experience of individual human consciousness. This observation establishes a link between yoga practices recommended in Yoga Vasishta and improved experience of consciousness as observed by science. Both Yoga Vasishta and Science view 'micro consciousness' as a subjective experience of an individual. Yoga Vasishta says vibration of consciousness is the trigger for creation to begin that align with scientific observations on how quantum fluctuations could have preceded big bang.[12]

Yoga Vasishta deals with both individual and cosmic consciousness and gives a way for the former to be in perpetual union with the latter whereas scientific inquiry on consciousness deals only with individual consciousness. However, efforts are in progress to understand and comprehend cosmic consciousness such as Panpsychism, Integrated Information Theory. Yoga Vasishta associates 'consciousness' with non-physical soul (spirit-centric) whereas Science associates 'consciousness' with physical brain (matter-centric).

While we recognize the need for a more detailed study on this subject, there are some important implications and future research opportunities that we could recognize. We attempted to integrate philosophical views with scientific approach to explore possible synergism between the two. What we have discussed here as implications and opportunities can be considered as possible outcomes of such a synergism. This approach proposes to use philosophical and scientific knowledge to unravel some unanswered questions and better understand some unexplained phenomenal experiences.

- Enhanced experiences of 'individual consciousness' through practice of yoga, pranayama and meditation can result in upheaval of 'societal or collective consciousness' which can possibly catalyze holistic social development[3] and growth

- In an era of artificial intelligence, there exists an opportunity for us to build a society of 'inclusive consciousness'—symbiotic relationship of higher order Carbon-based (humans) and possibly a lower order Silicon-based (machines) consciousness [13–14] where scriptural wisdom of Yoga Vasishta can be used in establishing a framework for governing ethical aspects in machines
- Can the blissful union of individual and cosmic consciousness explained in Yoga Vasishta possibly be explained scientifically through principles of Quantum Theory of superposition and entanglement based on the exchange of quantum information between microcosm and macrocosm?
- Can eternity of 'pure consciousness' be the time entanglement of past, present and future?
- Can better empirical understanding of 'cosmic consciousness' give any clue for the elusive 'Theory of Everything' that physicists are looking for?

From our analysis, it appears that the effort to study consciousness in an integrated perspective of combining philosophical tenets with empirical research is a suitable and necessary approach that merit more detailed research. We conclude that Yoga Vasishta presents as one of the greatest scriptures that has not only incorporated thoughts on consciousness but also has useful wisdom for the 21st century society. Yoga Vasishta can be studied in a larger context to elucidate so many other concepts that it has talked about and interpret the embedded knowledge in the context of empirical research especially quantum mechanics. Any efforts of holistic studies on consciousness that are anchored on philosophy-science synergism are not only applicable and valuable for today's Age of Information but also for tomorrow's Age of Machine Intelligence. Philosophy-Science synergism can well be the directional thinking we need for the 'Theory of Everything'.

---

[3] Holistic social development is concerned with the social development of the human being from the perspective of developing capacities into nine domains: (a) temperament, personality and self-views, (b) cognition and thinking, (c) affect and emotions, (d) conation volition or self-regulation, (e) physical and bodily-kinesthetic, (f) social/ interpersonal, (g) spiritual/ transpersonal, (h) moral character and (i) citizenship-Approaches and Strategies for Holistic Social Development by Radhika Kapur, Arts and Social Sciences Journal, 2015, 6:3 https://www.omicsonline.org/open-access/approaches-and-strategies-for-holistic-social-development-2151-6200-1000119.php?aid=59242

References

1. Edelman, Gerald M., Joseph A. Gally, and Bernard J. Baars, "Biology of Consciousness", Frontiers in Psychology 2 (2011): 4. PMC. Web. 6 June 2018 https://www.ncbi.nlm.nih.gov/pmc/articles/PMC3111444/
2. https://futurism.com/new-find-may-explain-how-the-brain-creates-consciousness/
3. http://www.sciencecodex.com/burning_more_calories_linked_with_greater_gray_matter_volume_reduced_alzheimers_risk-177663
4. http://integratedinformationtheory.org/
5. https://www.sciencedirect.com/science/article/pii/S0732118X15300039#fn3
6. https://www.frontiersin.org/articles/10.3389/fpsyg.2017.00420/full
7. http://www.psychology4all.com/psychologyofconsciousness.htm
8. https://www.ncbi.nlm.nih.gov/pubmed/11958969
9. https://eocinstitute.org/meditation/dhea_gaba_cortisol_hgh_melatonin_serotonin_endorphins/
10. http://nopr.niscair.res.in/handle/123456789/6832 and http://nopr.niscair.res.in/bitstream/123456789/6832/1/IJTK%205%282%29%20% 282006%29%20177-180.pdf
11. https://timesofindia.indiatimes.com/city/hyderabad/vedic-chant-can-help-improve-test-score/articleshow/57802728.cms
12. https://www.sciencedirect.com/science/article/pii/S221268641300037X
13. http://theconversation.com/will-artificial-intelligence-become-conscious-87231
14. http://www.scholarpedia.org/article/Machine_consciousness

— × —

Experiencing Divinity: Kamakshi, Meenakshi, Visalakshi through the eyes of Muthuswami Dikshitar

Vinay Varasani

Abstract

In Carnatic music, Muthuswami Dikshitar (1775–1835) is celebrated as one of the musical Trinity. Dikshitar composed extensively on several Gods and Goddesses of the Hindu pantheon during his travels across India. Some of his kritis (compositions) contain visible patterns, as they belong to a series. This paper is a glimpse into the wondrous world of Dikshithar, and will research on the inter-connectivity created by Muthuswami Dikshitar in his kritis on Kamakshi, Meenakshi and Visalakshi: mantra shastra, mythic imagery, musical knowledge and some tenets of advaitha-vedanta(non-dualism). The intended effect of this inter connectivity in these kritis have a positive influence on the sadhana (spiritual pursuit), for the musician and devotee alike.

Introduction

In Puranic lore, *Kamakshi*, *Meenakshi* and *Visalakshi*, (present in the temples of *Kanchi*, *Madurai* and *Kasi* respectively) are referred to as a trio. The reason is that their *shakti* is focussed in their eyes, giving them the suffix *"akshi"*. Several other connections exist between these forms.This esoteric knowledge is evidently understood by Dikshitar, an initiate in *Sri-Vidya Upasana* himself. (the occult knowledge of *Sri*, the Mother-Goddess). He presents this knowledge in common frameworks he has used in structuring his kritis addressing these three Goddesses. Some of those frameworks include: Netra-Shakti Vivarana, Sthala-Purana-Smarana, Samayaachara-Upasana, Sodari-Sodara Tatva, Matru-Bhava. These patterns and frameworks are hidden at first glance, creating scope to research upon. This paper attempts to explore the frameworks used by Muthuswami Dikshitar to structure the *kritis* in praise of *Kamakshi, Meenakshi* and *Visalakshi.*

***Muthuswami Dikshithar*:** Muthuswami Dikshithar (1775–1835) is one of the celebrated trinities of Carnatic Music. While his contemporaries, Shama Shastri (1762–1827) and Tyagaraja (1767–1847) wrote on their favoured deities, Kamakshi and Rama respectively, Muthuswami Dikshithar is the only one of the trinity who wrote compositions on Gods and Goddesses extensively across various shrines in India. Several of these compositions were written during his pilgrimages. What pours forth in Muthuswami Dikshithar's music is not only the rich technical flavour of the ragas, but also his deep understanding of Sanskrit. Amongst the trinity, he was the only one who composed a majority of his compositions in Sanskrit. He has to his credit several groups of Kritis: Navagraha Kritis, Kamalamba Navarana Kritis, Tyagaraja Vibhakti Kritis, Abhayamba Vibhakti Kritis and so forth.

These above kritis fall into the category of Kshetra Kritis. Kshetra kritis can be referred to as a category of compositions in praise of certain Gods and Goddesses at certain holy sites These sets of Kritis show a clear connection amongst each other, depending on the series they belong to. For example, each kriti in the series of Kamalamba Navavarna describes each avarna, or realm of the Sri chakra and the ruling deities.

Muthuswami Dikshithar was initiate into the occult worship of the Mother-Goddess in a systematic, traditional format, known as Srividya Upasana. Being initiated in this paddhati, or system, he placed strong focus on embedding several aspects of Sri-vidya, or esoteric knowledge of the Devi into several of his kritis. With this belief in mind, I stumbled upon similarities in his kritis on Kamakshi, Meenakshi and Visalakshi, and discovered that he has used certain common frameworks in these compositions, though they do not appear so on first glance. In order to understand and analyse his kritis, a basic understanding of the background of these Goddesses is essential.

Kamakshi-Meenakshi-Visalakshi: While there are several other forms of Devi describing her eyes, three forms, namely Kamakshi, Meenakshi, Visalakshi enjoy a certain privileged status. In popular folk lore, they are referred to as 'Kanchi Kamakshi Madurai Meenakshi Kasi-Visalakshi'. Regarding this trio, there is iconography depicting the three Goddesses. What makes this trio so unique? The connection between them has several different aspects, when understood from the Shakta perspective.

Srishti-Stithi-Laya: The Lalitha Sahasranama, a text in the Bramhanda Purana, which describes Devi's glory through 1008 of Her names, contains all these three words:

Kamakshi: Beautiful eyed; Meenabha-Lochana: Fish Eyed; Visalakshi: Wide eyed.

However, as explained in Bhaskaracharya's commentary, a surface level meaning of this does not provide the significance of the names, for they merely explain external beauty. There are largely three processes involved in upholding the Universe-srishti: creation, stithi: sustenance, laya: dissolution. Devi as Kamakshi represents the process of creation, while as Visalakshi, she uses her wide eyes to observe, and then sustain (Annapoorna). Finally, as Meenakshi, she dissolves the world: attrivuted to the ability of the motherfish to take her children in her mouth when a predator is sensed, and release them when it is safe again. Similiarly, Devi takes the Universe back into her, and then the process begins again.

Icha-Gyana-Kriya Shakti: Shakta texts describe the concept of Srishti-Stithi-Laya, the process of creation, sustenance and dissolution of the Universe. The unmanifest Paramatma, uses his resolve, or sankalpa shakti to perform these tasks. This shakti splits itself into three parts: Icha shakti, Gyana shakti, and kriya shakti. Icha shakti represents the desire, gyana shakti represents the knowledge required for creation, and kriya shakti represents the activity of creation. These three are essential to uphold the Universe. Kamakshi represents icha shakti, Visalakshi represents gyana shakti, and Meenakshi represents kriya shakti.

Lalitha-Shyamala-Varahi The *Lalitopakhyaanam*, found in the *Bramhanda Puraana* describes the narrative of Lalitha Mahatripurasundari, the form of Devi who killed the demon Bhandasura. The story states that as Lalitha was preparing for war, she yoked two prominent shaktis from within Her: Varaahi and Raja Shyamala Devi. They too then formed a trio, which went on to vanquish Bhandasura. The slokam describing this trio is:

Bhaje Sri-Chakra Madhyasthaam Dakshinotharayo Sadaam
Shyaama Vaarthali Samsevyaam Bhavanim Lalithambikaam

Essentially eulogizing Lalitha Devi, flanked by Devi Shyamala and Varahi standing to her Southern and Northern sides respectively. Geographically speaking, a map of India depicting Kanchi at the center shows perfectly how Madurai is to it's south, while Kasi is to it's north. Thus, one can say that this slokam clearly depicts that Devi Lalitha resides at Kanchipuram, Raja-Shyamala at Madhurapuri (modern day Madurai), Varahi at Varanasi. This is evident, temple wise as well.

It is essential for us to understand that the idols in the temples are not the only aspects of the energies there, the idols are representatives of the *sahaja-siddha-bhoomi*, or naturally energized sites. The energy in these places becomes intensified by the penance of rishis and yogis. That essentially means that the power of the Goddess can be experienced anywhere in that area. This observation helps understand two things:

(i) it explains how even though the temple at Madurai houses an idol of Meenakshi, the kshetra is that of Raja Shyamala.

(ii) This observation is a key factor in understanding Muthuswami Dikshithar's common framework in his compositions addressing these Goddesses, infifteen compositions on Kamakshi, thirteen compositions on Meenakshi,(including a set of eight called the Madhuramba Vibhakti Kritis) and two compositions on Visalakshi. While the number of his compositions on Visalakshi are lesser in number than works in praise of the other two, Dikshithar's scholarly understanding is aligned to the Shastras, evident in the fact that he addresses several Goddesses in Kasi as forms of Visalakshi herself. (Kritis such as Annapoorne Visalakshi bear testimony to this. However, while some scholars opine that Annapoorne Visalakshi was written at the *kshetra Kuzhikkarai*, this kshetra was known as dakshina Kasi, as the patron deities there are Visalakshi and Vishveshwara).

Muthuswamy Dikshithar evidently understood these aspects of these *kshetras*, and embedded them into his compositions. This is made evident in several ways. These common characteristics touch upon different aspects of his strong knowledge of *Sri-Vidya* and principles of *Advaitha.*

Samarasya

Kalidaasa's famed work of poetry, *Raghuvamsham* begins with the iconic sloka:

Vagartha Vivasamprukthou Vakartha Prattipathaye,
Jagatah Pitaro Vande Parvathi Parameshwaro

While this sloka has layered connotations to it, a basic understanding of it is that just as a word and it's meaning cannot be separated, Shiva and Shakti cannot be separated from the other.

This concept of *Parameshwara* and *his Shakti* being equal and inseparable is known and explained by the word *Saamarasya.* This word appears in the Lalita Sahasranama (samarasya parayana). Shiva and Shakti are co-equal in nature, and prayers to one are to be followed with an obeisance to the other.This concept forms the basis of the first words in Adi Shankaracharya spiritual gems- The *Soundarya Lahari* and *Kanakadhara Stotram.* The former begins with the words '*Shiva Shakthya-yuktho*', while the latter begins with '*Angam-Harehe*', describing Shiva-Shakti and Lakshmi-Vishnu respectively. This concept is evident in Muthuswami Dikshithar's kritis on the three Goddesses, where he specifically makes a reference to Devi's consort Shiva in each of the three kshetras. In Kanchi, Shiva is worshipped as *Ekambreshwara*, in Madurai as *Somasundareshwara*, and in Kasi as *Vishvheshwara*. As opposed to a generic reference to Shiva, Dikshithar refers to the name of the Patron Deity in each of the places. These references are clearly demonstrated:

Goddess	Kriti	Part	Reference
Kamakshi	Kanjadalaayataakshi	Charanam (madhyama kala sahityam)	Ekamreshagruheshwari
Meenakshi	Meenakshi MeMudam	Charanam	Mahadeva Sundareshapriye
Visalakshi	Kasi Visalakshim	Anupallavi	Kasi Vishveshwara Manolaasa-karineem

Dikshithar has written compositions in praise of the forms of Shiva at the respective *kshetras* too. Staying true to this school of thought of *Saamarasya*, he has made references to Shiva's consort with the corresponding name.

Goddess	Kriti	Part	Reference
Kamakshi	Ekamranathaya Namaste	Charanam	Kamakshi Samethaya
Meenakshi	Sundareshwaraya	Anupallavi	Meenakshi Mohithaya
Visalakshi	Sri Vishwanatham Bhajeham	Anupallavi	Sri Visalakshi Gauri Sametham

Kshetra: As described earlier, certain *kshetras* contain certain energies. Owing to this power, *Kshetra-mahima*, or the power of these sites are that they confer their blessings even when their name is uttered. While in many of his compositions, Dikshithar makes indirect references to Kshetras, in the case of these compositions, he directly refers to the name of the Kshetras. A speculation at this point would be whether he specifically refers to the names of the Kshetras (also) because of the colloquial terminology: *'Kanchi Kamakshi-Madurai Meenakshi-Kasi Visalakshi'*, for in this saying, the names of the kshetra too are present.

Goddess	Kriti	Part	Reference
Kamakshi	Kanjadalaayataakshi	Charanam	Shri Kanchainibhasane
Meenakshi	Meenakshi Memudam	Charanam	Madhurapuri Nilayae
Visalakshi	Ehi Annapoorne	Charanam	Kasi Kshetra Nivasini

Sthala Puranas: Owing to the energy present there. each *kshetra* has certain legends about it, which are recorded in texts known as the *sthala puranas*. These describe in great length the legends, miracles and tales of events that have happened at the kshetra.

The sthala purana of Kanchipuram refers to the story of *Muka*—a mute devotee of Kamakshi. Despite being mute, his devotion to Kamakshi was unphased. One day, as he sat facing the sanctum sanctorum in the temple complex, Kamakshi emerged from the idol, and pleased with Muka's devotion, offered him betel leaves that she herself had chewed. In ecstasy, Muka opened his mouth, where Kamakshi placed the betel leaves. Such was the power of this *tamboolam* that a mute Muka was gifted the blessing of speech. In his immense gratitude, he composed five hundred slokas in praise of Kamakshi, known as the Muka-Panchasathi. This story of the sthala purana finds a reference in Dikshithar's kriti in *Saraswati* Manohari: *muka-vaak-pradaanakari:* one who blessed Muka with the power of speech.

The sthala purana of Madurai cites the story of Meenakshi, and her unmatched conquests across the world. Describing her glory as a warrior, the sthala purana alks about Meenakshi who took upon the title of 'Digvijayam', or conquering all the directions. Through her skills as an adept warrior, a perfect ruler and an excellent administrator, she went on to be known as a figure of bravery-prathapamurthi. This is depicted in the kriti Mamava Meenakshi, where Dikshithar refers to her as 'Digvijayaprathaapini'.

The Kasi Mahatymam, the text describing the occult powers of Kasi and the divine forces who reside there, focusses on one central aspect-Kasi as a seat of Moksha or salvation. 'Kasyaath Maranaath Muktihi', is the Sanskrit saying, meaning that death in Kasi frees a soul from the cycle of birth and life. According to Shakta Sampradaaya, Devi is the doer, while Shiva is the observer. That is to say, Shiva acts through Shakti. Thus, the one conferring moksha or salvation is Devi, and in this case, Visalakshi gives the soul salvation, leading them to Vishveshwara himself. This is captured in lines in his compositions-Kasi Visalakshim Bhajeham and Annapoorne respectively: 'Pasha Mochanim', 'Moksha Prada Chature'.

Goddess	Kriti	Part	Reference
Kamakshi	Saraswati Manohari	Charanam (madhyama kaala saahityam)	Muka Vaak pradaanakari
Meenakshi	Mamava Meenakshi	Anupallavi	Digvijayapartaapini
Visalakshi	Visalakshim Bhajeham	Charanam	Pasha Mochanim

Sodari-Sodara Sambandha: The *Devi Bhagavatham* describes Vishnu and Parvathi as siblings, stating that they emerged from the same golden egg. Their relationship of being siblings is seen even in the *Lalitha Sahasramanama*, where Parvati is addressed as *'Padmanabha Sahodari'*. According to the sthala puranam of Madurai, Meenakshi is given in marriage to Sundareshwara by her brother, Vishnu—this tradition is seen in the temple icionography till date. This association of Vishnu and Parvathi as siblings is an underlying principle of tatva-essence. Both Vishnu and Shakti represent expansive energy, and thus Dikshithar makes references to Vishnu in his kritis, clearly highlighting this *sodari-sodara sambandha.* What is interesting is the way in which he attaches a descriptive name of Vishnu, sometimes describing his qualities, and in other cases, describing incidents associated with him. In his kriti on Kamakshi, he refers to Vishnu twice, once as *Kamajanaka*—the father of *Kamadeva/Manmatha*. In Meenakshi Memudam Dehi, he refers to Vishnu as the slayer of the demons Madhu and Mura (Madhuraripu), and in the case of Kasi Visalakshi, Vishnu is referred to as *Mukunda* (most pristine gem).

Goddess	Kriti	Part	Reference
Kamakshi	Kamakshi Shri Varalakshmi	Anupallavi	Kamajanaka Purna Phale
Meenakshi	Meenakshi Memudam	Charanam	Madhumuraripu Sodari
Visalakshi	Kasi Visakshim	Charanam	Mukundavarapradaayineem

Akshara Vidya: The word *Akshara* has multiple meanings—if it is split up, means that which is not destroyed. (A+kshara). This word is applied to *Bramhan,* the metaphysical reality, and alphabets/letters, both extolled in the Vedas, for technically speaking, neither can be destroyed. *Akshara-Vidya* deals with the knowledge pertaining these letters, which is much more than just knowing them by heart. It is the supreme most knowledge of identifying syllables as a form of the Divine. When *aksharas* are brought together in certain combinations, they give rise to *mantras*, or energetic sounds. *Mantra-shastra* says that these combinations are not arbitrarily put together, but exist in nature and are revealed to those capable of internalizing this. This is the reason why Rishis or seers are called *Mantra-drashtas*, or viewers of the mantra. The *Dhyana slokam* in the *Lalitha Sahasranama* refers to Devi being the essence of all *aksharas-'ahamityeva vibhaye Bhavanim'*. Shakta texts say that Devi resides at the heart of all mantras, giving her the title *Sarva Mantratmika* in the *Lalitha Sahasranama*. Comprehending her in this form slowly takes the devotee from viewing Devi as a physical form towards the occult practice of understanding that she resides as *shabda-shakti*, or the vibration of sound, produced by intoning mantras. This esoteric knowledge is reflected in Dikshithar's Kritis on the trio.

In his *kriti Saraswati Manohari*, Dikshithar identifies Kamakshi as the form of every letter, beginning with the primordial 'a'—*Akaaradyakshara Swarupini.*

In Sri Madhurambike, he refers to Meenakshi as the one who represents all forms of the alphabet: *Kaadi*, *Haadi* and *Saadi*-the three divisions according to which Sanskrit (and subsequent languages derived from it) is split into.

In '*Ehi Annapoorne*', he refers to Visalakshi as the embodiment of all the fifty letters-*Panch-Shad Varne.*

Goddess	Kriti	Part	Reference
Kamakshi	Saraswati Manohari	Charanam	Akaaradyakshara Swarupini
Meenakshi	Sri Madhurambike	Charanam	Kaadi Haadi Saadi Mantra Rupini
Visalakshi	Ehi Annapoorne	Charanam	Pancha Shad varne

Advaita Siddhantha: The philosophy of *Adviatha* talks about the true self-the *Atma* being identical to the metaphysical reality—the *Bramhan.* There is no difference between these two, however, there is a screen that prevents the atman from identifying with the *Bramhan,* this is known as *Maya*: power or the principle that conceals the true character of spiritual reality. ("Bramha Sathyam Jagan Mithya" corresponds to this.) However, Maya is an essential positive force required for sustenance of the Universe. Devi is *Mahamaya*—the great deluder. This is an essential component of *Advaitha* philosophy, for only when one understands *Maya*, can one cross over it, as the Lord himself says in the Gita. (Chapter 7, Sloka 14). Shakta principles in line with this concept talk about Devi as the creator and destroyer of Maya.

At the heart of his being, Muthuswami Dikshithar was a strong believer in the principles of *Advaitha.*, evident in several of his *kritis*, on multiple Gods and Goddesses, makes reference to *advaitha.*

In the case of this context, Dikshithar calls out to Kamakshi as the supreme representation of *Advaitha*: *Parama-advaitha-Rupini,*

He refers to Meenakshi as *tat-tvam-pada-artha-yugale*, meaning the true embodiment of the term: '*tath*'. This is a clear reference to the Upanishad saying 'Tat-tvam-asi', one of the four jewels of the *Advaitha* philosophy.

Visalakshi, in his words is *Vinoda Jaalinim*—one who playfully spins the illusory web of this world. This reference of his talks about the essential nature of Maya in creating the Universe.

Goddess	Kriti	Part	Reference
Kamakshi	Saraswati Manohari	Charanam	Paramadvaita Rupini
Meenakshi	Sri Meenakshi Gauri	Charanam	Tatvam Padaartha yugale
Visalakshi	Visalakshim Vishveshim	Charanam	Vinoda Jaalinim

Conclusion

Carnatic music is spiritual in nature, focused on elevating, rather than entertaining. This theme is taken upon by several composers. However, one does not often come across music where one uses spirtuality as the point of departure to connect the Rasika, the patron, and the musician, to aspects of esoteric philosophies. Muthuswami Dikshithar's compositions on *Kamakshi*, *Meenakshi* and *Visalakshi* stand testimony to the fact that his understanding of *Sri-Vidya* and *Advaitha Siddhantha* become the foundation of his compositional framework. He reinforces these beliefs by adding in elements of *Aksharas*, *mantras*, references to *sthala puranas*, all along adhering strongly to tradition. This common methodology he has used in putting together these compositions make them not only pleasing to the ear, but make them a deeply spiritual experience. The spiritual structure caters to the seeker, while the musical format caters to the musician and the patron. All in all, these compositions contain esoteric secrets of Devi, and they do so in such an endearing format, that they cease to become unapproachable testaments. The compositions come alive, as seen and felt by those who have heard and been touched by their renderings. This common structuring used in these *kritis* shows such a clear intended connection by the composer, that makes one stand in amazement at his forethought, for their commonality does not easily present itself. Keeping these aspects in mind, one can safely say this: Muthuswami Dikshithar cannot be referred to as a mere composer-musician. He is in fact, a Sangeeta Yogi, one who uses music as a medium to experience the divine bliss that resides within each of us-the essence of *Advaitha* philosophy, so subtly delivered.

—x—

III. History and Ideas

Philosophies of Inclusion and Pluralism: An Important Facet of Indian Culture for the Contemporary World

Jeffery D. Long

Abstract

The intent of this paper is *not* to present a romanticized picture of India as a place of unparalleled tolerance and openness to diverse worldviews, without any conflict or antagonism amongst members of different communities. The intent of this paper is to argue that India has produced numerous philosophical approaches to the diversity of views and practices which, were they to be implemented on a global scale, perhaps through a program of moral education, would have the potential to greatly mitigate conflict and foster a world in which difference is appreciated as a source of insight rather than feared as a threat to one's own identity.

At least since 1893, when Swami Vivekananda delivered his famous 'Sisters and Brothers of America' speech at the first World Parliament of Religions in Chicago, India has come to be seen by many in the West as home to a variety of philosophies inclusion and pluralism. The words of the *Ṛg Veda—ekaṃ sad-viprā bahuḍhā vadanti*—"Reality is one, though the wise speak of it in a variety of ways," are widely quoted as an affirmation of the idea that many diverse philosophical and religious views can co-exist as so many differing perspectives on a shared reality.[1] Though the idea that this is the original intent of this verse has been challenged by some, it is certainly how it has been read and understood by many in the modern world.

Historically, even as the adherents of various Indian philosophical sects debated each other and refuted one another's arguments and claims, on the popular level, pluralism has often been the norm. It is still not uncommon in India for members of different religious communities

[1] *Ṛg Veda* 1.164.46c.

to celebrate one another's festivals, to attend one another's places of worship, and even to share worship space. Jains, for example, celebrate the holiday of Dīpāvali, or Diwali, alongside Hindus, and also revere shared deities, such as Gaṇeśa, Lakṣmī, and Sarasvatī.[2]

To be sure, the intent behind this paper is *not* to present a romanticized picture of India as a place of unparalleled tolerance and openness to a diverse range of worldviews, with no conflict or antagonism whatsoever amongst members of different communities. As Alexis Sanderson has documented, there were cases of violence and religious persecution in ancient and medieval India. Though, "Indian and Southeast Asian states generally propagated tolerance in matters of religion" and "the religions that flourished during the early mediaeval period in the Indian subcontinent and Southeast Asia enjoyed in many regions an enviable degree of peaceful co-existence," there is also "evidence of sporadic outbreaks of intolerance and persecution." It is also important to note that Sanderson does not attribute the overall state of peaceful co-existence in India to the teachings of the religions or the philosophical systems themselves, but interprets this state of affairs, rather, "in terms of a balance of influence in which no one religious tradition was in a position of such strength that it could rid society of its rivals, a balance of power sustained by the policy of governments."[3]

In other words, it was the very diversity of religions and philosophies in pre-modern India that helped to ensure a state of relative harmony, at least in comparison with many other parts of the world during this same period.[4] No single community was able to promote itself at the expense of the others, at least in most regions of India, because no single religion or philosophy commanded the assent of the majority of the population. Government policy typically supported this state of affairs, one might presume, for the sake of maintaining order and keeping Indian society relatively free from destabilizing communal violence.

Government policy, though, is generally not purely pragmatic in nature. Ideology plays an important role as well. The case of the Maurya emperor Aśoka provides a very striking case of an ancient Indian ruler who promoted harmony amongst religions in his realm, based not only

[2] Long, Jeffery D., 2009, *Jainism: An Introduction*, London: IB Tauris.

[3] Sanderson, Alexis, 2015, 'Tolerance, Exclusivity, Inclusivity, and Persecution in Indian Religion During the Early Medieaval Period', pp.155–224, in *In Honoris Causa: Essays in Honour of Aveek Sarkar*, ed. by John Makinson, Northwood, Middlesex, UK: Allen Lane, p.159.

[4] Gier, Nicholas F., 2014, *The Origins of Religious Violence: An Asian Perspective*, Lanham, Maryland: Lexington Books.

upon pragmatic considerations, such as maintaining social and political stability, but also because the philosophy to which he personally adhered mandated such an approach. To be sure, the pragmatic concern to avoid communal conflict in a realm of diverse religions was certainly present in Aśoka's case. As Bruce Rich notes:

> Respecting, reconciling with, and giving equal support to both *Brahmanas* and *Sramanas* [the groups today identified, on the one hand, with Hinduism, and on the other, with the Buddhist, the Jain, and the now-extinct Ājīvika tradition, respectively] are major aspects of Ashoka's promulgation of religious tolerance in his edicts.[5]

According to Rich's account, though, Aśoka goes much further than is required by pragmatism. It is Aśoka's own philosophy of life, strongly shaped by the Buddhist tradition to which he adhered, that also provided the impetus behind his policies of promoting toleration and mutual respect. We know this because Aúoka himself says as much, proclaiming his philosophy to all in the various edicts that he had carved upon stone throughout his empire:

> The seventh rock edict is the first of two please for religious toleration. Ashoka 'wishes that all [religious] sects may dwell in all places, for all seek self-control and purity of mind.' ...The twelfth rock edict is [also] a proclamation of toleration for all religions and philosophical sects, and what this implies. The proclamation of toleration is in itself an extraordinary act for the third century BC but not totally unprecedented in ancient history since Cyrus the Great [of Persia] also issued an edict of religious toleration when he conquered Babylon. But Ashoka goes much further. He says all sects have an essential doctrine that he seeks to actively support through 'gifts and various forms of recognition.' He says it is his desire that 'all sects should be well informed and should teach that which is good.' Everywhere, Ashoka proclaims, the adherents of different religions should be told that he 'does not consider gifts or honor to be as important as the progress of the essential doctrine of all sects.' This is, for the time, a revolutionary statement since Ashoka seems to be saying that beneath the outward form all religions and beliefs have an essential core that aims for the good, and that it is his policy to support the progress of all sects because they aim essentially for the same.[6]

---

[5] Rich, Bruce, 2010, *To Uphold the World: A Call for a New Global Ethic from Ancient India*, Boston: Beacon Press, p.23.

[6] *Ibid.*, pp.118, 119.

Aśoka thus represents a situation in which the pragmatic considerations of governance—the need to rule a large and religiously diverse population with a minimum of communal conflict—coalesce with the personal philosophy of the ruler, who sees diverse religions as varied manifestations of and paths toward a shared desire for transcendence and the realization of the an ideal of the good.

The thesis of this paper is that our global situation, not unlike that of pre-modern India, is one in which there are a great many religions and philosophies which are competing, sometimes violently, for adherents, or for supremacy over other religions and philosophies in terms of power and resources. This situation is further overshadowed by the phenomenon of climate change, due to which it is highly likely that, as the twenty-first century continues to unfold, resources will be ever more scarce. We are in a situation in which pragmatic considerations—the need to cooperate and co-exist on a fragile planet—have given rise to a need for ideas supportive of such cooperation.

In this search for ideas, for compelling philosophies which can support and sustain human co-existence rather than undermining it—as more conventional, competitive approaches have done—India is an amazing resource: an ancient culture with abundant examples of modes of thought that promote, as Aśoka's philosophy did, inter-religious harmony.

A comprehensive overview of Indian philosophies of inclusion and pluralism will not be possible given the constraints of this paper. It is hoped that this paper will serve, rather, as a brief snapshot or, to use another metaphor, an 'appetizer' of the possibilities that are offered by Indian systems of thought as resources for imagining a world in which difference is cherished rather than feared.

Indian Philosophies of Pluralism and Inclusion

The introduction has already mentioned the *Ṛg Vedic* dictum: "Reality is one, though the wise speak of it in a variety of ways." As Sanderson has outlined in the article cited previously, it has not always been the case that the adherents of the various Vedic schools of thought that now make up what is known as Hinduism took this dictum to be an indicator of how they should view diverse worldviews. Indeed, the polemics, not only between Vedic and non-Vedic traditions, such as Jainism and Buddhism, but even amongst the Vedic schools of thought—Sāṃkhya, Yoga, Nyāya, Vaiśeṣika, Pūrva Mīmāṃsā, the various systems of Vedānta, Vaiṣṇavism, Śaivism, and so on—have often been quite fierce. The understanding of truth articulated in many of the texts of these systems is not that different from the binary view of truth often found in Western thought: the idea that there can be only one true system of thought and that all others are false.

Other approaches, however, are also articulated in these systems of thought. As Wilhelm Halbfass documents, many Indian philosophical texts express an *inclusivist* model of truth.[7] This is especially the case in the doxographical literature generated by scholars representing a variety of Indian schools of thought: Vedāntic, Buddhist, and Jain. A *doxography*, a text often termed in Sanskrit either a *samuccaya* or a *saṃgraha*—a 'collection' or 'gathering'—is a text that enumerates the views of various schools of thought. Such texts are a rich source of knowledge about what the Indian systems of philosophy affirmed and the arguments they advanced for their varied claims. As Halbfass notes, the doxographic literature often arranges the various systems of Indian thought known to the author based on a hierarchy of truth. The idea is that systems of thought are not simply true or false, being made up of interlinked sets of truth-claims, but that the truth or the falsehood of systems of thought can admit of degrees. There are 'more true' systems of thought and 'less true' systems of thought.

The criteria for determining what is true are set by the system of philosophy to which the author of a given doxography adheres. Thus, if the author is a Mahāyāna Buddhist of the Yogācāra school, Yogācāra Buddhism will be taken to be the truest system of philosophy available. It will represent the *siddhānta*: the 'perfected' or final conclusion of philosophical inquiry. It may be, for this reason, listed first in the doxographic text, with the next truest system of thought listed as the second (the one which is in closest agreement with Yogācāra Buddhism), and so on, with the final system listed being the furthest from the truth. (This dubious position is held by the Cārvāka or Lokāyata system of materialist philosophy in most surviving Indian doxographic literature.) It is also possible that the least true system will be listed first in a doxographic text, and then each succeeding system of thought will represent a further stage of conceptual evolution, or a step up the ladder toward the highest truth, which is then listed and elaborated last.

This traditional Indic hierarchical conception of truth, as admitting of degrees, is quite well articulated in the modern period by Swami Vivekananda, when he says:

---

[7] Halbfass, Wilhelm, 987, *India and Europe: An Essay in Understanding*, Albany: State University of New York Press.

> Man never progresses from error to truth, but from truth to truth, from lesser truth to higher truth—but it is never from error to truth. The child may develop more than the father, but was the father inane? The child is the father plus something else. If your present state of knowledge is much greater than it was when you were a child, would you look down upon that stage now? Will you look back and call it inanity?
>
> Why, your present stage is the knowledge of the child plus something more.[8]

Inclusivism of this kind has been criticized on the basis of the paternalism which it can be seen to exhibit toward traditions or schools of thought that are seen as 'less developed'—as the perspective of the 'child' rather than of the 'adult.' Clearly, no one wishes to see their worldview or system of belief as 'childish' or as a less developed form of some other view or tradition. In the Christian tradition, this view is associated with Karl Rahner and his idea of 'anonymous Christians.'

Paul F. Knitter refers to this approach to religious diversity as the 'fulfillment model,' in which one's own religious tradition is seen as the 'fulfillment' or the ideal toward which all other religions are evolving or developing: Swami Vivekananda's 'higher truth.'[9] Inclusivism, though, certainly represents an advance over exclusivism: the idea that one's own religion or philosophy alone is true and that all others are false. It is the idea, as Vivekananda has said, that there is some truth in every perspective. The idea that the truth of systems of thought can admit of degrees also resonates intuitively with the understanding that a religion or philosophy is a complex system of claims. One has certainly had the experience of encountering a particular religion or philosophy and agreeing with some of its claims, but not all of them. For a thoughtful believer, even one's own tradition—the one to which one adheres and with which one identifies—is not always a perfect match with one's personal belief system. Certain things make sense to us and resonate with our experience and our intuitions, and some do not. To quote another Indian master, Sri Ramakrishna, "The scriptures contain a mixture of sand and sugar."[10]

---

[8] Vivekananda, Swami, 1979, *Complete Works, Volume Two*, Mayavati: Advaita Ashrama, pp.365–366.

[9] Knitter, Paul F., 2010, *Introducing Theologies of Religions*, Maryknoll, New York: Orbis Books, pp.63–108.

[10] Nikhilananda, Swami, 1942, *The Gospel of Sri Ramakrishna*, New York: Ramakrishna-Vivekananda Center, p.543.

The insight that no system of thought that can be expressed in words and that is subject to human interpretation—including interpretations that are conducive to the exploitation of the poor by the powerful, or to inter-communal violence—leads to yet another way of thinking about diverse worldviews: namely, pluralism. Pluralism moves beyond inclusivism. Although inclusivism moves beyond the simplistic idea of only one true system of belief and practice, with all others being false, in favor of the idea that there is some amount of truth in each system, it nevertheless remains wedded to the idea of only one fully true system of thought, or a 'truest' system of thought. Pluralism takes the next step after allowing that truth admits of degrees, and that there can be some truth and some falsehood in any given system, by affirming that there is no neutral or objective basis for affirming that any one system of thought is the truest or the best. Phrased positively, pluralism is the idea that there is at least some truth to be found in many diverse perspectives, and that no single system of practice or belief is clearly superior to all the rest. All are to be respected. One can learn something from all of them. And they all have their flaws and limitations.Pluralism in this fuller sense is articulated most famously in the modern period both by Sri Ramakrishna and by Mohandas K. Gandhi. Ramakrishna was well known for having practiced a great variety of religious paths: various Hindu paths, as well as, to a limited extent, both Islam and Christianity. His conclusion, on the basis of his practices, resonates with Aśoka's teaching that a common essence underlies all religions:

> ...'I have practiced,' said he, 'all religions—Hinduism, Islam, Christianity—and I have also followed the paths of the different Hindu sects. I have found that it is the same God toward whom all are directing their steps, though along different paths. You must try all beliefs and traverse all the different ways once. Wherever I look, I see men quarreling in the name of religion...But they never reflect that He who is called Krishna is also called Śiva, and bears the name of the Primal Energy, Jesus, and Āllāh as well—the same Rāma with a thousand names.'[11]

Along similar lines, Gandhi writes:

> I believe in the fundamental truth of all great religions of the world. I believe that they are all God-given and I believe that they were necessary for the people to whom these religions were revealed. And I believe that if only we could all of us read the scriptures of the different faiths from the standpoint of the followers of these faiths,

[11] *Ibid.*, p.35.

> we should find that they were at the bottom all one and were all helpful to one another.[12]

Gandhi and Sri Ramakrishna, it seems, are both tapping into a deep well of what could be called a 'popular pluralism' that has been an important facet of Indian culture since ancient times: again, the willingness, at the popular level, to accept and even to participate in varied religious practices. This popular pluralism occasionally finds expression in formal writings of the adherents of the various systems of thought, as well as in the proclamations of leaders like Aśoka. Although it was often derided by previous generations of scholars as an unthinking 'syncretism,' it is really an approach to truth which displays profound cultural wisdom. Even as one adheres to or identifies with a particular philosophy or religion as matching the most closely of any other available with one's own intuitions and beliefs, this need not prevent one from drawing appreciatively upon other sources of wisdom. Ramakrishna's radically pluralistic practice, engaging with a particular mode of spirituality to the point where he achieved an altered state of consciousness, probably marks the limit of what is humanly possible in this regard.

Growing numbers of people in the West, however, define themselves as 'spiritual but not religious' precisely because they draw from many religious sources for inspiration, and to reflect and sustain their worldview. This is actually a very ancient mode of practice that has been common in India for many centuries. And it has not only been practiced amongst the traditions indigenous to India. Hindus and Muslims have frequently drawn on elements of one another's practice, and there have even been times and places in Indian history where the boundaries between Hinduism and Islam, though they often appear quite stark today, have been blurred.[13]

I have not had the scope within this article to explore such concepts as the Jain doctrines of relativity—*anekāntavāda*, *nayavāda*, and *syādvāda*—which, collectively, articulate a view of truth as being amenable to multiple interpretations, thus rendering invalid absolutist claims regarding the nature of reality, or the Buddhist concept of *upāya kauśalya*, or 'skillful means,' according to which truth is articulated in

[12] Gandhi, Mohandas K., 1982, *The Words of Gandhi*, New York: Newmarket Press, p.78.

[13] Gottschalk, Peter, 2000, *Beyond Hindu and Muslim: Multiple Identity in Narratives from Village India*, Oxford, UK: Oxford University Press.

different ways by awakened masters according to the needs of different groups of people.

It seems unlikely that simply promoting ideas of this kind will, by itself, lead to a peaceful world where there is no religious or communal conflict. These ideas were all present in ancient and medieval India, which nevertheless suffered from occasional bursts of violence and religious persecution. And in the modern world, which has experienced the teachings of such figures as Sri Ramakrishna, Swami Vivekananda, and Mahatma Gandhi, such violence seems to have increased in frequency and magnitude. Indeed, Gandhi was murdered in part for his commitment to the ideal of pluralism, or at least for how he chose to translate this ideal into action. As David Ray Griffin notes, however, belief systems do matter, and do have an impact on the kinds of decisions people make in their day-to-day lives:

> Advocates of this movement [for pluralism] do not hold the naively utopian belief that the success of this movement would bring about a global society of universal and lasting peace, harmony, and happiness, in which all spiritual problems, social conflicts, ecological destruction, and hard choices would vanish. There is, after all, surely a deep truth in the testimony of the world's religions to the presence of a transcultural proclivity to evil deep within the human heart, which no new paradigm, combined with a new economic order, new child-rearing practices, or any other social arrangements, will suddenly eliminate...No such appeal to 'universal constants,' however, should reconcile us to the present order, as if it were thereby uniquely legitimated. The human proclivity to evil in general, and to conflictual competition and ecological destruction in particular, can be greatly exacerbated or greatly mitigated by a world order and its worldview. Modernity exacerbates it about as much as imaginable. We can therefore envision, without being naively utopian, a far better world order, with a far less dangerous trajectory, than the one we now have.[14]

It is with the hope that Indian philosophies of inclusion and pluralism might mitigate the current world situation, in which religious divisions and ethno-nationalisms have been asserted with new force—

[14] Griffin, David Ray, 2000, 'Introduction to SUNY Series in Constructive Postmodern Thought', pp.xxi–xxvi, in *Spiritual Titanism: Indian, Chinese, and Western Perspectives*, by Nicholas F. Gier. Albany: State University of New York Press, pp.xxv–xxvi.

and just as climate change is reaching a tipping point—that these philosophies need to be explored.

References

1. Gandhi, Mohandas K., 1982, *The Words of Gandhi*, New York: Newmarket Press.
2. Gier, Nicholas F., 2014, *The Origins of Religious Violence: An Asian Perspective*, Lanham, Maryland: Lexington Books.
3. Gottschalk, Peter, 2000, *Beyond Hindu and Muslim: Multiple Identity in Narratives from Village India*, Oxford, UK: Oxford University Press.
4. Griffin, David Ray, 2000, 'Introduction to SUNY Series in Constructive Postmodern Thought', in *Spiritual Titanism: Indian, Chinese, and Western Perspectives*, by Nicholas F. Gier, Albany: State University of New York Press, p. xxv-xxvi.
5. Halbfass, Wilhelm, 1987, *India and Europe: An Essay in Understanding*, Albany: State University of New York Press.
6. Knitter, Paul F., 2010, *Introducing Theologies of Religions*, Maryknoll, New York: Orbis Books.
7. Long, Jeffery D., 2009, *Jainism: An Introduction*, London: IB Tauris.
8. Nikhilananda, Swami, 1942, *The Gospel of Sri Ramakrishna*, New York: Ramakrishna-Vivekananda Center.
9. Rich, Bruce, 2010, *To Uphold the World: A Call for a New Global Ethic from Ancient India*, Boston: Beacon Press.
10. Sanderson, Alexis, 2015, 'Tolerance, Exclusivity, Inclusivity, and Persecution in Indian Religion During the Early Medieaval Period', pp.155–224, in *In Honoris Causa: Essays in Honour of Aveek Sarkar*, ed. by John Makinson, Northwood, Middlesex, UK: Allen Lane.
11. Vivekananda, Swami, 1979, *Complete Works, Volume Two*, Mayavati: Advaita Ashrama.

—×—

Origins and Development of Asceticism and Its Influence on Hinduism

Ramdas Lamb

Abstract

There can be many ways in which one can approach the study of ascetic practices in the world. Herein, three general groupings of individuals will be considered for whom asceticism has played an significant role connecting with the non-human realms and entities who reside in them. The first is comprised of the myriad shamanic-type traditions found all over the world; the second involves the different renunciants and communities in the Abrahamic religious traditions; the third brings together the individuals, groups, and practices that took birth in the various Indic traditions. It examines *tapasya* in various contexts but will focus primarily on the Hindu context. The focus of my paper will be on the early rise of asceticism and yoga, speculating on possible reasons for their origins, and the roles they have played in the evolution of the India and its religious culture.

Excavations in the Indus Valley reveal that a highly advanced civilization for the time period existed there at least 4 millennia and possibly longer ago. Evidence suggests people had many of the necessities of life that fostered a relatively comfortable daily existence. These likely included ample water for their crops and for themselves, food, clothing, toys for children, clean homes, etc. There were also images that appear to represent humans and deities, both male and female and that suggest the presence of a religious culture. At the same time, clay tablets depict what seems to be the likely roots of yoga. Taken together, we can speculate that the Indus Valley laid the foundation for much of what is found in the Hindu tradition today. The focus of my paper will be on the early rise of asceticism and yoga, speculating on possible reasons for their origins, and the roles they have played in the evolution of the India and its religious culture.

In discussing asceticism (*tapasya*) and ascetics, it is important from the outset to acknowledge that most of what has been written about them throughout the history of India has not been by ascetics themselves but by observers standing outside the life style and often misunderstanding what they were seeing. Throughout most of their existence, those who traditionally chose to pursue the path of transcending material attachments likely had little or no interest in memorializing on the material level their experiments and experiences. Consequently, the bulk of our understanding of these are, at best, theoretical speculation based on the way ancient records of others have presented and interpreted the early ascetics, along with what we know of contemporary asceticism.[1]

That said, the presence and performance of *tapasya*, in one form or another, has been a significant part of cultures around the world since ancient times. The practices referred to here are those specifically done to restrict certain enjoyable physical, mental, and psychological experiences and comforts. Although there have been a variety of reasons for such undertakings, among the most common has been the gaining of control over one's body, mind, and emotions. On the purely material level, ascetic practices have been the tools of athletes, those in the military, and others seeking the attainment of physical or mental power and abilities. They have also been used by shamans to connect and communicate with beings in the spirit world, and they have been practiced in the Abrahamic religions to please, placate, or seek forgiveness from the doers' chosen deity. On a still more sublime level, various forms of *tapasya* have served as tools for renunciants seeking to go deep within themselves to gain an understanding and experience of a transcendent reality and their connection with it. Additionally, asceticism has been used as a foundational vehicle for traversing the path to realizing inner peace and liberation from the dualism of the material world. Much of the determinant of how and why such practices are done and how they are utilized comes from the culture or religious tradition of the practitioner. Today's discussion will take a look at *tapasya* in various contexts but will focus primarily on the Hindu context.

There can be many ways in which one can approach the study of ascetic practices in the world. Herein, three general groupings of individuals will be considered for whom asceticism has played an significant role connecting with the non-human realms and entities who reside in them. The first is comprised of the myriad shamanic-type

[1] The earliest uses of tapasya was to break one's involvement with and attachment to pleasant sensual experiences and various comforts.

traditions found all over the world; the second involves the different renunciants and communities in the Abrahamic religious traditions; the third brings together the individuals, groups, and practices that took birth in the various Indic traditions.

Shamans and Asceticism

Indigenous cultures throughout history have typically had within them individuals whose task it has been to communicate with spirit world and serve as intermediaries between the spirit and human realms. This may occur during a particular time of year or event, or it may be at the request of one or several individuals. In academia today, the term "shaman" is most commonly used for such a practitioner. In some cultures, shamans are believed to be chosen by the spirit beings for whom they will serve as mediums, and they may be given their abilities by these spirits from birth or at an early age with some event in their lives that awakens their powers. Others may be chosen and trained by existing shamans. One grouping of spirits with which shamans are said to communicate include divinities. These beings are believed to aid humans through control of or at least influence on nature and natural phenomena, human emotions and abilities, and/or human thoughts and actions. They may give blessings and protection, but they may also punish and condemn. Another category of spirits is comprised of departed human ancestors of the village, tribe, or community in which the shaman lives or functions. These are supplicated in hopes they can provide assistance from the spirit world for their descendants, for living family members, or for the community at large. Lastly are those spirits who may be labeled demonic. In many cultures, they are also propitiated for various reasons, including keeping them from hurting particular humans, but also for having them take out their wrath on someone as per the request of the shamans' clients. Depending upon the cultural milieu, a shaman may be called upon to communicate with any or all such beings.

In most cultures, shamans will enter into trance or possession states during which communication with spirits will take place. In preparation for these, some form of ascetic activity is commonplace. This can include periods of fasting, celibacy, solitude, bodily mortification, etc. Shamans typically also perform rituals, chants, or practices to help them temporarily break their attachment or loosen their connection to the physical body so they can enter the realm of the spirits (trance) or so spirits can enter their bodies and work through them (possession). While some of these practices are similar to those done by religious renunciants, the shamans' goal is typically not personal spiritual elevation or insight but instead being mediums for their human clients who seek information, protection, guidance, healing, or other types of worldly gain from the spirit world. Thus, the role and rules of morality may or may not play a part in the practices done or goals sought. Instead, a sort of quid pro quo relationship exists between the shamans and the deities or spirits they propitiate. Most who function as shamans do so only when called upon or on specific occasions. When not involved in those activities, their lives have generally been much like others in their community, following traditional occupations such as farmers, fishermen, laborers, craftsmen, etc. Most have also been married and have had children. The practice of worldly renunciation or seeking personal spiritual evolution has not typically been a part of their lifestyles.

Unlike the occasional ascetic practices of shamans, religious ascetics have traditionally dedicated all or much of their lives to their practices, which have typically included various forms and degrees of physical renunciation from normal involvement in society. In stepping away from the material world in which they were raised, they enter a way of life circumscribed by vows that limit their interactions with others, with material goods, and with sensually enjoyable experiences. Their lifestyles have often been almost diametrically opposed to the kind of lives that most others seek out. This can been seen quite clearly in the case of males, since they are members of the primary, if not exclusive, gender group in nearly all renunciant traditions or orders throughout history and even in present times. Males in most cultures have been evaluated on the social and materials level by their possessions, their powers, and their prowess. The more they have, the more they accomplish in the material realm, the more influence they have on the world, and the more people they control, the more they are respected and/or feared, and the more power they have. Conversely, renunciants give up possessions, renounce material power, and seek to accomplish little or nothing in the material realm. They have sought a life that essentially rejects that which others aspire for and desire. Nevertheless, not all renunciants and renunciant groups have undertaken their practices for the same reasons or with the same goals in mind. More specifically, the traditional bases for renunciation in the Abrahamic faiths and those in the Indic religions have often been fundamentally different.

Abrahamic Asceticism

Renunciation in the Abrahamic religious traditions originated out of a desire to please or placate a divinity. Early forms of ascetic practice were done by individuals and groups to encourage their deity to interfere on their behalf in events in the world, as a way of repentance for sins committed, to help purify the practitioners from the natural pollution of being human, to assuage feelings of guilt, to avoid temptation or evil, to gain the favor of their deity, or to help to make themselves candidates for salvation and eternal paradise. In nearly all cases, something seen as tangible to the practitioners was and often still is sought, resulting in a sort of quid pro quo relationship. The earliest Abrahamic ascetics were the Jewish Essenes, who lived in the few centuries preceding the Common Era. Males and females are believed to have lived a renunciant life together in their own communities. Possessions were minimal and communal. Purity and repentance were very important. Some groups practiced strict celibacy, while there is some evidence to suggest that others allowed for marriage and families. They lived apart from the rest of society in a simple and austere way waiting for their Messiah, whom they believed would establish a Jewish theocracy for them.

The earliest Christian renunciants appeared in the late first or early second century of the Common Era. They followed some of the same practices of the Essenes, except female participation was rare and celibacy was often mandatory. Because Christianity emphasized the belief that humans are all born in sin and need to repent, ascetic followers renounced sensual pleasures and comforts in hopes of purifying themselves from this original sin and making themselves worthy of salvation. They also lived in wait for the return of their own Messiah, Jesus. In subsequent centuries, various Christian groups evolved their own sets of practices, but all with the same essential goals in mind, i.e. salvation and eternal residence in a Christian heaven.

The origins of Sufism, also known as "Mystical Islam" are uncertain, although many point to eastern Persia during or just before the 8th century. Some of the earliest writings place their presence in what is now Iran, Iraq, and Turkey, and reveal an ascetic and mystical approach to life, with a focus on the inner self. In many ways, Sufism was a response to the political aggressiveness and violence that was integral to early Islam and its expansion in the Middle East. Sufi practitioners sought a more interior, self-reflective life and drew upon Christian ascetic activities of the day, as well as the influence and presence of Buddhist and Hindu thought. Renunciation, celibacy, and ascetic vows became common place among Sufis, as did the goal of accessing an inner reality that transcends external categories. Once Sufism arrived in India near the end of the 12th century, its practitioners drew more deeply upon both Hindu ascetic and devotional approaches and philosophies. Although most Sufi groups remained closely allied with mainstream Islam in their philosophies and teachings, which was often necessary for their survival, some sought independence and more freedom of thought and practice. Unfortunately, many of these were killed by the more fundamentalist Muslim rulers of their day. As a whole, then, with the exception of some Catholic monastic orders and some Sufi schools, asceticism in the Abrahamic traditions was undertaken with goals that to them were seen as tangible. Again, these included forgiveness of sins, purity, the attainment of salvation, but on occasion, political and material goals as well. In addition, in both Christianity and Islam, evangelism and conversion of non-believers have long been central themes, and some ascetics have also undertaken and endured various austerity practices for these purposes as well.

Asceticism in India

In the Indus Valley, *tapasya* has been a part of the culture and practices since ancient times. Unlike asceticism in the shamanic and Abrahamic traditions, the roots and reasons for Indian *tapasya* seem to have had little to do with material tangible desires or fears. In India, the concepts and practices of renunciation and *tapasya* appear to have originated or were at least elaborated in the ancient civilization in the Indus region in a stable, peaceful social and cultural milieu in which people's material needs were generally satisfied. Such a context is significant and is noted in a 2015 article, published in *Current Biology*, by a group of research scholars theorizing on the rise of morality systems and asceticism in world religions.[2] In it, they posit that as economic plenty, social stability, and leisure time increased in certain areas of the world, so did the move away from short-term gain strategies that focused on "resource acquisition and coercive interactions" as primary goals in life toward one in which long-term strategies involving "self-control techniques and cooperative interactions" became more emphasized, including the

[2] Nicolas Baumard et al, "Increased Affluence Explains the Emergence of Ascetic Wisdoms and Moralizing Religions" in *Current Biology*, Vol.25, Elsevier Ltd., January 5, 2015:1–6.

concepts of morality and asceticism. The authors go on to suggest that along with self-control and asceticism, compassion also developed as a virtue in these societies. They see this process as having taken shape during what Karl Jaspers calls the "Axial Age" (roughly between 500 BCE and 300 BCE) in three areas of the world, i.e. in the region surrounding the Yellow and Yangzi rivers in what is now China, in the Ganga Valley, India, and in the eastern part of the Mediterranean.[3] They make a good case for their theories regarding the connection between affluence and asceticism, but they ignore the fact that the ways of life they describe appear to have been prevalent in the Indus Valley several millennia before the time period of Jaspers' "Axial Age."

Based on archaeological discoveries, early descriptions, and other available information on early asceticism, combined with later sectarian writings from various ascetic orders, we can surmise several significant points. One is that the material needs and comforts of the early renouncers were probably met, since that is what they gave up. Another is that their efforts were individualized and personal as they sought something beyond the material. The early Vedic seers, who seemed both distant from but also intrigued by the ascetics and ascetic practices of their day, mentions a variety of diverse groups and individual practitioners with such labels as *vratya*, *muni*, *vanaprasthin*, *tapasvin*, *kesin*, etc. Each of these terms serve to identify a particular characteristic or practice. By the time of the Upanishads, the influence of ascetic beliefs and practices was apparent in the broader Vedic culture. *Tapasya*, *tyāga* (renunciation), and *vairāgya* (non-attachment) had come to be accepted as important tools for those who sought to renounce materialism and sensual pleasures and replace these with transcendental wisdom and liberation from bondage to the cycle of birth and death.

There arose a variety of ascetic-influenced schools during the first millennium BCE, although only Jainism and Buddhism survived. In both, renouncing worldly desires and attachments was and is consider a given for those seeking liberation from suffering and the birth/death cycle. Later in the millennium, the *Yogasūtra* of Patanjali further provides evidence of the various practices that were important to ascetics. Taken together, the limbs of yoga as described circumscribe the life of a renunciant practitioner, not someone for whom material attainment and possession were the goals.

---

[3] Karl Jaspers. *The Origin and Goal of History*, Routledge and Kegan Paul, 1953, 1–3.

Hindu Asceticism

Because of the uniqueness of the goals and practices of ascetics, and the emphasis on individual interiorization efforts, several key concepts seem to have arisen within the overall lifestyle that have become an integral part of the broader Hindu tradition. Practices such as separation from family life and householder existence, renunciation, vow-taking, silence, and dwelling in the jungles and forests are among early manifestations. An emphasis on both *ahimsa* (non-violence) and *satya* (truth) appear as well. These latter are also promoted by both Mahavira and Buddha, and they are among the first rules in Patanjali's text. The combination of the concepts of karma, *punarjanama*, and *moksha* also appears to have come from the ascetic path, since it is not found as such in the early Vedas. The necessity of learning spiritual practices (*sādhanā*) unique to and relative to the personality of each individual to do regularly led to the need of an experienced teacher, and thus came about the development of and emphasis on the teacher/disciple (guru/shishya) relationship. Lineages were thereby created that naturally lead to the eventual rise of differing ascetic orders and *sampradāyas*.

The first millennium CE saw the birth of various groups and movements, both antinomian and orthodox, that drew from the well of ascetic beliefs and practices. Of the former, the *bhakti* poets and movement and the various tantric schools predominated, and each integrated aspects of asceticism in their respective traditions. In the matter of devotion, the Alwars and Nayanmars, commoners and householders, spread the message of emptying one's heart of worldly desires and attachments and replacing these with devotion to one's chosen deity. The tantric schools were started by ascetics themselves, and they inspired followers to break free of orthodox categories and doctrines and replace these with individual rituals and practices to awaken the powers within on the path to liberation. While Shankara established his orthodox order, in which renunciation and asceticism were integral, the sectarian Upanishads combined ascetic concepts with the ritual use of *bīja* and other tantric mantras as part of devotional practice meant to call on the presence and power of the deity or deities focused upon in each text.

During the last millennium, additional renunciant orders have arisen and have adopted and elaborated the myriad of forms of *tapasya* and added to the corpus of yogic practices. Several have also inspired householders to include aspects of these and daily *sādhanā* in their lives as well. The Nath Sampradaya is significant in this regard. However, largest among such orders is the Ramananda Sampradaya, begun in the 14th century by Swami Ramananda. His birthplace is in present day Allahabad, but as a youth, he traveled to Varanasi, where he adopted the renunciant life and eventually established his order. In doing so, he rejected the prevalence of caste restrictions on membership in renunciant orders and opened his to everyone. This is often expressed in the order in a verse attributed to him, "*jati pati pucha na koi | jo hari ko bhajan so hari ka hoi ||*" ("Do not ask anyone about caste and the like. Whoever prays to God, belongs to Him."). He had disciples from all castes, male and female, rich and poor, Hindu and non-Hindu. Among his main disciples was Kabir, who was from a Muslim weaver family.

There are very few writings attributed to Ramanandacharya, as he came to be called, although the *Adhyātma Rāmāyana*, a Sanskrit telling of the Ram story, is believed by most Ramanandi scholars, to be either written by him or by one of his disciples. The text expresses his theological and spiritual beliefs and values and was the telling of the story that most inspired Tulsidas, also a Ramanandi, as he composed his own Hindi version of the tale, the *Ramcharitmanas*. Much of the credit for the popularity of the text and the Ram *bhakti* tradition as a whole in northern India belongs to Tulsidas, but also to the Ramanandi *sgdhus*, who have carried with them his writings and teachings as they have wandered throughout the region during the last six centuries, meeting villagers and initiating them into Ram *bhakti*.

Contemporary Asceticism

Although asceticism remains an important part of the Hindu tradition, in the last half century the number of ascetic practicing renunciants has declined in India at an increasing rate. It has paralleled the decrease in the belief and participation in traditional religious practices. Where such traditions once provided a foundation for many upon which to base their relationship to family, community, and themselves, these are being replaced by a focus on the accumulation of material possessions and the temporal sensual pleasures they provide. This has not only affected and infected a significant percentage of the population of India but of the world as a whole. While immediate pleasures are gained, what gets lost is a foundation for a stable, meaningful, and contented life based on self-knowledge and awareness.

For many, increasing urbanization, the lessening of family contact and support, and the push to accumulate have led to increased social isolation and loneliness. Add to this the social and economic competition that are prevalent, and all these factors can lead to depression. When the external is all that one considers important, then the situation can become oppressive and hopeless. Ironically, it is in the west where many young people are taking cues from the Indian renunciants of the past. One example is a movement called Minimalism. A website of the movement explains its philosophy:

> "Minimalism is a tool that can assist you in finding freedom. Freedom from fear. Freedom from worry. Freedom from overwhelm. Freedom from guilt. Freedom from depression. Freedom from the trappings of the consumer culture we've built our lives around. Real freedom."[4]

Are they not seeking the same thing as did the ascetics of old? The young Indians who are lost, depressed, and in danger of suicide need to look to their ancient past, as are many in the west. Mahavira, the Buddha, and so many others taught that desires and attachments are what cause suffering. Renunciation and ascetic practices, including all the limbs of *ashtanga yoga,* instead of just *āsanas*, can provide invaluable tools for minimizing this affliction. As one moves down along the path to self-awareness, then one can experience joy that is not solely dependent upon things. For millennia, Indian householders turned to renunciants to ask for guidance in finding happiness. Indians today, especially the young, need to look to the past and the guidance and wisdom that was available then, and that still is today.

Notes

Baumard, Nicolas et al., 2015, "Increased Affluence Explains the Emergence of Ascetic Wisdoms and Moralizing Religions" in *Current Biology*, Elsevier Ltd., Vol.25:1–6.

Eliade, Mircea, 1964, *Shamanism: Archaic Techniques of Ecstasy*, New York, Bollingen Foundation.

Hutton, Ronald, 2001, *Shamans: Siberian Spirituality and the Western Imagination*, London and New York: Hambledon and London.

Jaspers, Karl, 1953, *The Origin and Goal of History.*

Lamb, Ramdas, 2005, "Rāja Yoga, Asceticism, and the Rāmānanda Sampradāy," in *Essays on the Theory and Practice of Yoga*, ed. by Knut Jacobsen, Leiden, the Netherlands: E.J. Brill, 317–331.

Lamb, Ramdas, 2011, "Sādhus, Sannyāsis, and Yogis," in *Brill's Encyclopedia of Hinduism*, ed. by Knut A. Jacobsen, Helene Basu, Angelika Malinar, Vasudha Narayanan, Leiden.

[4] https://www.theminimalists.com/minimalism/

References

1. Baumard, Nicholas et al., 2015, "Increased Affluence Explains the Emergence of Ascetic Wisdoms", *Current Biology*, Vol.25, Jan.5, 2015.
2. Bhagat, M.G., 1976, *Ancient Indian Asceticism*, New Delhi: Munshiram Manoharlal Publishers.
3. Bronkhorst, Johannes, 1993, *The Two Sources of Indian Asceticism*, New York: P. Lang.
4. Jaspers, Karl, 1953, *The Origin and Goal of History*, London, Routledge & Kegan Paul Publishers.
5. Kaelber, Walter O., 1989, *Tapta-Mārga: Asceticism and Initiation in Vedic India*, Albany: State University of New York Press.
6. Lamb, Ramdas, 2008, A Devotion, Reincarnation, and Rebirth in the Rāmānanda Sampradāya." *Cross Currents*. NY: Association for Religion and Intellectual Life.
7. Lamb, Ramdas, 2011, "Sādhus, Sannyāsis, and Yogis." in *Brill's Encyclopedia of Hinduism*, ed. by Knut A. Jacobsen, Helene Basu, Angelika Malinar, Vasudha Narayanan, Leiden, the Netherlands: Brill Academic Publishers.
8. Müller-Ebeling, Claudia et al., 2002, *Shamanism and Tantra in the Himalayas*, Rochester: Inner Traditions.
9. Olivelle, Patrick, trans., 1992, *Samnyasa Upanisads: Hindu Scriptures on Asceticism and Renunciation*, New York: Oxford University Press.
10. Scheckel, Msgr. Roger J. "Seeking Sanctification Through the Practice of Mortification." https://mariancatechist.com/seeking-sanctification-through-the-practice-of-mortification/ [accessed June 6, 2018]
11. What Is Minimalism? https://www.theminimalists.com/minimalism/ [accessed June 2, 2018]
12. Wimbush, Vincent L., Richard Valantasis, 1975, *Asceticism*, New York: Oxford University Press.
13. Zysk, Kenneth, 1991, Asceticism and Healing in Ancient India, Delhi: Motilal Banarsidass Publishers, therlands: Brill Academic Publishers, 262–278.

—×—

The Hindu Monastery in South India

Nalini Rao

Abstract

South India is the home of innumerable types of ancient and living Hindu ascetics, who have renounced worldly life. But the origins of institutionalized renunciation are relatively obscure. The Hindu *matha* or monastery is the residence of the ascetic guru who has played an important role in the religious life of the community. However, the Hindu monastic system encompasses a great variety of monastic orders and 'denominations'. The paper is an attempt to understand the nature of the Hindu monastery or *matha* as an ascetic and educational religious establishment of the residential monk from the 9th C CE. onwards. The area of investigation is Karnataka, with a particular focus on their origins and growth.

India has been the home of countless, ascetics and monks, who have maintained a tradition of philosophical speculation, religious practice and teaching. Whatever be his religious denomination, sect or school, the ascetic was revered. He was known by various names, such as *sanyāsī, sādhu, ṛṣi, sant, ācārya, paṇḍita, swāmi, yati* and guru. The ascetic is revered by all the three '*dharma*' traditions of India, Jainism, Buddhism and Hinduism and his status does not depend on his 'belongingness' to any particular denomination or fold. Hindu ascetics have greatly influenced the trajectory of Indian philosophy and culture, as well as the religious, social and political institutions. Their value to society is derived from renunciation of worldly pleasures, and more importantly, from their role as a teacher or guru. Despite their power to shape the growth of Hinduism, there are not many institutions or great architecture that were built for the simple saffron robed monk. The Hindu *devālayas* (temples) contain numerous images of gods and goddesses, but rarely do we find images of saints (although they must have played a key role in the construction of temples). Instead, the institution that was organized around the guru was the Hindu monastery known as a *maṭha.*

The term guru means a teacher, in the narrow sense of the term, but a guru within the institution of a *maṭha*, is more than a teacher; he is an ascetic, and a philosopher-monk. He follows specific rules and norms, beliefs and practices affiliated to the original founder of the organization of the particular *maṭha*. He maintains the *guruparamparā* (lineage of gurus) and is responsible for the interpretation of religious doctrines. Today, an additional function of the guru is the proper guidance in matters of religious and spiritual at various levels. Although known by various terms, such as *jagadguru* (world teacher), *swāmi*, *ānanda* and *tīrtha*, the most common epithet for the head of the monastery is *ācārya* or simply Guru.

The chief aim of the Hindu monastery is to preserve the body of religious doctrine formulated by its founder (or later Gurus), and to transmit these traditions. The ultimate religious purpose of the *maṭha* is to help the individual to attain *mokṣa* from *samsara.* Often, the Guru solves disputes, and even functions as a fund raiser. His learning, and charismatic leadership elicits admiration and respect from the community. Thus, *maṭhas* have preserved and helped in the transmission of religious and philosophical traditions thereby playing an important socio-religious role.

Maṭhas are religious institutions, distinct particularly to South India and serve as schools which perform the function of feeding, boarding, lodging, and rest houses for pilgrims. A *maṭha* may be defined as an organized integral system of education, worship, feeding, and lodging, consisting of a community of disciples and headed by a Guru, who is normally an ascetic. Scholars have defined it as a monastery or a monastic institution The Hindu *maṭha* has a more expansive function that includes education, worship, feeding, and lodging, and consists of a community of disciples who adhere to a set of beliefs affiliated to the original founder and headed by an ascetic guru. These characteristics are more noticeable during late medieval period, from the 11th centuries CE.

Origins of the Hindu Monastery

The earliest reference to the term *maṭha* has been found in stray Jain texts of 2nd and 5th century CE. They were educational organizations of gurus who moved from place to place as evidenced in the inscriptions from Paharpur in Bengal. With the migration of the Jain saint, Bhadrabahu with his disciple Chandragupta Maurya, the theater of Jain monasteries shifted to the Deccan. It then flourished in Karnataka under the Ganga kings, Eastern Chalukyas and Hoysalas (5th–10th centuries CE). An early reference to a Hindu *maṭha* can be found in the inscription of Samudragupta, which stated that it was a hostel for students. Numerous inscriptions provide interesting aspects about the early function of a *maṭha* during the Gupta and post-Gupta periods (6th–7th centuries CE).

However, a history of Hindu monasteries can begin only with an introduction of existing Buddhist *saṅghas* (monasteries) which have been known to exist from as early as 2th century BCE, and flourished in almost all parts of India till 9th–11th centuries CE. It may be said that they inspired the Hindu Gurus to establish their own orders. Unlike the large Buddhist institutions, Jain monasteries (also known as *maṭhas*) were small and largely in remote areas. Supported by powerful kings, Hindu monasteries were wealthy, popular and powerful, particularly in Andhra Pradesh, and Tamil Nadu. Although the beginnings of Hindu monasteries go back to 3rd century CE, it is only between the 9th and 12th centuries that they developed into seminal institutions.

The Ascetic Tradition

In order to uncover the origins of monasteries, inscriptional evidences are insufficient by themselves. Two relevant sources that are often overlooked, are two socio-religious *sāmpradayas* (traditions) of *sanyāsa* (asceticism) and *ācārya* (teaching) that provided inspiration. Asceticism flourished in India from about 2500 BCE particularly in the Indo-Gangetic doab. The Jains attached the highest importance to it, and Buddha resorted to the golden middle path of avoiding self-indulgence, and practicing self-denial. Numerous Vedic seers practiced *sanyāsa* which was passed down through oral tradition and eulogized in texts such as *Dharmasūtras, Bhagavad Gīta, Āśrama Upaniṣad*, and *Sanyāsa Upaniṣad*. The ascetic shaves his head, cuts the sacrificial string, performs the *sāvitrī* rite, sacrifice, and deposits the fires in the self, and takes the vows of celibacy and non-attachment. He is now a *sanyāsi*, and continues to practice these values, by internalizing them. The orange robe is one of the most powerful symbols of asceticism, of the triumph of virtue, discipline, renunciation, liberation, physical control, order, vigilant striving for divinity and spiritual strength—the characteristics of a yogī. He is not attached to a site or place wanders monk except for the rainy season when he lives in a fixed place. The ascetic nature of a guru was helpful in cultivating and teaching discipline, love, dedication, passion for knowledge and service to society.

The ascetic was known by various names, such as *santa, ṛṣi, sanyāsi, sādhu, bhikku, sanyāsin, muni, yati, acārya, sādhu, mahāpūruṣa, yogī, bābā* or *mahārāja*. These terms specifically applied to the varieties of saints/monks/gurus who maintained the continuous ascetic tradition of the past 3000 years. Seventeen out of eighteen Upaniṣads deal with *sanyāsa*, practiced under different names: *bhikṣu, sanyāsin, parivrajaka, avadhūta* and *paramahaṃsa*. It viewed the ascetic and hermit life as an essential part of its system which prescribed the path of four Āśramas, namely *brahmacārin* (student-hood), *gṛhastha* (householder), *vānaprasthya* (retired) and *sanyās*i (renunciate). It was a remarkable system headed by *sanyāsis* or married *acāryas*, and pandits.

The Teaching Tradition

Being an ascetic did not appear to be contradictory to the function of teaching. Ancient India had a teaching tradition that goes back to the Vedic and Epic periods, with *gurukulas* and individual teachers. Many *sanyāsis* were teachers or gurus. Both ascetics and householders were teachers. There were a number of categories of teachers, and the titles used for a teacher were *acārya, guru, sadguru, śāstrī, ācārya, paṇḍita, adhyāpaka*, who spread or taught the philosophy and religious studies. The title of guru was the most popular and seen as one who was an authority on the knowledge of the *Vedas* (Books of knowledge), *Purāṇas* (quasi-historical texts) and *Śāstras*. Although these titles, *śāstrī, acārya* were all related to education, teaching and learning, it is the *paṇḍita* that was most strongly identified with the figure of the guru.

The most commonly used term for the teacher was guru. He has been described as one who brings light, meaning divine reality. There is actually no English word that can be used to translate the word guru, which has been connected only to Hindu/Buddhist and Jain traditions. The guru in the *Maṇḍūka Upaniṣad*, is defined as one who is well versed in the Vedas and one who is absorbed in the *brahma*n. The guru, in the Upaniṣadic tradition, was a realized individual, while in the epic tradition, it meant ascetics, and householders with *āśramas*. In the *Bhagavad Gīta* (2.54) it is mentioned that gurus were those who were steeped in *brahmavidyā* (science of understanding *brahman*). Thus the grace of the guru became invaluable for learning.

All the scriptural traditions agreed that the term guru was one who imparted *vidyā* (knowledge), particularly spiritual knowledge. Imparting knowledge to a pupil (*vidyopadāna*), so as to make him/her a *śikṣita*, a learned person was given great importance. *Vidyā* was accorded a high place and regarded as a third eye that gave insight into life. It is well known that ancient India had a comprehensive system of educational philosophy, theory, and classification along with steps of learning, complexity of subjects.

The ritual of commencement of studies (*vidyārambha* or *akṣara abhyāsa*), was a *samskara* that was (and is still) performed at the beginning or commencement of primary education in the fifth year. The first stage of student life was that of the *brahmacāri* which demarcated the period of education from the 5th or 6th year, from the period of *vidyārambha* (commencement of education) till the 16th year, the *samartha*. This was generally followed by specialization in arts and sciences. In this system, *vidya* and guru, were both considered sacred. The importance of a guru was so great that he was accorded a high place in society and his status equaled that of the gods.

The teaching and ascetic traditions came together in the traditional school system of *gurukula* and later during the medieval period, in the monastic culture of Ādi Śaṅkarācārya (788–820 CE) who systematized the Hindu monastic system. Thus the amalgamation of the two systems of asceticism and teaching can also be seen in the rise of the Buddha, who was an ascetic and teacher, which was synthesized in the institution of the Buddhist *saṅgha*. It may be added that the Hindu monastic system was an institution that was largely influenced by the earlier order of the Buddhist *saṅgha*, although the traditions of asceticism and teaching *was* pre-Buddhist.

Although the early history of Hindu monasteries has been difficult to trace, it is reasonable to assume that by 7th century CE they functioned as a hostel for students, and a residential college. In addition, they grew to be a place of Vedic studies, devoted to a particular school of the Vedas. Later medieval inscriptions came to refer to them as an academic institution. Although they were situated near temples, there has been no reference to a deity or to an ascetic as the founder of a *maṭha*. However after the decline of Buddhism, Hindu *maṭhas* become formidable institutions particularly with the rise of the earliest Saiva monasteries. After the gradual waning of Buddhist *saṅghas*, various types of educational institutions arose. Hindu education was in the ascendancy around 7th century CE (and many Hindus consecrated their lives to a life of celibate study). However, it was only after the decline of Buddhist *saṅgha* that Hindu monasticism arose as an institution with an ascetic as the head of the order.

Growth of *Maṭhas*

The foundations of the monastic system can be said to have been laid between the 5th and 9th centuries CE. While maintaining a rough chronological order, and religious differences, recognizing their parallel expansion; they include:

(1) A foundational period between the 5th and 9th centuries CE.

(2) An evolutionary period (9th–12th century CE) when they grew to be independent institutions, in three different regions—the Śaiva Siddhānta *maṭhas* in Central India and Tamil Nadu and Pāśupata and Kālamukha *maṭhas* in Karnataka; and

(3) a mature period with the rise of the multifaceted Vedānta *maṭhas* (9th–14th century CE). These include: the Advaita Vedānta *maṭhas* (that arose in the 9th century CE) Viśiṣṭādvaita *maṭhas* (between 11 and 12th centuries CE); Dvaita *maṭhas* between the 13th and 14th centuries CE. However, all *maṭhas* (except the Pāśupata, Kāpālika, and Kalamukha monasteries) continued to develop and divide. The Vedanta and Veerasaiva *maṭhas* are still living institutions and are popular religious institutions in South India.

In Central India, from about 7th centuries CE, Saivite *maṭhas* flourished. In the forest lands of Gopaacala or modern Gwalior (7–14th centuries CE) and the Dahala region (between Yamuna and Narmada rivers (10–13th centuries CE), lived Śaiva ascetics in *āśramas* that grew into *maṭhas* affiliated to Śaiva Siddhānta doctrine as well as Pasupata and Kalamukha beliefs. The early medieval Saivite *maṭhas* in Karnataka adhered to Pāśupata, Kālāmukha, and Kāpālika doctrines, and were followers of Lakulisa *siddhānta*. Kālāmukha temples and *mathas* existed in Hassan, Kadur, Chitradurga, Mysore, Bangalore, Tumkur, Kolar and Shimoga districts, as well as in Abbalur, Hangal, Gadag, Sri-Parvata (Srisaila) in Kurnool District and generally all over Kannada-speaking country as well as in parts of Andhra.

An important contribution of Saivite *maṭhas* was the adherence to the ancient system of guru—lineage that provided additional legitimacy to the institution. In addition, they aligned themselves with royal houses, and were *rajagurus* to powerful kings. With the spread and construction of large temple complexes patronized by royalty, *maṭhas* began to play a central role in Karnataka. *Maṭhas* were normally located near temples and functioned as feeding centers. In Tamil Nadu there were both *brahmin* and non-*brahmin maṭhas*. These multifaceted institutions with functions of feeding, teaching, boarding, lodging, consisting of a pluralistic community, and headed by Gurus. A significant center of Kālāmukha *maṭha* (and temple) system in Karnataka was at Balligame (in Shimoga District), capital of the kingdom of Banavasi kingdom. Inscriptional evidences clearly support the fact that the 12th C *maṭhas* were not sectarian institutions, particularly those in Balligami and Golakki. Here apart from Hindu maṭhas, Jain *basadis* and Buddhist *vihāras*, there were many temples. Whatever be the circumstances of their evolution, the growth of Saivite *maṭhas* as centers of both secular and religious education laid a solid foundation for the growth of *Vedānta maṭhas* that institutionalized the system of monasticism.

Vedānta Maṭhas

Numerous *Śaiva maṭhas* spread to various parts of South India and flourished particularly in northern Karnataka, Tamil Nadu and Andhra. But, between the 9th C and 13th C CE there arose a parallel system in Karnataka, namely the *Vedānta maṭhas*. Among the three main *Vedānta maṭhas*, the *Advaita maṭha* was the earliest that arose in 9th C CE, the *Viśiṣṭādvaita maṭha* in 11th C and the *Dvaita maṭha* in the 13th C. They based their doctrines on the Upnishadic theistic philosophy, rooted in the authority of the *Vedas*. Their three main sources were the *Upaniṣads, Brahma Sūtras*, and the *Bhagavad Gita*, the three together known as the *Prasthānatrayī* (sources of philosophy).

Unlike the *Śaiva maṭhas*, the *Vedānta maṭhas* were founded by an individual *ācārya*. The *Advaita maṭha* was established by Śrī *Ādi Śaṅkarācārya* (788–820 CE) who began to articulate commentaries on the *Upaniṣads*. A few centuries later, *Rāmānujācārya* (1017–1137 CE) founded *Viśiṣṭādvaita maṭhas* and in the 13th C, *Dvaita maṭhas* were founded by Śrī *Madhvācārya* (1199–1278 CE).[1] The three major *Vedānta maṭhas* were large organizations headed by ascetic whose Guru-teacher lineage, ideology and practices had a great impact on society.

The major contribution of *Ādi Śaṅkarācārya* was to establish *maṭhas* in the four corners of India, where the philosophical tradition could be preserved and practiced by ascetic scholars. As he was influenced by Buddhist and Jain system of organization, he was convinced of the necessity of building major monastic centers, instead of few localized ones to revitalize Vedism and to preach *Advaita* philosophy and *sanātana dharma*. His noble achievement was that he founded four *maṭhas* with ascetic heads in the four zones of the subcontinent to propagate Advaitic religious philosophy.[2] Four major *maṭhas* were established in four different zones: *Śringeri*,[3] *Dwāraka*, *Puri*, *Badrināth* (and in addition, Kanchipuram) as principal seats of learning. The

---

[1] Other philosophical schools include Nimbarka, 1162, Vallabhācārya, ca.1500 and Gaudiya Madhva traditions

[2] Cenkner, 2001: p.110.

[3] According to sawai *Śringeri* math was an abode for sannyasins, a center for philosophical study, and a site for worship, Sawai, 1992: p.31.

Śaṅkara maṭhas[4] were each headed by an *ācārya*, titled *Śaṅkarācārya*, and recognized as *Jagadgurus* or world teachers who claim direct lineage from the founder.[5] *Ādi Śaṅkarācārya* sent his four disciples to the *maṭhas* in four quarters of India, *Badarikāśrama, Puri, Dvārkā and Śringeri* (and Kanchipuram).[6] He selected the disciples for posting in the *mathas* on the basis of their affiliation to a particular *Veda*. Each *matha* was again given a special formula as the symbol of philosophical quintessence of pure monism.[7] The head of each branch had to supervise the administration of this *maṭha*, regulating the life and conduct of monks there.

(a) *Padmapāda* was affiliated to the *Ṛgvedic* school, and head of the *Govardhana maṭha* of the eastern zone. Govardhan was given a sacred formula for *Prajñānam Brahma* or true knowledge in *Brāhmaṇa*.

(b) *Dvārka* was the seat of the *Śarada* Center of the western region, and Suresvara was in charge. The *mahāvakya* of this *maṭha* was *Tat-tvam-as*i or That Thou Art, and had to take care of the teaching of *Sāmaveda*.

(c) The Joshi (or Jyotir)-*maṭha* at Badarikasrama in the north, was under *Totakācārya*. The center followed the *Atharvaveda*; its sacred formula was *Ayamātmma Brahma* or I am *Brāhmaṇa*. The branches attached to this *maṭha* were *Giri*, *Parvata* and *Sāgara*.[8]

(d) *Hastamālaka* was deputed to *Śringeri* and was in charge of the southern countries as Andhra, Dravida, Kerala and Karnataka. The center was concerned with the orders of *Sarasvati*, *Bharati* and *Puri*.[9] He was affiliated to *Yajurveda* and the formula, *Aham Brahmāsmi* I am *Brāhman*.

---

[4] Cenkner, 2001:ix.

[5] The *mathas* were: Jyotirmatha at Badri in the North; Saradapith at Dvaravati (Dvarka) in the West, Govardhan-matha at Puri in the east.

[6] There is a disagreement regarding the name of the monk who was dispatched to a prticualr matha.

[7] Anandagiri, an early biographer of *Śaṅkarācārya*, confirms the fact that Śaṅkara had many disciples and the two headed many *maṭhas*, four of 5 headed by his foremost pupils: Suresvara, Padmapāda, Taotaka, Hastamalaka from whom the lineage for the *Śaṅkarācāryas* evolved through the centuries.

[8] Since the death of its head Ramkrishna Svami, the temple was in charge of nambudri Brāhmaṇas and now the *maṭha* is headed by *Svāmi Brāhmāṇanda*, learned scholar of Benares.

[9] F.N. Śaṅkara is said to have made Sureshwara in charge of *Śringeri* and Kanchi Matah too, as a guardian of the seven year old boy, *Sarvagynātman*.

Ādi Śaṅkarācārya institutionalized the tradition of the sanyasin and teaching lineage in the *maṭha* and began an orderly way of spreading the religion in four different parts.[10] Under the leadership of these 'Guru-sannyasins,' *maṭhas*, became educational and philosophical institutions with their own system, pilgrimage sites, organization, ritual, philosophies which were distinct from earlier Buddhist *sanghas*. From the time of *Ādi Śaṅkarācārya*, the *maṭhas* were headed by ascetics of *Śaṅkarācārya* orders and came to called as *Jagadgurus* (preceptor of the world).[11] Although heads of *mathas* are described as *Jagadgurus*,[12] those belonging to *Sringeri matha* tradition and of *smarta* tradition are called *Śaṅkarācārya*s as well, including those in Dvarka, Puri branches as well.[13]

Viśiṣṭādvaita Maṭhas

About four hundred years after *Ādi Śaṅkarācārya* organized the *maṭha* system, *Rāmānujācārya* (1017–1137 CE) formulated the philosophy of qualified monism, by which he refuted *Śaṅkarācārya*'s doctrine of *maya* or illusion, and incorporated the concept of *bhakti* or devotion turning to Vaisnavism. Rāmānuja, refuted *Śaṅkara*'s doctrine of spiritual monism which negated *bhaktivada*, the doctrine of love and faith. He argued that if there is only one universal spirit, there is no scope for love or devotion which necessarily postulates two separate entities—the lover and the beloved. Rāmānuja placed the *bhakti* cult on a firm philosophical basis by expounding the doctrine of qualified monism or *Viśiṣṭādvaita* which recognized three eternal principles, individual soul, the insensate world and the supreme soul (the creator), thus reconciling his philosophy of qualified non-dualism with bhakti.[14] He disagreed with *Śaṅkara* that both *jivātman* and *paramātma* are one and same, while propounding the death of *Advaita*, he postulated a a more realistic theory of qualified monism.

[10] Although this model existed in the Buddhist monastery as well as in Saivite *maṭhas*.

[11] The heads were not merely *jagadgurus*, but were also *sankarcharyas* in spirit. However the basic tradition of *maṭhas* as educational institutions, vidyapithas or seats of learning continued. Although the tradition of lineage of gurus, existed in the Saivite *mathas*, the lineage of gurus to disciple, (not guru to son) who adhered to a particular philosophy was established.

[12] Sawai, 1992: p.31.

[13] *Smarta* (relating to memory) is a movement of Vedic Hinduism. It is a synthesis of *Advaita*, Yoga and *Mīmāṃsā*. Followers of this tradition accept all major Gods. Known as the panchayatana form of worship, they venerate Śiva, *Viṣṇu*, Devi, Surya and Gaṅeśa.

[14] *Brāhmaṇ*, according to *Rāmānujācārya* manifests as *Viṣṇu*.

Dvaita Maṭhas

With the coming of *Madhvācārya* (1238–1317 CE) the trajectory of *mathas* takes a different turn.[15] *Madhvācārya* was the historical founder of the *Dvaita* system of philosophy. *Madhvācārya* appears on the philosophical scene when the two systems, *Advaita* and *Viśiṣṭādvaita* had been well established. "Due to doctrinal differences and ideological dissatisfaction with contemporary trends and schools of thought,"[16] he founded a new school of thought, called *Tattvavada* or Realism, popularly known as *Dvaita* or Dualism, which believes that *Viṣṇu* as *paramatma*, supreme soul and *jivatma* or individual soul are independent realities.[17] His philosophy has not been considered as the main line of Upaniṣadic thought particularly in the west, although it is in which the fundamental thought of the *Veda-śastras* has been preserved meaningfully and consistently. But due to certain negligible philosophical differences between his disciples, the Dualist *maṭhas* (also known as *Madhva maṭhas*), began to divide which led to the emergence of branch *maṭhas*, when ascetic disciples set up their own *maṭha.*[18] These were known as Asthamathas and Desastha *mathas*.

Madhvācārya had eight disciples who chose to stay in Udupi and founded their own *maṭhas*, which came to be known as the Asthamaṭhas (Eight *maṭhas*) Each *maṭha* assumed the name of a school of thought, which were denominations of Madhva's *Dvaita* philosophy: Hrishikesa *Tīrtha* of Palimaru *Maṭha*, Narasimha *Tīrtha* of Adamaru *Maṭha*, Janardhana *Tīrtha* of Krishnapura *Maṭha*, Upendra *Tīrtha* of Puttige *Matha*, Vamana *Tīrtha* of Sirur *Maṭha*, Vishnu *Tīrtha* of Sode *Maṭha*, Srimara *Tīrtha* of Kanayur *maṭha*, Adhoksaja *Tīrtha* of Pejavara *Maṭha*

---

[15] According to Madhvācārya, there are two realities in the world: independent and dependent.

[16] Sharma, B.N.K., 1962:xv.

[17] According to Madhva philosophy, *jagat* or world is real, it is dependent and the only independent entity is *paramatma* or *Brahman*. Every *jiva* is inherently different or *svarupatha*. God impels each *jiva* into activity and provides benefits in conformity to the karma performed by the *jiva*. This *siddhanta* or belief system of mutual gradation is bitter truth and established by *Vedas*, Itihasas and Purāṇas (*vaidika dharma*). The cause of inequality between each *jiva*, according to *Advaita* is *māyā*. According to *Madāhvacārya* it is *karma*. God is the creator of *jivas*, he grants sorrow and joy, and discriminates between *jivas* due to ones karmas.

[18] Such was the case with the Vyasa Raja, who had established his *maṭha* on river Kabini, near T. Narasimhapura near Mysore. Śrī Vyasaraja *Maṭha* split into Kundapur Vyasa Raja *Maṭha* and the Sosale Vyasa Raja *Maṭha*.

The division into Asthamathas reflect very slight differences in the philosophical stands of the pontifical heads. Each *maṭha* has a different *guruparampara* (guru lineage). Today, each of the eight *maṭhas* in Udipi contains valuable manuscripts, idols of *avataras* of Vishnu which is handed down to generations of Guru.

The Desastha *Mathas* owe their organization to the four disciples of *Madhvācārya-Padmanabhatīrtha*, *Naraharitīrtha*, *Madhvatīrtha* and *Aksobhyatīrtha* (earlier distinguished scholars of *Advaita*) who continued the traditions of their founder. These include Uttaradi *maṭha*, Sosale Vyasarja *maṭha*, Kundapura *maṭha*, Raghvendra Swamy *maṭha*, Sripadaraja *maṭha* at Mulabagal, Majjigehalli *maṭha*, Kudli *maṭha*, Balegaru *maṭha*, Gokarna-Partagali-Jivottama *maṭha* Kasi *maṭh* and others.

While the *Śaiva mathas* during the early medieval period had grown to be multifarious institutions, the *Vedānta mathas* became formidable institutions and had a more rigid order, with a hierarchy of organization, a large body of followers, and grounded in the philosophy of the founder. *Vedānta mathas* were founded by one main guru, and more importantly, were always headed by ascetics who were also philosophers and learned scholars and their commentaries themselves became scriptures. One of the reasons for the growth of *mathas* was the influence of *bhakti*, and its leaders. Thus Gurus were able to rephrase, reinvent traditions, interpret philosophy, rituals, and yet maintain a sense of continuity, echoing Vedic and Upaniṣadic thoughts. Hindu monastic organization underwent a growth in function, and practice. The Hindu monastery in South India was more than a static institution and its meaning and role changed periodically. It was a flexible, multi-faceted institution that could adopt to changing historical circumstances. Today, *mathas* have adopted gods, and have grown to be large pilgrim centers.

References

1. Altekar, A.S., *Education in Ancient India*, New Delhi: Gyan Publishing House, 1965.
2. Bradford, N.J., "The Indian Renouncer: Structure and Transformation in the Lingayat Community," In *Indian Religion*, ed. by R. Burghart and A. Cantlie. London/New York: Curzon Press/St. Martin's Press, 1985.
3. Cenkner, William, *A Tradition of Teachers: Śankara and the Jagadgurus Today*, Columbia: South Asia Books, 1983, first ed., Delhi: Motilal Banarsidass, 1983, reprint, 1995, 2001.
4. Chakraborti, Haripada, *Asceticism in Ancient India: in Brahmanical, Buddhist, Jaina and Ajivika Societies from the Earliest Times to the Period of Sankaracharya*, Calcutta: Punthi Pustak, 1973.

5. Chitnis, K.N., "Vira Saiva Mathas in the Keladi Kingdom," *Journal of the Kamalak University (Social Sciences)*, Vol.III, 1967.
6. Desai, P.B., *A History of Karnataka*, Dharwar: Kannada Research Institute, Karnatak University, 1970.
7. Dutt, Sukumar, *Buddhist Monks and Monasteries of India: Their History and Their Contribution to Indian Culture*, London: G. Allen and Unwin, 1962.
8. Govindacharya, Bannanje. *Acharya Madhwa: Life and Works.* Translated into English by U.P. Upadhyaya, Udipi: Isavasya Pratishanam, 2011.
9. Govindacharya, B, *Udupi: Past and Present*, Udupi: Pejavara Matha, 1984.
10. Govindacharya, B, "Dvaita In Karnaktaka", in *Avalokana: A Compendium of Karnataka Heritage*, ed. Krishna Swamy, Bangalore: Directorate of Kannada culture, 1985.
11. Govindacharya, Bannanje, ed. *Madhva Rgbhasya in Sarvamulagrantha*, Vol.4, Udipi: Akhila Bharata Madhwa Mahamandala, 1973.
12. Ishwaran, K., *Speaking of Basava: Lingayat Religion and Culture in South Asia*, Boulder: Westview Press, 1992.
13. Karashima, N., Subbarayalu, Y., and P. Shanmugam, P. "Mathas and Medieval Religious Movements in Tamil Nadu: An Epigraphical Study". *Indian Historical Review* 37 (2) 217–234 (2011).
14. Karashima, Noaboru, *South Indian History and Society: Studies from Inscriptions (AD 850–1800)*, Delhi: Oxford University Press, 1984.
15. Krishnamani, M.N. *Shankara: The Revoltionary*, New Delhi: Rajan Publications, 2001.
16. Kumara, S and others, ed. *Bhagavad Sri Ramanuja's Contribution to Four Swayamvyakta Kshetras-Kanchipuram, Srirangam, Tirupati and Melkote.* Melkote: Academy of Sanskrit Research, 2015.
17. Lorenzen, David, The Kapalikas and Kalamukhas: Two Lost Saiva Sects, Berkeley: University of California Press, 1972.
18. Madugula, I.S., *The Acharya: Sankara of Kaladi*, Delhi: Motilal Banarsidass, 1985, reprint 2006.
19. Misra, R.N., *Ascetics, Piety and Power*, *Saiva Siddhanta Monastic Art in the Woodlands of Central India*, New Delhi: Aryan Books International, 2018.
20. Olivelle, Patrick, *The Āśrama System: The History and Hermeneutics of a Religious Institution*. New York: Oxford University Press. 1993.
21. Padmanabhacharya, C.M., 1983, *Life and Teachings of Sri Madhvachariar*, 2nd ed., Bombay.
22. Rao, B.A. Krishnaswamy, *Outline of the Philosophy of Sri Madhwacharya*, Bangalore: Swetadweepa Publications, 2003.
23. Rao, Hayavadana: *Poornaprajna Vijaya: Life and teachings of Sri Madhwacharya*, translated from Kannada by Dhadra Krishnamoorthy, Chennai: Sri Krishna Sri Raghavendra Trust, 2010.
24. Rao, Krishna: *Udupi: A Great Religious Center*, Manipal Rotary Club., Manipal, 1989.
25. Sarma, Deepak, *An Introduction to Madhva Vedanta*. Aldershot, Hampshire, England; Burlington, V.T. S: Ashgate, 2003.

26. Sawai, Yoshitsugau, *The Faith of Ascetics and Lay Smartas: A Study of the Sankaran Tradition of Srngeri*, Publications of the De Nobili Research Library, Vol.XIX, ed. by Gerhard Oberhammer, Institute for Indology, Vienna: University of Vienna, 1992.
27. Sharma, B.N. Krishnamurti, *Philosophy of Sri Madhvacarya*, Delhi: Motilal Banarsidass Publishers, 1962, rev. ed. 1986, reprints, 1992, 2002, 2008.
28. Sharma B.N. Krishnamurti, *Madhva's Teaching in his own Words*, ed. K.M. Munshi, R.R. Diwalar, Bombay: Bharatiya Vidya Bhavan, 1961.
29. Sharma B.N.K., *History of the Dvaita School of Vedanta and its Literature from the earliest beinnings to our own times*, Delhi: Motilal Banarsidass Pub. Delhi, first ed. 1981, third rev. 2001, reprint 2008.

Making the Invisible Visible: The "Woman Factor" in the Stepwells of Gujarat

Purnima Mehta Bhatt

Abstract

My paper explores and documents the role women have played in the building, patronage and as inspiration for the water architecture of Gujarat, Western India. Based on archival research, fieldwork and folklore, I provide an historical analysis and visual documentation of stepwells, thereby contributing to a better understanding of the intricate relationship between women, water, religion, and aesthetic expression. Historians and scholars have in recent years become increasingly aware of the fact that women have generally been overlooked and ignored in historical texts and literature. Women's contributions, their experiences, their perspectives are seldom represented in historical writing. History has mostly been written by men and deals with the lives of men. This paper, which grew out of my research work over the past ten years is an attempt to rectify this and focus on women as the principal actors.

Introduction

My paper examines and documents the role women played in the building and patronage of and as inspiration for the numerous stepwells of Gujarat from the seventh to the nineteenth centuries.[1] My research provides a historical analysis and visual documentation of the stepwells, thereby contributing to a better understanding of the relationship between women, water, architecture and religion. My work takes a unique perspective: it examines the stepwells primarily as a distinct space for women. It focuses on the unique perspective of "the woman factor". More often than not, women appear as silent spectators in history, not active participants. Recent scholarship points to an urgent

[1] This paper is based on my book, *Her Space, Her Story: Exploring the Stepwells of Gujarat*, New Delhi, Zubaan, 2014.

need to call into question why women's lives and their contributions have been so vastly neglected. There is a compelling urgency, I believe, to correct the historical record to more accurately reflect women's perspectives and achievements, to hear their voices, which have remained silent for so many centuries.

I first encountered stepwells nearly half a century ago when, on a summer vacation, I visited my grandparents in Ahmedabad. My grandmother arranged for me to join a daylong sightseeing tour of the architectural marvels and historical sights in and around Ahmedabad. It was during the course of this trip that I first visited the stepwell of Adalaj and was struck by its unique grandeur and artistic beauty.

Many decades later, I learned that these stepwells, which are a familiar feature of the landscape of Gujarat, once numbered in the thousands. In the dry, arid and parched land where water is scarce and the rains are scanty, these wells provided life-giving water to humans and animals, and enabled the land to become fertile. What was even more intriguing was that of the several hundred stepwells that have been excavated, around 25 per cent were actually built by women—queens, royalty, wives of rich merchants, ordinary women, courtesans and servant girls who hoped to gain religious merit and possibly immortality through the gift of water.

Not, only, did women commission many of the stepwells as patrons and donors, they also frequently served as the inspiration—stepwells were built to honour and were named after a virtuous wife or a benevolent mother, a local goddess or a beloved mistress. As new research is undertaken with a greater sensitivity to gender issues, it is exciting to envision that more women will emerge as patrons of art and architecture. 'Women's agency' in art will receive the attention it merits. The art of the stepwells honours and celebrates the feminine principle, the creative force in the Universe. The goddess in her manifested forms is visible everywhere in the stepwells, occupying not the servile position of the Brahmin wife, but a place of pre-eminence. Were these wells an indication of women's growing power and wealth in society, their striving to place themselves in history's gaze and thereby challenge the stereotypes of their passivity?

Women gathered at these stepwells to obtain water but also to appeal to the local deities for health, happiness and children. They performed rituals to ensure their own fertility, to ask for the gift of sons, to ask the goddess to intercede on their behalf so that milk would flow from their breasts to nurture their newborn. These age-old rituals in and around the stepwells continue even today. The stepwells became a favorite subject in folklore. Every step of these stepwells yields tales of love and betrayal, courage and sacrifice. I have attempted to identify and translate some of these songs that tell us about the inner lives of the women whose voices still echo in these now crumbling and dilapidated structures.

These stepwells are unique structures because they were not merely utilitarian buildings; they served a dual function—providing water but also as a site for ritual and propitiation of the local deities. They linked three worlds: the subterranean, the earthly, and the celestial. There is much we can learn by giving a voice to the countless women forgotten and neglected by history. In doing so, we will have succeeded in some measure in "making the invisible, visible."

Significance and Sanctity of Water in India

It goes without saying that water is essential for survival. From the very beginnings of human culture it played a vital role in the birth and flowering of civilisations. In a dry and arid landscape like that of Gujarat, water can make the difference between life and death. Rainfall is scarce, except during the monsoons, and most rivers are devoid of water during the dry season. As early as the 6th century CE, inhabitants of this region developed strategies for storing and preserving the water from the annual monsoons by digging deep into the ground to utilize the underground sources of water. They built steps leading to the water, which became the first stepwells.

The stepwell is referred to in Sanskrit as "Vapi" or "Vapika" and in Gujarati as "vav" or "bauli."[2] It is a rectangular or octagonal structure containing a flight of steps leading down to the water. In contrast to wells, the stepwells did not require a rope or any other device to draw water.In a parched land, the gift of water was precious and quenching the thirst of humans and beasts was viewed as meritorious—an act that gained great merit for the giver. In the Vedic tradition, water is said to be endowed with transformative and magical powers (Rig Veda I.23; 17–22). It is stated in the Padma Purana that whoever builds water buildings will enjoy thousands of years of paradise. One attains all merits by the endowment of water and goes straight to heaven.

Wells were also said to be invested with supernatural powers, their water seen as the dwelling place for spirits. The water contained medicinal properties to heal the sick and cure the afflicted. It is evident

---

[2] In Marathi and Hindi, it is known as "Vavdi" and "Bavdi", or "Baori". There is an ancient text dealing with the construction of stepwells known as *Vapi Shilpa Shastra*.

that the healing and curative powers residing in the waters of the wells caused them to be venerated. Various types of offerings were made at the wells that include sweets, sugar, honey, betel nuts, flowers, milk and coconuts.

The region of Gujarat was a vital link in the trade between the north and south. It was located at the crossroads of trade routes. From times immemorial, caravans laden with cotton textiles, silk, indigo dye, pearls, carpets and other goods traveled through this region carrying precious cargo bound for distant lands. In the old days, prior to the introduction of modern systems of transportation comprising of railways and highways, merchants known as "Vanjaras" traveled long distances with their merchandise and trade goods loaded on their bullock carts and camels. These traders and merchants often traveled at night guided by the stars and tried to avoid the fierce midday sun taking rest for several hours. The stepwells, thus, provided not just water for them and their animals but also a dark, cool place, where they could avoid the scorching sun and rejuvenate themselves surrounded by the presence of the gods and goddesses. Women, pilgrims, itinerant traders, troops on the march, and royal hunting parties used these step wells for water and rest. The landing platforms and ornamental galleries decorated with figurative carvings of deities, animal and plant motifs served as an escape and distraction from their monotonous journeys. Thus, *Vavs*, in contrast to ordinary wells, were more elaborate structures, often multistoried. They also differed from wells in that they often contain elaborate decorations and embellishments on the walls, which were profusely decorated with designs of flowers, vines, leaves and animals.

The step wells of Gujarat, thus, represent a unique form of water architecture, which is both functional in nature as well as aesthetically beautiful. An examination of these step wells constructed under the patronage of Hindu and Muslim dynasties, reveals the unique attitude of religious tolerance and a spirit of assimilation rarely witnessed elsewhere. These step wells successfully transcend religious differences and sectarian conflicts.

Women and Space

From the very earliest of times, in virtually all societies, women have been relegated and confined to the 'domestic' sphere while men's activities link them to the 'public' realm. The underlying assumption here is that it is their biological role, the fact that they give birth to children, which would explain their being identified with the private realm. Being confined and restricted to the home implied that women fewer or no opportunities to move into the public realm, to establish crosscutting networks of support and to seek and exercise power.The step wells are in a sense unique because they provided women a socially legitimated opportunity to move out of the domestic (albeit just for a few hours daily) and step out into the public domain. This enabled them to escape the oppression of their daily lives, the exploitation and restrictions they experienced in a deeply patriarchal society.

Thus, the step wells where women went to fetch water daily afforded them a brief measure of freedom and autonomy. It allowed them to express their sorrows and frustrations and perhaps seek solace and support from other women. Wells and step wells provided women with a measure of social freedom and served as a "safety valve". The step well, thus, served as a substitute for her *piyara* or childhood home.The women often lacked spatial and psychological space of their own. The stepwells and wells offered them that space where they came to laugh and cry, to share their joys and sorrows, and to while away an hour or two and enjoy leisure, something they rarely possessed. The songs and folklore emanating from these encounters provide a glimpse into the inner lives of women in a gendered society about which we know so little and which give us invaluable insight into the lived experience of these women.

In the nineteenth century when stepwells became obsolete and no longer served their original purpose, women once again repossessed them, establishing a claim on these structures and transformed them into shrines for the worship of local mother goddesses. In so doing, they asserted their right to carve out some space for themselves and create their own identities. They came here to restore the order in "their" universe and to renew themselves.

The Woman Factor in Stepwells

It is estimated that of the several hundred stepwells in Gujarat, perhaps, one-fifth or more were built or commissioned by women. Through the patronage of stepwells, these women were demanding a place in the pages of history and vying for immortality. Women's patronage of water buildings can also be understood in view of the fact that the responsibility of fetching water fell on womenfolk and thus, the building of wells represented a noble activity which benefited a large number of women, while conferring great merit on the donor.It is tempting to suggest that one of the chief motivations of commissioning wells was precisely to insert themselves into history to prevent being forgotten. They wanted to bestow their name to posterity. When women become patrons of art and architecture, they call into question and challenge the prevailing notions of their passivity. It also enables them to exert some power and establish their separate identity in a patriarchal society.While the pre-eminent gods of Hinduism—Shiva, Vishnu and Brahma are featured in some of the step wells, it is mainly the veneration of the local goddesses that is the focal point of the art.

Voices from the Deep

Stepwells and wells serve as the inspiration for countless songs and poems that describe the emotions and inner feelings of the young women who go to the wells to get water. This also led to chance encounters and liaisons which are reflected in the folk literature. One such song goes:

How can I go to fetch water, O friend of mine
How can I go to fetch water?
A stranger standing at the steps of the well
Made me bashful and lose all control.
How can I go to fetch water, my dear friend?

Women took great pride in their shining, glistening pots which they scrubbed till they shone like the golden rays of the sun. In one such poem, a young girl expresses her longing for a beautiful pot:

"I am not going to draw water from
A copper pot.
O mother,
I yearn for a golden one".

The women came to the wells, stepwells and ponds to fetch water for bathing, washing and cooking, however, these places were also a popular site for the performance of rituals and religious rites. The rituals performed near the stepwell or river very often centered on fertility and a woman's yearning for children—a common concern for all women. This emotion was particularly intense in India where fulfillment came from becoming a mother of many sons and childlessness was considered a curse. A popular song in the Kheralu area focuses on this theme:

I am coming fast with the water-pot filled with water,
O Rannade![3] *Please give me the one who would pull*
Me by the skirt
O Mother! The taunts of childlessness are unbearable.[4]

---

[3] Rannadé refers to the wife of the Sun, a Female deity.

[4] Gaudani, 'Panihari Ane Panisherado', *Lokgurjari*, 1968.

This above refrain is a common one. Women who are unable to bear children suffer the taunts and humiliation in society and appeal to the mother goddess to bless them with a child. No humiliation was greater than the curse of barrenness. The frustrations and despair of the maiden mad in love who goes out on the pretext of fetching water is expressed in the following song:

The rope is forty arm lengths long,
Yet could not reach the water;
While waiting for the beloved one,
The day, after all is about to end?

While she drops the pot inside the well, she looks down into the well but thinks only of her beloved, and sees his reflection in the water. The maiden does not let the pot sink into the water lest the reflected face of the lover be disturbed! The terror of the mother-in-law and the scarcity of water in the Vāgada region is reflected in the following:

O grandfather! Kindly do not give your daughters, like me,
In marriage to someone in the Vg̲gada region;
The quarrelsome mother-in-law of Vg̲gada is difficult to deal with.
O grandfather! She makes me grind corn during the day, and spin during the night;
Sends me to fetch water late at night prior to the break of dawn, O grandfather!

The pitcher sinks not, since the rope reaches not the water
My sun has arisen and set on the bank of the well.
O flying birds! Take my message to my grandfather
That your granddaughter has fallen into the well. O grandfather!

No sacrifice was seen as too great to quench the thirst of the village and ensure survival. The sacrifice of human life was regarded as necessary for the well being of the community. Many folk songs deal with this theme. The best known is about the Madhavav

For twelve long years, we dug a well
But could not locate the underground stream, O My Dear!
Astrologers of fame were summoned who predicted, O My Dear!
The sacrifice of our son and his wife;
We hope, profuse water could be located, then.

The couple descended down to the fifth step,
The water in the well flowed and immersed them upto the neck.

As they stepped down to the sixth and seventh step,
The head dress and the silken sari were found floating on the water![5]

Thus, according to the legend, the sacrifice by the young couple filled the stepwell with water.

Stepwells Today

These beautiful stepwells that represent the finest examples of water architecture ceased to be built after the establishment of British rule in India in the nineteenth century. The British administration viewed the stepwells with horror and disdain. They regarded the waters in these wells as unclean, unhygienic and a source of potentially hazardous infections. Regulations imposed by the British prohibited the use of the stepwells for drinking water. After nearly a thousand years, the stepwells became obsolete and were replaced by taps, pumps and tube wells. Many were sealed off and declared off limits while others crumbled to the ground, victims of neglect and disuse. Those that survived are silent reminders of the past when they were alive with the sound of laughter and the voices of women who came here to fetch water and others who spent a few hours here to rest and drink the cooling waters.

During my numerous visits to the stepwells in various parts of Gujarat, I was struck by the fact that some of these wells, are, once again being reclaimed, mostly by women and have been transformed into, "embryonic shrines for the worship of local goddesses and female deities". Women are once again claiming these structures as their unique space for the performance of rituals and worship centered on fertility, abundance, health and prosperity.

Women have reclaimed these stepwells and appropriated them for their own ritual purposes. Often a shrine for a local goddesses that contains a sculptural representation of the goddess is constructed in or adjacent to the step well. She is dressed in silk and satin with gold and tinsel, and is often accompanied by her 'vahan' or mount and holds weapons in her arms. Women from the surrounding neighborhood come here to perform rituals of fertility and pray for the blessings of sons, health, long life and prosperity. These often 'gaudy' images of the 'Devis' become the magnet which attracts the local women who converge here just as women did when they went to fetch water at the stepwells. The goddesses are given offerings of marigold flowers,

[5] The headdress refers to the 'Paghadi', worn by men, especially in Saurashtra.

silk scarves, sweets and coconuts. Young girls come here to invoke the blessings of the goddess to ensure that they will find good husbands and happiness in marriage. Others bring offerings to pray for fertility and sons. During a recent visit to one of the stepwells on the outskirts of Ahmedabad, I noticed a mound of clay pots in a corner of the stepwell discarded after the completion of rituals. This has once again become "woman's space" and serves the useful function of preserving these structures and protecting them from neglect and destruction.

Some stepwells—neglected, crumbling and dangerous—teem with all forms of life. Plants and creepers grow defiantly from the crevices of the stone structures, cooing pigeons and flying bats shatter the silence with the arrival of a stranger in their midst, parrots the color of spring green share the space with snakes, squirrels, frogs, fish and turtles in the waters of the well. The birds and other carved creatures on the walls are being replaced by these new inhabitants of the stepwells.

The world of nature with birds and animals, as well as humans and divine figures carved on the walls and pillars still astonish us with their beauty, a reminder of a time and unique worldview in which birds and animals were our companions and equals in the spirit world, a world in which anything was possible, one in which mystical transformations took place between the human, animals and divine worlds.

In the last few decades, the stepwells have once again been revived and revitalized, not just as a focal point for the worship of local goddesses but they are also being put to new uses—as the setting for concerts and classical music and dance festivals. Recently, I had the opportunity to attend a Water Festival at Adalaj Stepwell, which was organized to celebrate World Heritage Day. The magnificently lit stepwell glowed and shone in the night and reverberated with the sounds of story telling of Manbhatt (a member of the traditional community of oral historians, folklorists and bards) and the rhythms of the electric guitar and tabla performed by a maestro. Nearly a thousand people, old and young gathered at the stepwell on a cold, starry night to celebrate the thousand-year architectural heritage. Perhaps, listening to the fusion music and the rhythms and melodies, the new generation of youth are rediscovering ancient buildings like the Adalaj stepwell and in the process learning and rediscovering the legacy of their past. Queen Rudabai, who commissioned this step well would have smiled for the prophecy was coming true that "as long as the sun and moon shine, may there be joy and steadfastness."[6]

[6] Inscription at Adalaj.

References

1. Abbot, J.E., "Bai Harir's Inscription at Ahmedabad", AD 1499, in *Epigraphia Indica*, Vol.IV, 1896, pp.297–299.
2. Acharya, G.V., *Historical Inscriptions of Gujarat* (in Gujarati), 3 Vols., Shree Forbes Gujarati Sabha Series, No.15, Bombay, 1933–35.
3. *Agni Puranam*, A Prose English Translation by Manmatha Nath Dutt Shastri, Vol.1, Chowkhamba Sanskrit Studies, 1967, Delhi, 1984, dum Vol.1, Sept. 2006, No.2, pp.95–105.
4. Bayley, Edward Clive, "Local Muhammadan Dynasties, Gujarat," in *The History of India as Told by its Own Historians,* London, 1886.
5. Bhattacharyya, B. (ed), *Aparajitapraccha*, Gaikwad Oriental Series No.CXV, Oriental Institute, Baroda, 1950.
6. Briggs, Henry G., *Cities of Gujarashtra*. Bombay: Times Press, 1849.
7. Burgess, James and Henry Cousens. *The Architectural Antiquities of Northern Gujarat, Most Especially of the Districts Included in the Baroda State*, 1902; Reprint, Bhartiya Publishing House, Varanasi, 1975.
8. Burgess, James, *Report on the Antiquities of Kathiwad and Kachh*, 1874–75, Archaeological Survey of Western India, 1971.
9. Burgess, *Architectural Antiquities of Northern Gujarat*, Asiatic Society of Western India IX, ASI (NIS), XXXII, 1903a.
10. Burton-Page, John. *Ahmedabad*, ed. By George Michell and Snehal Shah, Bombay: Marg Publications, 1988.
11. Chaghatai, M.A., "Muslim Monuments of Ahmedabad through their Inscriptions", *Bulletin of Deccan College Research Institute*, Vol.III, 1941–42, pp.77–180.
12. Chaube, J., *History of the Gujarat Kingdom*. Munshilal Manoharlal Publication, 1973.
13. Commissariat, M.S., *A History of Gujarat, Including a Survey of its Chief Architectural Monuments and Inscriptions,* 2 Vols., Bombay and London, 1938.
14. Coomaraswamy, A., 'Transformations of Nature in Art', in Vatsyayan, K. (ed.), Indira Gandhi National Centre for the Arts, Sterling Publishers, New Delhi, 1995.
15. Cousens, H., *The Architectural Antiquities of Western India*, London, 1926.
16. Dehejia, Vidya, *Devi: The Great Goddess: Female Divinity in South Asian Art,* Washington D.C., Arthur M. Sackler Gallery, Smithsonian Institution, 1999.
17. Dehejia. Representing the Body: Gender Issues in Indian Art, Kali for Women; New Delhi, 1997.
18. Dosabhai, Edalji, *A History of Gujarat* from the earliest period to the present time. Asian Educational Services, New Delhi, 1986.
19. Enthoven, R.E. & A.M.T. Jackson, *Folklore of Gujarat*. Second Edition, Vintage Books, 1989.
20. Enthoven, R.E., *Folklore Notes,* Vol.1. Gujarat, Bombay, 1914.
21. Forbes, Alexander, Kinloch, *Ras Mala*, Vol.1, Oxford University Press: London, 1924.

22. Hope, T.C. & Furgusson, T.C. *Architecture of Ahmedabad*, 1866.
23. Foucault, Michel, "Space, Power and Knowledge," in *Cultural Studies Reader*, Routledge, London, 1999.
24. Gaudani, Harilal, "Panihari and Panisherdo" Lokgurjari, Vol.5, 1968. Gujarati Rajya Loksahitya Samiti, Ahmedabad, 1968.
25. Gaudani, Harilal, "Vadthal ni Vav" in *Mahagujarat na Shilpa ane Sthapatya*, pp.150–154, Ahmedabad, 1980.
26. *Gazetteer of the Bombay Presidency*, Vol.2, Surat and Bharuch, ed. R.M. Nilkanth, Bombay, 1888.
27. *Gazetteer of the Bombay Presidency*, Vol.3, Kathiawar, Bombay.
28. Goswami, Prangiri, "Kutch na Vav Kuva nu Sthapatya", Lokgurjari.
29. Harper, Katherine Anne, *Iconography of the Sapatamatrikas: Seven Hindu Goddeses of Spritual Transformation*, Edwin Mellen Press, 1989.
30. Howard, R.W., "Stepwells at Ahmedabad" *Architectural Review*, Sept 1967.
31. Jackson, A.M.T. & R.E. Enthoven, *Folklore of Gujarat*, Vintage Books, 1989.
32. Jadav, Joravarhsinh, *Prachin Bharat na Jala Vihara and Jalakuunda*, Ahmedabad, 2006, pp.48–54.
33. Jain-Neubauer, Jutta. *The Stepwells of Gujarat in Art—Historical Perspective*. New Delhi: Abhinav Publications, 1981Ahmedabad, 1957.
34. Kadikar, Yashwant, "Adalaj ni Vav", *Pathik*, Oct–Dec 2000.
35. Keith, A.B., *Religion & Philosophy of the Veda & Upanisad*, Harvard Oriental Series Vol.31, Cambridge, Mass., 1925.
36. Kumar, Savitri V., *The Pauranic Lore of Holy Water-Places: With Special Reference to Skanda Purana*, New Delhi: Munishiram Manoharlal, 1983.
37. Livingston, Morna, *Steps to Water: The Ancient Stepwells of India*, Princeton Architectural Press, 2002.
38. Livingston, Morna, "Temples for Water: The Stepwells of Western India", *Natural History*, May 2003.
39. Majumdar M.R., *Cultural History of Gujarat*, New York: Humanities Press, 1966.
40. Mankodi, Kirit, *The Queen's Stepwell at Patan*, Project for Indian Cultural Studies Publications, Bombay: Franco-Indian Research, 1991.
41. Marshall, John, *Cambridge History of India*, Vol.3, Cambridge University Press, 1928.
42. Masani, R.P., *Folklore of Wells, Being a Study of Water Worship in East and West*, Bombay, 1918.
43. Mehta, Mridulabehn, H. "Gujarat ni Kala Kushal Be Behno". *Pathik*, Sept–Oct 1973, pp.70–72.
44. Mehta, R.N. and Kantawala. "Bhoj ni Vav no Sheelalekh". *Swadhyaya*. Vol.16, pp.192–196, London: Oxford University Press, 1921, 3 Vols.
45. Merutunga, Acharya, *The Prabandha Cintamani or Wishing- Stone of Narratives*, (History of Chaulukya Kings of Anhilvad, Gujarat, 746–934 CE Published ca.1350 CE), Translated from Original Sanskrit by C.H. Tawney, Indian Book Gallery, Delhi, 1982.
46. Miller, B.S. (ed). *Exploring India's Sacred Art: Selected Writings of Stella Kramrisch*, University of Pennsylvania Press, Philadelphia, PA, 1983.

47. Mookerjee, Priya, *Pathway Icons: The Wayside Art of India*, Thames & Hudson, New York, 1987.
48. Moore, Charles, *Water and Architecture*, New York: Harry N. Abrams, 1994.
49. Pandya, Mahesh Chandra, "Uttar Gujarat ni Vavo: CE 942–1500, *Pathik,* Dipotsav Ank, Nov–Dec 1999, pp.87–100.
50. Parikh, Rasiklal Chotalal and Hariprasad G. Shastri, ed. B.J. Vidya Bhawan. *Gujaratno Rajakiya ane Sanskrutik Itihas.* Vol.4, Solanki Kala, ed. by B.J. Institute, 2005.
51. Parmar, Khodidas, *Folksongs of Gujarat*, Sahitya Academy, Delhi.
52. Pathak, Ramanlal, *Gujarat na Jalashayo*, M.S. University, Baroda, 1997.
53. Raja Dinkar Kelkar Museum. *Birds and Animals in Indian Art and Crafts,* Raja Dinkar Kelkar Museum, Poona, 1985.
54. Rawal, Mukund. "Gujarat na Vav-kuva", July 1973, pp.53–63.
55. Rousselet, Louis, *India and Its Native Provinces: Travels in Central India and the Presidencies of Bombay and Bengal*, New York: Scribner, 1876.
56. Sadani, Jaikishandas, *Underground Shrine: Queen's Stepwell at Patan*, B.J. Institute of Learning and Research: Ahmadabad, 1998.
57. Sandesara, B.J. ed., *Mirat-i-Ahmadi: A Persian History of Gujarat*, Gaekwad Oriental Series No.146, 1965.
58. Sankaliya, H.D., *The Archeology of Gujarat*, Bombay: Natwarlal & Co., 1941, 1991.
59. Shastri, Hariprasad G., "Gujarat ni Prachin Vavo," *Gujarat Diwali Issue*, no.2020, 1964, pp.286–288.
60. Shastri, Hariprasad G., *Gujaratno Rajkiya ane Sanskrutik Itihas* (Chaulukyas of Gujarat: History and Culture of Gujarat During the Chaulukya Period), B.J. Institute, Ahmedabad, 2005.
61. Sivaramamurti, C., *Approach to Nature in Indian Art and Thought*, Kanak Publications, New Delhi, 1980.
62. Valand, Narottam, "Gujarat ni Vavo", *Gujarat Dipotsavi*, 2000.
63. Yagnik, Hasu, *Folklore of Gujarat*, trans. by Dr. N.M. Kansara, National Book Trust, India, 2002.

— x —

Sacred groves among the Jaintia community of Meghalaya in Northeast India: a case of the Thadmuthlong and Mukhla *Khloo Blai* (sacred groves)

Evelinda Suchiang

Abstract

Sacred groves among the Jain community of Meghalaya in Northeast India have a deep rooted religious significance which is tied to the notion of the relationship between man and nature. The present paper thus attempts to discuss the sacred groves of West Jaintia Hills District of Meghalaya with reference to Thadmuthlong and Mukhla villages in an attempt to draw into historical perspectives the myths of origin on such beliefs about natural landscapes and the socio-cultural beliefs, taboos and various ritual practices associated with the sacred groves and further attempts to explore the consequent role of women in such traditional practices since ancient times.

Sacred groves among the Jaintia community of Meghalaya in Northeast India have a deep rooted religious significance which is tied to the notion of the relationship between man and nature. The origin of such a tradition perhaps dates back to pre-agrarian times and with the advent of agriculture, it was necessary for indigenous communities to manage and protect their forests from indiscriminate slash and burn. In addition to the State legislative measures to protect the forest of Meghalaya, what is noteworthy is the persistence of such belief systems that entails the protection and conservation of these virgin forests by means of traditional customary practices and societal laws that stress on the sacredness of the forests, and hence ensuring the protection of the groves. In Jaintia matrilineal society, individual land is owned by the mother and thereafter inherited by her daughters. However, in the case of the sacred groves or *khloo blai*, they are held jointly by the whole village under the leadership of the *Doloi*. The present paper thus attempts to discuss the sacred groves of West Jaintia Hills District of Meghalaya with reference to Thadmuthlong and Mukhla villages in an attempt to draw into historical perspectives the myths of origin on such beliefs about natural landscapes and the socio-cultural beliefs, taboos and various ritual practices associated with the sacred groves.

Sacred groves are forest fragments of varying sizes, which are communally protected, and which usually have a significant religious connotation for the protecting community. The country with the highest number of sacred groves is said to be India but these forests are dwindling due to various reasons.[1] The concepts of "sacred" and "nature" have long been interlinked. Various cultural aspects such as religion, faith and traditions act to bring people closer to nature. Sacred groves are one such example, which have a deep-rooted significance to a community and it is seen that such groves are left undisturbed due to abiding beliefs.[2] By definition, sacred groves refer to tracts of usually virgin forests of varying sizes which are communally protected, and which usually have a significant religious connotation for protecting the community.[3] Biologically they are rich patches of undisturbed forests and serve as a natural habitat for many endemic, rare, primitive and economically valuable plants along with a good number of wild animals, birds, reptiles, amphibians, variety of butterflies and insects Sociologically they signify many aspects of the society such as religious and cultural beliefs. Hunting and logging are usually strictly prohibited within these patches.

In many societies, if not all, such areas are protected, not by state legislation but by societal laws. These laws stress on the sacredness of the groves, thereby leading to their protection. Many societies live close to nature and their life is largely influenced by its forces which becomes a part of their life and is interwoven in their socio-cultural beliefs. The local communities establish rules that vary from grove to grove: these often prohibit the felling of trees and the killing of animals, but do allow for the collection of firewood, fodder, and medicinal plants.

The people of Meghalaya believe that the sacred groves are the abode of deities. The sacred grove serve as sites for several social and cultural rituals and religious ceremonies. In Khasi hills the sacred groves are of three kinds:[4]

---

[1] see Chandrakanth et al., 2004.

[2] see Marak and Ghimire, 2012.

[3] see Gadgil and Vartak, 1975.

[4] Tiwari et al., 1998.

1) Law Lyngdoh are the groves ruled by the priest Lyngdoh.

2) Law Niam are the places of traditional religion Niam trai.

3) Law Kyntang are the groves where the area is under control of the village headman.

In Jaintia, sacred groves are known as Khlaw U Blei or Khloo Blai, while in Garo they are known as Asong Khosi. The sacred groves bestow the welfare of the people, their cattle & land, and keep the evil spirits away. Those who do not obey the traditional norms of these groves may have to face the wrath of the deity. A religious belief is one of the major factors for conservation of plant resources in such groves. Local people believe that the deities would be offended if trees are cut and twigs, flowers, flowers fruits, etc. are plucked carelessly. These groves are considered as one of the most species-rich areas for plants, birds, and mammals. The mythological stories and indigenous knowledge associated with the groves have been the principal factor in preserving the sacred groves in an immaculate condition.

Historical background of the community

The present study is based on empirical data acquired from Thadmuthlong and Mukhla Nongrim villages in Jaintia Hills District of Meghalaya in May and June 2018. The district lies between 25°3'North and 25°45'North latitude and 91°59' East and 92°45' East longitude and covers an area of 3819 square kilometers. Thadmuthlong village, is located towards the east of Jowai town, the headquarters of the district, on the Jowai Garampani Road which is about 15 kilometers from Jowai towards Garampani Kupli hydro project. A qualitative research method was used employing interviews and participant observation.

The family[5] is the smallest and most important social unit, followed by clan.[6] It is believed that there were three sisters searching for livelihood thereby came to settle in Jaintia hills. Their names were *Chai, Doh* and *Wa* hailing from Nongstoin side West Khasi Hills Khasi. Chai settled in a place now called Tuber. *Wa* settled in the present Ialong and *Doh* settled in a particular place known as *Chnongrim* where the sacred groves of the Thadmuthlong exists now. Her clan is known as *Lyngdoh.* Later on the *Lyngdoh* clan was joined by other clans such as *Papiah, Kanai*, *Tang* and *Suchiang* from different places.

Due to frequent wars and fightings, the village was forced to shift to another location called Muthlongrim very close to Shangpung for

---

[5] *chi-yung.*

[6] *kur.*

security sake. From there they cultivated rice in a more fertile area nearby. Slowly they settled near their own paddy fields so that it is easier for them to take good care of their crops. In this way they settled in a third village called *Thadmuthlong* the present one. The population of Thadmuthlong is about 7000 comprising of 1000 households. Its area is about 8 sq. kilometers. The term Jaintia is used to denote various groups of people inhabiting West and East Jaintia Hills, viz Pnar, Bhoi, Hadem, War, Lalung, and Biate. The village is inhabited by the Pnars and they have their own dialect. There are two religions here namely the Niamtre[7] and the Christians. The latter are just a handful and the Niamtres are almost 900 families. Thadmuthlong village is being looked as one of the strongest villages in preserving the indigenous beliefs viz *Niamtre* religion. People from other villages come to Thadmuthlong to get directions from God in the names of Shyngkhan, Blai Kupli, Ram Lakhon etc though through human beings who are not themselves during such moments called *Hiarblai*. During such times people ask questions about what is going on and directions as to how to live their daily lives and do their different activities. The conscience of the people is thin. They are God fearing in general with a few exceptions. The Pnar indigenous religion is termed as *Ka Niam* but with the coming of Christianity the word Tre (original) was added. Thus Ka Niam became *Ka Niam Tre*. The Pnar has one Supreme Being known as Blai (God). Like two sides of the coin, one of His sides is known as *U Blai Wa Booh Wa Thoo* or U Tre Kirot (God the Creator) and on the other side Ka Blai Shynchar (the goddess who rules). The other parts of the Supreme Being just like the different parts of the body are deitified in a number of smaller deities. Thus Ka Blai Kupli would refer to the goddess of the Kupli river, and U Blai Lum would refer to the God of the hills ('lum' meaning 'hills').

Sacred groves of Thadmuthlong and Mukhla Raij

Mukhla Nongrim is a village situated 3 km away from the sub-headquarter Thadlaskein and 10 km away from the district headquarter, Jowai. The sacred grove *(khloo blai),* of Thadmuthlong, is in *Chnongrim* (where the first village was) and the Mukhla *Khlooblai* is right in the heart of a Village called Mukhla Nongrim lage. The *Khloo Blais* are being looked after by the villagers, both Niamtre and Christians in Thadmuthlong in case the same is being attacked by any one but in Mukhla it is being looked after only by the *Niamtres*. Normally the land

[7] indigenous believers.

belongs to the lady since it is a matrilineal society but with regards to *Khlooblai* the land belongs to the community as a whole. But ladies have an important role to play at home. All things required for the rituals are being prepared by the ladies. Before the rituals take place meetings are being held in the house of the lady and ladies have the freedom to give their opinions. Thadmuthlong *Khlooblai* is about 30 acres in area. Its location is to the south of the main village. There are of varieties of trees and shrubs here. Like any other village in Meghalaya the *Thadmuthlong* and *Mukhla* too, believe that God resides in the *Khlooblai,* and for this reason no one is permitted to cause damage to them by lumbering or indulging in any injurious activity. Some of the observances in the grove include the following:

1. A visitor to the forest should not cause any damage to the flora and fauna. He/she can only admire its beauty. Even plucking a flower or cutting a branch is strictly forbidden.
2. All kinds of littering like throwing garbage or urinating is strictly forbidden. Such acts are considered an insult to the guardian spirits of the forest and as such the culprits would be punished.
3. Anyone who visits these sacred grounds should observe decency. Use of foul language is considered a taboo, as well as having impure and evil thoughts while one is inside these places.

Rituals at Khloo Blai

Thadmuthlong village is being looked as one of the strongest villages in preserving the indigenous beliefs viz *Niamtre* religion. People from other villages come to Thadmuthlong to get directions from God. Presently *Blai Kupli* speaks to the people of Thadmuthlong and other villagers through a woman named *Smt Ioi* from the clan *Tang*. The *Kupli* chooses her due to her holiness. *Shyngkhan* is a male deity but presently he speaks to the people through a woman whose name is *Smt Ongbha* From the clan *Papiah*. *Ram* and *Lakhon* are also male deities speaking to the people presently through a woman again by the name Smt. Ri from the clan Lyngdoh. Beef consumption is prohibited by Kupli, *Shyngkhan*, Ram and Lakhon. If anyone disobeys the directions of the deities they pay the price for their own actions. Normally people of this village do not face any natural calamities, nor attacked by any gundas because the deities are protecting the village. So we are safe so far.

For the welfare of the village *two* rituals are being performed in the *khlooblais* in both the villages i.e. Thadmuthlong and Mukhla Raij. For the Thadmuthlong, before performing the rituals, the Langdoh (priest) seeks directions from *Shyngkhan, Kupli, Ram* and *Lakhon*. Accordingly they will be told about their days not dates and the materials needed for the rituals. The days are counted as *Musiang, Muchai, Pyngkat Wanpyngkat Muksow, Khyllaw, Pynsin and Mulong*. The rituals must be performed on Pyngkat of a particular month and week of whichever God wants.

(1) *Thoh-Langdoh* is a ritual being performed in the month of March–April before sowing seeds i.e before agriculture starts. It is believed that *Blai* will protect the seeds from being eaten by pests and rodents, make them sprout and grow abundantly.

(2) *Khie-ator* is a ritual performed in the month of August–September before harvesting sets in so that God protects the crops from damage by insects and natural calamities and bestow a bountiful harvest for the people.

In *Mukhla Raij* the names of the rituals are (1) *Ka Knia Syiem Khlam Ram Shyllong* performed in the month of March and August. (2) *Ka Knia Ryngkaw* (*Thoh Lyngdoh*) performed in the month of April. The purposes of both the rituals are almost the same as that of Thadmuthlong.

Although there are works on the sacred groves of the Khasis[8] and comparative studies between the Meghalaya sacred forest and African forest,[9] except for the work by Marak and Ghimire (2012) nothing is much is written about the Jaintia sacred forest. Since the traditional religion or *Niamtre* still persist among the locals, there is a continuing reverence for these forests at the study sites. All rituals conducted in the sacred forest seems to be linked to reasons such as these. Such rituals are linked to the welfare of the local community offering prosperity, wealth and protection from diseases and attacks from neighbouring villages. They are performed for the protection to crops (from pests and droughts and to ensure a rich harvest), of domestic livestocks, from water such as water borne diseases, drowning and other natural calamities.

Presently there are over 100 prominent community forests in the state, of which only 41 have been declared as Community Conserved Areas (CCAs). Remaining forests and sacred grooves are reportedly facing increasing threats from commercial exploitation of bio-resources and unsustainable *jhum* especially on steeper slopes. However, their conservation status has not been ascertained. Recently, Meghalaya Forest Department has listed as many as 125 sacred groves in the state

[8] see Jeeva et al., 2006; Samati and Gogoi 2007; Kharkongor and Tiwari 2017.

[9] Ormsby, 2012.

including those which need to be recognized and notified.[10] Although sacred groves are declared under the United Khasi and Jaintia Hills Autonomous District (Management and Control of Forests) Act, 1958 and Garo Hills Autonomous District (Management and Control of Forests) Act 1961 yet these forest has fragmented in size and extent. Many communities lost their customary rights of forest management to the government that led to dwindling of sacred areas.[11] Tiwari et al. (1998) and Khan et al. (2008) suggest the problems pertaining to management of sacred grooves in Meghalaya. The erosion of traditional conservation practices, and neglect of religious beliefs towards nature have been the major reasons for loss and degradation of sacred groves. Economic factors particularly poverty, socio-cultural changes, loss of traditional ways of resource use are the other factors. In addition, whatever sacred forest now survives in the Jaintia Hills is due to the practice of the old traditional religion that continues that conversely played an important role in biodiversity conservation. As reported by MBSAP (2017), there is no institutional mechanism to monitor or assess the status of community forests, enhance awareness and education programs for communities. Better awareness and education can play a vital role in sustainable forest use, which can provide continued benefits to communities. The community in the study area perceive the sacred forest as part of their identity and are struggling hard to have access to government support to protect the surviving forest of the region for the promotion of tourism. The strict customary laws maintained by the villages have also resulted in the conservation of a wide diversity of flora and fauna. With effective conservation support from the government through a community resource management framework, such sacred groves may offer great potential for ecotourism in the region in *Thadmuthlong and Mukhla Nongrim* and the region as whole.

References

1. Chandrakanth, M.G., M.G. Bhat & M.S., Accavva, 2004, Socio-economic changes and sacred groves in South India: protecting a community-based resource management institution, *Natural Resources Forum* 28: 102–111.
2. Gadgil, M. and V.D. Vartak, 1975, Sacred groves of India: A plea for continued conservation, *Journal of Bombay Natural History Society* 72 (2): 313–320.
3. Jeeva, S., B.P. Mishra, N. Venugopal, L. Kharlukhi and R.C. Lalo, 2006. Traditional knowledge and biodiversity conservation in the sacred groves of Meghalaya, *Indian Journal of Traditional Knowledge* 5 (4): 563–568.

[10] see MBSAP, 2017.

[11] Marak and Ghimire, 2012:346.

4. Khan, M.L., A.D. Khumbongmayum and R.S. Tripathi, R.S. 2008. The sacred groves and their significance in conserving biodiversity: an overview, *International Journal of Ecology and Environmental Sciences* 34(3), 277–291.
5. Kharkongor, B.M and B.K. Tiwari. 2017. Sacred groves of Meghalaya: A Review, *International Journal of Science and Research* 6 (3):346–349.
6. Marak, Q and S. Ghimire. 2012. How sacred are *Khloo Blai*? A look into the Pnar Jaintia concept of sacred groves, *The Eastern Anthropologists* 65 (3–4):339–354.
7. *Meghalaya State Biodiversity Strategy and Action Plan (MBSAP) 2017.* Wildlife Institute of India.
8. Ormsby, A. 2012. Perceptions of Tourism at Sacred Groves in Ghana and India, *Recreation and Society in Africa, Asia and Latin America* 3 (1):1–18.
9. Samati, H. and R. Gogoi. 2007. Sacred groves in Meghalaya, *Current Science* 93 (10):1338–39.
10. Meghalaya State Biodiversity Strategy and Action Plan (MBSAP) 2017. Wildlife Institute of India.
11. Tiwari, B.K., S.K. Barik and R.S. Tripathi, 1998, Biodiversity value, status, and strategies for conservation of sacred groves of Meghalaya, India, *Ecosystem Health* 4(1):20–32.

Oral Sources

Interview with Buhlut Suna, 40 yrs old, Raij Mukhla elder, Mukhla Nongrim village: 9th May 2018.

Wanbha Lyngdoh 37 yrs old, Priest cum Secretary of Raij Mukhla, Mukhla Nongrim village: 16th May 2018.

Ruhi Tang one of the ladies who knows and lives her religion well: 27 May 20–18.

Anthony Lyngdoh 60 years old, Headman-cum-Advisor of Raij Muthlong, Thadmuthlong Village: 3rd June, 2018.

Kol Suchiang 65 years old, the priest of the Suchiang clan: 21st June, 2018.

Paucity of Coinage in Early Medieval India: A Reappraisal

Gautam Jantakal and *Purnanand Sanket*

Abstract

This research papers examines the proposed paucity in metallic coinage as suggested by Sharma, the methodologies applied thereon and its shortfalls. Newer methodologies are adopted to evaluate coin volumes. Additionally, relevant data gleaned from contemporary epigraphs, coinage and literature are utilized. The research presented in this paper is currently limited to Deccan India and it does not address the implications of the new outlook on the broader theories of declining overseas trade, de urbanisation and feudalism. The authors then adopt newer methodologies; present relevant data gleaned from contemporary epigraphs, coinage and literature and thereby propose a newer outlook on the stated paucity.

Since its invention, coinage has served mankind in an unprecedented way. Coins have eased trade and commerce, enabled simpler taxation and book keeping. Coins have brought large geographies together in a common exchange network, thereby promoting not only commerce but also cultural and social exchanges. Long after its circulation life, coins from the past are today important sources of history, be it political, economic, religious or cultural. This is particularly true for India where there are no continuous written historical records prior to the 12th Century CE.

While studying coins as a source of history, two sets of attributes of a coin have to be considered. One is its intrinsic attributes such as the coin's motifs, legends, typology, weight, dimensions, fabric, metal, purity. These parameters shed light on the political, economic, religious and cultural history of the issuing dynasty as well as the degree of technological expertise in metallurgy. The other set is the extrinsic attributes of a coin such as the coin's provenance (i.e find spot) and volume of mintage. These parameters shed light on the geographical extent of rule/influence as well as the degree of monetization. More the volume of mintage, more is the degree of monetization and vice-versa. However, the volume of mintage during ancient and medieval periods is not readily available to us, hence a systematic and scientific study of the available coins in museums and private collections has to be conducted to deduce coin volumes. In the work on early Indian medieval society, it has been stated by Sharma[1] that a paucity in metallic coinage existed in early medieval India, particularly during 500–1000 CE. This has been subsequently used to support his theory of declining overseas trade and the resulting de urbanisation and birth of feudal mode of agricultural production. This research paper aims to examine the proposed paucity in metallic coinage.

Findings of Sharma and Research methodology adopted

In his work, Sharma[2] has suggested that a paucity of metallic coinage existed in almost all dynasties of early medieval India, including the Deccan.

"By and large, after the sixth century, for about 400 years the south Indian dynasties seem to have discarded the practice of issuing coins. A careful study of coin finds in the Deccan and south India shows very little metal money after the sixth century. Between AD 600 and AD 1000 we witness the rule of the Pallavas, Pandyas, the Badami Calukyas and the Colas, but very few coins can be attributed to them."

For determining early medieval coinage volumes, Sharma has mainly used coins available from museums across the country. This approach however has some shortcomings, in that, the dataset gleaned from museums tend to be skewed owing to its subjectivity such as personal choices, eye appeal, availability, financial budgets etc. Additionally, no die studies were conducted to calculate number of unique dies and in turn extrapolate coin volumes. Lastly, references to coins from contemporary inscriptions were not utilised to understand coin usage scenarios, possible coin volumes and instances of coin re-melting.

One of the early works which debated on Sharma's postulations was of Deyell.[3] He perceives that Indian numismatists have focused mostly on collecting, identifying and attribution of coins based on coin appearance, metrology, metal type and script. He goes on to suggest that

---

[1] Sharma, R.S., 2003:126.

[2] Sharma, R.S., 2003:128.

[3] Deyell, John, 1990.

the methodology used in regards to coinage studies should also be based on sources of metal, area and period of circulation and most importantly, should also calculate the volume of coins in the context of time and space. Deyell's work gives a numismatic perspective of early medieval India based on coin hoards and its analysis. But the main focus of his study is the period 11th to 13th century CE. Also, he concentrates more on the coinage of central and north India like the *Gadhaiya* paisa, *Laxmi* type gold coins and the bull and horseman type billon coins. His study has however gives us a great deal of numerical data for the period and geography he has focused. Using Deyell's studies, it was concluded by subsequent scholars that there was a *revival* of coinage post the 10th Century CE. Bhandare[4] delves further into this subject by listing many coinage series which existed between the 6th to 10th century CE across the Indian sub-continent. In Deccan India, he lists various important coinages, eg. *Krishnaraja Rupakas* in Maharashtra, *Vishnukundin* fabric coins of the bull type and *Rashtrakuta* coins. In *Karnataka* and *Andhra*, he mentions that there was a long series of the lion type *Vishnukundin* typology coins issued by the eastern *Chalukyas* with the inscribed coins of this type bear the *brahmi* legend *Vishamasiddhi*. He has provided inscriptional evidences for some of the coin series. Thus Bhandare concludes that there was no paucity of coinage in the early medieval period. He further highlights the need to employ numismatic methodologies such as die analysis and typological studies for any research being undertaken on circulating coin volumes. Bracey[5] has reiterated the methodologies which were earlier suggested by Deyell and Bhandare. He has chosen his scope of study to a couple of centuries i.e. 6th and 7th Century CE and for north India. He suggests that there must have been a partially demonetized economy in this period where in some of the transactions became barter and there were also land grants. The coins which were earlier in circulation must have continued in this period. Additionally, crude issues of the familiar *Kumaragupta* and *Skandagupta* coins must have been minted in large numbers during this period which needs to be classified as posthumous issues. Bracey agrees with Deyell but then moves a step further and opines that hoard analysis as to the type of coins in a hoard, die analysis of a particular type of coin which circulated for a long time and the mentions of such coins in inscriptions should be considered which would yield a more holistic view on coin volumes and hence the economy of that period. To

---

[4] Bhandare, Shailendra, 2015:159.

[5] Bracey, Robert, 2017.

summarise, the above scholars have all highlighted the need for newer numismatic methodologies to extrapolate coin volumes for any particular time period.

New Data presented by the Authors in the context of early medieval Deccan coinage

Before going into the new research data, it would be relevant to have a quick survey of the political landscape of early medieval Deccan. The complete demise of the *Satavahana* Empire in 3rd Century CE resulted in smaller kingdoms making an appearance. The *Vishnukundin* dynasty controlled a large part of Deccan and *Orissa* in the 5th and 6th Centuries. Their copper alloy coins are characterized by a lion on obverse and these coins circulated in large parts of the Deccan region. The *Vishnukundins* were ultimately defeated by *Pulakesin* II of the *Badami Chalukyas*. His brother *Kubja Vishnuvardana* was appointed the governor of this region in 624 CE. In the conquered regions, these *Chalukya* kings issued coins which were similar to the earlier *Vishnukundin* coins. The later rulers of *Vengi* became independent and this branch is called eastern *Chalukyas* (*Chalukyas* of *Vengi*) and they continued to use the lion motif on their coins.

The *Kalachuris* with their capital at *Mahismati* (*Malwa*) rose in the 6th century and controlled large parts of *Gujarat*, *Madhya Pradesh* and *Maharashtra*. Their most well known coins are the *Krishnaraja* silver *Drammas/Rupakas*. These coins are characterized by the bust of king on obverse and a bull along with name of king i.e. *Krishnaraja* on reverse. The *Kalachuris* thus followed the pattern of the earlier *Gupta* coins which were present in the region. Their reign came to an end in the 7th Century when they were defeated by the *Chalukyas* of *Badami*. Regarding the coinage of the *Badami Chalukyas*, only a few gold coins are known. To summarise, the major powers in the Deccan in the 6th Century were the *Kalachuris* and the *Badami Chalukyas* which controlled a major portion of Deccan India.

The *Kadambas* of *Banavasi* came into power in the early 4th Century CE after the demise of the *Satavahana* rule. They were the contemporaries of the western *Gangas* and have issued a large number of coins in potin alloy. The *Kadambas* of *Banavasi* were defeated by *Pulakesin* I in the 6th Century CE.

The imperial *Rashtrakutas* were initially feudatories to the *Badami Chalukyas* but they gained independence under *Dandidurga* around mid 8th Century. It was earlier thought that they have not issued any coins but during the last decade, many inscribed coins in silver and copper have come to light which have been attributed to the *Rashtrakutas*. Some of them have been conclusively attributed to *Dhruva Dharavarsha*, *Krishna* II *Shubatunga* by Bhandare. Additionally there is a range of uninscribed silver *drammas* and copper units which are also typologically attributed to the *Rashtrakutas*. These typically bear a seated *garuda* on the obverse and an elephant rider on the reverse. *Rashtrakutas* were defeated by the Western *Chalukyas* in the later part of 10th Century CE.

The Western *Gangas* started their rule in *Kolar* in the 5th Century CE and later shifted their capital to *Talakad*. They minted their own coins in gold which has elephant on the obverse and a flower scroll on the reverse. They were feudatories of the *Badami Chalukyas* and later ruled as feudatories of the *Rashtrakutas*. Their rule came to an end in the 10th Century CE when they were defeated by the *Cholas*.

With this political background of early medieval Deccan, the authors now set out to apply the newer numismatic methodologies to some of the coinages of this period. Additionally, the authors will extensively use contemporary inscriptions that refer to coins and its usage. The research has been carried out under five streams, namely, Die Studies, Typological Continuations, Borrowed Coins, Coin Usage Scenarios and Metal reuse for new coinage.

'Die' Studies

Coins in the early medieval period were mostly die struck and rarely casted or punch marked. The dies used for manufacturing these coins were metallic and handmade (as against machine made) and hence each die had a degree of uniqueness to it. Additionally, each die also had a life expectancy which depended on the metal it was used upon. Dies for gold coins had the longest life and then came silver and copper. By studying the coins currently available, the number of dies can be derived. Assuming a suitable life span for the die, the total number of coins minted can be extrapolated. European estimates show that for silver coins, about 5000 coins can be struck from a die pair (obverse and reverse die) until one of the die breaks. The same estimate will be used in the following case study.

Case Study: Until the year 2000, no coins were definitely attributable to the *Rashtrakutas*. However as of today, we known many coin types of the *Rashtrakutas*, both inscribed and uninscribed. For the current case study, one particular *Rashtrakuta* coin type with legend *Gunatunga* is taken up for die studies. The following illustration shows a collection of eighteen *Gunatunga* coin obverses, all struck from different dies. This dataset has been gathered from accessible coin images of auction houses and private collections.Extrapolating from these eighteen different dies, we end up with a coin count of $18 \times 5{,}000 = 90{,}000$ coins. And this is just one coin variety. Today, we know as much as forty different *Rashtrakuta* coin varieties across gold, silver and copper coinage albeit gold coins are very rare. So the total number of *Rashtrakuta* coins that can be extrapolated from known specimens is numerous.

Die studies are imperative to understand coin volumes. Till the year 2000, we hardly had a single coin that can be conclusively attributable to the *Rashtrakutas*. Now with the help of die studies, we know at least 90,000 coins could have been minted for the coin variety under question. And this is only a conservative figure considering the fact that there are many more coins of this variety to be discovered and attributed. And if this exercise is to be done to all known coin varieties, then the overall extrapolated coin mintage would be substantial.

Typological Continuations

A popular coin type that was issued usually stays on in circulation for a long time albeit in a degraded design. This is in line with the *Law of Numismatic Continuity* and can be seen in various coinages and across different time periods. Thus, there presents an opportunity to study popular coin types and based on the degree of degradation, assign the degraded coins a time period which is much later than the time when these coin types were originally issued. This then spreads the coin volumes of the particular coin type across a wider time zone and helps to come up with a more accurate deduction of the coin volumes for any specific time period.

***Case Study*:** The *Vishnukundins* controlled large parts of Deccan India between the 5th and 7th Centuries. They issued copper alloy coins in various weight standards. These coins usually had a lion with paw raised on the obverse and a *Kalasha* (sacred pot) with lamp stands on the reverse and they circulated for nearly two hundred years. When *Pulakesin* II defeated the *Vishnukundins* and captured their territories, he issued copper alloy coins similar to the *Vishnukundin* style which was already in circulation. He added his epithet *Satyashraya* written in *brahmi* script on top of the lion. His brother *Kubja Vishnuvardhana* was appointed as viceroy of the newly captured territories and he must have become independent after *Pulakesin* II was killed in battle with the *Pallavas*. On *Vishnuvardhana's* coins. we see the legend *Vishamasiddhi* written in *brahmi* on top of the lion. A wide number of uninscribed coins of different weight standards of the similar design and fabric are also known. Over a period of time the coins become crude in terms of representation of lion which became more of a series of dots for the head and mane of the lion. Some other coins from this region with the same coin fabric depict a bull on the obverse instead of the lion. They are thought to be issued by the *Pallavas* who had captured the *Vengi* territories.

The *Vishnukindin* coins were very popular over large parts of Deccan India. To maintain this acceptability among the masses of the former *Vishnukundin* territory, the eastern *Chalukyas* minted their coins in the prevailing pattern with minor additions i.e. the additions of the rulers name. These can be assigned to the time period 7th Century CE with the help of the legends. We however also see a large number of crude variations of these eastern *Chalukya* coins of which the crudest coins could be tentatively assigned towards the fag end of the dynasty i.e. 10 Century CE. Thus it could be suggested that eastern *Chalukya* coins were emitted for more than three hundred years. On the same lines, detailed coin volume studies of any popular coinage would need to partition the coin volumes based on degree of degradation or crudeness that the coins exhibit.

Borrowed Coins

Coin types with good and consistent metal fineness enjoy acceptability of the masses and tend to be used across political entities and time periods.

***Case Study*:** The *Anjaneri* (State: *Maharashtra*) plates[6] of *Bhogasakti* dated to early 8th Century CE tells about taxes to be levied at various places which correspond to places in and around current day *Nasik* district. The copper plate engraving talks about taxes to be paid in *rupakas* and mentions taxes from villages to be collected in *Krishnaraja rupaka*. *Krishnaraja* was a *Kalachuri* king who ruled parts of present day *Maharashtra, Gujarat* and *Madhya Pradesh* in the later part of 6th Century CE. His silver coins followed the pattern of the *Guptas* and featured a bull on the reverse.

The *Krishnaraja rupakas* were silver coins with consistent fineness. It can be inferred from the above mentioned *Anjaneri* plates that these coins were very popular and widely used by the *Badami Chalukyas* even 200 years after the issuer's reign. So any exercise to understand the monetization of the *Badami Chalukyas* or for that matter any coinage series should also consider such instances of borrowed coin usage.

[6] Padigar, Shrinivas V., 2010:179.

Coin Usage Scenarios

Early medieval period provides us with a lot of copper plates. Although most of these talk about land donations, there are also quite a good number of them that additionally talk about fees to priests, taxes and tolls being collected in cash in the form of gold and silver coins. This has a very important bearing to understand the degree of monetization of that period.

Case Study: *Rashtrakuta* copper plate inscriptions[7] talk about coin names such as *Gadyanas*, *Drammas*, *Kalanju, Pana, Suvarna*. These coins were used in monetary transactions such as fees to priestly class, donations for poor and for taxes. These usages are possible only when the coins are minted in sufficient volumes. A statistical analysis on number of occurrences for each type of coin usage i.e. fees, donations, taxes is herewith presented to give a sense of the degree of coin monetization.

Coin Usage Scenario	Details	Name of the Coin	Number of References
Donation to Temples	Temple Diety Poojas	*Gadyana*	1
	Fees to Priests	*Gadyana*	1
	General Temple or *Basadi* offerings	*Gadyana, Dramma, Suvarna, Kalanju*	13
	Lamp oil for Temple	*Gadyana*	1
	Food offerings to Diety	*Gadyana*	1
	Fruit basket to *Basadi*	*Pana*	1
Donation to Brahmins	General offerings	*Gadyana, Dramma, Suvarna*	3
	By Village Headman	*Gadyana*	1
Donation to Beggars	Clothes to Beggars	*Dramma* (Gold)	1
	Financial Aid to Beggars in difficulty	*Dramma*(Gold)	1
	Religious books to beggars	*Dramma*(Gold)	1
	General offerings to Beggars	*Dramma*(Gold), *Dramma*	2
Tariffs , Taxes, Fines	Payment to local administrators	*Dramma, Pana*	2
	Fines for breaking rules	*Dramma*	1
	Tax collection	*Dramma*	1
	Property Tax	*Kalanju*	1
Loans	Loan from temple	*Kalanju*	1

[7] Bharathi, B.R., 2011.

Few important coinage references gleaned *Rashtrakuta* copper plate inscriptions: Land purchase tax of forty gold *Kalanjus* was nullified by a buyer Ammadevi when she purchased land for a temple. This shows that there was a practice of collecting land tax in coins.

A loan of forty gold *Kalanjus* was obtained by a group of people from the temple treasury. This shows that loans were offered in coins.

There was a tulabhara of *Govinda* IV during his accession to the throne. During that time, eight hundred villages, four lakh *Suvarnas* and thirty two lakh *Drammas* were donated to the diety. Additionally, 600 Agraharas and 3 Lakh Suvarnas were donated to Brahmins.

Contemporary *Rashtrakuta* Inscriptions have yielded a good number of references of coin usage for different scenarios of every day commerce, important being taxes, loans and donations. Four different coin names in gold and silver metals are referred. All these are clear indications of a well monetized economy.

Metal reuse for New Coinage

While we have sufficient evidences of a good degree of coins monetization from contemporary inscriptions, the question arises as to why these coins are extremely rare today. While there may be several factors to this, one important factor that can be gleaned again from inscriptions is the reusability of metal from older coins to mint current coinage.

Case Study: An interesting inscription is present at the *Kumaraswami* Temple, *Kudatini*, *Bellary* District.[8] It is dated to 1098 CE during the reign of the *Chalukya* king *Tribuvanamalla*. It tells about certain goldsmiths who are engaged in converting *Lokkiponnu* into *Navilaponnu* and the weight should correspond to the latter coins. The name *Navilaponnu* was given as the coin has an image of a peacock. The remnant gold after reminting was to be made to twelve *Gadyanas* every year and offered to the Lord *Kumaraswami*. We can deduce that the *Lokkiponnu* had a higher weight standard to the *Navilaponnu* (*Navilaponnu* about eight tenth's of *Lokkiponnu*). The *Lokkiponnus* are thought to have been minted at *Lokkigundi* which is a small town currently in *Gadag* district, *Karnataka*. The town today has ruins of as many as fifty temples and was an important town during the *Kalyani Chalukyas*.

The *Kumaraswami* Temple inscription gives us an insight on how these coins were melted and reused and each region had coins of

[8] Sastri, Shama R., 1939:164.

varying weight standard which necessitated the reminting of coins for use in a particular region. It can be inferred that there were many mints which were producing gold coins.

Interestingly, the *Kurugodu* inscription[9] of *Satyashraya Pulakesin* II talks about the established system of currency and mentions the *Naviluponnu* to be used for transactions. This was the gold coin which was the *current currency* in and around *Bellary* region. The *Naviluponnu* must have been a popular coin in the *Bellary* region from the 7th to 11th century but hardly any coins exist today. This must be due to the reminting of coins which was very prevalent as can be gleaned from the previously mentioned 11th century inscription of king *Tribuvanamalla*. The later dynasties like the *Hoysalas* and *Yadavas* must have used these coins for reminting their own gold coins which has led to the *Naviluponnu* to become a rare coin.

There was not a single series of coins being circulated in a kingdom. There was a localized currency system in which coins of varying fineness and types were being minted and used at major trading centres. When such coins were to be used in another regional trading centre, they were exchanged with the local currency and were subsequently melted to make the local currency. The *Naviluponnu* was popular and seem to have been minted for a long time. But, this is now a rare coin and very few seen. Thus, it can be inferred that these *Naviluponnu* coins must have been melted in large quantities by the subsequent dynasties like the *Hoysalas* and *Yadavas* to mint coins for funding trade, commerce and expansion of their kingdoms.

In the above case studies, the application of proven numismatic methodologies to known coinages as well as references to contemporary inscriptions have demonstrated that early medieval coinage was prolific and also not bereft of precious metals. While the case studies above cover specific coinages and kingdoms, the authors see a research potential to utilise the approach outlined in this paper to examine other early medieval coinages.

References

1. Bhandare, Shailendra, 2015, *Evaluating the Paucity of metal currency in Medieval India*, *Landscapes in Early Medieval South Asian History*, Routledge, Delhi, ed. Himanshu P. Ray.
2. Bharathi, B.R. (ed.), 2011, *Rashtrakutara Shasanagalu*, Vols.I and II. Kuvempu Institute of Kannada Studies Mysuru University.

[9] Padigar, Shrinivas V., 2010:52.

3. Bracey, Robert, 2017, *Money Supply, Quantitative theory and Feudalism in Sixth Century India*, European Research Council grant Beyond Boundaries: Religion, Region, Language and the State in Asia.
4. Deyell, John S., 1990, *Living without Silver*, Oxford India Paperbacks.
5. Padigar, Shrinivas V. (ed.), 2010, *Inscriptions of the Chalukyas of Badami*, Indian Council of Historical Research, Southern Regional Centre, Bangalore.
6. Sastri, Shama R. (ed.), 1939, *South Indian Inscriptions*, Vol.IX, part 1, No.164.
7. Sharma, R.S., 2003, *Early Medieval Indian Society, A Study in Feudalisation, Chapter 4*, Orient Blackswan.
8. Coin Images are from Classical Numismatic Gallery, Todywalla Auctions, Oswal Auctions, Bombay Auctions and Rajgors Auctions. Access date 30th May 2018.

—×—

Understanding of Indian Culture-Role of Ancient Texts: A Study of *Manasollasa* of King Someshwara III

Vithal D. Potdar

Abstract

The ancient Sanskrit work Manasollasa (also known as Abhilashtartha Chintamani) by Raja Someshwara III of Kalyani Chalukyan dynasty, throws light on different aspects of Indian life, and culture. This paper hopes to examine some of functions and role of kings, arts, literature and society during his times and its contribution to the sources of history of Karnataka.

Someshwara III of Kalyani Chalukyan dynasty wrote *Manasollasa* (1129 CE) which throws much welcome light on different facets of life, including Indian culture. The king was a versatile person, an erudite Sanskrit scholar, a great warrior, an able administrator and a benevolent ruler of his subjects. One can look upon this king as *Rajarshi*. The meaning of the title of the work *Manasollasa—Manas* means the mind, and *ullasa* is rejoicing or delighting i.e. if you read this work, your mind is very much delighted. The work is also known as *Abhilashitartha Chintamani* which can be translated as 'a precious gem that fulfils the wish (of a reader)'. The work consists of 8022 verses (*Shlokas*), 5 Sections (*Prakarana*) and 100 chapters (*Adhyaya*). Further, it throws much light on geographic, social and cultural aspects of the world of the 11–12th century. The volume can be considered as a 'source book' relating to the cultural studies of ancient Karnataka. In ancient times, a ruler was expected to be an expert in 64 branches of knowledge (*Chausasti kale*). It is heartening to note that the ruler was much an expert in these branches of knowledge. The work has more character of a *Dharmashastra* (work on Law) than that of a *Nitishastra* (work on Polity).

Social and Cultural Aspects in *Manasollasa*

This encyclopaedic work which deals with different aspects of life also explains the prominent cultural features of India in general and ancient Karnataka in particular. The encyclopaedic work covers the topics such as polity, governance, ethics, economics, astronomy, astrology, rhetoric, veterinary medicine, horticulture, perfumes, food, architecture, sports, recreational activities, painting, poetry, dance and music. It has the topics like social services, education, family life, health, justice and the role of a physician in the welfare of a state and rearing of elephants for both domestic use and at the time of wars.

The work talks about the 'universal welfare' which is based on 'moral duties'. Someshwara III, the author who ruled from 1127 to 1138 AD called this work as *Jagadacharya Pustakah*, i.e. 'a book which tutors the whole world'. The king declared 'I am working on *Manasollasa*, which is useful for the welfare of the world'. 'It is a real teacher and is an important book in the world'. 'It is very wide like the hundred branches of *Kalpataru*. 'The book is also like a *Kamadhenu* declared the author.

Regarding *Dandaniti,* he states that its purpose should be to protect the subjects and not merely to collecting money or punishment. He adds that the punishment by a king ought to be like 'the administration of *medicine* by a physician, any mistake by both of them will have the fatal consequences'. 'By the help of *Danda* the king should proceed on the religious path'. It also regards *Dharma* as the foundation for building a strong state. Hence, the enforcement of law or *Danda* is essential for the existence of the state. During the period of king Someshwara people entertained high principles in respect of religion, religious faith and practices. Ultimately, *Dharma* originates from the existing good customs in a given society. Relating to war strategies, the author said 'a ruler should always wield a sword of high quality not to kill the people, but to uphold the social, cultural heritage of our country'. This unique statement highlights the cultural undercurrent which flows in India for generations.

The realization of *Trivarga* was an ideal of the state. The king was advised to follow *Dharma, Artha*, *Kama* in their moderate limitations, without hurting the interests or sentiments of others. Someshwara has mentioned in detail the religious duties of a king without deviating from the existing principles in the society. The king fulfilled *Trivarga* by protecting *Svadharma* of his subjects. *Svadharma* is the particular duty of each individual in every group in a society. After acknowledging on the whole all the principles of *Svadharma*, king Someshwara yet mentions *Samana Dharma*, the duties and responsibilities common to all castes and groups. He felt that by protecting *Svadharma* of his subjects, he receives one-sixth of the fruit of the religious merit of his subjects.

The continuous process of acquiring knowledge with unwavering devotion and untiring efforts was absolutely necessary for the growth and development of human culture. Learning was considered to be the holiest of the holy things in the world'*(Nahi jnanena sadrsam, pavitram ihavidyate)*. Education imparted with devotion and dedication, enabled the society to be mentally alert to face the increasing challenges posed by the changing times.Someshwara attached great importance to education without which it was difficult to make the nation great. The system of education was well-planned. His work emphasizes more upon the acquisition of knowledge, which was made obligatory for the three upper castes. The institutions known as the *Gurukulas* headed by *Kulapatis,* were the centres of learning and excellence.

Ethics and ethical conduct for ruler and his subjects is the focal point in ancient works like the *Smrtis* and works on *Dharmasastra.* The ethical standards stipulated by these works are the 'cultural indicators' for the Indian society. Someshwara is also bound by these values when he discusses '*Raja Guna Dharma*' in the early part of his work. He gives an elaborate list of *dos* and *don'ts* to a king/administrator. He is expected to desist from telling lies, eating stale food, arrogance, companionship other ladies, flattery and others. Further, the monarch is expected to adopt these qualities to be a successful administrator: 'Give alms, good speech, good deeds, devotion towards the God, respect towards brahmins and cows, remembering the elders, feeding the guests, worship of the teachers, meditation and taking a holy dip in the sacred rivers. Apart from this, he should protect and support the poor and destitute, servants and all others who are dependent on him.' All these good deeds will help ruler in retaining his power in the state.

The work also covers different modes of entertainment for the common people. War games have a cultural dimension. People engage in them, depending on different festive occasions and they are purely meant for entertainment. He mainly describes the games like wrestling, cock fight. Wrestling is an adventurous game, whereas Cock fight is an indicator of geographical, social, regional and cultural tastes of the people. These sports can be studied from social, economic, geographical and ethnographic points of view. The rulers and the elite in the society also engaged themselves in hunting which was considered as social prestige. But nobody was allowed to cross the social limits and engage oneself in fighting and violence. It was considered as an offence, and the violator was punished severally by the king who was the 'upholder of values in the society'.

Arts in *Manasollasa*

Someshwara was an authority on 64 branches of knowledge. He was much influenced by Bharata's *Natyashastra*. Out of 64 branches, the art is called as *Alekhya* i.e. which is not available in the written form, but it is drawn. The work talks about a balance between *Yoga* and *Bhoga* which will bring an equilibrium in the lives of the people. Hence, under *Bhoga*, it lists the activities like taking a bath with perfumed water, decorating oneself, eating the betel nut and betel leaves (*Tambula*), anointment of the body (*Gandha lepana*) and wearing dress with expensive jewellery (*Vastropabhoga*). Thus it brings about a balance between sensual pleasures and spirituality (*Yoga bhogayatanam shareeram*).

The *Manasollasa* covers several subjects like dance, music, prosody, architecture and sculpture including painting. There is a great stress laid on the close relationship among the fine arts like dance and music. It is a compendium of the then available knowledge relating to fine arts. The work throws a flood of light on the state of civilization that existed in those days. Dance and its different forms are dealt elaborately in the work. The king opines that dance was the first form which man adopted in his cultural evolution. Someshwara has drawn from earlier texts about dance He describes both contemporary and popular forms of dance with specific details and follows a different style and pattern while writing about this unique art form. For the first time, he records some striking features of the dance form in his work, which were never brought to light by earlier authors on this art form. He is described as a distinguished teacher *(Lakshanika)* in this branch of knowledge. Firstly, he gives all the details of his earlier authors including the technical details. But later he deviates from the path of the earlier authors and gives his explanation in a unique way. This localised version was later termed by his successors as the native one (*Desi* style). Among such later works, *Manasollasa* occupies a prominent place in the Cultural History of India. Added to it, it is the first of its kind work which describes much about the native styles (*Desi* style). Bharata's *Natyashastra* and Someshwara's *Manasollasa* works represent the two prominent styles viz. *Marga* and *Desi* styles respectively. Furthermore, Someshwara states in his work that 'a king himself should learn to dance with the knowledge of *Rasa* and *Bhava*'. He himself was well versed in all types of Dance (*Nrtya*). He might have learnt this skill from his mother who was known as *Nrtya Vidyadhari*. It is evident that members of the royal family used to be well-versed in dancing since the period of early Chalukyan rulers and the legacy continued even during the period of Someshwara III.

Someshwara of Chalukyas of Kalyana is called as an authority on music. The dynasty has been referred to by C.R. Day in his work on music in South India as 'The most flourishing age of Indian music was during the period of native princes, a little before the Mohammadan conquest'. An authority on the ancient music in ancient India Sarangadeva has also eulogised king Someshwara as 'an authority on music' (*Paramardi cha Somesho Jagadeka mahipatihi*). Indian musical instruments have a long history when references to these musical instruments are found in the ancient texts. The instruments are also depicted in old paintings, sculptures and their remains are also found in archaeological excavations.

The work contains greater details about paintings and iconography, compared with other works. Relating to the rules about the materials and the colours, the author gives more freedom to the artists with an advice that the 'paintings should be reasonable, of good taste, befitting and pleasant to the eyes on account of beautiful colour combination (*Chitra Lakshana Samyuktam*). The work refers to a class of painting called *Bhava Chitra* and explains it as a painting which manifests *Rasa* such as *Sringara*.Thus, the work is a comprehensive guide relating to almost all aspects of fine arts and extensively deals with its components like sculpture, painting, architecture, music and the dance.

Social Life in *Manasollasa*

The author deals with issues like health, food and even the art of cooking, in order to see a healthier society in the present and future times. A healthier and an ethical society can only contribute in a better way for its cultural development. Someshwara states that the *Krura karma* of an individual is the cause for a disease. Ancient Indian works specially recommend *Dana, Japa, Homa* and *Vrta* etc. as the better remedies for a disease than recommending more medicines. The king said that *Dana* and *Japa* are not only capable of curing the disease, but also powerful in destroying the root cause i.e. sin of the individuals. The king writes, 'If a person follows the rules of *Brahmacharya* and practices *Tapa, Indriya Nigraha, Japa, Dhyana, Pranayama, Samadhi* and other *Niyamas*, he gets even the difficult desires fulfilled by maintaining a good health.' While advising his subjects to develop healthy food habits, he said that 'health is more important than the kingdom.' Further, he said that only a healthy person can become a good administrator.

The Institution of Marriage has drawn the attention of almost all the philosophers and the thinkers of ancient India, which is even true with Someshwara. In any given society, marriage is one of the most important social institutions. In the Indian context, the whole ceremony is supported by the concept of *Dharma*. The marriage is contracted between a man and a woman in accordance with the principles laid down in the form of *Dharma*. Hence, it cannot be dissolved so easily. It is one of the important Samskaras an adult undergoes to fulfil his social obligations in an ethical way in a society. The purpose of dealing multiple subjects in the work was to see to it that a healthy, everlasting society existed in India.

Games and Amusements in *Manasollasa*

The work makes its reading interesting due its treatment of diverse subjects. The ruler has dealt with the subjects relating to man's mind, body, senses, creativity and also recreation for self and the society. The recreational activities are meant to bring in much needed social harmony in a given society. The author talks about recreational activities in groups not necessarily by involving the members of the royal family, but even by involving the common people. The noteworthy aspect of games and amusements is by involving oneself in much eco-friendly activities. The king also gives the tips for cultivating eco-friendly forests in the state. He further says that 'for the well-being, improving your health condition, to get name and fame, to become a winner, and ultimately to be victorious in life one has to cultivate eco-friendly forests in one's own country.' This aspect highlights the king's concern for ecological conservation.

Many local and traditional games for entertainment find prominent place in this work. The description of native sports with new ecological dimensions have also a cultural dimension, and they throw much light on socio-cultural aspects while organising them. The examples of *Sechana Krida* (water sports), *Shadwala Krida* (Game played on green pasture), *Waluka Krida* (sport on sand dunes), *Jyotsna Krida* (game on full moon day) and *Sasya Krida* (playing a game in well-grown greenery) highlight the fact that much diversity and variety existed during that time.

The social life also includes the entertainment for mind and body. *Prahelika Krida* is one such game which provokes one's thinking and reasoning ability. Similarly, the *Chaduranga Krida*, game of chess was played and is much related to one's intellectual capacity. *Pashaka Krida* (game of dice), *Waratika Krida*(another game of dice) and *Fanida Krida* (game of hand and wrist movement) highlighted an individual's skills. These games can also be studied for their cultural backgrounds. *Fanjika Krida* was exclusively meant for the women folk.

The different games explained in the work can be studied for their social and cultural affinities. These games and amusements represent the cultural legacy of our past. The ruler asks the people engaged in these modes of entertainment to be a little bit cautious as they are meant for entertainment. Hence, they should not be played to earn money or it should not become a sin or a bad habit. Further, they should not become a cause in disturbing the social fabric and harmony in the society.

The social health of a given society will remain on its tracks when the physical, mental, emotional, financial needs of the individuals are addressed effectively under an ethical framework. There lies the culture of a country and its society. Someshwara was aware of these different needs of the individuals. The work exhaustively discusses subjects like the sexual needs of the individuals within a legal and moral framework. The last chapters of the work deal with the games and amusements like *Timira Krida*, *Prema Krida* and *Surata Krida* which include most challenging subjects like the physical urges of men and women, the conjugal relationship between the two sexes, the art of love-making etc. These sensitive subjects are very much included in most of the ancient works because the four *Purusharthas* i.e. *Dharma*, *Artha, Kama* and *Moksha* (Dharmartha *Kama Mokshanam Faladanatra Samshaya—Sri Mad Bhagavad Gita*) should be addressed on an equal footing by an individual to achieve the final goal in one's own life (attainment of Salvation-*Moksha*).

The king concludes his marathon discussion on varied subjects with a wish that 'a reader who reads this work with much seriousness will develop interest in *Dharma*, expertise in *Arthashastra* (science of administration and governance) and leadership qualities and wisdom in *Rajanitishastra* (science of polity).' Further, people belonging to different sections of society will be able to enhance their skills in their respective trades or professions. 'One will develop the urge to serve the society, develop more expertise and knowledge in literature, skills in the art of warfare, music and in other prominent areas. The work is like a *Kamadhenu,* the sacred cow which fulfils all the wishes of the human beings. The author proudly declares that 'no other work can be compared with this scholarly treatise (*Shastra*).

Almost all branches of knowledge which existed in ancient India have been discussed in this voluminous work. It serves as a store house of information on all leading topics of learning. Critical scholarship and poetical faculty are very perfectly combined in this work. The author-king had mastered all branches of knowledge and they are found their prominent place in his work. As a literary artist, Someshwara stands second to none. His thoughts and ideas are so profound that they make one to infer that he must have had liberal education in a systematic manner. His imaginative faculty is wonderful and sometimes lofty. His work suggests clearly that in his early life he must have spared no pains to widen his intellectual capacity and to develop his all-round knowledge. Further, he advises to the kings that they must keep their citizens always happy, for which they should study this anthology of knowledge *Manasollasa*. They should also study this keeping in mind the interests of their subjects. Scholars should study it for the enhancement of their knowledge. The work caters to the needs of people of all classes. This fact proves that Someshwara's contribution to the world of knowledge is undoubtedly unique. It can be called as a 'guide to the mankind'.

References

1. Mallepuram Venkatesh G. (ed.), *Manasollasa*, Vols.5 (Text, Translation & Notes), Karnatak Samskrit University, Bengaluru, 2015.
2. Joshi Mahadev N., *Art and Science in Manasollasa*, New Bharatiya Book Corporation, Delhi, 2003.
3. Joshi Mahadev & Hebballi B.S., *Manasollasa and Ayurveda*, Sharada Publishing House, Delhi, 2004.
4. P.B. Desai et al., *History of Karnataka*, Karnatak University, Dharwad,
5. Karthik S., *Kalyanada Chalukya Vamshada Sangeeta Shastrakara Rajaru* (in Kannada), Ragadhanasri Magazine, Vols.119, 120, Nov–Dec, 2017.
6. Majumdar R.C. et al. (ed.), *The History and Culture of the Indian People*, Vol.V: *Struggle for Empire*, Bharatiya Vidya Bhavan, Bombay, 1966.
7. Day C.R., *The Music and Musical Instruments of Southern India and the Deccan*, B.R. Publishing Corporation, Delhi, 1974.
8. Shrigondekar G.K., *Manasollasa of King Bhulokamalla Someshwara*, Oriental Institute, Baroda, 1967.
9. Shamashastri R., *Abhilashitartha Chintamani of Someshwara*, Part I, Oriental Research Institute, Mysore, 1926.
10. Dikshit G.S., *Local Self Government in Medieval Karnataka*, Karnatak University, Dharwad, 1964.

—×—

IV. Arts and Historical Method

Cham Arts in the 11th and 12th Centuries: Trade Relations between the Cholas and Champa Kingdom

Tran Ky Phuong

Abstract

The kingdom of Champa was located on the sea route connecting between the South India and South China, and it built a midway transportation system with its prosperous port-cities/port- polities for import-export commodity demand. The similarities and transformations in the arts of Champa, between the 11th and 12th Centuries CE in regard to trade, and artistic influences, in terms of iconography, religious concepts, architectural ramifications, style as well as artistic technique in comparison to that of the Chola Empire and other states of Southeast Asia is remarkable and will be explored including original researches.

Introduction

The cultural and art influences of South India on Champa were first noticed by art historians such as Boisselier[1] and Baptiste.[2] However, there has not been any study of the particular aspect of the effects of the Chola empire on the Champa kingdom through religious artworks, and especially with regard to the context of maritime trade relations between South India and South China. In the early 11th century, circa 1025, Chola king, Rajendra I, carried out the naval expeditions noted in his inscriptions, "despatched many ships in the midst of the rolling sea"; and he also took over many port-cities of the famous Southeast Asian kingdom of Srivijaya in Sumatra as well as on the Malay Peninsula.[3] It was the only warlike incident occurred in the long peaceful and cultural relationship between India and its neighboring kingdoms in

[1] Boisselier 1963:26, 27, 135.

[2] Baptiste 2010:151–87.

[3] Coedès 1968:142–43.

Southeast Asia.[4] During the last centuries of the first millennium CE, maritime trade activities had been continuously developed between India and Southeast Asia, but it is often believed that from the 11th century, the spread of Indian culture through the Bay of Bengal slowed down. Indeed, before the 11th century, Buddhism and Hinduism had profoundly imprinted on the emergence of the Mainland and Island Southeast Asian cultures. The first striking influence of South India was often associated with the famous Buddhist art of Amaravati and the earliest Pallava Grantha inscriptions in the 5th century CE found in present-day Indonesia and at the Mỹ Son sanctuary of Champa kingdom in Central Vietnam, followed by the stronger impacts of the art and architecture of Pallava and Chola to Southeast Asia.[5] However the great conquests of Chola over Srivijaya in 1025, followed by other smaller naval conquests in ca.1070, remains a conundrum for historians.[6] In 1955, Nalakanta Sastri raised the question "why was this expedition against the king of Kadalam [Srivijaya] undertaken and what were its effects?" and he suggests that "We have to assume either some attempt on part of Srivijaya to throw obstacles in the way of the Chola trade with the east, or more probably, a simple desire on the part of Rajendra to extend his *digvijaya* ['world conquest'] to the countries across the sea so well-known to his subjects at home, and thereby add lustre to his crown."[7] While Majumdar suggested that the conquests of Chola to Southeast Asia in the early 11th century may be interpreted in two ways as, "It may be that Rajendra Chola threatened to invade Kambuja and its king tried to avert the disaster by conciliating him. It is, however, equally, or even more likely in view of the language of the record, that the King of Kambuja was eager to enlist the support of Rajendra against an enemy who threatened his Kingdom."[8] The suggestion of Majumdar perhaps corresponded to the case of Champa that is discussed below.

Political Relations in the 10th Century with a New Perspective

From the perspective of Champa, the expeditions of Rajendra to Southeast Asia in the 1070s can be explained from the view of Cham history which is a necessary background for this study. According to Vietnamese historical records, in the year 982, Lê Hoàn, king of Đại [Cô] Việt (Vietnamese kingdom) attacked the capital city of Champa.

[4] Kulke 2009:xiii.
[5] Kulke 2009:xiii.
[6] Kulke 2009:xiv.
[7] Sastri 1955:218–20.
[8] Majumdar 1961:341.

The Vietnamese king had taken plenty of Cham soldiers, a hundred of palace maids, and an Indian monk; he had destroyed fortresses, religious foundations; and remained in Champa for a year.[9] In 984, after Lê Hoàn had withdrawn from Champa, one of his generals namely Luu Ký Tông seized power. The Viet usurper officially proclaimed himself king of Champa and in 986 he notified the court of China of his accession.[10] Although, Luu Ký Tông had usurped the throne for only a short period, he cruelly dominated the Cham people as the contemporary witnesses who were Arabian merchants have stated, "Abu Dulaf said: At the time when I was in India [around the middle of the 10th century], the king who ruled Campa was called Lagin. The monk of Nadjran told me that at that time [980–986], the king [of Campa] was a king of Lukin [Luu Ký Tông] who had occupied Campa, ravaged her and enslaved all her peoples."[11] The year and the name of the king of Champa and the historical events that the Arabian travelers indicated that it corresponded to those of the Vietnamese historical records as mentioned above.

This important event was also recorded by the Chinese book of Song Hui Jigao, (around 1080) and that there was war between Champa and Đại [Cồ] Việt; king of Đại Việt is Lê Hoàn who wanted to offer 93 Cham war prisoners to the Sung court. In 985, a Cham ambassador had complained that his territory was occupied by Giao Châu (Đại [Cồ] Việt) at the same time with the escape of the Cham people to the Song's territory to avoid the attacks of the Vietnamese. In the end of 986, a Song administrative unit in Hainan noted that there have been about 100 Cham people who escaped into this island.[12] Thus this historical event was echoed in India and South China, and perhaps impacted their trade relationship. This was the first invasion of Đại Việt to the political, economic and religious center of Champa; it caused serious damages to the North Champa hence the economic activities in this region probably were completely suspended.[13]

Although, the northern parts of Champa were fallen into the turbulent period from the end of 10th to the early 11th centuries because of the incessant wars with Đại Việt;[14] we have learned that the southern parts of the kingdom remained reasonable stable and were reigned by other powerful kings as mentioned in several inscriptions found at the

[9] Toàn Thu 1993:122; Coedès 1968:124.

[10] Coedès 1968:124–25.

[11] Ferrand 1913: 123.

[12] Wade 2011:143–45.

[13] Trân Ky Phuong 2017:597–601.

[14] Coedès 1968:139–41.

Po Nagar Nha Trang sanctuary and in Panduranga region (modern day Ninh Thuận province). These inscriptions state about the power of the kings and their donation to rebuild several royal religious foundations during that period.[15]

Hence, the Cham kings in the South, including the regions of Panduranga[16], [17] Kauthara (today's Khánh Hòa province) and Vijaya, asked for military help from the Cholas in order to retrieve the northern kingdom that had fallen to the hands of Đại Việt army and to rebuild their own kingdom? If so, we may compare this suggestion that coincides deeply with Sastri's arguments, "We shall see later that one of the successors of Rajendra, Virarajendra I, claims to have conquered Kadaram and restored it to its ruler who supplicated for it before the conqueror. In any case, there is no evidence to show that the Colas made any attempt to rule these lands as provinces of their empire."[18]

Related to the above suggestion, the other historical fact for comparison is that, after having regained the kingdom from the Đại Việt, the Cham king contemporarily known as Harivarman (1071–84) who brought back peace and stability to the kingdom probably under the military assistance of Chola (?); his merit was praised in the inscriptions found at Mỹ Son sanctuary, as follows, "The enemies had entered into the kingdom of Campā and installed themselves as masters; having taken possession of all the royal property and the wealth of the gods; having pillaged the temples, the monasteries ...; having ravaged everything in the provinces of the kingdom of Campā; having plundered the temple of Śrīśānabhadreśvara and all the objects which the kings of past times had granted as endowments to Śrīśānabhadreśvara; having taken all the riches of the god and carried away the men belonging to the temple, the dancers, musicians ... Then His Majesty Vijaya Śrī Harivarmadeva, yāñ Devatāmūrti ascended the throne. He completely defeated the enemies, proceeded to the Nagara Campā and restored the temple of Śrīśānabhadreśvara ... And reestablished... with all the crops destroyed... The kingdom of Campā became prosperous as of old times. Then Harivarman celebrated his coronation ..."[19] As a result, under

[15] Gozio 2004:128–35 [C.30B3], [C.122], [C.39], [C.95], [C.31A2].

[16] Coedès 1968:143.

[17] According to Coedès, an inscription of Rajendra I found at the temple of Tanjore, dated in 1030–31, states that the king conquered successfully several lands in Southeast Asia, amongst them there was a placename so-called 'Valaippanduru' that he argues, perhaps, the name of Pandur[anga] or Phan Rang of Champa (Coedès 1968:143, notes 79, 82).

[18] Sastri 1955:220.

[19] Majumdar 1985, III:159–161; Gozio 2004:136–137 [C.94].

the reign of Harivarman, the Chola art influences created substantial imprints that can be seen on the Cham temple-towers built at the royal sanctuaries such as Mỹ Son and Po Nagar Nha Trang.[20]

Role of the Cholas and the Chams on the maritime trade route

In the 11th century, after occupying the whole of Southern India, the Chola empire was able to control the maritime trade route linking South India and Southeast Asia and extended up to South China; thus, the trade interactions between Tamil merchants and those of the Quanzhou, the port-city of Fujian province, China, and other port-cities of Southeast Asia had become very prosperous.[21] During this period, Cholas sent no less than three missions of a diplomatic and commercial nature to the Song court of China in 1017, 1025 and 1077.[22] The Chola merchants had built many Hindu temples in Quanzhou from the 11th–13th centuries to serve the Tamil merchant guilds and other Hindu believers who lived there. Today there still remain more than 300 vestiges of the Hindu temple architecture and sculpture in this port-city.[23]

The major economic event which occurred in the early 12th century that encouraged trade development between the two regions of South India and South China was the advantageous financial policy and the new technique of copper coin casting together with the open maritime trade policy of the Southern Sung dynasty (1127–1279). This had a positive influence on trade throughout Southeast Asia and impacted Champa as this kingdom was in close proximity to South China to exchange luxury forest products.[24]

In this context, Cham port-cities must have played an important role as a midway point in the bustling maritime trade route connecting between the two lands of South India and South China. According to the historical book of An Nam Chí Lược/ [Abbreviated Historical Records of An Nam/Vietnam] published in 1335, until the early 14th century, the port-cities of Champa were the first place in which Chinese merchant ships had to be disembarked to obtain fresh water and firewood for their cruise to the further south.[25] Thanks to its role as a major intermediary in the maritime trade relationship and the full promotion of the convenient network of port-cities as the entrepôts supplying precious forest products

---

20 Baptiste 2010:151–187; Trân Ký Phuong 2009:155–86.

21 Kulke 2009:xiii–xx; Sen 2009:61–75.

22 Dehejia 1990:xiv.

23 Guy 2001:296–302.

24 Wade 2009:222–231.

25 Lê Tăc 2002:72–73.

to the international market; hence, the economy of Champa was highly prosperous during that time.

In Indian cultural tradition, donating to build religious works has been highly respected. This customary practice was particularly encouraged by the Cholas from the 9th–13th centuries. The Tamil merchants under the protection of these great dynasties contributed large donations to build many Buddhist and Hindu temples for pilgrims. Among them the most remarkable one is the famous Buddhist temple of Nagapattinam in South India that was originally built under the reign of Narashimhavarman II in the late 7th century, ca.695–722; and it was honored by rich donations under the reign of King Chola Rajaraja I in 1006. This temple was built to serve foreign traders;[26] besides, there have been several other Hindu temples built by Tamils in Quanzhou during the 12th–13th century.[27] Such religious activities of Tamil merchants created profound cultural influences on contemporary Southeast Asian kingdoms, including Champa.[28]

In order to build costly religious works throughout the kingdom, the Cham kings may have received extensive donations from the royal aristocratic elite and the foreign merchants who stayed in the port-cities of the kingdom. Recently, in the late 1990s, the new findings at Mỹ Son site of the Cham royal sanctuary have provided evidence regarding donations to the Cham Hindu temple. During the excavations for restoration at the Mỹ Son G temple-group, the Italian experts discovered three bricks of decorative corner pieces (pièce d'accent) on which were those engraved the Old Chinese characters of Chen (Trân in Vietnamese);[29] they are now displayed at the Mỹ Son Site Museum. The character of 'Chen' is more likely to be the family name of a Chinese merchant who contemporarily lived in Champapura (Chan-ch'eng in Chinese; Đại Chiêm Hai Khâu in Vietnamese, meaning Port of Great Champa, the Ancient Town of Hội An in present time), and offered donations for the construction of the royal temple of king Jaya Harivarman in 1157/58.[30] Such contributions to build the main temple of the king at the royal sanctuary also brought prestige to the donors among the community of foreign traders in Champa,[31] and among them

[26] Dehejia 1990:77–78; Ray 2014a:1–18.

[27] Lee 2009:240–245.

[28] Levin 2008:85–99; Ray 2014b:1–18.

[29] Zolese 2009:197–237.

[30] In my email exchanges with Qian Jian and Geoff Wade, the two historians have confirmed that the family name 'Chen' of Chinese merchants was popular in the southern Fujian province during the 12th century (Email on 14 May 2015).

[31] Hardy 2009:111; Hall 2018:22.

the Chinese merchants may have played a significant role. This can be confirmed by the Mỹ Son G temple-group built in the middle of 12th century. According to historians, foreign traders living in the large port-cities of Champa may include Arabs, Tamil, North Indian, Chinese, Malay, Khmer and Vietnamese, so on; as a result, the Cham language has adopted many vocabularies from those foreign languages.[32]

Artistic Exchanges between Chola and Champa Kingdoms

In 2006, I had the occasion to survey the Bujang Valley ruins in Kedah, Malaysia. This is the most abundant Hindu and Buddhist monument in this region and was developed over centuries from the 8th–13th century CE.[33] This ruin is located in a large river estuary which played the role of an important port-city on the Indian Ocean trade routes. In 1025, King Chola Rajendra I had conquered this port-city and named it as Kadaram (Kedah).[34] Here, I studied a square sandstone pedestal with its composition, art stylistic and decorative patterns look very similar to those of the Cham sculptural works created in the 11th–12th centuries. The size of the Bujang pedestal measures in 88 cm wide × 87 cm long × 47 cm high, and is represented by a stylized lotus flower combined in two horizontal moldings with a well-proportioned layout (Fig.1). The upper side was perforated, at the middle, a multi-edged square hole to mount with another part; this is a kind of altar so-called 'bali-pitha' or offering-altar which is installed in front of the main temple in a complex temple-tower of Chola art period.[35]

In Cham sculptural art, this type of offering—an altar 'bali-pitha' and the temple-base (sousbasement)—represented a highly stylized lotus composition and appeared commonly only during the 11th and 12th centuries. The typical sculptural works of this type including the well-known sandstone pedestal known as the 'Dancer of Trà Kiệu' created in the second half of the 11th century, is on display at the Danang Museum of Cham Sculpture now (Fig.2). The other one is the square sandstone pedestal carved with four elephants found at Triên Tranh site, Duy Trinh district, Quang Nam province, which measures by 76 cm wide × 75 cm long × 63 cm high, and is now display at the Museum of Sa Huỳnh-Champa Culture in Trà Kiệu, Quang Nam province now.[36] Besides, there are several temple-bases composed in such stylized lotus shapes, made

[32] Maspero 1928:7, note 4.

[33] Rahman, Yatim 1990:1–42; Hassan, Chia, Isa 2011:27–50; Adaya 2011:69–94.

[34] Christie 1998:254.

[35] Sastri 1955:707–709.

[36] Trân Ký Phuong 2018:222–225.

Fig.1. The unique square pedestal in the form of lotus petals represented by horizontal moldings found at Bujang Valley, Kedah, Malaysia. Made in sandstone in the 11th–12th century. (Photo: Trân Ký Phuong)

Fig.2. The well-known pedestal so-called 'Tra Kieu Dancers'. Made in sandstone; dated in the second half of 11th century. On display at the Danang Museum of Cham Sculpture, Vietnam. (Photo: Trân Ký Phuong)

in sandstone and brick, which belonged to the Mỹ Son temple-complexes (Fig.3).

Fig.3. The The Mỹ Son B5 temple of Mỹ Son sanctuary composed with a curved roof, double pilasters and horizontal molds in lotus shapes that influenced from Chola art, built in the 10th century and restored afterwards. (Photo: Trần Ký Phuong)

Thời kỳ thứ 1

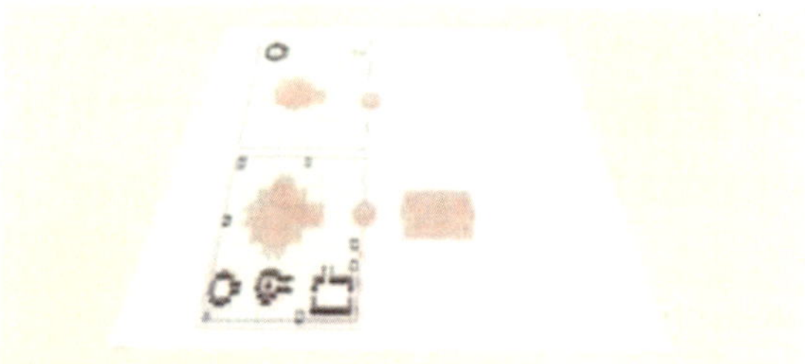

Thời kỳ thứ 2

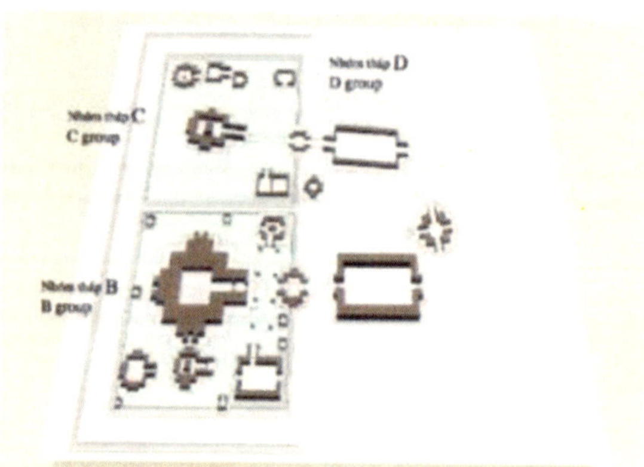

Thời kỳ thứ 3

Fig.4. The process of the temple complexes of the Mỹ Son B-C-D groups through the three architectural stages. The first stage: ca. the 7th to 8th century; The second stage: ca. the 9th to 10th century; The third stage: ca. the 11th to 13th century. In which the third stage had strongly received the art influences from Chola. The composition of a complex of temple-towers in this stage comprised: kalan (main temple) + gopura (gate tower) + mandapa (exterior hall) + secondary shrines and kosagrha (fire-tower) + enclosures. Drawing is displayed at the My Son Site Museum (Trân Ký Phuong, Akiko, Toshihiko 2005:22).

Although the art influence of Chola has clearly appeared in Cham art during the 11th–13th centuries, until now, there have not yet been any inscriptions in the Tamil language that have been discovered in the territory of the Champa kingdom, although many inscriptions written in Tamil have been found in most of ancient kingdoms in Southeast Asia as well as in Quanzhou, Fujian. In a later period, according to Ma Huan's book of *Ying-Yai Sheng-Lan/* (The Overall Survey of the Oceans Shores) written in ca.1434–1436 it was noted that the contemporary king of Champa was noted that he most probably belonged to Chola or Indian lineage.[37] Thus under the influence of religious architecture techniques from Chola in this art period, the Cham temple construction techniques were perfected, as can be demonstrated by the large buildings constructed in the Amaravati state (present-day Quàng Nam province), such as the full improvement of the temple-complexes the groups of A-B-C-D at the Mỹ Son sanctuary.[38] In terms of form and function, influence of Chola aesthetics is certain.[39]

Epilogue

This is a preliminary study of the relationship between Chola and Champa. I also hope to provide further understanding of one of the most remarkable empires of South India and its prominent role on Indian Ocean and Pacific Ocean in the 11th century.[40] Were the Chola expeditions purely political and military aims or might they have reinforced the indispensable trade relationships between South India and South China and the other neighboring states in Southeast Asia, in which Champa was an outstanding trading intermediary? In the contexts of the Cham political and economic turmoil during the end of 10th to the mid-11th century, the Chola naval expeditions can be considered as not only the military assistance to recover peace for Champa but also to "establish trading rights for Tamil-speaking merchants in those areas, a trade from which the ruler, the merchants and the Cola bureaucracy could expect sizable profit" as historians pointed out.[41]

As a literary artist, Someshwara stands second to none. His thoughts and ideas are so profound that they make one to infer that he must have had liberal education in a systematic manner. His imaginative faculty is wonderful and sometimes lofty. His work suggests clearly that in his early life he must have spared no pains to widen his intellectual capacity

[37] Ma Huan 1970:79, note 6.

[38] Trân Ký Phuong, Okiko, Toshihiko 2005:22.

[39] Levin 2008:85–99; Devara 2009:184–186; Shanmugam 2009:208–26.

[40] Kulke 2009:xv.

[41] Kulke 2009:xiv.

and to develop his all-round knowledge. Further, he advises to the kings that they must keep their citizens always happy, for which they should study this anthology of knowledge *Manasollasa*. They should also study this keeping in mind the interests of their subjects. Scholars should study it for the enhancement of their knowledge. The work caters to the needs of people of all classes. This fact proves that is better than *Kama*. But Artha should always be first practiced by the king for the livelihood of men is to be obtained from it only. Again, Kama being the occupation of public women, they should prefer it to the other two, and these are exceptions to the general rule." (Burton 1995:14)

Kamasutra: The Exploration of the Spiritual and the Erotic through Indian Art and Literature

Dr. Alka Pande

Keywords: Vatsyayana, Kamasutra, Spirituality, Indian Erotic, Indian Art, Indian Aesthetics, Purusharthas, Medieval Indian Literature, Bhakti, Post Colonialism

The aim of the paper is to explore spiritual and the erotic features of Kamasutra through Indian art and literature and relook at its relevance within the ambit of the contemporary Indian culture. The Kamasutra is the mother of all erotic writing in India, partly by virtue of its age, having been composed around the third century CE, but also because of its scope and ambition. Vatsyayana's Kamasutra is the first systematic text on erotic and carnal desires. Ever since Vatsyayana first collated it, it has been the muse for a number of writers and artists through the many centuries to come. The paper attempts to raise a few questions with scope to answer them: Is, it part of Dharma Shastra? What is the Kamasutra: ls, it a book of sexual acrobatics, where men stand on their heads, having sex with a woman? Is, it a book of orgiastic delight, where a man is satisfying three women at the sometime? Is, it a book of same-sex love? Is, it a book of aphrodisiacs where men and women are in a slate of inebriated pleasure? Is, it a book which helps men to have large extended penises which turn men into stallions of sexual energy?

Some Indian philosophies following the *purusharthas* "four main goals of life", says, "*Dharma* is better than *Artha*, and *Artha* is better than *Kama*. But Artha should always be first practiced by the king for the livelihood of men is to be obtained from it only. Again, Kama being the occupation of public women, they should prefer it to the other two, and these are exceptions to the general rule." (Burton 1995:14)

1. *Dharma*: Virtuous Living
2. *Artha*: Material Prosperity
3. *Kama*: Aesthetic and Erotic Pleasure
4. *Moksha*: Liberation

The Kamasutra actually transcends each one of these misconceptions and concerns itself with the realm of the spiritual. It educates the reader on their journey through life and gives practical advice with regard to one of the three life goals these goals are *dharma, artha* and *kama* needed before being able to achieve the fourth and final goal i.e. *moksha* (Haksar 2011:73).[42] In fact, Vatsyayana explicitly expresses this aim in his conclusion, in which he writes:

> "A person acquainted with the true principles of this science, who preserves his Dharma (virtue or religious merit), his Artha (worldly wealth) and his Kama (pleasure or sensual gratification), and who has regard to the customs of the people, is sure to obtain the mastery over his senses. In short, an intelligent and knowing person attending to Dharma and Artha and also to Kama, without becoming the slave of his passions, will obtain success in everything that he may do."[43]

These three goals compose the meaning of life, so how can a person achieve *ananda* or sublime bliss without at some point turning their attention to Kama? It is for this, the very practical, reason that the Kamasutra was created, and a proper understanding of the history of the book and Hinduism should help to emphasize this.

Interplay of Spiritual and Erotic

The medieval India is replete with examples of several artists composing poems, plays, novels, philosophy and visual arts on the practice and theory of erotic sentiment.[44] The wealth of this literature shows that people were preoccupied with the erotic and that life in antique India was influenced by the pleasure principle. Poems and novels openly chronicled love affairs, sexual adventures, faithfulness and infidelity. Male and female sexual beauty was celebrated with men having great arms like 'plantain trees', torsos 'like the face of an ox' and eyebrows 'like a strong bow'. Women, meanwhile, possessed faces 'like the full moon' and were 'long-eyed', 'tiny-waist' and 'broad-hipped'.[45]

At this time, Indian society was nearly male-dominated and most of the prominent writers and artists were men. Women, however, were not a less powerful. While it is true that the upper classes were polygamous and viewed women as private property, being bound by caste restrictions and seen as valuable war prizes, the writings of the day emphasize that men's first duty, and pleasure, was to cherish their women, make them as happy as possible and never treat them brutally. Husbands were to spend lavishly on gold and jewels for their wives so as to proclaim their social status. The art of this period shows both sexes wearing elaborate strings of jewels in their hair along with precious necklaces, rings, armlets, anklets and hip girdles.[46]

Eroticism in Indian Art and Literature

In some ways the medieval period becomes the most fertile soil for the production of *sahitya* (literature). The literature of this period is a clear reflection of the luxurious culture of the courts and aristocracy. Poets and writers, dependent on the higher classes' patronage, catered to their lords' increasing demand for erotica. Court poets who wanted to remain in favour had to constantly flatter their patrons by writing erotic literature.[47] Most scholars place *bhakti* as a post-Vedic movement that began primarily in the same period as the epic but it continued and prospered especially in the medieval period. The Sanskrit noun *bhakti* is derived from the verb root *bhaj*,[48] which means attachment, devotion, fondness for, devotion to the universal god. It also is used in terms of human relationships, where it describes the relationships of 'beloved-lover, friend-friend, parent-child, and master-servant. A final common usage may refer to devotion to a *guru* or spiritual teacher as *guru-bhakti*, to a personal form of God, or to divinity without form *nirguna* (Ranjana Malik)'.[49]

Bhakti can be used in the Hindu traditions of Shaivaism and Vaishnavism alike. Also, often seen as the *adwait* philosophy, it is the union of *atma* with *paramatma*, which is shown through a sensual and erotic rasa i.e. *shringara*. This is manifested by the *bhakti* (devotion) movement, which was begun by Tamil poets, it spread across the subcontinent propagated by a vast number of *bhakti* saints such as Kabir, Mirabai, Nanak, Tulsidas, Lalla, Tukaram, Ravidas, Chaitanya and more.[50] The central tenet of this devotional movement was a yearning for oneness with god or the absolute achieved through unconditional love and erotic plea to the god. In the *Bhakti* period, the act of eroticism undergoes a transformation and is dominated by a feeling of yearning. From the copulation of the *tantric* in the ancient period where the union of Shiva and Shakti leads to liberation, to the *Bhakti* period where erotica is expressed through the longing of the union of the *atma* and *parmatma*, the change in the definition of eroticism is remarkable.[51]

It also occurs in compounds where it means 'being a part of' and 'that which belongs to or is contained in anything else.' *Bhajan* or devotional singing to God, is also derived from the same root. Devotion —the most widely used English translation for *bhakti*—does not fully convey two important aspects of the term—the sense of participation that is central to the relationship between the devotee and God, and the intense feeling that is more typically associated with the word love.[52] An *adwaitic* interpretation of *bhakti* goes far beyond devotion and instead defines it as the realization of union with the essential nature of reality as *ananda* or divine bliss. Bhakti is sometimes used in the broader sense of reverence toward a deity or teacher. *Bhakti marga* is usually used to describe a *bhakti* path with complete dedication to one form of God.

Temple architecture and sculpture of this period mirror the inquisitive state of mind. Temples for Vishnu and Shiva resembled a palace for the deity to hold court, attended by gods and dancing girls. The erotic charm of these girls hinted at the rapture to be enjoyed by uniting with God. In some cases, the lovers are shown in complete union, although their peculiar acrobatics—think of the Khajuraho lover seen standing on his head—makes their love an ideal fantasy. This fevered sexuality might have been caused by the strain in medieval India, where sex, condemned in real life, became celebrated in art and religion. Sculptural art in this period centred on the human figure; moving away from the earlier Buddhist visual representations of Bharhut and Sanchi, all the animal and vegetal patterns were pushed out of the narrative onto the borders and panels. In the centre of these rich vegetal patterns of decorations was the human figure. Here the body was youthful, smooth with a transparent luminosity of texture (Kramrisch 1946:173–175).[53]

The *Riti kavya* also known as *Ritis magra*, which was primarily devoted to Krishna *Bhakti*, reached its apogee during the medieval period. The *bhakti* of this genre translated into *shringara* or the erotic aspects of Krishna's life, i.e. his *leela* or play with the *gopis* of Braj. The two genres of *riti kavy* (full of rhetoric) and *riti mukta* (free from rhetoric) contributed greatly to the pool of erotic literature. Two major *riti mukta* poets were Bihari and Ghananand Das. The former wrote the *Sat Sai* and the latter wrote in a spontaneous manner, describing powerful feelings of love, desire and longing in his iconic works *Sujana-Sagara*, *Rasa-Kelivalli* and *Kripa-khanda* (Bahadur 1990:34).[54]

The beginning of the medieval period saw a shift towards the feudal tendencies that determined the productive and economic basis of medieval Indian society. Feudal beginnings are seen in the land grants made in the time of the Gupta rulers. The Kamasutra prescribes the attributes of a *nagaraka* as a man of *grahita vidya* or learning and collector of wealth who should be a householder. However, there are examples that indicate the weakened position of the *nargaraka* class from the seventh century CE onwards. As in all feudal societies, the society witnessed the rise of several grades of landed intermediaries. Overt sensuality and the pursuit of a pleasurable life are two of the hallmarks of this age. So, despite the near male domination of the period, the literature should be celebrated as, specifically in the *Gathasaptasati* of Satavahana Hala, there is an emergence of women's voices and autobiography that is built upon in medieval literature. A few examples of this potent early feminine literature should be proof enough of the strength of the female sexual character at this time:

'A scorpion's bitten her,' they cried,
And as she thrashed about,
Her shrewd friends in her husband's presence
Rushed her to her physician-lover. (Mehrotra 2008:23)[55]

Conclusions

With the British colonialization came in the Western idea of beauty in India. In the realm of the visual arts, painting, sculpture and architecture that was produced under these socio-political conditions showed a marked influence of Western cultural influences. The understanding of carnal desire as a study moves into a more physical space nearly spilling over into the domain of pornography where it is a commodity of hedonistic pleasure.[56] The commodification of the female form as sexual objects: the sensuousness and voluptuousness of feminine beauty in Indian aesthetics has largely been replaced by the notion of crossing the line of coy mistress. Far from describing female sexuality as passive as in Western thought, Indian art and literature is a celebration of the Indian beauty in its fullest form. The current state demands a deep conceptual re-reading of the Kamasutra. Doniger and Kakar (2009:89)[57] rightly states: "The cultural context is urbane and cosmopolitan with a real consciousness of the possible regions of India." She further added, "It is not, as most people think, about positions in sexual intercourse. It is a book about the art of living—about finding a partner, maintaining power in a marriage, committing adultery, living as or with a courtesan, using drugs—and also about positions in sexual intercourse."

The contemporary understanding of the aesthetic of the erotic within Indian culture has moved beyond its singular appealing appraisal. It concerns itself with the indigenous systems around the body and related constructs of otherness, masculinity and femininity, health and sexuality, cultural connotations and personal identity. Contemporay Indian art and literature often delves and dips into the many readings, historical narratives and myths, transforming and translating Pauranic stories within contemporary narratives. In the process new stories, modern forms of storytelling, and retellings have emerged. The ideology of polyphony is embedded in today's expressions. The words carry different meanings and resonances according to varying audiences. This is the age of interpretation: the author's word is not the final one. Any fixity of meaning is denied; a piece of work could contain different analysis and versions. Therefore, these forces of development, from the ancient to the contemporary, have affected the depiction of the notion of erotic thoughts in India.

In my opinion, the basic tenets of love, longing, lust and desire, as expounded in Kamasutra, remain as relevant as they were more than 2000 years ago. The human emotions cuts across boundaries of geography, race, and community. The ethics of conjugal life have not shifted dramatically. What emerges through the social reading of society is that the narrative is driven by the dynamics of hypocrisy and double-standards. The *purusharthas* as stated in Kamasutra have lost their ethical significance as stated in the text in the in the current context of contemporary life. The paper attempts to draw attention to the notion that how the exploration of the spiritual and the erotic through Indian art and literature is still a source of great inspiration for writers, artists and even sophisticated city dwellers/*nagarka* of the Kamasutra, to lead an enriching, joyous, abundantly sensual and fulfilling life.

References

1. Appadorai, Angadipuram. (1992) *Indian Political Thinking: Through the Ages*. New Delhi: Khama Publishers.
2. Bahadur, K.P. (1990) *Rasikapriya of Keshavadas*. New Delhi: Motilal Banarasidass Publications.
3. Burton, Sir Richard and Arbuthnot, F.F. (trans.) (1995) *The Kamasutra of Vatsyayana*. Ware: Wordsworth Classics.
4. Carman, John B. (2005) 'Bhakti' in *Encyclopaedia of Religion* Vol.2. 2d, edited by Lindsay Jones, 856–860. Detroit, MI: Macmillan Reference.
5. Dehejia, Vidya. (1997) *Indian Art*. New York: Phaidon Press.
6. Dehejia, Vidya. (1997) 'Issues of Spectatorship and Representation', in *Representing the Body: Gender Issues in Indian Art*, edited by Vidya Dehejia. New Delhi: Kali for Women.

7. Desai, Devangana. (1975) *Erotic Sculpture of India: A Socio-Cultural Study*. Tata McGraw-Hill Publishing Company, New Delhi.
8. Doniger, W., and Kakar, S. (2009) *Kamasutra by Vatsyayana*. Oxford: Oxford University Press.
9. Flood, Gavin. (1996) *An Introduction to Hinduism*. New York: Cambridge University Press.
10. Geaves, Ron. (2008) 'Bhakti Movement' in *Encyclopaedia of Hinduism*, edited by Denise Cush, Catherine Robinson, and Michael York, 89–97. London and New York: Routledge.
11. Gupta, C. (2002) *Sexuality, Obscenity, Community: Women: Muslims and The Hindu Public in Colonial India.* New York: Palgrave.
12. Haksar, A.N.D. (trans.) (2011) *Kamasutra: A Guide to the Art of Pleasure by Vatsyayana*. New Delhi: London: Penguin.
13. Lutgendorf, Philip. (2003) 'Medieval Devotional Traditions: An Annotated Survey of Recent Scholarship' in *The Study of Hinduism*, edited by Arvind Sharma, 200–260. Columbia, SC: University of South Carolina Press.
14. Kramrisch, Stella. (1946) *The Hindu Temple*. Calcutta: University of Calcutta.
15. Malla, K. (1964) *Ananga Ranga: Stage of the Bodiless One: The Hindu Art of Love*. New York: Medical Press of New York.
16. Mehrotra, A.K. (2008) *The Absent Traveller: Prakrit Love Poetry from the Gathasaptasati of Satavahana Hala*. New Delhi: Penguin Classics.
17. Malik, Ranjana. *Devotion—A Necterine Bliss*, available at https://www.speakingtree.in/allslides/devotion—a-necterine-bliss. (Accessed on June 2, 2018).
18. Paniker, K. Ayyappa. (1997) *Medieval Indian Literature: An Anthology—* Volume One, edited by Paniker, K. Ayyappa. New Delhi: Sahitya Akademi.
19. Pollock, S. (2006). *The Language of the Gods in the World of Men: Sanskrit, Culture, and Power in Premodern India.* Berkeley: University of California.
20. Rawson, Philip. (1984) *Oriental Erotic Art.* New York: Omega Books.
21. Schelling, Andrew. (trans.) (2019) *Erotic Love Poems from India: 101 Classics on Desire and Passion.* Berkeley: Shambhala Publications.
22. Available at http://shodhganga.inflibnet.ac.in/bitstream/10603/26519/8/08_chapter%203.pdf (Accessed on May 20, 2018).
23. Tharu, Susie and Lalita, K. (1991) *Women Writing in India Volume I –600 BC to the Early Twentieth Century*. New Delhi: Oxford University Press.

Kamasutra: The exploration of the Spiritual and the Erotic through Indian Art and Literature

Alka Pande

Abstract

The Kamasutra validates the timeless philosophy of a civil, balanced, prudent and a good life as evidenced through Indian art, literature and thought. *Vatsyayana's Kamasutra*, the first systematic text on erotic and carnal desires has raised few questions. However there are intriguing questions: Is it a book of sexual acrobatics, where men stand on their heads, having sex with a woman? Is it a book of aphrodisiacs where men and women are in state of inebriated pleasure? Was it a part of Dharma Shastra With these questions this paper beyond these multiple reductive interpretations.

The aim of the paper is to explore spiritual and the erotic features of Kamasutra through Indian art and literature and relook at its relevance within the ambit of the contemporary Indian culture. The Kamasutra is the mother of all erotic writing in India, partly by virtue of its age, having been composed around the third century CE, but also because of its scope and ambition. Ever since Vatsyayana first collated it, it has been the muse for a number of writers and artists through the many centuries to come. The paper attempts to raise a few questions with scope to answer them:

What is the Kamasutra: Is, it a book of orgiastic delight, where a man is satisfying three women at the sometime? Is, it a book of same-sex love? Is, it a book which helps men to have large extended penises which turn men into stallions of sexual energy? The paper provides a dynamic juxtaposition with the Victorian notions of a voyeuristic, patriarchal gaze where the commodification of women is foregrounded. It attempts to highlight the need to draw a balance between religion, spirituality, philosophy and a life of pleasure.

Some Indian philosophies following the *purusharthas* "four main goals of life", says, "*Dharma* is better than *Artha*, and *Artha* is better than *Kama*. But Artha should always be first practiced by the king for the livelihood of men is to be obtained from it only. Again, Kama being the occupation of public women, they should prefer it to the other two, and these are exceptions to the general rule." (Burton 1995:14). The

Kamasutra actually transcends each one of these misconceptions and concerns itself with the realm of the spiritual. It educates the reader on their journey through life and gives practical advice with regard to one of the three life goals these goals are *dharma, artha* and *kama* needed before being able to achieve the fourth and final goal i.e. *moksha* (Haksar 2011:73).[58] In fact, Vatsyayana explicitly expresses this aim in his conclusion, in which he writes:

> "A person acquainted with the true principles of this science, who preserves his Dharma (virtue or religious merit), his Artha (worldly wealth) and his Kama (pleasure or sensual gratification), and who has regard to the customs of the people, is sure to obtain the mastery over his senses. In short, an intelligent and knowing person attending to Dharma and Artha and also to Kama, without becoming the slave of his passions, will obtain success in everything that he may do."[59]

These three goals compose the meaning of life, so how can a person achieve *ananda* or sublime bliss without at some point turning their attention to Kama? It is for this, the very practical, reason that the Kamasutra was created, and a proper understanding of the history of the book and Hinduism should help to emphasize this.

Interplay of Spiritual and Erotic

Medieval India is replete with examples of several artists composing poems, plays, novels, philosophy and visual arts on the practice and theory of erotic sentiment.[60] The wealth of this literature shows that people were preoccupied with the erotic and that life in ancient India was influenced by the pleasure principle. Poems and novels openly chronicled love affairs, sexual adventures, faithfulness and infidelity. Male and female sexual beauty was celebrated with men having great arms like 'plantain trees', torsos 'like the face of an ox' and eyebrows 'like a strong bow'. Women, meanwhile, possessed faces 'like the full moon' and were 'long-eyed', 'tiny-waist' and 'broad-hipped'.[61]

At this time, Indian society was nearly male-dominated and most of the prominent writers and artists were men. Women, however, were not less powerful. While it is true that the upper classes were polygamous and viewed women as private property, being bound by caste restrictions and seen as valuable war prizes, the writings of the day emphasize that men's first duty, and pleasure, was to cherish their women, make them as happy as possible and never treat them brutally. Husbands were to spend lavishly on gold and jewels for their wives so as to proclaim their social status. The art of this period shows both sexes wearing elaborate strings of jewels in their hair along with precious necklaces, rings, armlets, anklets and hip girdles.[62]

Eroticism in Indian Art and Literature

In some ways the medieval period becomes the most fertile soil for the production of *sahitya* (literature). The literature of this period is a clear reflection of the luxurious culture of the courts and aristocracy. Poets and writers, dependent on the higher classes' patronage, catered to their lords' increasing demand for erotica. Court poets who wanted to remain in favour had to constantly flatter their patrons by writing erotic literature.[63] Most scholars place *bhakti* as a post-Vedic movement that began primarily in the same period as the epic but it continued and prospered especially in the medieval period. The Sanskrit noun *bhakti* is derived from the verb root *bhaj*,[64] which means attachment, devotion, fondness for, devotion to the universal god. It also is used in terms of human relationships, where it describes the relationships of 'beloved-lover, friend-friend, parent-child, and master-servant. A final common usage may refer to devotion to a *guru* or spiritual teacher as *guru-bhakti*, to a personal form of God, or to divinity without form *nirguna* (Ranjana Malik)'.[65]

Bhakti can be used in the Hindu traditions of Shaivaism and Vaishnavism alike. Also, often seen as the *adwait* philosophy, it is the union of *atma* with *paramatma*, which is shown through a sensual and erotic rasa i.e. *shringara*. This is manifested by the *bhakti* (devotion) movement, which was begun by Tamil poets, it spread across the subcontinent propagated by a vast number of *bhakti* saints such as Kabir, Mirabai, Nanak, Tulsidas, Lalla, Tukaram, Ravidas, Chaitanya and more.[66] The central tenet of this devotional movement was a yearning for oneness with god or the absolute achieved through unconditional love and erotic plea to the god. In the *Bhakti* period, the act of eroticism undergoes a transformation and is dominated by a feeling of yearning. From the copulation of the *tantric* in the ancient period where the union of Shiva and Shakti leads to liberation, to the *Bhakti* period where erotica is expressed through the longing of the union of the *atma* and *parmatma*, the change in the definition of eroticism is remarkable.[67]

It also occurs in compounds where it means 'being a part of' and 'that which belongs to or is contained in anything else.' *Bhajan* or devotional singing to God, is also derived from the same root. Devotion —the most widely used English translation for *bhakti*—does not fully convey two important aspects of the term—the sense of participation that is central to the relationship between the devotee and God, and the intense feeling that is more typically associated with the word love.[68] An *adwaitic* interpretation of *bhakti* goes far beyond devotion and instead defines it as the realization of union with the essential nature of reality as *ananda* or divine bliss. Bhakti is sometimes used in the broader sense of reverence toward a deity or teacher. *Bhakti marga* is usually used to describe a *bhakti* path with complete dedication to one form of God.

Temple architecture and sculpture of this period mirror the inquisitive state of mind. Temples for Vishnu and Shiva resembled a palace for the deity to hold court, attended by gods and dancing girls. The erotic charm of these girls hinted at the rapture to be enjoyed by uniting with God. In some cases, the lovers are shown in complete union, although their peculiar acrobatics—think of the Khajuraho lover seen standing on his head—makes their love an ideal fantasy. This fevered sexuality might have been caused by the strain in medieval India, where sex, condemned in real life, became celebrated in art and religion. Sculptural art in this period centred on the human figure; moving away from the earlier Buddhist visual representations of Bharhut and Sanchi, all the animal and vegetal patterns were pushed out of the narrative onto the borders and panels. In the centre of these rich vegetal patterns of decorations was the human figure. Here the body was youthful, smooth with a transparent luminosity of texture (Kramrisch 1946:173–175).[69]

The *Riti kavya* also known as *Ritis magra*, which was primarily devoted to Krishna *Bhakti*, reached its apogee during the medieval period. The *bhakti* of this genre translated into *shringara* or the erotic aspects of Krishna's life, i.e. his *leela* or play with the *gopis* of Braj. The two genres of *riti kavy* (full of rhetoric) and *riti mukta* (free from rhetoric) contributed greatly to the pool of erotic literature. Two major *riti mukta* poets were Bihari and Ghananand Das. The former wrote the *Sat Sai* and the latter wrote in a spontaneous manner, describing powerful feelings of love, desire and longing in his iconic works *Sujana-Sagara*, *Rasa-Kelivalli* and *Kripa-khanda* (Bahadur 1990:34).[70]

The beginning of the medieval period saw a shift towards the feudal tendencies that determined the productive and economic basis of medieval Indian society. Feudal beginnings are seen in the land grants made in the time of the Gupta rulers. The Kamasutra prescribes the attributes of a *nagaraka* as a man of *grahita vidya* or learning and collector of wealth who should be a householder. However, there are examples that indicate the weakened position of the *nargaraka* class from the seventh century CE onwards. As in all feudal societies, the society witnessed the rise of several grades of landed intermediaries. Overt sensuality and the pursuit of a pleasurable life are two of the hallmarks of this age. So, despite the near male domination of the period, the literature should be celebrated as, specifically in the *Gathasaptasati* of Satavahana Hala, there is an emergence of women's voices and autobiography that is built upon in medieval literature. A few examples of this potent early feminine literature should be proof enough of the strength of the female sexual character at this time:

'A scorpion's bitten her,' they cried,
And as she thrashed about,
Her shrewd friends in her husband's presence
Rushed her to her physician-lover. (Mehrotra 2008:23)[71]

Conclusion

With the British colonialization came in the Western idea of beauty in India. In the realm of the visual arts, painting, sculpture and architecture that was produced under these socio-political conditions showed a marked influence of Western cultural influences. The understanding of carnal desire as a study moves into a more physical space nearly spilling over into the domain of pornography where it is a commodity of hedonistic pleasure.[72] The commodification of the female form as sexual objects: the sensuousness and voluptuousness of feminine beauty in Indian aesthetics has largely been replaced by the notion of crossing the line of coy mistress. Far from describing female sexuality as passive as in Western thought, Indian art and literature is a celebration of the Indian beauty in its fullest form. The current state demands a deep conceptual re-reading of the Kamasutra. Doniger and Kakar (2009:89)[73] rightly states: "The cultural context is urbane and cosmopolitan with a real consciousness of the possible regions of India." She further added, "It is not, as most people think, about positions in sexual intercourse. It is a book about the art of living—about finding a partner, maintaining power in a marriage, committing adultery, living as or with a courtesan, using drugs—and also about positions in sexual intercourse."

The contemporary understanding of the aesthetic of the erotic within Indian culture has moved beyond its singular appealing appraisal. It concerns itself with the indigenous systems around the body and related constructs of otherness, masculinity and femininity, health and sexuality, cultural connotations and personal identity. Contemporay Indian art and literature often delves and dips into the many readings, historical narratives and myths, transforming and translating Pauranic stories within contemporary narratives. In the process new stories, modern forms of storytelling, and retellings have emerged. The ideology of polyphony is embedded in today's expressions. The words carry different meanings and resonances according to varying audiences. This is the age of interpretation: the author's word is not the final one. Any fixity of meaning is denied; a piece of work could contain different analysis and versions. Therefore, these forces of development, from the ancient to the contemporary, have affected the depiction of the notion of erotic thoughts in India.

In my opinion, the basic tenets of love, longing, lust and desire, as expounded in Kamasutra, remain as relevant as they were more than 2000 years ago. The human emotions cuts across boundaries of geography, race, and community. The ethics of conjugal life have not shifted dramatically. What emerges through the social reading of society is that the narrative is driven by the dynamics of hypocrisy and double-standards. The *purusharthas* as stated in Kamasutra have lost their ethical significance as stated in the text in the in the current context of contemporary life. The paper attempts to draw attention to the notion that how the exploration of the spiritual and the erotic through Indian art and literature is still a source of great inspiration for writers, artists and even sophisticated city dwellers/*nagarka* of the Kamasutra, to lead an enriching, joyous, abundantly sensual and fulfilling life.

References

24. Appadorai, Angadipuram. (1992) *Indian Political Thinking: Through the Ages*. New Delhi: Khama Publishers.
25. Bahadur, K.P. (1990) *Rasikapriya of Keshavadas*. New Delhi: Motilal Banarasidass Publications.
26. Burton, Sir Richard and Arbuthnot, F.F. (trans.) (1995) *The Kamasutra of Vatsyayana*. Ware: Wordsworth Classics.
27. Carman, John B. (2005) 'Bhakti' in *Encyclopaedia of Religion* Vol.2. 2d, edited by Lindsay Jones, 856–860. Detroit, MI: Macmillan Reference.
28. Dehejia, Vidya. (1997) *Indian Art*. New York: Phaidon Press.
29. Dehejia, Vidya. (1997) 'Issues of Spectatorship and Representation', in *Representing the Body: Gender Issues in Indian Art*, edited by Vidya Dehejia. New Delhi: Kali for Women.
30. Desai, Devangana. (1975) *Erotic Sculpture of India: A Socio-Cultural Study*. Tata McGraw-Hill Publishing Company, New Delhi.
31. Doniger, W., and Kakar, S. (2009) *Kamasutra by Vatsyayana*. Oxford: Oxford University Press.
32. Flood, Gavin. (1996) *An Introduction to Hinduism*. New York: Cambridge University Press.

33. Geaves, Ron. (2008) 'Bhakti Movement' in *Encyclopaedia of Hinduism*, edited by Denise Cush, Catherine Robinson, and Michael York, 89–97. London and New York: Routledge.
34. Gupta, C. (2002) *Sexuality, Obscenity, Community: Women: Muslims and The Hindu Public in Colonial India.* New York: Palgrave.
35. Haksar, A.N.D. (trans.) (2011) *Kamasutra: A Guide to the Art of Pleasure by Vatsyayana*. New Delhi: London: Penguin.
36. Lutgendorf, Philip. (2003) 'Medieval Devotional Traditions: An Annotated Survey of Recent Scholarship' in *The Study of Hinduism*, edited by Arvind Sharma, 200–260. Columbia, SC: University of South Carolina Press.
37. Kramrisch, Stella. (1946) *The Hindu Temple*. Calcutta: University of Calcutta.
38. Malla, K. (1964) *Ananga Ranga: Stage of the Bodiless One: The Hindu Art of Love*. New York: Medical Press of New York.
39. Mehrotra, A.K. (2008) *The Absent Traveller: Prakrit Love Poetry from the Gathasaptasati of Satavahana Hala*. New Delhi: Penguin Classics.
40. Malik, Ranjana. *Devotion—A Necterine Bliss*, available at https://www.speakingtree.in/allslides/devotion—a-necterine-bliss. (Accessed on June 2, 2018).
41. Paniker, K. Ayyappa. (1997) *Medieval Indian Literature: An Anthology—* Volume One, edited by Paniker, K. Ayyappa. New Delhi: Sahitya Akademi.
42. Pollock, S. (2006). *The Language of the Gods in the World of Men: Sanskrit, Culture, and Power in Premodern India.* Berkeley: University of California.
43. Rawson, Philip. (1984) *Oriental Erotic Art.* New York: Omega Books.
44. Schelling, Andrew. (trans.) (2019) *Erotic Love Poems from India: 101 Classics on Desire and Passion.* Berkeley: Shambhala Publications.
45. Available at http://shodhganga.inflibnet.ac.in/bitstream/10603/26519/8/08_chapter%203.pdf (Accessed on May 20, 2018).
46. Tharu, Susie and Lalita, K. (1991) *Women Writing in India Volume I–600 BC to the Early Twentieth Century*. New Delhi: Oxford University Press.

Growth and Development of Indian Craft from Manufacturing Perspective

Muralidhar Lakkanna and *Tombing Vungsonching*

Abstract

Indian crafts have deep historical significance, rich cultural heritage and their distinct literary style have an awesome legacy. Most of their developmental detours are primarily attributable to the gaps in value chain, anomalous need-fulfilment, unorganised network with imperfect backward-forward integration, unregulated economy has led vulnerability to high risk and significant drudgery owing to high reliance on obsolete technology. So, the well-thought over proposition for preservation was to lead crafts towards inclusive manufacturing prospects. This will prompt all stake-holders to participate and derive a dignified set of derivatives, its sustenance depends on the extent of transparency, trust level, participation/teamwork, truth, courteous tolerance and tenacity.

Indian crafts have deep historical significance, rich cultural heritage and their distinct literary style have an awesome legacy. Most of their developmental detours are due to the disrupts in value chain, anomalies in need-fulfillment and unorganized networking with imperfect backward-forward integration. Review of this unregulated economy has revealed a serious risk vulnerability and significant drudgery owing to excessive reliance on obsolete technologies. Only an inclusive value chain can render opportunities for all stakeholders to contribute their full potential and get a dignified set of derivatives. The perspective here is to preserve these slumping fortes to vital contributors for development.

Scholars, forums, international organizations, researchers, dictionaries, and national associations articulate crafts by many definitions in several contexts. Crafts are products produced by (i) manual effort[1] (ii) a substantial level of skill or expertise (iii) a

[1] with least or no input from machines.

significant level of tradition and (iv) largely typify the legacy of survival.[2] In 1989, Development Commissioner of Handicrafts, Government of India provided a simple and functional definition as "Items made by hand, often using simple tools, and... generally artistic and /or traditional in nature". They include objects of utility and/or objects of decoration. Another definition is "A skilled activity in which something is made traditionally with the hands rather than being produced by machines in a factory, or an object made by such an activity."[3] Likewise, UNESCO/ UNCTAD/WTO defines it as "artefacts are made by craftspeople, either completely by hand, or using hand tools or even mechanical means, as long as the direct manual contribution of the artisan remains the most substantial component of the finished artefact. Crafts derive their distinctness from the characteristic features of the artefacts or the artisan's noesis, that include utilitarian, aesthetics, creativity, cultural significance, decorative, functional, traditional, religious and socially symbolic".

The Indus valley civilization is known for its practice of essential crafts like earthen pots, ceramic beads, combs, metal sculptures, seals, painting on pottery, as well as attires.[4] Artisans were objectively fulfilling food, clothes, utensils, shoes, and other essential necessities for the whole community. This virtue won the royal patronage of medieval rulers and elite classes; their encouragement had fostered several crafts triumph to their helms across the country. Mainly because of this political clout, craft practices also underwent acculturative blending amongst indigenous indwells and foreign invaders, thus evolving crafts significantly across India. During the British period, India came to be a source for cheap imports. raw fibres were imported from India at cheap rates and finished fabrics were exported to India for premium rates. Farmers were constrained to produce raw materials and supply at cheaper rates much less than their cultivating expense. Indian consumption was regulated and controlled through shrewd taxations. Thus, coerced Indian consumers to buy their imported products rather than native Indian products. This allure strife crippled the livelihood of almost all stakeholders; the unjust exploitation accrued huge losses and; scrupulously eroded traditional Indian craft economy into a steep recession.[5] During the National movement, and the boycott of British cloth, rise of 'Swadeshi' goods and Khadi movement and ensued

[2] Liebl and Roy 2003.

[3] Cambridge Dictionary.

[4] Kenoyer, 2004.

[5] Jena, 2010.

empathetic post-independence public policies. These policies resurged the deep concerns across several craft value chains for contemporary needs was a renaissance in Indian crafts economy. Like oppressed domestic value chains were restored deliberately in the 1st five-year plan (FYP) and; unfairly ignored crafts were encouraged emphatically in the 2nd FYP. Adoption of Industrial Policy on LPG by the government of India in the early 1990s, pitched competition in craft economy as well.[6] Liberally allowing foreign goods enabled demand for higher value needs. Similarly, globalization also opened global markets for Indian crafts.[7] Subsequently, uplifting the overall standard of the craft sector like asset capitalisation, affordable developments and export orientation were envisaged in the 3rd to 7th FYP.[8]

Literature

For over centuries, crafts have prompted harmony among over 3000 castes, 432 tribal communities, believers of different religions who speak over 1650 dialects.[9] The communal diversities among artisans have culminated as varieties in craft practices. Like crafts ascribe history, ethnic styles, often culture and sometimes religion only to each state, region, geography, etc., For instance, varied styles of weaving exemplify their state of origin on a basis of design, colour, yarn, thickness, and so on. Some of these transformations are narrated with textile crafts, metal crafts, wood crafts, earthen crafts, stone crafts, and leather crafts. Crafts is the second largest economy engaging most Indians, besides agriculture; so to enhance value accession and sustaining their entire value chain a visionary transformation is imperative for national development.

Craftspeople are primary stakeholders making artefacts at the beginning of value chains. They are often at the grassroots and their demographic distribution, status, engagement level, wisdom, and entrepreneurship establish the prospect of aggregate value accession. However, value means different things for a diverse group of people or individual stakeholders. Since there are several craft practices and distributed over several value chains; ranking and ordering their networks is too complicated. So from an inclusive manufacturing perspective, products involving many stakeholders with cumulative

[6] Liberalization, Privatization, Globalization.

[7] Jena, 2010.

[8] Jadhav, 2014.

[9] Kapur and Mittar, 2014.

revenue earnings from a craft practise are considered together as the net worth of a craft value chain in this script to annotate growth and development of Indian crafts; Figure 1 depicts this value.

Figure 1: *Dispersion of craftspeople and revenue in different crafts* (Viswanathan 2013).

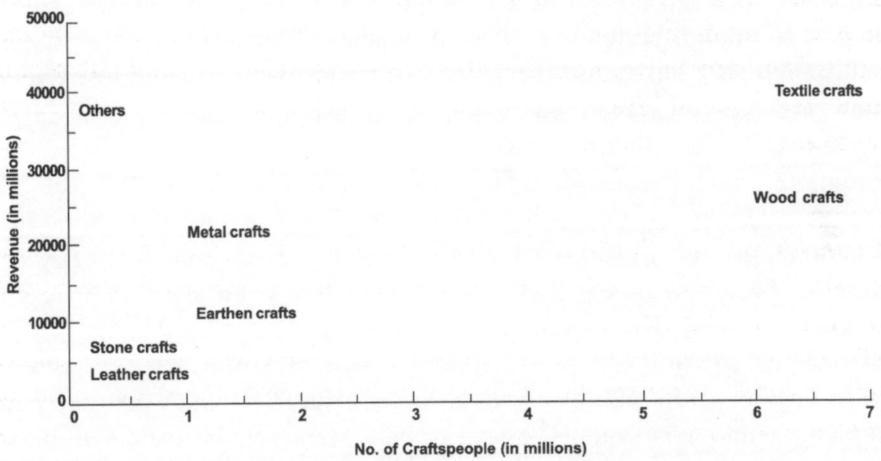

Textile Crafts

Textile crafts of India are vibrant colourful, have rich traditional significance and cultural heritage. Costumes of Indus valley civilization in anthropologist records thousands of years of rich heritage of textile craft in India. Each Indian state has unique costume ethnicities; like Kalamkari in Andhra Pradesh, Muga Silk in Assam, Bandhani in Gujarat, Zardosi in Lucknow, Panja Durries in Haryana, and so on. Altho' their style, design and raw material differ; together they make textile craft the largest in India. Bandhani, Zardosi, and Kalamkari are discussed to illustrate their growth and development. Some of the metal crafts in India are Bidri craft of Andhra Pradesh, Dhokra craft, Silver filigree, beaten silver engraving in West Bengal and the Brassware of Moradabad. Usually bronze, copper, silver, gold, and iron artefacts were atypical. Many historic crafts like damascening a weaponry craftsmanship of inlaying gold and silver wires and wafers on swords, shields, armour and other iron objects have lost contemporary relevance. Koftagiri, the craftsmanship of encrusting one metal over another to rituals and festivities by the elite classes.[10] Brassware of Moradabad has evolved through contemporary need and earned the city a name as "Peetal Nagri" or Brass City. Since pre-medieval era, woodcarving, and wooden artefacts were mainly utilised for construction of buildings, temples, palaces, chariots, houses, carts and so on. So most historical monuments across India exemplify the excellence of skills, designs, and proficiency of wood craftsmanship. The diversity of these varieties of wooden crafts depends on origin, purpose, wood, etc. Unique styles and exclusive cultural preferences were in practice in each state; these styles and preferences have rendered proficiency with distinct identities. Every state ascribes its traditional wood crafts and customary practices to accentuate their innate creativity.[11] Wooden toys of Varanasi, the exquisite and intricate Marapani wood carving for houses in Kerala, wooden cutlery of Udayagiri in Andhra Pradesh and the infamous Khatamband ceiling craft of Kashmir. The design and intricacy of diverse Indian wooden crafts have attracted popularity in foreign markets as well. Khatamband, a craft of binding wooden patches is narrated as a case study below. Extensive use of earthen clay in pottery is an ancient craft.[12] Using a wheel to centrifugally mould the clay and forming it into axis symmetric pots or pans were popular craft than hand moulding practice into a non-axis symmetric form. Besides, utensils earthen crafts involved toys, decorative vases, figurines, roofing tiles, etc. Typical earthen craft examples are the terracotta horse of Panchmura from Bankura, West Bengal; blue pottery crafts of Jaipur; Longpi coiled pottery of Manipur; Glazed pottery of Uttar Pradesh; black pottery of Azamgarh and so on. This script discusses below Blue pottery earthen craft as a representative case. Since the use of small stones to make weapons like arrowheads or spears for hunting in the evulsion as art, tradition, and culture; stone crafts have profound history. Each state in the country has a different style of sculpting several forms and many purposes are in practice. Usually, many gods, goddesses, and tiles are sculptured on soft stone, marble, and granite. Historically evident monuments, temples, statues, deities or figurines illustrate the excellence, and adeptness of stone sculptors. The abundance of marble and scarcity of wood encouraged the growth of marble craft in Rajasthan. This script discusses below skilful sculpting of granite, the hardest of all stones in Bihar as a representative case. Since primitive

[10] Ranjan and Ranjan, 2005.
[11] Majumdar, 2011.
[12] Pratap, 2016.

hunting, leather crafts have a long antecedence of making attire, costumes, leather shoes with intricate designs and vibrant ornaments. Eventually, they have evolved to making of saddles, shoes, bags, water bottles and so on. The basic raw material comes from the hides of various animals like the popular Masak made from goatskin which is used to sell cold water along the streets of markets.[13] Besides, protection leather is considered as the insignia of wealth, fashion, and royalty. Mojaris of Gujarat and Rajasthan; Kolhapuris of Kolhapur, Maharashtra and; Leather puppets of South India are few famous leather crafts. This script discusses Mojari craft as a representative case.

Case Studies: Bandhani and Zardosi

The Sanskrit verb bandh is a traditional embellishment craft of type dyeing fabrics most pervasively.[14] Bandhani involves high skill folding, twisting, knotting the fabric, tying them tightly with a thread at several points and pulling them out to develop through the knots. Producing a pattern variety like Chandrakala, Bavan Baug, Shikari etcetera depends on the distinct wrap design technique. These Bandhanis are then hand plucked with fingernails to form decorative figurative designs by patterns of many tiny knots, typically a meter length of cloth can have thousands of tiny knots known as "Bheendi" in local Gujarati language; these knots form a pattern once opened after dyeing in bright colours. Dot, square, wave, and stripe Bheendis are popular design patterns formed from Ekdali,[15] Trikunti,[16] Chaubandi,[17] Dungar shahi,[18] Boond,[19] kodi,[20] laddu jalebi[21] and leheriya.[22] The costing depends on the number of tie-ups in the fabric/garment; the most intricate design in a saree will have nearly 75,000 dots or tie-ups. Yellow, red, green, black are chic colours and are mostly bright, deep and dark shades. Each colour has a special significance, such as red for marriage; saffron for divinity; yellow for the spring season or the start of a new venture and; finally, black and maroon are for mourning. The dyes are mostly natural organic and made from leaves, roots, and flowers. As the colours tend to fade

---

[13] Soofi, 2017.

[14] "to bind, to tie-up".

[15] *single knot.*

[16] three knots.

[17] four knots.

[18] mountain pattern.

[19] small dot with a dark centre.

[20] teardrop shape.

[21] round Indian sweets.

[22] waves.

while wet washing instead needs dry cleaning; to preserve their strength and vibrancy low heat setting must be ensured while ironing either by covering it with a muslin cloth before ironing.[23]

Women do the tedious process of tying knots on the garments while men do the dying part along with managing the business. The craft has outgrown from familial practice to community-based practice. As in Rajput paintings, men wearing leheriya turbans and women wearing Bandhani blouses manifest the distinct culture. There are multiple styles, colours, motifs and designs involved in Bandhani. Leheriya, a tie-dye type, is used mainly for men in turbans and dupattas of women. Traditional varieties are 'khombhi', 'Ghar Chola', 'Chandrakhani', 'Shikari', 'Chowkidaar', 'Ambadaal' and other categories. Each sub-community and tribe have their own unique Bandhani design that distinguishes them from the rest. Because of this, the cultural codes of Rajasthan assimilate Bandhani.[24]

Bandhani has its traces from Indus Valley Civilisations and since 4000 BC around Gujarat, Rajasthan, Sindh, Punjab and Tamil Nadu region;[25] however, Kutch in Gujarat and Rajasthan were the major centres of Bandhani craft. According to the legend, a holy sadhu visited a khatri's house, and when the sadhu was meditating[26] and knots appeared on the cloth that was meant to be dyed. The cloth was dyed just the way it was, and when the knots were opened, an exquisite pattern emerged. Since then khatris pay attention to the way they form it and have continued working on it. This later became referred to as Bandhani, the first Bandhani saree was worn in a royal marriage at the time of Barra Bhatt's Harshacharita,[27] the history of King Harshavardan of Kannauj. So, wearing a Bandhani saree as bridal wear is considered to bring a good future. Wall paintings of Ajanta have stood as a testimony of evidence for Bandhani sarees.[28]

The wall paintings[29] depicting the life of Buddha found on the wall of Cave I at Ajanta is the earliest evidence seen so far, where maidservants are wearing blouses with visible tie-dye patterns; large bright dots and rings on almost transparent dark violet fabrics. In the Bagh cave paintings, garments with long-sleeves have greenish yellow

[23] Fitzgerald, 1992.

[24] Jain and Tiwari, 2012.

[25] where it's locally known as Sungudi.

[26] jap.

[27] 606–648 AD.

[28] Wada 2012.

[29] 6th CE.

tunic decorations with a single white dot in circle motif. Alike illustrations also occur in Jain scriptures from the 12th CE of women wearing tie-dye. In Gujarat, the earliest surviving pieces of bandhani were fragments of silk bandhani used by Jain monks to interleave manuscript pages in the medieval period onwards. These exquisite printing of cotton fabrics also finds mention in the texts of Alexander the great. Khatri community-dwelling around Kutchh, Saurashtra and Sindh region are believed to be the primary practitioners of Bandhani. Being the main source of income and their affluence attracted East India Company into this business of exporting these tie-dyed silk Bandana textiles like the famous handkerchiefs, rumals and scarfs across Europe and around the world in the late 1720s. The Indian origin Bandhani exported from Bengal to London by the East India Company have made appearances in many British paintings from that time period. Indian bandhani also travelled to other British colonies such as West Indies and East Africa.

During its peak in the early 19th century; many merchants and traders of Rajasthan began wearing bright coloured Bandhani turbans with pride. However, by early 20th CE screen printing competed stiffly and subdued the demand for Bandhani. Besides, they closely guarded its craftsmanship knowledge and that eventually led to its rapid decline; today around 5000 artisans are only practicing this craft.[30]

Zardosi

"Zardosi" hyphenates two Persian terms "Zar" etymologizing *gold* and "dosi" etymologizing *work*; implying gold work. So it's a Persian embroidery craft that's omni-practiced in India since the 12th century. Artisans use gold and silver threads to embellish elaborate three-dimensional textures on royal attire. They used them to decorate wall hangings, curtains, scabbards, paraphernalia of regal wrappings on horses and elephants of emperors. Further, magnificent crafts were made by studding pearls and precious stones that eventually became priced possessions. Its practice was traditionally in Lucknow, Bhopal, Agra, Kashmir, Ajmer, Kolkata and lately around Delhi and Andhra Pradesh. During its peak, Zardosi value chain was lucrative and well-organized three-tier system comprising exporters or traders in the first tier, karkhanedars or commission agents in the second tier and skilled artisans known as karigars in the third tier. Karigar task was the most arduous but least remunerating in the entire value accession system.

[30] Acharya and Samani, 2017.

Karigars sit cross-legged around the addaa[31] with their tools. These tools include curved hooks, needles, salmaa pieces,[32] sitaaras,[33] round-sequins, ceramic and plastic beads, dabkaa[34] and kasab. Next they trace a design on the fabric like silk, satin or velvet. They then stretch the fabric over the wooden frame and the embroidery work begins. A needle is used to pull out each zardozi element and integrated into the basic design by pushing it into the fabric itself.

Patronage of Akbar glorified Zardosi in the 17th century, but the disdain of Aurangzeb and his successors relinquished it. As the royal patronage descended the cost of practicing this craft rose while the revenue declined. This trounced the affluence, the relinquishes overthrew the livelihoods of many artisans and compelled many of them to migrate away to other regions in search of an alternate vocation for a living.[35] However, 19th century industrialization mechanized the karigar drudgery to economise Zardosi craft. Besides advancements in technology have introduced new forms of textiles, so there is more scope for these alternate mechanized karigar viz Zardosi craft to become relevant for contemporary needs, more artistic and better traditional value. Using actual gold or silver threads for the crafts got substituted by economical metallic or coated strings.

Kalamkari hyphenates two terms "Kalam" that etymologize *pen* and "kari" that etymologize *work*; in a slangy reference to painting with a pen. Costumes and draperies in the Ellora and Ajanta frescoes with Kalamkari designs are its earliest evidence.[36] Kalamkari crafts were formally practiced to make chiktrakatta artistic paintings on canvas as a religious tapestry. Vagabond storytelling dancers, poets, singers, and painters used these chiktrakattas to depict stories from Hindu mythology and roamed around the villages. Their distinctive folk beliefs fashioned and popularised the craft. The Muslim rulers transformed it as secular craft and Kalamkari artisan community was recognized as "Qualamkars" and patronized particularly by the Sultans of Golconda. Owing to these patronages, the glory of Kalamkari crafts rose during the Mughal Era to an extent of exporting the fabric in large quantities to many foreign countries from east to west. This economy attracted East India Company in the 18th century to also trade in large quantities to UK. This British

[31] a wooden frame.

[32] gold wires.

[33] metal stars.

[34] thread.

[35] Sherry and Mehta, 2008.

[36] Chandra, 2015.

demand obligated transformation in its style for their foreign consumer preferences. The impressive demand it garnered in international markets made it flourishing merchandise for British.[37] Late 17th century industrial and automation advents in the textile industries reversed the supply chain and by the early 18th century cheap British made fabrics with Kalamkari replica were sold in India. Neither these cheap British made replicates reined the true historical value of Kalamkari nor their Indian base fabric and that devolved its demand and incited protest against its import. In 1701, the British government retaliated this protest by banning the import of Indian textiles in all forms. This ban along with the rise of the Batik industry in Indonesia led to the decline in the craft. Altho' most craftspeople took this skill to their graves; few foresighted craftspeople transferred their knowledge by facilitating its inheritance to ensure the survival of this craft. However, the scarcity of organic stains and the tedious process to prepare natural dyes has made it expensive, while the use of alternate inexpensive chemical dye is deterring its traditional value.

Kalahasti and Machilipatnam in Andhra Pradesh are its two major centres practicing Kalamkari. Kalahasti crafts persons paint only in hand while Machilipatnam craftspeople also use block printing along with hand painting. Kalamkari products have evolved from portraits, wall hangings in temples to clothes, bedspreads, prayer mats and so on. Today, there are over 300 crafts persons practicing some aspect of *kalamkari* work, from preparing cloth and dyes, to designing motifs and formatting the layout, to final painting and execution.

Brassware, Khatamband—Blue Pottery

The golden lustre of brass articles symbolizes prestige and sanctity in traditional rituals. So, brass was extensively used in everyday life in the form of utensils like thalli, pots, pans, tumblers, trays, etc., since time immemorial. Muslim craftspeople incursion into India brought newer skills, improved tools and diversified crafts for making various other artefacts. Eventually in the Mughal regime, the art of making brassware led to forming a largest brassware cluster in Moradabad, Uttar Pradesh, India. Most articles were made by cast, forged, extruded, rolled, formed, etc., with specialized skills at each stage of production and detailed fine engravings were carved on them to improve value. However, they were largely organized on individual proprietorship, so traders and dealers were inevitable for the supply of raw materials and distribution of

[37] Purohit, 2013.

finished goods as well as retailers for selling their finished artefacts. Thus, low value acceding intermediaries commanded major cost while the high-value acceders got only a meagre about 20% of the cost.[38]

With the British regime, East India Company took the brassware articles and artefact to foreign markets and that leads to the dispersal of craft practice to the neighbouring areas including places like Benaras, Lucknow, Agra and Jalesar. This increase in crafts persons infused higher competition and scrambled income. These ill-effects and poor living conditions deterred the interests of the next generation brassware crafts persons into this practice. However, modern technologies like electroplating, lacquering, powder coating etc. found their way to this craftsmanship.[39] Instead of adopting appropriate technology, their heavy reliance on empirical methods and casual slaying of resources is trifling the art. Besides, brassware utility in households is now getting limited for occasional rituals and religious functions while foreign subs from Thailand and China are offering a tough competition; thus, brassware economy is receding. Like in 2008–09, the Moradabad brassware cluster had 1,800 SSIs locally designated as karkhanedars and 25,000 unregistered household units; together they employed 3,60,000 people. But today, there're around 1,80,000 artisans altogether.[40]

"Khatam" in Arabic means *patch* and band in Persian means *lock*; Khatamband is a slangy reference to the craft of locking patches with its origin tracing to 14th century sultanates. As per local legend, an Iranian Sufi saint migrated to Kashmir accompanied by Iranian craftspeople who later taught the art of Khatamband to the local craftspeople. Originally the Geer communities were the only ones practicing and inheriting Khatamband.[41] Khatamband is a skill of panelling and binding small pieces of wood in the ceiling to get geometric patterns of folding and braiding intricate pieces without using nails or glue. Its uniqueness is, it can be disassembled and reassembled at different locations or any other moments without destroying the primary piece. Many palaces, public buildings, colonial residences, and temples were decorated with khatamband ceilings. By the early 19th century, it was even exported to England and by the late 19th century Kashmiri boat owners started decorating their boats with Khatamband to attract tourists. As their insulating property kept the houses warm even in the cold climate of

[38] Sajid, 1989.
[39] Saha, 2004.
[40] Sachan, Munagala and Chakravarty 2013.
[41] Mirani, 2006.

Kashmir; thus, Khatamband became popular and reached its peak.[42] Its characteristic drudgery deposed affordability and its value trifle wasn't appealing anymore to its core consumers, owners of boat houses. Besides the scarcity of raw materials and expensive labour cost are together deterring the next generation to pursue Khatamband as a profession. Since the conservatively inherited Khatamband skill is descending its relevance to contemporary needs, its practitioners are imparting their skills to artisans beyond Geer community. About 300 Khatamband artisans have registered with the Marketing and Service Extension Centre, Srinagar, office of the Development Commissioner Handicrafts, Ministry of Textiles Government of India. It's estimated that the total annual turnover of Khatamband amounts to C10.71 crores.[43]

Blue pottery is a blend of Chinese glazing and Persian decorative craft. Its characteristic acronym is from the dominant blue colour got from the mixture of copper oxide with sugar or salt used for this craft. As per local legend, once Maharaja Sawai Ram II was watching his kite-master compete with others, surprisingly the imperial kite's thread was cut by that of two potter brothers, Churamani and Kaluram, who had coated their string with the blue-green glass-like dust they were using in their pottery. Their theme impressed Maharaja and he nominated them to the Royal school of art, Goonga Mehra ki Gali, Gangori Bazaar. This patronage led blue pottery to Jaipur and encouraged the craft to thrive formally.[44] The eventual blue Jaipur potteries embarked on mass production of tiles for embellishing mausoleums, catacombs, fortresses and eventually became popular for decoration throughout Jaipur.[45] The craft was practiced as a household vocation predominantly involving family members; where typically women ground and prepared the pigments while men moulded them into pottery forms, painted and burnt them.

Over time several communities including Muslim, Rajput, Natt, Kumhar, Regar, etc., have also begun practicing blue pottery crafts. As Jaipur blue pottery craft thrived thro' 18th century and during the periods of Sawai Jai Singh and Sawai Ram Singh II; Ram Singh II set up a school of art in 1886 and encouraged formal craft training to learn and practice the skill.[46] However, with the closure of this school of art in

---

[42] Kapoor, 2013.

[43] Aen, Alam and Ahmad, 2015.

[44] Ranjan and Ranjan, 2005.

[45] Mathur and Shukla, 2014.

[46] Gupta, 2011.

1952, the craft has trifled to around 300 craftspeople left now, who are manufacturing for export of blue pottery art.

Pathar Kama (Stone Craft) and Mojari Jootie

Stone carvings are in practice since the pre-medieval era, it's evident from the monuments and structures like Ashok pillar at Sarnath that stone craft was dominant around Bihar in Mauryan era. During its peak in the Mauryan era, more than 10 villages were engaged in stone carving only.[47] Royal patronage of Rani Ahilyabai of Indore flourished this craft in the 18th century. Like around 1300 gaud brahmin craftspersons were engaged to renovate the Vishnupad temple in Bihar. Stone crafts gained popularity within the country as a traditional art and in foreign countries for its creativity along with the spread of Buddhism religion. Household wares of convenience like mortars, pestle, thali, bowls, tubs, etc., kept the craft in usance. Its skill was inherited thro' the Gaud Brahmin clans till independence, post-independence it was taught beyond Gaud brahmins to all communities as well. Now there are around 190 families from different backgrounds and castes are still practicing stone craft.[48]

Overtime to bid with substitutes, stone artisans are alienating the artistic affluence of Pathar Kama towards simple artefact making. Besides, they have diversified from high-value essential need fulfilment to low-value complimentary artefacts. As a result, Pathar Kama stone craft has a tedious labour-intensive stone carving than creative artistic value accession. Moreover, the undue exploitation of stone quarries is making the required raw material scarce and expensive; making the artisans and consumers apathetic.

In the 16th century, fourth Mughal Emperor Saleem Shah, popularly known as Jahangir patronized Mojari or Khussa style footwear craft beyond functionality as a symbol of royalty, social and religious status. Their insoles and linings were made of one-piece traditionally using tanned buffalo, camel, cow or buffalo leather and mantled with textile vamp with intricate embroidery designs, welts embedding precious stones, brass nails, cowry shells, mirrors, bells and ceramic beads.[49] Eco-friendly, bright golden and ornate cotton threads, enmeshing leather fibres for better strength were used to bind the stack of the upper welt to leather lining and the bottom sole. The distinct ornamental style, shape, appearance and unique insulating and durability characteristics make

[47] UMSAS, 2018.

[48] Patther Katti, 2013.

[49] Srivastava and Sharma, 2014.

Mojaris craft artistic and behold cultural significance. The craft has a unique feature of a 'priori customising user feet/preferences by actually wearing them and also there is not any distinction between left and right. Althou' with each artisan practicing uniquely, the skill has evolved into several varieties in design, colours, encapsulating the cultural diversity, local ethos, and ethnicity.

Mojari making involves many communities like the leather selection and processing are done by "Chamars"; dying of the finely processed leather is done by "Rangaras" and; cutting, assembling several leather pieces and stitching the final pair of Mojari is done by "Mochis". Typically cutting, pasting and stitching above the sole is done by men and women do the delicate embroidery. Traditional natural tanning is time intensive, expensive and requires expert handling; the dearth of such expert crafts persons was coercing raw material preparation, so chemical tanning is now in practice.[50] Mojari Jootie craft is still in practice thro' traditional inheritance around Rajasthan and Gujarat but is scrambling to meet the consumeristic need, preferences of the present generation and competitive significance over alternate forms of footwear. Artificial materials are now in use for decorating the upper canvas to reduce cost and owe to a higher value than competing artefacts.

Organization

Physiological, safety, belongingness, and esteem are the four most fundamental, basic, essential and crucial needs for the very existence of the human race are "deficiency needs" or "d-needs" in accordance to Maslow's hierarchy; the various pursuits to endure with these d-needs have surged as crafts. Crafts have further accustomed to social changes and organized to aptly meet contemporary utilitarian needs; thus are a means of creativity, skill, and intelligence.

Most crafts began as individual's knowhow and later scooped to collectively practice by groups of people; this contiguity evolved to households, communities, clusters, cottage industries, small-scale enterprises and so on. As with household crafts, most of the adult members took an active part in the production process and often by distributing the process among them. Every habitation settlement (village) in pre-medieval era, started by having one craftsman of his calling in the community, these artisans were respectable members of that small community who were living by bartering their produces or

[50] Bhansali and Jangid, 2015.

exchanging their services for equal occupational standing. Sometimes artisans were also nomads, like potters moving around the village meeting to the needs of different villagers as long their services were needed, mostly such crafts persons didn't have any proper value accession structure or organization. Progressively, each family member's practice became specialised to a few activities in the value chain and they acquired their specialty skills or individual expertise. Also, as their families grew, separated and spread; groups practicing a particular craft of its kind got associated around a cluster of villages of their own; like 150 carpenters or 100 smiths in some villages. All those dwelling around such areas were practicing the same or similar occupation or sharing common objectives, innately cooperated with each other. This socialisation prompted local structuring with compassion among stakeholders of specific crafts and tagged geographical indexes with those regions.[51] Cultivators, herdsmen, financiers, traders, and artisans got together to form their own ascensive clans and castes. Each of these influential communities got recognition, and their leaders wielded considerable authority as they were often consulted by kings.[52] These communities received fixed allowances from politically higher groups like land grants or other concessions, free residence, food and clothing. Through guilds, craft persons could inclusively address their problems among themselves and got better prospects to represent for collective action.[53]

After independence, craft persons practicing the same craft came together ignoring caste differences to form a better-organized guilds structure for representation as craft clusters. These clusters were a geographical concentration of micro, small, medium and large enterprises making the same or a similar range of artefacts.[54] As a cluster, they could deal with common or similar sets of threats[55] and opportunities.[56, 57] Cluster activities also emphasize heavily on skilling, developing technologies, promoting advanced knowledge through regular workshops for active craft people, exposing to modern fabrication methods, using novel materials and prompting awareness on

---

[51] Mahapatra, 2012.

[52] Ramesh, 2016.

[53] S. Kramrisch, 1958.

[54] Goods or services.

[55] E.g. product obsolescence or lack of markets.

[56] E.g. increasing turnover through quality upgradation or introduction of new artefacts and increasing exports through targeted marketing.

[57] Bhattacharyya, 2014.

the contemporary need for artefacts.[58] Craft enterprises are mostly MSMEs and unorganised unlike huge regular factories in China; mainly because of sterner labour regulations and the risk of unionization hindering overall development.[59]

In the early medieval period, with the increase in the need for the utilitarian items, many people were practicing various crafts. By the medieval period, more people got involved and their skills also became specialised; this steady increase was due to finer meeting of need despite changing needs as showed in Figure 2. This increase was mostly owing to the skill dispersion from individual to family members, inheritance and legacy. However, the incursion of foreign traders during the latter part of the medieval era acceded contrastive skills from around the world into India, likewise Indian crafts also reached to foreign consumers. Most craft practices reached their covets mainly owing to the state patronage; relevance to their artefacts to societal life like never before; the dependence of most stakeholders on artefact for sustenance and; diversification of most trendy crafts into several derivative artefacts which was increasing production quantity. This en-masse organising and broadening range of crafts led to various other occupations, vocations and enabled many other ancillary livelihoods.

The neoteric aggregators often adopted state patronage to command foothold. Especially while the Mughal regime rose, their state administration

Figure 2: *Chronicle of the number of people involved in crafts.*

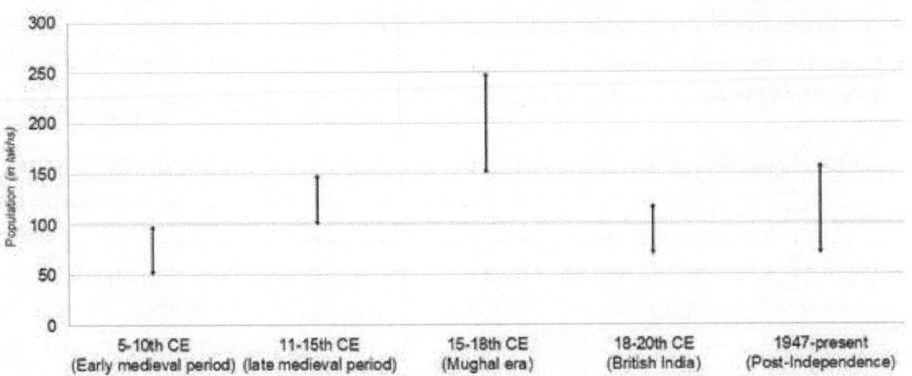

[58] Ghosh, 2012.

[59] Liebl and Roy, 2003.

meticulously controlled craft economy by veiling avid command over the entire value chain. They encouraged Islamic bias and that transpired to thoroughly secularise crafts such that the acculturing of crafts ensued its economic glory. Like the elocute demands of royals, noble and elite class motivated artisans to passionately produce peerless artefacts specifically for them, some of which are best even today. The exquisite use of precious stones, vivacity of colours, the traditionalism of manufacturing processes, intricate designs and large requirements inspired development of creative rigour, enthused artisans to demonstrate their best-in-class professional talents, this intensified overall competence of some tasks and a few artisans specialised some skills. The callous imposition of greedy policies by the invading Britishers for commercial exploitation of thriving craft economies led to outright seizure as seen in Figure 2 and wrecked the livelihood of all stakeholders depending on the crafts; like even popular or master craft persons had to seek alternate employments for fulfilling their basic needs. The British outrage eventually drew most artisans to abandon crafts and that quickly decreased active artisans from almost all craft practices. Further the affluence of East India company into the lucrative crafts value chain led to introduction of many neoteric artefacts. These incursions pre-empted many customary practices, disordered established methods, ridiculed native creativity and jealousy countered the heritage. The neoteric artefacts differed largely from those made by traditional practices, primarily compromising the zest of creativity and ingenuity. Traditional crafts were either family, community and/or location specific and were mainly made out of locally available materials. Collectively as the family or a group of families of artisans assumed the customary responsibility for procuring raw materials, processing, making of artefacts, storing and selling, while the neoteric manufacturing fragmented these activities and squared them to compete with intra commercial interests. Rapid decline in the number of individuals thoroughly disrupted the entire crafts value chain and quelled the overall revenue of the sector as showed in Figure 2. Post-Independence, successive policies are strategically fetching more artisans to active practice and apparently recuperating the craft economy as in Figure 2. But, there is acute dearth of master crafts persons, experts, skilled and intelligent artisans; the divergence of characteristic features on the artefacts and contemporary needs is too wide; most of the practices active today are accessing poor value and heavily dependent on obsolete technology instead artisans have to pursue adoption of state-of-the-art technology explore higher value accessing and; artisans have to pursue eco-friendly methods, performance, efficiency and frugality are essential to sustain growth.

Value

Among the casually acquired hobbies and relives of pre-medieval period; few virtuosi had promising value and they got transformed to serious professional skill for manufacturing artefacts of utility. Alike talented folks came together, their aggregate value accession and skills coalesced common value chains along with tradition. Since the transience of knowledge was conservatively through inheritance and their skills got fragmented into specialities; active stakeholders among affluent crafts value chains got associated through religious cults, castes and culture as a societal system. Specialised artisans with manufacturing excellence made high value artefacts and started bequeathing recognition through state patronization by rulers, elite classes and even temples. This inspired more admiring artisans to creatively fulfil different needs as well, thereby prospering crafts economy. Most crafts reached their prosperity covet as Mughal regime arose because early Mughal rulers wooed them by state patronage. Like endorsing the extensive use of precious stones, expensive and rare raw materials as royalty, traditional, cultural and monetary values as shown in Figure 3.

Figure 3: *Chronicle of approximate net worth (in crores).*

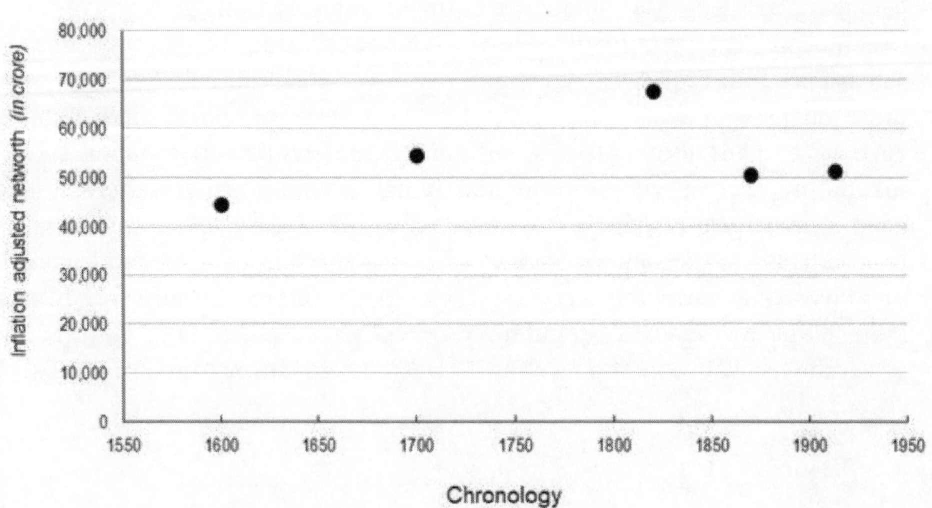

During the two-decade British colonisation in India, greed to skim higher profits thoroughly ripped the long-established values amongst most craft value chains. The insane exploitation of British regime widely provoked all stakeholders, including artisans to rebel and distracted them towards the freedom struggle by 1857; these aspects disrupted the value chains and deterred the relevance of artefacts to competently meet evolving modern needs. This rapid decline in the overall craft economy is illustrated in Figure 3, likewise the post-independence efforts to revive the craft economy aren't effective. The anomalies mainly owe to incompetent bureaucracy; technological insentience; breaches in value chains; delineation of artefacts by meeting psychological needs[60] instead of physiological[61] needs and; dearth of skilful of artisans, schools of practice, master trainers and neglect to research. However, it's clear that the reverberating societal memoir, rich cultural heritage, and awesome legacy of the distinct literary styles of craft economy allude a higher prospect of phenomenal contribution.

Conclusion

Since the neoteric tumble of craft economy was sooner than it grew in the medieval era, so rejuvenating value accession thoroughly is a socioeconomic imperative for holistic development. Enabling cumulative value across the chain is essential[62] to ensure fair wealth generation and dignified living for all stakeholders[63] and to sustain its contributions towards the overarching economy of India. Recuperating crafts is not just for economics, it's just for social reasons as well because establishing a conducive craft economy is a promising avenue to empower marginalised and the fringe section of society with subsistence.[64] It requires many small-cap investments to enable crafts, as those business models will stimulate active participation at the ground zero level and; their actions will make real world differences like incubating innovative solutions and scalable opportunities. There is a need to synergise responsibility and compassion among all stakeholders' from artisans to consumers; instead of deposing them to compete, square or cross one over another. Besides, governments should restrain themselves for ensuring regulatory compliance, audits, and statutory governance. The extent of supports need to go deeper thro' all most

[60] Mostly decorative.

[61] Basic.

[62] SDG17.

[63] SDG8.

[64] SDG1.

all value chains, restructure linkages and converge as a national transformation movement.

Being the second largest livelihood sector in India after agriculture, crafts economy is a sunrise enabler hence its renaissance through inclusiveness can certainly make India great. The post-independence attempts through consecutive five-year plans and their policies were moderately effective in revitalising of the craft economy, but there is more scope to feat. From afore review of crafts economy context and to the best of our apprehension, there are less than 1000 promising crafts natively practiced with indigenous skillsets that can generate more than C1,00,000 lakh crore revenue per annum and add to the national economy.

References

1. Acharya, P.A., and V.S. Samani. "Review Study on Detailing Traditional Motifs and Techniques of Bandhani and Its Changes of Saurashtra Region." *International Journal of Home Science 3,* no.1 (n.d.):377–79.
2. Aen, Mir Farhatul, Mir Junaid Alam, and Farooq Ahmad Mir. "LEGAL PROTECTION OF KASHMIRI KHATAMBAND: POST-GI ISSUES AND CHALLENGES." *International Journal of Research in Management & Social Science* (2014):9–17.
3. Bhattacharyya, D. "Cottage Industry Clusters in India in Improving Rural Livelihood: An Overview." *International Journal of Humanities & Social Science Studies* 1, no.1 (2014):59–64.
4. Chandra, Sharad. "Kalamkari, the Art of Painting with Natural Dyes." *Chitrolekha Journal on Art and Design* 5, no.2 (2015):82–88.
5. Ghosh, A. "Triggering Innovation and Creativity in Traditional Handicrafts Sector—an Indian Perspective." *Management Insight* 8, no.1 (2012):67–71.
6. Gupta, S. "An Interactive Design Study of Jaipur Blue Pottery." *Need Assessment Survey Report, MSME Design Clinic Scheme*, 2011.
7. Jadhav, Shreya. "Indian Handicrafts: Growing or Depleting." *IOSR Journal of Business and Management*, no.2 (2014):7–13.
8. Jain, Ruby, and Ambika Tiwari. "An Insight into the Traditional Bandhej Craft of Sikar City of Rajasthan." *Indian Journal of Traditional Knowledge* 11, no.4 (2012):733–37.
9. Jangid, Govind, and Shrenik Bhansali. "Mojari Craft: Craftmark." Accessed March 30, 2018. http://www.craftmark.org/sites/default/files/Mojari%20Craft_0.pdf.
10. Jena, Pradeep Kumar. " Indian Handicrafts in Globalization Times: an Analysis of Global-Local Dynamics." *Interdisciplinary description of Complex Systems* 8, no.2 (2010):119–37.
11. Kapoor, S. "Rebirth of Katambandh." *Deccan Herald*, November 15, 2013.
12. Kapur, H, and S Mittar. "Design Intervention & Craft Revival." *International Journal of Scientific and Research Publications* 4, no.10 (2014):1–5.

13. Karren, Sherry, and Balwant Singh Mehta. "Wages and Productivity of Child Labour: A Case of the Zardosi Industry." *IHD Working Paper Series 1–20*, 2008.
14. Kenoyer, Jonathan Mark. "Ancient Textiles of the Indus Valley Region." Essay. In *Tana Bana: The Woven Soul of Pakistan*, edited by Noor Bilgrami, 18–31, 2004.
15. Kramrisch, Stella. "Traditions of the Indian Craftsman." *Journal of American Folklore* 71, no.281 (1958):224–30.
16. Liebl, M., and T. Roy. "Handmade in India, Preliminary Analysis of Crafts Producers and Crafts Production." *Economic and Political Weekly* 38, no.51/52 (n.d.):5366–76.
17. Mahapatra, S. "Guild, the Institutional Economic Base of India." *International Journal of Social Science & Interdisciplinary Research* 1, no.9 (2012):165–74.
18. Shukla, D, and AK Mathur. "Managing Dwindling Glaze of Jaipur Blue Pottery: a Case of Rajasthan." *International Journal of Advanced Research in Management and Social Sciences* 3, no.12 (2014):35–43.
19. Mirani, H. "The Art of Khatamband." *Kashmir Newz*, March 31, 2006. *An Interactive Design Study of Stone Craft*. Patna: Need Assessment Survey Report, MSME Design Clinic Scheme, 2013.
20. Pratap, A. "The Archaeology of Childhood: Revisiting Mohenjodaro Terracotta." Edited by Vasant Shinde. *Ancient Asia: Journal of the Society of South Asian Archaeology* 7, no.5 (2016):1–8.
21. Purohit, Pooja. "The Study of Traditional Hand Painted Kalamkari to Design a Set of New Age Prints." Dissertation, Department of Design Space, 2013.
22. Ramesh, Y. "Origin and Development of Guilds in Early Medieval India—A Review of Literary Sources." *Imperial Journal of Interdisciplinary Research*, 2016, 928–34.
23. Ranjan, Aditi, and M.P. Ranjan. "Handmade in India." Ahmedabad: National Institute of Design, 2005. Chakravarty, Saswati, Sachan Nita, and Venkat Munagala. Rep. *Innovation Cluster in the Brassware Industry at Moradabad, Uttar Pradesh*. National Innovation Council, Indian School of Business, 2013.
24. Saha, H. "Intellectual Property and the Development of Cultural Districts National Examples." *Department of economics, Universitë di Torino*, 2004.
25. Sajid, M. "Development of Brassware Industry of Moradabad," 1989. http://ir.amu.ac.in/2090/1/DS%201583.pdf.
26. Soofi, Mayank Austen. "The Goat-Skin Bag' in City Secret—The Vanished Mashak, The Delhi Walla, Mushtaqeem Chai Stall," May 3, 2017.
27. Srivastava, Meenu, and Neha Sharma. "Changing Trends in Traditional Mojari Craft." *Asian Journal of Home Science* 9, no.2 (2014):555–60.
28. "Stone Carvings (Patharkati)." Upendra Maharathi Shilp Anusandhan Sansthan. Dept. of Industries. UMSAS, n.d. Accessed May 30, 2018.
29. Viswanathan, Brinda. "Enumeration of Crafts Persons in India, Monograph 25 for Madras School of Economics." *Crafts Council of India*, 2013.

—x—

The Pilgrimage of Balarama: A Religio-Cultural Study

Sneha Nagarkar

Abstract

The present paper seeks to investigate the cultural and religious aspects of the different sites mentioned in the course of Balarama's pilgrimage and their bearing as well as impact on Indian culture. The study will be conducted using historical and archaeological evidences combined with traditional accounts. An attempt will also be made to juxtapose the entire theme of Balarama's pilgrimage with the more comprehensive context of the Mahabharata and the Bhagavata Purana.

A pilgrimage to a sacred site is a universal feature common to almost all world religions. Rana B.P. Singh, an authority on pilgrimage studies, defines pilgrimage as "a spiritual quest, a search for wholeness". In the Indian religious tradition, our texts are replete with references to legendary kings, sages, and the common populace traversing long distances to visit places which have an aura of holiness around them. The Mahabharata, as stated by S.M. Bhardwaj, considers a pilgrimage superior to a sacrifice. The Mahabharata hero Arjuna goes on a tirtha yatra as a mark of repentance for violating the privacy of Draupadi and Yudhisthira. It is a well-known fact that Balarama, the elder brother of Krsna chose to remain neutral during the great Bharata War and refrained from participating in the fratricidal conflagration. Texts like the Mahabharata and the Bhagavata Purana contain a detailed description of Balarama going on a pilgrimage to numerous holy sites including those on the banks of the once mighty Sarasvati. The present paper seeks to investigate the cultural and religious aspects of the different sites mentioned in the course of Balarama's pilgrimage and their bearing as well as impact on Indian culture. The study will be conducted using historical and archaeological evidences combined with traditional accounts. An attempt will also be made to juxtapose the entire theme of

Balarama's pilgrimage with the more comprehensive context of the Mahabharata and the Bhagavata Purana.

A pilgrimage is a process of self discovery combined with the establishment of a communion with the divine. In the context of Hinduism, Rana P.B. Singh, an authority on pilgrimage studies states that, "pilgrimage is a sacramental process that both symbolizes the participation of the pilgrim in the spiritual realm and actively establishes a two-way reciprocal relationship between the pilgrim and the divine" (Singh 2013, 8). Mahamohopadhyaya P.V. Kane in his iconic *History of the Dharmasastras* states that, "Though India was divided into many kingdoms and people of India followed several cults and sub-cults, pilgrimages tended to foster the idea of the essential and fundamental unity of Indian culture and of India also" (Kane 1953, 553). In the opinion of S.M. Bhardwaj, a noted scholar of pilgrimage studies, "Tirtha yatra not only means physical act of visiting holy places but implies mental and moral discipline" (Bhardwaj 1973, 2). If we consider Hinduism or Sanatana Dharma alone, the tradition of a pilgrimage is as old as the Vedic period, with references in the *Brahmanas* about *sattras* or sacrificial pilgrimages along the banks of the once mighty Sarasvati River. The oldest testimony to the practice of pilgrimage is the *Aitareya Brahmana* (Keith 1920). However the 'pilgrimages' described here are not the prototypes of pilgrimages, as we understand today. The first text which presents elaborate descriptions of pilgrimages which have continued to the present day is the *Mahabharata*. In the *Tirthayatra Parvan* of the *Vana* or *Aranyaka Parvan* of the same text, sages Pulastya and Dhaumya describe the various *tirthas* throughout India, though the main focus is on the *tirthas* of north India (Mahabharata Volume II, Sections 80–90)(Bhardwaj, 1973, 15). Apart from these descriptions, the Mahabharata is replete with details of the *tirtha yatras* undertaken by Arjuna and Balarama. In fact, the same text considers a pilgrimage higher than a sacrifice. The *Puranas,* specially those like the *Bhagavata, Padma* and *Brahma Puranas* shed valuable light on the practice of pilgrimage and the numerous *tirthas* which dot the map of India. In the cases of both the *Mahabharata* and the above mentioned *Puranas*, many *tirthas* cannot be accurately identified, but nevertheless they give us precious information about the religious practices of the concerned times.

In Hinduism, a pilgrimage is referred to as a '*tirtha yatra*', the fundamental aspect being '*tirthas*' or sacred centres (Ibid). The word *tirtha* is derived from the Sanskrit root *tr* which means to 'cross' a river or water body. In India a *tirtha* or a sacred space is invariably associated with a water body—in most cases a river, but in some instances like Pushkara we find a lake closely connected to a sacred place. In some well known sacred sites like Dvaraka on the coast of Gujarat and Puri on the coast of Odisha, the *tirthas* are closely linked to the sea. In the case of almost all *tirthas*, the water bodies are significant players in defining the greatness or *mahatmya* of a particular sacred space.

Rana P.B. Singh has given the classification of *tirthas* based on the *Brahma Purana (Brahma Purana*, Chapter 37, 147) (Singh 2013, 55–56). According to this classification, holy sites are divided into four categories—

1. *Daiva Tirtha* (Divine Sites)—Sites related to obtaining the grace or *anugraha* of certain divinities.
2. *Aasura Tirtha* (Demonic Sites)—Sites associated with trouble-making demons who performed penance at these sites.
3. *Arsha Tirtha* (Sage Related Sites)—Sites associated with realized sages.
4. *Manusha Tirtha* (Human Perceived Sites)—Sites which do not fit into any of the above categories but are worshipped by people.

From the topographic perspective, *tirthas* are categorised into—

a. *Jala Tirtha* (Water Sites)—Sacred sites where people take ritual baths
b. *Sthana Tirtha* (Temples or Shrines)—Associated with a certain deity or sect where pilgrims worshipping that particular deity or adhering to that particular sect come
c. *Ksetra* (holy territory)—A cosmic *mandala* where a *parikrama* of the sacred site gives the pilgrim religious merit (*punya*)

The focus of this paper is the pilgrimage of Balarama, the elder brother of Krishna, as described in the *Mahabharata* during the great Bharata War. The Harivamsa, the *khila* text of the Mahabharata does not mention this pilgrimage at all. The general focus of the sections in the Mahabharata describing various pilgrimages is the Ganga—Yamuna doab. (Bharadwaj 1973, 33). The reason for this is explained by S.M. Bhardwaj in the statement that, "The appellation of the Ganga Yamuna Doab is suggestive of both fertility and the pre-eminent sanctity of the region" (Ibid). Another important sector for a pilgrimage, as exemplified by Balarama's *tirtha yatra* in the *Mahabharata* is the Sarasvati River and *tirthas* associated with her. Praised as *nadi-tame, ambhi tame* in the *Rig Veda*, in the *Mahabharata,* the river comes forth as a mere shadow of her former self and references like the Sarasvati disappearing underground appear in the description of the Yadava scion's pilgrimage along the most worshipful river in the *Rig Veda.*

Balarama's Tirtha Yatra in the Mahabharata

The description of Balarama's pilgrimage comes in the ninth book of the Mahabharata—the *Shalya Parvan*. Within the *Shalya Parvan*, the *Tirthayatra Parvan* , *Adhyayas* 33–53 deal with this pilgrimage. Krishna had always favoured and helped the Pandavas where as Balarama on the other hand had his predilection for the Kauravas. As the great war became imminent, Balarama had asked Krishna to help the Kauravas but Krishna did not show much inclination to do so. Enraged, Balarama told his brother that he will neither help the sons of Dhritarashtra nor the sons of Pandu and instead go on a pilgrimage. The Great Bharata War had almost reached its end and the most awaited mace dual (*gada yuddha*) between Bhima and Duryodhana was about to take place. Balarama, the great Yadava king, with the mark of a palm tree on his banner (*taladhvaja*) and a plough as his weapon appeared on the scene to witness the dual. Balarama was the guru of both the rival cousins. The whole description of the pilgrimage is in the form of a dialogue between King Janmejaya and Sage Vaishampayana, the disciple of Sage Krishna Dvaipayana Vyasa. The epic gives elaborate details about the entourage of Balarama which consisted many of Vrishnis (the clan to which Krishna and Balarama belonged), Brahmanas, horses, mules, camels, elephants, chariots etc. Taking the ritual fire with him, Balarama left with his entourage of officiating priests and others along the banks of the Sarasvati. Balarama sojourned from the mouth of the Sarasvati at Prabhasa all the way up to its source at Plaksha Prasravana in the Siwalik Hills. The duration of this pilgrimage was forty two days. In this paper, the candidate has dealt with only select *tirthas*.

The Sarasvati River has been mentioned in seventy two *rks* in the *Rig Veda* (Kalyanaraman 2008, 20). According to the account given in the *Rig Veda*, the Sarasvati was situated between the river Sutlej (Vedic Satudri) in the west and the Yamuna in the east. The same *Veda* describes Sarasvati as 'seven sistered' or 'one of seven sisters' (Danino 2010, 39). In *Rig Veda*, the Sarasvati is a flowing river and the *suktas* referring to her reaffirm this point. The Sarasvati is many a times spoken in the context of her tributary Drishadvati. The Yajur Veda mentions Sarasvati having five tributaries which is similar to her description in the Rig Veda as 'seven sistered' (Danino 2010, 40). Later Vedic texts like the *Pancavimsa Brahmana* and *Jaiminiya Upanisad Brahmana* mention the disappearance of the Sarasvati at a place called Vinasana. This indicates that the Sarasvati which had a strong flow in the early Vedic period had dried up considerably by the later Vedic period. The

Mahabharata mentions Vinasana in the context of Balarama's pilgrimage and indicates that the river had partially dried up. However at every tirtha along the Sarasvati which is visited by Balarama, there are references to his 'touching the waters' and bathing in the river. The Sarasvati finds mention in the Puranas as well as texts like Banabhatta's Harshacarita written in the 7th century CE. The Mahabharata describes the Sarasvati as *'anatahsalila'* or an underground stream. Sarasvati reappeared at sites like Camsobheda and Udapana which attained fame as sacred *tirthas* on the Sarasvati. At the same time, the epic in the *Vana Parvan* describes the river as "*Sarasvati Mahapunya Hrdini Tirthamalini*" (Mahabharata Volume II, 90.3, 314) which implies that from the epic's point of view, Sarasvati was a river to which great merit was attached and her banks were dotted with a series of *tirthas*.

Dvaraka

Dvaraka was the city founded by Krishna after he and the Vrishnis relocated from Mathura on the coast of Gujarat. Texts like Mahabharata, Harivamsa, Bhagavata, Vayu, Matsya and Visnu Puranas refer to the migration of Krishna and Balarama along with the Vrishnis to Dvaraka (Rao 1995–96, 61). For his new residence, the younger Yadava prince chose a site on the coast of Anarta (Gujarat) named Kusasthali which had been established by his ancestor Kakudmin Raivata. He enlarged the site and named it Dvaraka (Ibid). The fortified city of Dvaraka has been described in texts as Varidurga and Udadhimadhyastham so marine archaeologists explored the modern city of Dvaraka on land and island of Bet Dvaraka.

After setting out from Dvaraka, Prabhasa is the first tirtha visited by Balarama. In the opinion of Dr. Anand Damle, Balarama must have commenced his journey at the end of the monsoon season at Prabhasa. (Damle 2012, 14). The Mahabharata refers to Prabhasa as the foremost *tirtha*. According to the epic, the *tirtha* is known as Prabhasa as the moon regained his radiance back after bathing in the Sarasvati (*prabha* means radiance). As per the legend given in the Mahabharata, the moon was emancipated from the curse of Daksa Prajapati. The site of Camsobheda is mentioned in the Mahabharata in connection with Prabhasa. Balarama stayed here for a night and gave donations to the needy. It was near this spot that the Sarasvati met the sea.

In the context of Udapana, the Mahabharata says that this site is replete with herbs and the soil here is cool. According to some scholars, the coolness or moistness of the soil could be because of the Sarasvati flowing underground. It is because of this reason that though the

Sarasvati has been destroyed, the Siddhas are well aware of her. The Mahabharata also makes references to the presence of wells (Damle 2012, 15). Wells have been constructed in the Indian sub-continent right from the age of the Sindhu-Sarasvati civilization and well architecture researches its apogee in the step wells of Gujarat, the Rani Ki Vav at Patan being the finest example. Certain scholars identify modern day Patan with the tirtha of Udapana. (Ibid). Damle further states that Patan may have been originally Pattana and this could indicate that like Dholavira and Surkotada, Udapana could have been a riverine port. (Ibid). The Mahabharata discusses the greatness of Udapana with reference to the legends of Sage Trita and his brothers whose father was a sage called Gautama. The epic states that Trita lived in a pit and drank the Soma juice. The Mahabaharata narrates the story of sages Ekata, Drita and Trita who were the sons of Sage Gautama. Once, while trying to save himself from a wolf, Sage Trita fell into a pit. In a bid to come out of the pit he offered a sacrifice there and pleased the gods who rescued Trita from the pit after conferring a boon on him. It is said that the Sarasvati emerged in the pit and brought Trita out along with her flow.

Vinasana is the place where according to the Mahabharata, the Sarasvati disappeared because of her hatred for the Sudras and Abhiras. This particular legend may have arisen because of the disappearance of the Sarasvati due to tectonic activities in the region of her flood plain (Valdiya 2012, 81). O.P. Bharadwaj has given a detailed analysis of the site of Vinasana in his scholarly article titled 'Vinsasana'. Medieval Sanskrit lexicons like the *Sabda Kalapadruma* define the place Vinasana as the site where Sarasvati (present day Ghaggar) disappears underground (Bharadwaj 1983, 69). We have already stated that the Sarasvati was the most venerated river in the Rig Veda and this sacredness was invariably transferred to her site of disappearance as well. Texts like the Mahabharata and the Kurma Purana attach a lot of greatness to Vinasana. The *Krityakalpataru* of Laksmidhara incorporates it as a prominent *tirtha* on the Sarasvati. Thus Vinasana gained fame as the foremost among the *tirthas* specially for the conduct of *sraddha* rites. Sacrificial rites like the Sarasvat and Darsadvat, known as *yatta satras* came to be performed here (Ibid).

O.P. Bharadwaj opines that the site of the disappearance of the river constantly changed because the flow of the river became shorter as the rainfall on the lower Himalayan slopes lessened (Bharadwaj 1983, 71). He further elucidates that the term Vinasana was not confined to a particular tirtha only but came to imply an entire region or *janapada* (Ibid). In the *Baudhayana Dharmasutra,* Aryavarta is defined as the country to the east of Adarsana (Vinasana), west of Kalakavana, south of the Himalayas and north of Pariyatra (Bharadwaj 1983, 72). Texts like the *Vasistha Dharmasutra*, *Mahabhasya* and *Manusmrti* also give a similar definition of Aryavarta and locate Vinasana on the western end of Aryavarta or Madhyadesha (Ibid). The *Vana Parvan* of the *Mahabharata* places Vinasana at the top of the desert (Ibid). In *Salya Parvan*, Vinasana is placed near the territory of the Abhiras, Sudras and Nisadas (Salya Parvan (36.1). The Sudras were a tribe mentioned by the Greek writers as Xodraka and Ptolemy specifically states that it was region on the left bank of the Indus (Ali 1966, 144). The Sudra Janapada could be in the region of Uch-Khanpur region of Bahwalpur in modern day Pakistan (Ibid). The Abhiras, a pastoral tribe had their province on the Indus as well. B.C. Law states that the Abhiras along with the Yaudheyas lived in the Rajputana (Rajasthan) region (Law 1943, 63). In Patanjali's *Mahabhasya,* like the *Mahabharata*, the Abhiras are associated with the Sudras (Law 1943, 79). In the opinion of the great epigraphist Buhler, the Nisadas lived in the area around Bhatner (modern Hanumangarh in Rajasthan) (Bharadwaj 1983, 73).

O.P. Bharadwaj states that the location of Vinasana should be in the northern part of the desert of Rajasthan (Ibid). According to the *Pancavimsa Brahmana*, anyone going along the Sarasvati Sattra, received initiation at Vinasana and then travelled along the eastern bank of the river towards its source at Plaksa Prasravana where the sacrificial journey would end (Bharadwaj 1983, 74). Bharadwaj uses numerous textual and archaeological evidences to identify the Sindhu-Sarasvati civilization site of Kalibangan, along the modern Ghaggar River with the epic site of Vinasana. Kalibangan is a site situated on the left bank of the Ghaggar or the Vedic Sarasvati (Lal 1998, 19). The settlement at Kalibangan was divided into the Lower Town and the Citadel, and the southern part of the citadel had many raised platforms on which there were architectural features which were identified by the excavators as fire altars (Lal, 1998, 93). In the Citadel area, one of the platforms had seven altars adjacent to each other where remains of ash and charcoal were found (Ibid). A small mound to the east of the Lower Town yielded remains of only fire altars with a surrounding wall. (Lal 1998, 96). In the opinion of B.B. Lal, these fire altars may have been for what he calls 'community worship' (Ibid).Bharadwaj connects the discovery of these altars with the sacrifices that the pilgrims would perform during the *sattras* along the Sarasvati and the Drishadvati (Bharadwaj 1983, 87). We conclude the discussion on Vinasana with a quote from Bharadwaj where he states, "The location of Kalibangan satisfies all the attributes that we set out to find in the site of Vinasana. It is located on the eastern bank of the Sarasvati below its confluence with the Drishadvati above the upper edge of the desert of Rajasthan. And finally it provides ample evidence of sacrificial activity as well as occurrence of a fierce–tectonic upheaval antecedent to the occupation of the site. Only linguistically there is nothing common between Kalibangan and Vinasana" (Bharadwaj 1983, 86).

Subhumika

From Vinasana, Balarama travelled to the tirtha of Subhumika. The epic tells us that this place was also located on the banks of the Sarasvati. Subhumika was famous as the sporting of celestial beings like *apsaras*, *gandharvas* and the *pitrs*. The *apsaras* are described as fair skinned damsels. The epic refers to this site as the shrine of *Brahman*. What is striking here is that there is a reference to the shrine of Brahman, a concept which defies any proper definition. No shrine of Visnu or Siva has been referred to.

Gargasrota

Balarama after visiting the tirtha of the Gandharvas, reached the *tirtha* of Gargasrota. Garga was the family priest of the Vrsnis and he is considered the author of the *Garga Samhita,* a text on astronomy. Garga is said to be the astrologer of Prthu Vainya. As per the Mahabharata Index, Garga practised severe austerities on the banks of the Sarasvati and pleased Siva who blessed him with the knowledge of time and its sixty four branches. He further blessed him with a thousand sons. The life times of Garga and his progeny were extended to ten million years according to the epic.

Sankha

The next *tirtha* visited by Balarama was Sankha and there he beheld a large tree called Mahashanka on the banks of the Sarasvati. According to the epic, this tree was as large as Meru and like a white mountain. This *tirtha* was the abode of a number of semi-divine beings like *Yakshas, Vidyadharas, Pisacas* and *Siddhas*. This tree was considered as the source of this sacred *tirtha* on the Sarasvati. N.L. Dey identifies the Meru or Sumeru Mountain with the Rudra Himalayas in Garhwal where the Ganga has her source (Dey 1927, 196). This mountain is said to have five peaks and it is therefore known as '*Panca Parvata*'. The five peaks are called Rudra Himalaya, Visnupuri, Brahmapuri, Udgarikantha and Svargarohini. The *Matsya Purana* mentions that this mountain is flanked by Uttara Kuru in the north, Bharatavarsha in the south, Ketumala in the west and Bhadravarsha in the south. Dey further states that the

Kedarnatha Mountain is also considered as the Sumeru Parvata (Dey 1927, 197).

There is a reference here to Balarama donating copper and iron vessels to Brahmanas at this site. References to copper and iron vessels in the Mahabharata are much more than those of gold and silver (Laud 1983, 50). The metal vessels of copper (*tamra*), bronze (*kamsya*) and iron (*ayasa or lauha*) have been referred to in the epic as *bhanda* and *bhajana* (Ibid). The earliest evidence of copper-bronze metals goes back to the period of the Sindhu-Sarasvati Civilization where sites like Mohen-jo-daro and Harappa have yielded such artefacts. A surprising fact is that the Chalcolithic and Iron Age cultures which followed the Sindhu Sarasvati Civilization have produced numerous metal artefacts but no metal utensils. Metal utensils only appear in the archaeological records around 6th century BCE (Ibid). Metal vessels became common household objects only from the Mauryan period (c. 300 BCE) onwards (Ibid). In the words of Dr. Gouri Laud, "The references to them (metal vessels) in the Mahabharata may therefore be credited to this period of Indian history" (Laud 1983, 50–51).

Sapta Sarasvata

The Sarasvati which had taken a turn eastwards again took a turn westwards (the original direction) at the spot called Sapta Sarasvata. The Sapta Sarasvata, from the descriptions given in the epic was a highly forested place. The epic names trees like *badari, inguda, kashmarya, plaksha, ashvattha, vibhitaka, panasa, palasha, karira, pilu* and other varieties. *Badari* is the Indian *ber* tree, *inguda* has been identified as the desert date, *kashmarya* is barberry, *plaksha* is papal, *ashvattha* is the religious fig tree, *vibhitaka* is myrobalan, *panasa* is jackfruit, *palasha* is flame of the forest, *karira* is *capparis deciduas* and *pilu* is *salvadora oleoides*. Groves of trees like *parushas* (not identified), *bilva (bel*), *amarakatas* (wild mango), *kashanda* (not identified) and *parijata* (night jasmine) have also been mentioned (Debroy 2015, 460). In the epic, Vaishampayana states that Seven Sarasvatis envelop the entire universe. Wherever she is summoned with great power, Sarasvati appears there. The Seven Sarasvatis are Suprabha, Kancanakshi, Vishala, Manasharada, Sarasvati, Oghavati, Suvenu and Vimalodaka.

1. Suprabha: Sarasvati appeared at the great tirtha of Pushkara (Rajasthan) as Suprabha where Brahma performed a great sacrifice.

2. Kanchanakshi: There was a huge congregation of sages in the Naimisha forest (eastern Uttar Pradesh) who intended performing a sacrifice which could not be completed in the absence of the Sarasvati. The sages remembered her and she appeared there as Kanchanakshi.

3. Vishala: In Gaya (Bihar), Gaya was performing a sacrifice and the Sarasvati appeared there and the sages assembled named her as Vishala.

4. Manasharada: The Sarasvati is described as originating from the mountains and rapid in her flow. The great sage Ouddalaka who is frequently mentioned in the Upanishads performed a sacrifice here and a number of sages gathered for this purpose. The site of the sacrifice was to the north of the Kosala region. Before the commencement of the sacrifice, the sage remembered the Sarasvati and she appeared at the site. As she was summoned through the mind, she came to be known as Manasharada. Kosala is the region around modern Ayodhya and was divided into two parts- north and south. Sravasti (the site hallowed by the presence of the Buddha) was the capital of the former and Kusavati of the latter. By the Mauryan times it was incorporated in the Magadhan Empire.

5. Oghavati: King Kuru, the ancestor of the Kauravas and Pandavas had performed a sacrifice here. Sage Vasistha summoned Sarsvati here and she was known here as Oghavati.

6. Suvenu: Daksha was performing a sacrifice here at Gangadvara (modern Haridvara, where the Ganga enters the plains) and Sarasvati appeared there as Suvenu.

7. Vimalodaka: Brahma had performed a sacrifice on the slopes of the Himalayas and Sarasvati appeared there as Vimalodaka.

The epic also associates this place where the young sage Mankanaka practised celibacy here. One day he beheld a beautiful damsel in the waters of the Sarasvati and his semen fell into the water. He picked it up and placed it in a pot. His semen got divided into seven parts and from each part was born a sage. These seven sages became the progenitors of numerous Maruts. Maruts are Rig Vedic deities who are associated with Rudra. They represent strong winds and are represented as malevolent deities. The number of Maruts is generally considered to be forty nine. The legend of sage Mankanaka's euphoric dancing and Siva preventing him to do so is narrated in the *Vana Parvan* of the epic. The epic tells us that Mankanaka attained *siddhi* here.

Sapta Sarsvata is the tirtha where these seven streams have their confluence. Geographically speaking this place can be located in the Kurukshetra region of modern Haryana. These seven Sarsvatis could suggest either tributaries or palaeo channels of the great river.

8. Vasisthapravaha: During his pilgrimage Balarama visited the tirtha of Sthanu where sage Vasistha had his hermitage. This particular tirtha is associated with the rivalry between the two sages-Vasistha and Vishvamitra. This antagonism dates back to the age of the Rig Veda.

The two sages had their hermitages on the opposite banks of the Sarasvati. The epic narrates how Vishvamitra ordered the Sarasvati to get Vasistha and how she saved Vasistha from being killed by Vishvamitra. The river was cursed by Vishvamitra to flow with blood for an entire year because of her defiance. The story of the birth of Skanda Kartikeya as *Devasenapati* has been narrated here in detail.

9. Plaksha Prasravana: Balarama was extremely keen to see the source of the Sarasvati and he climbed the slopes of the Siwaliks or lower Himalayas to reach this site. There was a hermitage with varied flora like the trees of *madhuka*, mango, *plaksha, nyagrodha,bilva* and jackfruit. Lord Visnu had performed austerities here and a Brahmana maiden had observed brahmacarya at the same site. From here Balarama went to the site called Karapacana . This was Balarama's last spot along the Sarasvati. From there he traversed to the site which had the hermitage of the Vedic gods Mitra and Varuna on the banks of the Yamuna.

Analysis of Balarama's Tirtha Yatra

The Critical Edition of the Mahabharata has dealt extensively with the pilgrimage of Balarama and therefore this may not be treated as a very late interpolation. Traditionally speaking, the Mahabharata is dated to the Dvaparyuga and it is said that in this age Kurukshetra on the Sarasvati was the main tirtha and in the Kaliyuga the whole focus of pilgrimage would change to the Ganga (Pargiter 1922, 313) (Benedetti 2014, 226). Though much of the action in the Mahbharata takes place in the Ganga-Yamuna Doab, the Great Bharata War takes place at Kurukshetra on the Sarasvati which has been described in the Bhagvad Gita as '*dharmakshetra*'.

The pilgrimage of Balarama is similar to what has been described as '*yat sattras*' in the *Brahmana* Texts. These were sacrificial journeys along the Sarasvati and Drishadvati where the *yajamana* would be a *brahmana.* However here the *yajamana* is Balarama, a *kshatriya* of the Vrishni clan. Here a connection is established between later epic tradition and the older Vedic tradition (Kalyanaraman 2000, 731). The tradition of *sthala mahatmyas* which reached its maturity in the *Puranas* has its origin in the descriptions of the pilgrimages in the epic. Balarama's journey is a case in this point where the religious and cultural significance of every tirtha has been presented in great detail. The epic has devoted a lot of attention in recounting the legends associated with different *tirthas.* These legends themselves have many Vedic elements and references to Vedic divinities like Maruts, Mitra and

Varuna thus further strengthening the link between the Vedic and epic traditions. As stated by Dr. Kalyanaraman, "Many legends (related to the *tirthas*) are paralleled in the legends mentioned or briefly indicated in the rcas of the four Vedas" (Ibid).

Temples or shrines are the fundamental elements of early medieval, medieval and modern pilgrimages. However, references to shrines or temples as such are missing in the account of Balarama's pilgrimage. The only reference to a shrine is that of Brahman (an abstract concept) in the context of Subhumika. Balarama in contrast to the Puranic tradition, is not represented as a divinity but as a strong and brave leader of the Vrishni clan. Balarama's role itself in his pilgrimage is understated. His acts at every tirtha are almost repetitive with hardly any variations. In other words his acts are very stereotypical. Martin Haigh (Haigh 2011, 179–193) has interpreted this pilgrimage in the context of Gaudiya Vaishnavism where he has assigned to Balarama the role of the *Adi Guru*. However the candidate does not agree with Haigh as the data given in this particular section of the epic does not support this proposition.

Balarama's pilgrimage is an important source of information of a now dead practice of the pilgrimage along the banks of the Sarasvati. The whole idea of a pilgrimage has been dealt with in detail by the *Mahabharata* and this tradition was later continued in the *Puranas*. The fact that our texts have produced such an ocean of data with respect to the practice of pilgrimage underlines the role played by this practice in the growth and development of Indian Culture.

References

1. Ali, S.M. 1966. *The Geography of the Puranas*. New Delhi: People's Publishing House.
2. Benedetti, Giacomo. 2014. "The Chronology of Puranic Kings and Rgvedic Rsis: In Comparison with the Phases of the Sindhu-Sarasvati Civilization". In *Sindhu-Sarasvati Civilization-New Perspectives*, ed. by Nalini Rao, 220–246. Los Angeles and New Delhi: Nalanda International and D.K. Printworld.
3. Bharadwaj, O.P. 1986. *Studies in the Historical Geography of India*. Delhi: Sundeep Prakashan.
4. Bharadwaj, O.P. 1983. "Vinashana". *Journal of the Oriental Institute of Baroda,* Vol.33, nos.1–2:69–88.
5. Bhardwaj, S.M. 1973. *Hindu Places of Pilgrimage in India: A Study in Cultural Geography*. Berkeley: University of California Press.
6. *Brahma Purana*. Samvat 2073, Fourteenth Edition. Gorakhpur: Gita Press.

— x —

Colonial Roots of the Aryan Invasion/ Migration Theory and the Contemporary Archaeological Evidence in Western Sources

Kundan Singh

Abstract

The distortion on Indian History and Hinduism, encountered in the California Textbooks for school going children, is primarily because of the colonial legacy that the American educational system has inherited. The distortions however have calamitous effects on the psychological well being of Indian-American children involving their ancestral heritage, culture, and history because of which it is extremely important and pertinent that the skewed narrative is set right. The prescription for cure will be faulty if the diagnosis is not correct. This presentation will focus on a complete analysis of James Mill's *History of British India*, which he wrote without even visiting India. This "historical" document is a case study in the misuse of colonial power to distort the history of nation, country, or people.

William Jones famously, by identifying close linkages between Sanskrit and European languages, gave birth to research into the common ancestry between Indians and Europeans. In the earlier years of contention on the matter, India was considered the cradle of civilization and Sanskrit as the mother of all Indo-European languages. With the rise in the imperial power of Europe over India, the cradle of civilization began to shift outside India and ultimately landed in Europe. Simultaneously, the idea of invasion of India by the "Aryan race" or the Aryan Invasion Theory (AIT) was promoted. Since then however, one archeological find over another, have consistently refuted the AIT, proving it as false. As flawed as it remains, this theory has nonetheless persisted and morphed in its current form as the Aryan Migration Theory or AMT, and continues to find mention and favor in contemporary academic discourse. In mainstream academia today, whether in grade-school texts or in texts meant for undergraduate and graduate study, whenever India and Hinduism are mentioned, the coming of Aryans from outside of India and establishing Hinduism and civilization in India is discussed as a veritable fact. By examining the theory in anticolonial and postcolonial contexts, we show that despite considerable archeological evidence refuting the theories of the invasion or migration of Aryans into India, its colonial embeddedness in the notion of the racial superiority of the Europeans or people with European ancestry that the theory does not fade into oblivion.

Genesis of the Aryan Invasion Theory

With the following famous passage in 1792, William Jones outlined the connection between Sanskrit and European languages, and thus the recognition of a common ancestry between Indians and Europeans took root:

> The Sanskrit language, whatever may be its antiquity, is of a wonderful structure; more perfect than the Greek, more copious than the Latin, and more exquisitely refined than either, yet bearing to both of them a stronger affinity, both in the roots of the verbs and in the forms of grammar, than could possibly have been produced by accident; so strong, indeed, that no philologer could examine them all three, without believing them to have sprung from common source which, perhaps, no longer exists: there is a similar reason, though not quite so forcible, for supposing that both the Gothick and the Celtick, though blended with a very different idiom, had the same origin with the Sanskrit, and the old Persian may be added to the same family.[1]

The common ancestry theory was not born with Jones as Bryant (2001) demonstrates. Such conjectures were prevalent even before him. Scholars such as Pere Coeurdoux, in as early as 1768, had contended that Sanskrit, as the language of the Brahmins, came to India from Caucasia. There were others such as Nathaniel Halhed and James Parsons, physician and fellow of the Royal Society and of the Society of the Antiquities, who in the year 1776 had already drawn a connection between Indian and European languages. It was the reputation and stature of William Jones, who was a judge in the Supreme Court in Bengal, which engraved this idea in stone.[2] In the initial years of common Indo-European ancestry, India was the cradle of the

[1] (Bryant 2001:15–16).

[2] This section of the book chapter is largely inspired by the research work of Edwin Bryant (2001). Adequate attention has been paid to give credit to his ideas.

civilization. Thinkers of the Modern Era, such as Voltaire, Sonnerat, Schelling, and Schlegel argued that the epicenter of civilization was India, and that Europe owed its cultural and philosophical origins to India. Monboddo (1774), Halhed, Schlegel, and Kennedy (1828) believed that Greek and Latin were derived from Sanskrit. The mother tongue of all the Indo-European languages was Sanskrit. This theory however, did not remain static. With the political ascendency of Europe over India, the mother-tongue theory began to fade into oblivion. One of the first people to challenge it was Frantz Bopp, who felt that there was instead an "original" tongue out of which Sanskrit as well as European languages was derived, though Sanskrit was able to preserve its originality better than others. The original tongue was termed the Proto-Indo-European language to which Sanskrit became one of the daughters, albeit the eldest of them all. For the people thus being represented by these ideas, the terms Indo-German, Indo-European, and Aryan came into use beginning in the nineteenth century (Bryant 2001).

With the decline of the status of Sanskrit as the original mother tongue of all European languages, India as the mother-region of all Indo-Europeans also began to recede. Fredrick Schlegel's brother, A.W. von Schlegel in 1842 asserted that instead of migration happening from India to Europe, there existed some central region from which people went in different directions to Europe and India. Benfey, consequently, contended that since Southern India consisted of "tribal" population (and hence by implication inferior given the prominent discourse of the times), they had to be subjugated by the invading "superior" Aryans from the North. Muir (1860), torturing the Sanskrit texts, claimed the gradual advance of Aryans from Northwest of India to East as well as South. The Aryan Invasion Theory (AIT) was thus born. Post the First War of Indian Independence against the British in 1857, as the British established its political suzerainty over most part of India, neither India as the home of the Aryans nor Sanskrit as the mother tongue of the European languages remained. Chakrabarti writes, "With the Raj firmly established, it was time to begin to visualize the history and cultural process of India as a series of invasions and foreign rules."[3]

Given that the colonizers and missionaries began driving the AIT hard. A common ancestry of the Hindus and Europeans was an idea that had made most of the missionaries and colonizers uncomfortable. Missionaries such as Alexander Duff and William Hastie and colonizers such as James Mill opposed the idea tooth and nail, and were more

---

[3] (Chakrabarti 1976:66–67).

inclined to emphasize the differences between Indians and Europeans rather than their similarities. Disparaging Indians—their culture, civilization, traditions, and religion—was the master note of their utterances instead of focusing on convergences or similarities. With the "discovery" by the Madras school of Orientalists that southern Indian languages and Sanskrit did not come from a common root (Bryant 2001), the aforementioned notion of "Aryans" invading the "Indians" began to gain further currency. The Vedas were further tortured to depict white and fair "Aryans," coming through the northwest, in conflict with the dark-skinned and flat-nosed "Dravidians," described as the original natives of the Indian subcontinent. The corollary to all this as Trautmann (1982) shows was that the European Aryans brought civilization and Sanskrit to India. The conclusion fitted extremely well with the "civilizing mission" notion of the Europeans: just as the Aryans of the past brought civilization, language, and culture to the Indians of the yore, the colonizers and missionaries were bringing a second wave of civilization to the inter-mixed and corrupted (hence by default inferior) Indians. The AIT served many different political ends—of missionaries, colonialists, and "native" Indians (for details, see Bryant 2001).

The movement of the Aryan homeland from India to "somewhere in Asia" to Europe also happened in successive stages. It was assisted by German philology. As an emerging nation, Germany had found itself lagging in becoming a colonial power as some other European nations such as England, France, Spain, Holland and Portugal, and it was desperately looking for sources that could bolster its national identity and ego. Sanskrit and India came in extremely handy for such an objective. If the Germans could show that they were the original Indo-Europeans, who were the cause of various European nations and India in history, their national pride would be stamped beyond question. This was at the basis of their quest for the pure Indo-German race. The Indo-Germans could consequently not have a homeland in Asia. Therefore, the homeland of the Indo Germans/Indo Europeans/Aryans had to be changed first and had to be moved to Europe.

The process began. Robert G. Latham in 1862 proposed a European homeland for the Indo-Europeans. In 1878, the German philologist L. Geiger contended that Indo-Europeans were blond and blue-eyed people, and these traits had become diluted and darkened in those places where there had been a foreign admixture of genes (Bryant 2001). Since the contention served the European sense of superiority, in no time it began to gather steam and get regurgitated. Finding evidence for unadulterated blond, fair, and blue-eyed Indo-European in the areas of

Germany, Austria, Switzerland, and Belgium was easy. And thus, this area became the original homeland of the Indo-Europeans. The rise of Nazism was exclusively related to this appropriation, though one must say that in the quest for the original home land of Indo-Europeans, scholars have virtually pointed to almost every part of Europe (Bryant 2001). In this melee, there emerged the German Indologist, Max Muller, who had been hired by the East India Company for the translation of the Sanskrit texts in its possession. He arbitrarily attributed the date of the Rig Veda around 1200 BCE. The arbitrariness of the dating was criticized by his contemporaries, to which he responded in 1890:

> I have repeatedly dwelt on the merely hypothetical character of the dates, which I have ventured to assign to first periods of Vedic literature. All I have claimed for them has been that they are minimum dates, and that the literary productions of each period, which still exist or which formerly existed could hardly be accounted for within shorter limits of time than those suggested.[4] If now we ask as to how we can fix the dates of these periods, it is quite clear that we cannot hope to fix a *terminum a qua.* Whether the Vedic hymns were composed [in] 1000 or 2000 or 3000 BC, no power on earth will ever determine.[5]

Consequently the coming of Aryans to India in 1500 BCE was determined—a date which gets regurgitated in all mainstream academic literature on India and Hinduism (for instance, Flood 1996). Before we address the contemporary archeological evidence regarding the AIT, the following are three points that emerge from the above: The issue of Aryans and India has not been static. Over a period of time, the spectrum has evolved from India being the cradle of the Aryan civilization to being invaded by fair, blond, and blue-eyed Aryans who had their homeland in Europe. It has changed with the changing fortunes of India. That the "Aryans" invaded India from the northwestern frontier was a theory developed during the times when suzerainty of the British over India was almost complete. The Aryan Invasion Theory is not divorced from—on the contrary contiguous with—the imperialistic designs of the colonialists and the evangelical zeal of the missionaries. Depending upon the political and missionary expediencies, the Aryan Invasion Theory was used by various parties involved.

The established and dominant narrative by the beginning of the twentieth century was that India knew no civilization before the coming

---

[4] (Bryant and Patton 2005:51).

[5] Ibid.

of the Aryans. This was to change when in 1924, the Director General of the Archaeological Survey of India, Sir John Marshall (through the excavations initiated by R.D. Bannerji and Daya Ram Sahni respectively), announced the discovery of two ancient Bronze Age Civilization cities—Mohenjo-Daro and Harappa—of what he called as the Indus Civilization (also known as Harappan civilization in the current discourse) as both the cities were situated in the river valley of Indus. The subsequent decade long excavations (excavations continued even later) revealed that the cities of the Indus civilization were massive and extremely well planned. They are marvels of urban engineering for the times in which they were built. They had roads intersecting at right angles with carefully laid out drainage and covered sewage system. Mohenjo-Daro, made use of baked bricks, which was quite unheard of in other Bronze Age civilizations. The houses of the inhabitants were well planned, with many of them at least two storied. They also had brick-lined wells, bathing facilities, privies, and drainage connected to city's main sewage system suggesting that town planning and cleanliness were of utmost importance to the Harappans (Possehl 2002).

Their economy was quite complex, with various craftspeople, metalworkers, seal cutters, architects, and engineers living in the city. The Harappans were wealthy people who traded as far away as with Mesopotamia, Sumer, and Egypt. The technological sophistication of the Harappan people can also be seen in making of metal alloys such as bronze, square seals, high quality faience, high quality ceramics especially stoneware, and jewelry—in the cutting, polishing, etching, and drilling of long carnelian beads. The metalworkers worked with copper, tin, arsenic, lead, silver, gold, and electrum. They also built small ships, which could sail as far away as 4000 miles to distant lands. The Harappan way of life was not possible without an in-depth knowledge of urban engineering, chemistry, and navigation (Possehl 2002).

The discovery of Mohenjo-Daro and Harappa struck at the very root of the then prevalent discourse that the Aryans came to India in 1500 BCE and consequently established civilization. One would think that with the massive amount of evidence against it, the AIT would suffer a fatal jolt. However, the ideas of European superiority and supremacy prevailed, and throwing all academic integrity to wind the new evidence was reinterpreted. The Aryans still came as invaders. This time instead of defeating the civilization-less original inhabitants of India—the "Dravidians"—they defeated the civilized Dravidians and pushed them to the southernmost corners of the Indian subcontinent.

The Vedic and Puranic texts were twisted and tortured for the desired outcomes. In 1944 when the Second World War was coming to a close, a Brigadier General of the British Army serving in the North African front, Robert Eric Mortimer "Rick" Wheeler was made the Director General of the Archeological Survey of India. Shortly after, he made a trip to Harappa which was in excavation at that point in time, and within a couple of hours of being at the site, he concluded that the mound at Harappa was a citadel—constructed to fend against the invading Aryans:

> The Aryan Invasion of the Land of Seven Rivers, the Punjab and its environs, constantly assumes the form of an onslaught upon the walled cities of the aborigines. For these cities the term used in the *Rigveda* is *pur*, meaning a "rampart," "fort" or "stronghold." ... Indra, the Aryan War god, is *puramdara*, "fort-destroyer." He shatters "ninety forts" for his Aryan protégé Divodasa.... Where are—or were—these citadels? It has in the past been supposed that they were mythical, or were merely "places of refuge against attack, ramparts of hardened earth with palisades and a ditch." The recent excavation of Harappa may be thought to have changed the picture. Here we have a highly evolved civilization of essentially non-Aryan type, now known to have employed massive fortifications, and known also to have dominated the river-system of north-western India at a time not distant from the likely period of the earlier Aryan invasions of that region. What destroyed this firmly settled civilization? Climatic, economic, political deterioration may have weakened it, but its ultimate extinction is more likely to have been completed by deliberate and large-scale destruction. It may be no mere chance that at a late period of Mohenjo-daro men, women and children appear to have been massacred there. On circumstantial evidence, Indra stands accused.[6]

Wheeler's contentions have not held the test of time. Excavations at Harappa and Mohenjo-Daro and the rest of the 1050 sites of the Indus Civilization (to date approximately 1052 sites of the civilization have either been identified or excavated; Possehl 2002), which many scholars would rather prefer to call as Indus-Saraswati Civilization. This is because of the finding of over 500 sites on the currently dried-up riverbed of a mighty ancient river, Saraswati, which is called Ghaggar in India and Hakra in Pakistan that flowed from the Himalayas to the Arabian Sea (Possehl 2002). Tectonic movements around the beginning of the second millennium BCE made a part of the river go paleochannel

---

[6] (Wheeler 1947:82).

and another meet the river Yamuna, which was not as big then as it is today (Agarwal and Sood 1982). Satellite images have proved the existence of this river in the past, and even today all over India there are Brahmin communities which name their *jati* by the name of the river Saraswati—they call themselves Saaraswat Brahmins, or Brahmins who lived by the banks of Saraswati at one point in time. Gregory Possehl (2002), who was engaged in archaeological research on Indus Civilization in both India and Pakistan for close to four decades, holds that the Indus Civilization began around 7000 BCE and entered its mature phase, called the Mature Harappan phase between 2500 BCE–1900 BCE in which its numerous cities flourished. These cities had declined much before the mythical invasion of the mythical Aryans. Mohenjo-Daro along with many other cities in Sindh, Baluchistan, and Cholistan came to an abrupt end around 1900 BCE, and as far as the other cities are concerned, there is either a progressive decline or a relocation of the civilization eastwards towards the Indo-Gangetic plain in the Late Harappan period (depending upon the region, the time span of this phase is either 1900 BCE–1300 BCE or 1900 BCE–1000 BCE). Possehl writes:

> There was an abandonment, or severe depopulation, of a number of important Indus settlements including Channu-daro, Kot Diji, Balakot, Allahdino, Kulli, Mehi, Nindowari, Nausharo, Kalibangan, Ropar, Surkotada, Dholavira, Desalpur, and Lothal. There was also a disruption in the Indus Economy. The production of a wide range of special materials, many of which seem to be have been luxury items, was curtailed.... [However] there was an increase in the number of settlements in the Punjab, Haryana, western Uttar Pradesh, and northern Rajasthan. The Harappans in Gujarat remained remarkably stable.[7]

Jonathan Kenoyer, who has conducted excavations and research both in Mohenjo-Daro and Harappa, having worked in western and central India, substantiates:

> One of the most important developments is the emergence of new peripheral centers in the Gangetic region concomitant with the eclipse of urban centers in the old core of the Indus Valley. This suggests that the Late Harappan period is not so much of a decline in the Indus Valley, but rather of social, economic, and political reorganization on a larger scale that includes both the Indus and Gangetic regions as well as the adjacent Malwa Plateau.[8]

[7] (Possehl 2002:237).

[8] (Kenoyer 2005:23).

Jim Shaffer, another archaeologist who has conducted extensive fieldwork in Neolithic and Bronze Age Civilization sites in both India and Pakistan—holding the drying of the river Saraswati as the cause—along with Diane Lichtenstein contend:

> Beginning in the late third millennium BC and continuing throughout the second millennium BC, many, *but not all*, Indus Valley settlements, including urban centers, were abandoned as a cultural response to the environmental "crisis."... Even within the Indus Valley, the cultural response of abandoning habitation sites varied. In Cholistan, along the Ghaggar-Hakra River, it was a dramatic response of abandonment. Yet all areas were affected in the Indus Valley. While the quality of the survey data is regionally variable, it is sufficient to show a gradual and significant population shift from the Indus Valley eastward into the eastern Punjab and Gujarat, beginning in the late third millennium BC and continuing throughout the second millennium BC.[9]

Focusing exclusively on Harappa, Kenoyer states:

> [Recent excavations at Harappa] indicate that the Late Harappan occupation at the site was much more widespread than originally thought.... Baked brick architecture was constructed with both newly made bricks as well as reused bricks from earlier structures. During the Late Harappan period there is evidence of over-crowding and encroachment rather than abandonment and decline (Kenoyer 1991).... *There is no concrete evidence for the appearance of a new biological population* (Hemphill *et al.* 1991; Kennedy 1992, 1995). This suggests that the changes and discontinuities reflect a transformation of the local population rather than the appearance of new people and the eradication of the Harappan inhabitants.[10]

We have mentioned earlier that the faience industry and bead making—an aspect of the lapidary industry—was quite developed in the Mature Phase of the Harappan civilization. Kenoyer notes that the making of stone beads became less common in the Late Harappan period and was substituted with glass beads. The production of glass beads in the Punjab continues all the way up to Painted Gray Ware Period (1400 BCE to 1000 BCE) and later till Northern Black Polished Ware Period, showing continuity between the Late Harappan period and the Early History. He writes: "Between 1700 and 800 BC, glass production developed into a common industry and became quite widespread throughout the northern subcontinent."[11] In effect, if we take

[9] (Shaffer and Lichtenstein 85–86, italics in original).

[10] (Kenoyer 2005:23–26, italics mine).

[11] (Kenoyer 2005:37).

the evidence of the beads and fiancee industry into account, there is a continuity coming to the current times. The state of Gujarat, which is the southernmost area of the Harappan civilization, still has the city of Surat as one the leading centers of the world even today in terms of the lapidary industry. The city is the biggest center in the world for the cutting and polishing of diamonds and gems.

What about the Citadel theory of Wheeler, standing on which he gave archeological evidence to the Aryan Invasion Theory? Possehl (2002) contends that the elevated mound was not a citadel—on the contrary, it was an elevated area, fortified with retaining walls to hold the mud used for its construction, on which the buildings of significance such as the Great Bath (taking the example of Mohenjo-Daro), Warehouse, and other large buildings could be built; it was some sort of an ancient Indian acropolis. If it were meant for defensive purposes, then the western side of the Mohenjo-Daro mound would not have been open to the Indus plains.

In the excavations at Mohenjo-Daro, there were some human remains that were found—a total of forty-two skeletons, interned in rather a hasty manner at different places within the city; no cemetery as yet has been found there. At one site which is called the "HR Area Tragedy" site—located in the HR-B Area, Block 2, House V, Room 74—a total of 14 skeletons (13 adult males and females and one child) were found. Wheeler immediately connected this to the invasion of the Aryans:

> That final blow has often enough been described. It is represented by groups of skeletons—men, women and children, some bearing axes or sword-cuts—which have been found lying on the topmost level in the sprawled or contorted positions in which they fell. They had been left there by raiders who had no further use for the city which they had stormed. In that moment Mohenjo-daro was dead.[12]

Dales (1964) and Kennedy (1982, 1984, 1994) have refuted these contentions. Kennedy, who investigated the skeletons, holds that though there was trauma on skeleton 10, the death did not seem to have occurred from the trauma because "the cut is not fresh and its margins are characterized by considerable bone absorption."[13] Or even if the death had been caused by the wound, the wound must have been caused anywhere between thirty to seventy days earlier. Therefore despite that there were skeletons found in one room, all but one did not have mortal

[12] (Wheeler 1959:113–114).

[13] (Kennedy 1984:429).

wounds. Though the skeletons suggest a hasty internment, there is no conclusive evidence to suggest that the people were put to death by any invading army. There are other three "massacre" sites where clusters of skeletons have been found. However all of them belong to a period (late Harappan Period) when civilization at Mohenjo-Daro had already come to an end. Possehl concludes:

> Some experts on ancient Indian history have faith in the preposition that these deaths were cause (sic) by invading Aryans. There are, however, many problems with this theory, not the least of which is chronological: While there may have been speakers of one or more Indo-European languages in the Greater Indus region earlier, there is a gap of centuries between the abandonment of Mohenjo-daro at about 1900 BC and the documentation found in the Ṛgveda, which probably dates to circa 1000 BC. Also note that the Rgveda is a not a text documenting the invasion and conquest of the Subcontinent, but speaks of the feuding among the Aryans as well as with the indigenous peoples. Sindh is a peripheral area in the Vedic literature: The center of this world was the Punjab. It is therefore noteworthy that there is no evidence for massacre at Harappa or any of the other Indus settlements in the geographical area described most prominently in the Vedas.[14]

Kenoyer seconds: "One of the most important results of the current work at Harappa is that there continues to be no support for the earlier interpretations of Vedic-Aryan invasions and the destruction of Harappan settlements."[15] The Aryan Invasion Theory thus stands refuted. But just like the earlier situation where the emergence of the ruins of the massive cities of Harappa and Mohenjo-Daro did not refute the Aryan Invasion Theory but rather was appropriated to continue the narrative, the profound refutation of the AIT has morphed into a new theory: the Aryan Migration Theory (AMT). The AMT now contends that the European Aryans may not have come as invading armies but they still came as wandering pastoralists. The idea of European Aryans was racist and imperialistic right from the very beginning and it remains racist and imperialistic today in whatever guise we may experience it—within its scholarly facade, it continues to deny India its history and the cultural, philosophical, spiritual, artistic, architectural, scientific, and technological accomplishments of its ancestors. What is most surprising is that the same archeologists, who refute the AIT promote the AMT

---

[14] (Possehl 2002:164–165).

[15] (Kenoyer 2005:44).

on either weak or no evidence, even when they have to contradict themselves. For instance, Kenoyer writes, "At the opposite end of the spectrum is the misconception that the Indus people as a whole represent the communities referred to in the Vedic literature."[16] This is despite the fact of his own contentions as quoted above: "During the Late Harappan period there is evidence of overcrowding and encroachment rather than abandonment and decline.... There is no concrete evidence for the appearance of a new biological population."[17] The non-appearance of a new biological population in Late Harappa should have been sufficient to contest the AMT theory. Kenoyer however takes a contrary route:

> According to many scholars, the chronological framework for the final phases of the Harappan and the Late Harappan occupation at Harappa does correspond broadly with the time frame for the Ṛg Vedic period. Therefore, it is not improbable that some communities referred to in the Vedas were passing through or living in the regions controlled by Harappa during both the Harappan (Period 3C 2250–1900 BC) and the Late Harappan times (1900–1700 or 1300 BC).[18]

This is also despite reporting the similarities in burial practices mentioned in the Vedas and found in the late Harappan period:

> The Rig Veda refers to several types of burial, including earth burials and cremation. It is clear from the careful reading the excavation reports of Vats that there is no evidence for cremation at Harappa, but there are earth burials in Stratum II of Cemetery H. In later texts dating to *c*.800 BC, there are detailed instructions on how to collect bones that have been either buried or exposed for a specified length of time and place them in a pot with a lid that is then buried in a pit.... Pot burials from the later Stratum I in Cemetery H could reflect an earlier example of this type of secondary or fractional burial. However, the limited nature of the data makes it impossible to make any conclusive statements about the presence or absence of Vedic communities at Harappa.[19]

With the above data, Kenoyer could have taken the position that perhaps both the dating of the Vedas as well as the coming of the Aryans into India are profound myths created to bolster and enhance the European supremacy over the native Indians of the Indian subcontinent. He, however, did not and perpetuated the AMT. This is despite his familiarity with the fact that the date of the creation of Vedas in 1200

[16] Ibid, 45.
[17] Ibid, 23–26, italics mine.
[18] Ibid, 46.
[19] Ibid, 45.

BCE on which the coming of Aryans in 1500 BCE was predicated is arbitrary—his colleague and fellow archaeologist B.B. Lal, as we saw earlier, has been quite vocal about it.

What has happened now is that the time of the coming of the Aryans has been moved backwards by a few centuries. The possibility that the Harappan civilization was an indigenous creation of Indian Aryans is yet to be acceded to by most western archaeologists. Gregory Possehl (2002), who as we have seen earlier, has comprehensively refuted the AIT. However, he too does not find the idea fantastical in that wandering pastoralists could create a massive civilization which made India the jewel in the crown of the British empire—after having achieved a golden age in the early centuries of the first millennium CE—but not indigenous people who already were massive city builders with a highly advanced civilization for its times, who would disappear without a trace or leave a little trace (particularly when they were not invaded and consequently decimated). Mere wandering herdsmen, because they simply were European, could become harbingers of a profound ancient Indian civilization, the full scope of achievements of which in the current times is yet to be fully traced and unfolded:

> I believe from linguistic evidence that the homeland of the Indo-European peoples was somewhere in the temperate forest regions of Eurasia, so they came to the subcontinent from somewhere else. When the speakers of an Indo-European language(s) first came to the Subcontinent is not known. They first appear in the Near East just after 2000 BC, but this is from linguistic evidence and they could have been there much before this, as would be the case for the Subcontinent.... No one knows for sure when the Indo-Europeans who spoke Vedic Sanskrit came to the Subcontinent, or how they got there. Speakers of other Indo-European languages were in the Near East early in the second millennium, and this may approximate the date of the Aryans into the Subcontinent. But there is no evidence for an invasion, and most contemporary scholars who deal with this issue think more in terms of the movement that characterizes cattle pastoralists because of their need for pastureland, than military conquest. Moreover, the Aryans may have come to the Punjab over a long period of time (a matter of centuries), not in a great rush, as an invasion would suggest.[20]

And they came so comprehensively that in no part of the world, they left any trace of their language, culture, philosophy, etc. other than the

---

[20] (Possehl 2002:249, italics mine).

Indian Subcontinent. Forget about evidence to refute the AMT, this theory militates against common sense. Given that Possehl earlier attests to the movement of Indus Civilization eastward after 1900 BCE, how does he explain the migration and the eclipsing of its fabulous urban centers? Comical as it may sound, Possehl holds that the Indus Civilization was so good that it failed. Its failure was not because of "flood, avulsion, drought, trade, disease, locusts, invasion, or any other of a myriad of 'natural' or 'outside' forces" but because of "sociocultural flaw."[21] It was a social system that achieved great heights because of "social harmony in human relationships and with the environment."[22] He states that it was too good for its own good. Citing Heesterman (1985), he feels that if a society does not have inner conflict, it cannot last for long because it is the inner conflict which allows the inhabitants to be in a "constant state of negotiating, resolving, dealing with maladaptation or lack of harmony in their lives"[23] and because the Indus Civilization built a system based on social harmony amongst and with one another, which included the environment, it collapsed under its own weight—it was too good for its own survival. The above position of Possehl is completely conjectural—as conjectural as the AMT. It is true there seems to be an absence of big temples and palaces within the Mature Harappan Civilization, quite unlike Mesopotamia and Egypt, but creating a comprehensive idea of an entire social system based on the lack of these artifacts is nothing but conjectural projection. Possehl is creating the radical "other" of the Egyptian and Mesopotamian civilizations in the Harappan Civilization, and basing his theory on it. He writes:

> One of the more interesting observations about the Indus Civilization is that no temples have been found. Nor is there much to be said of monumental architecture with a religious function or monumental architecture of any kind. The temples and pyramids of Dynastic Egypt and the ziggurats of Mesopotamia have no parallel in the Indus Valley.[24]

He contends further that it is not that religion was not there in the civilization; it certainly was as is evident from structures like the Great Bath in Mohenjo-Daro and various figurines that have been found. And the capacity to build monumental structures—the engineering and the work force—was there too and yet no such structures were built.

[21] Ibid, 244.
[22] Ibid.
[23] Ibid.
[24] Ibid, 148.

Similarly there are no palaces present either, much in contrast to the Egyptians and Mesopotamians: "Another contrast between Egypt and Mesopotamia and the Indus Civilization is the absence of palaces, the large abode of the heads of government and their powerful associates charged with managing the fortunes of the political apparatus."[25] The fact is that nothing conclusive is known about the social organization of the Harappans. Creating a social system completely in contrast to the Mesopotamians and Egyptians, based on the lack of similarity of structures found in the remains of the Mesopotamian and Egyptian Civilizations, is nothing but a sleight of hand—a pure work of fantasy and projection.

Then what really happened to most of the prominent cities of the Indus Civilization? The answer lies in the drying up of the Saraswati. There is a correspondence between the time that the Saraswati dried up and the abandonment or the decline (as the case may be) of the Harappan cities. Shaffer and Lichtenstein write:

> In the early second millennium BC, there was the capture of the Ghaggar-Hakra (or Saraswati) river system (then a focal point of human occupation) by adjacent rivers, with subsequent diversion of these waters eastwards (Shaffer 1981, 1982, 1986, 1993; Mughal 1990, 1997; Shaffer and Lichtenstein 1995, 1999). At the same time, there was an increasing tectonic activity in Sindh and elsewhere. Combined, these geological changes meant *major* changes in the hydrology patterns of the region (Flam 1981, 1993). These natural geological processes had significant consequences for the food producing cultural groups throughout the greater Indus Valley area.[26]

Further, they not only categorically refute the Aryan Invasion Theory but also are incisive about all attempts to twist data to show western influences on the rise of the prehistoric civilization in India. In their assessment, the most current archeological records show a remarkable continuity within the Indian subcontinent:

> The modern archeological record for South Asia indicates a history of significant cultural continuity; an interpretation at variance with earlier eighteenth through twentieth-century scholarly views of South Asian cultural discontinuity and South Asian cultural dependence on western cultural influences.[27]

---

[25] Ibid.

[26] (Shaffer and Lichtenstein: 84).

[27] Ibid, 93.

B.B. Lal, the erstwhile Director General of the Archaeological Survey of India and a renowned archeologist, validates the above-mentioned contention of Shaffer and Lichtenstein. Lal (2011) contends that many aspects and cultural practices, including the city building plan, of the Harappans, continued until historic times as is evidenced in the excavation of a six hundred BCE city of Shishupalgarh and its incorporation in the *Arthashastra* of Kautilya (1992), a text composed in the fourth century BCE. Lal (2009) has also shown how farming methods, plan of building houses, ornaments used by female populace including artifacts for wedding ceremonies, bedtime tales, lapidary methods, cooking methods including the use of pots and pans, games like chess, toys used by children, writing pad, etc. have continued to find their use in the current times in areas surrounding the Harappan civilization. In addition, figurines showing the traditional Hindu greeting Namaste, yogic poses later compiled in the Yoga Sutras of Patanjali, fire alters used in Vedic ceremonies, seals depicting the Hindu Deity Shiva, iconic representation of Shiva in the form of *Shivalinga* have been found in various sites of the Harappan culture. The above show the Vedic and indigenous roots of the Harappan culture rather than what the mainstream discourse argues for.

Shaffer and Lichtenstein are cognizant of the initiatives of various European nations to bolster their national identity and ego through the appropriation of the Aryan identity and Sanskrit—undertaken in the colonial era but not yet been abandoned:

> The scholarly paradigm of the eighteenth and nineteenth centuries in conflating language, culture, race, and population movements has continued, with historical linguistic scholars still assiduously attempting to reconstruct a proto-Indo-European language, and attempting to link that language to a specific "homeland," in order to define population migration away from the seminal geographic base. Suggestions for such a proto-Indo-European homeland range from Siberia to more recent efforts to tracing the homeland to Anatolia (Renfrew 1987) and the Ukraine (Gamkrelidze and Ivanov 1985 a, b; Gimbutas 1985; Mallory 1989; Allchin 1995), and these efforts now incorporate human genetic studies (Cavalli-Sforza et al. 1994) to verify the linguistic chronologies.[28]

Their reasoned view backed by the analysis of massive amounts of data gathered from various archeological sites and spread all over the Indian subcontinent is that there is neither western influence in the creation and

[28] Ibid.

shaping of the Harappan Civilization nor discontinuities in the cultural record of prehistoric Indian Subcontinent.

> The current archeological and paleoanthropological data simply do not support these centuries old interpretative paradigms suggesting western, intrusive, cultural influence as responsible for the supposed major discontinuities in the South Asian cultural prehistoric record (Shaffer and Lichtenstein 1999; Kennedy 2000; Lamberg-Karlovsky 2002).... It is currently possible to discern cultural continuities linking specific prehistoric social entities in South Asia into one cultural tradition (Shaffer and Lichtenstein 1989, 1995, 1999; Shaffer 1992, 1993). This is *not to* propose social isolation *nor* deny any outside cultural influence. Outside cultural influence did affect South Asian cultural development in later, especially historic, periods, but an identifiable cultural tradition has continued, an Indo-Gangetic Cultural Tradition (Shaffer 1993; Shaffer and Lichtenstein 1995, 1999) linking social entities over a period of time from the development of food production in the seventh millennium BC to present.[29]

The above by Shaffer and Lichtenstein is conclusive and is in line with the overwhelming amount of archeological data, which have been gathered over time. It also is in contradiction to the contentions of Possehl and Kenoyer, who despite the presence of such data perpetuate the AMT, following linguistics and philology, which continue to remain non-science despite their bellowing claims to be science—had they been science, the "Aryan homeland" would not have spanned and continue to span the different parts of Europe and most parts of Asia (minus India). It is time that modern academia backs off from perpetuating a colonial myth—either the AIT or the AMT—that continue to be used in textbooks all the way from primary and secondary levels to college to university levels of education. This theory is deeply and profoundly embedded in the racial superiority of Europeans or people with European lineage over the inferiority of Indians: it is quite explicit in the ways in which it was crafted. Evidence after evidence keep emerging but western academia, which controls the academic discourse in practically all parts of the world, keeps appropriating it and keeps shifting the goalposts. If it is not the AIT then it is the AMT; if it is not the AMT, then it will be something else. Once the Aryans came to India, they will keep coming, until we stand up and call out academia on the

[29] Ibid, italics in original.

racist nature of the AIT/AMT discourse. Seeing it any other way is tantamount to ignoring the huge white elephant in the room.

Distortion of history has been a mega project of the colonizers. The anticolonial writers were sophisticated enough to understand it. Though the postcolonial writers have built their legacy on the backs of the anticolonial writers, the analysis of distortion of history has not been such a serious undertaking among them, particularly when it comes to India. Eradicating the civilizational contributions of non-European people to humanity was the master-note on which the colonizers' representation of colonized cultures and nations played. By distorting the history, the colonial project destroyed the identity of the colonized. The destruction of identity led to destruction of their faith in themselves and hence to the resistance to the colonial rule. Whether it was Africa or it was India, the project was the same. Writing an introduction to Aimé Césaire's *Discourses on Colonialism*, Robin D.G. Kelly writes:

> An entire generation of "enlightened" European scholars worked hard to wipe out the cultural and intellectual contributions of Egypt and Nubia from European history, to whiten the West in order to maintain the purity of the "European" race. They also stripped all of Africa of any semblance of "civilization," using the printed page to eradicate their history and thus reduce a whole continent and its progeny to little more than beasts of burden or brutish heathens.[30]

By removing the "civilization" from the colonized, the European colonizers could turn the colonized "other" into primitives, which would then further and justify their civilizing mission. Kelly, commenting on Césaire, elucidates:

Césaire reveals, over and over again, that the colonizers' sense of superiority, their sense of mission as the world's civilizers, depends on turning the Other into a barbarian. The Africans, the Indians, the Asians cannot posses civilization or culture equal to that of the imperialists, or the latter have no purpose, no justification for the exploitation and domination of the rest of the world. The colonial encounter, in other words, requires a reinvention of the colonized, the deliberate destruction of the past-what Césaire calls "thingification."[31]

In the context of India, a systematic *primitivization* of the Indian culture and civilization, in particular of the Hindus, began with the publication of *History of British India* by James Mill (2015) in 1817. James Mill was hired by the East India Company (the corporation

[30] (Kelly 2000:22).

[31] Ibid., 9.

ruling India till the British crown took over after India's first war of independence in 1857), which funded his research for about 10 years leading to the publication of his three volume series on *History of British India.* Surprising as it may sound today, Mill did not visit India even once to write this work—in fact, he defends it quite vehemently in the opening pages, claiming that it is not necessary for an author to be familiar with the land to be writing its history. However, his work became an authoritative text on India—thanks to the colonial influence and power of the East India Company—and it was used by the East India Company to train its civil servants serving in India. In *Book II* of the *History of British India: Volume* One, Mill has written seven chapters on the Hindus. His agenda is quite explicit: to prove that Hindus are savages, barbarians, uncivilized, uncouth, rude, brute, unrefined, coarse, vulgar, etc. One would be hard-pressed to find one positive representation on the Hindus in the entire section. Let us present to you a slice of Mill's vitriol in which he defines or should we say denigrates the religion of the Hindus:

> No people, how rude and ignorant soever, who have been so far advanced as to leave us memorials of their thoughts in writing, have ever drawn a more gross and disgusting picture of the universe than what is presented in the writings of the Hindus. In the conception of it no coherence, wisdom, or beauty, ever appears; all is disorder, caprice, passion, contest, portents, prodigies, violence, and deformity. It is perfectly evident that the Hindus never contemplated the universe as a connected and perfect system, governed by general laws, and directed to benevolent ends; and it follows, as a necessary consequence, that their religion is no other than primary worship, which is addressed to the designing and invisible beings who preside over the powers of nature, according to their own arbitrary will, and act only for some private and selfish gratification. The elevated language, which this species of worship finally assumes, is only the refinement, which flattery, founded upon a base apprehension of the divine character, ingrafts upon a mean superstition.[32]

From the very first sentence in chapter one of *Book II*, Mill launches into showing how the Hindus and their civilization are barbaric. He begins with the premise that the uncivilized and brute nations claim a deep antiquity to their existence: "Rude nations seem to derive a particular gratification from pretensions to a remote antiquity."[33] For

[32] (Mill 2015:385–387).

[33] Ibid, 154.

this he takes the help of the division of time by the Hindus in terms of four *yugas*: *Satya Yuga*, *Treta Yuga*, *Dwapar Yuga*, and *Kali Yuga* that are arranged in the ratios of 4:3:2:1. If one takes into account the various texts where the *yugas* are described, the only commonality that one finds is that the *yugas* are arranged in the respective ratio of 4:3:2:1 and that the texts differ in terms of number of years for one unit. For instance, whereas the *Vishnu Purana* takes one unit as 432000 years (the number of years in *Kali Yuga*), *Manu Smriti* and other astronomy/astrology texts such as *Surya Siddhanta* take the unit as comprising of 1200 years—consequently, *Kali Yuga* from the perspective of these texts consists of 1200 years. Despite the fact that Mill is deeply familiar with the *Manu Smriti*—for he has liberally and selectively used the text to show the barbaric nature of the Hindus—he chooses to use the *Vishnu Purana* in order to substantiate his thesis about claims of the antiquity by a collectivity of people and lack of civilization. Had he used the time data in *Manu Smriti*, the Hindu civilization would only be in the range of 12000 plus years (4800 years of *Satya Yuga* + 3600 years of *Treta Yuga* + 2400 years of *Dwapar Yuga* + 1200 years of *Kali Yuga*). Ignoring the data, however he makes the claim that Hindus lack a sense of history and all that they are capable of is writing imaginary fiction:

> The offspring of a wild and ungoverned imagination, they mark the state of a rude and credulous people, whom the marvelous delights; who cannot estimate the use of a record of past events; and whose imagination the real occurrences of life are too familiar to engage. To the monstrous period of years which the legends of the Hindus involve, they ascribe events the most extravagant and unnatural: events not even connected in chronological series; a number of independent and incredible fictions. This people, indeed, are perfectly destitute of historical records.[34]

Given the influence that Mill's work came to have in academia due to the intersection of colonial power and "knowledge" production, it became engraved in stone consciously and unconsciously that Indians have no sense of history. Though we have only quoted the work of B.B. Lal above, there has been a host of archaeologists from India who have solidly refuted the AIT and AMT, yet it seems that academia, which is controlled by western discourse, does not seem to shift the needle. A host of their articles in international journals as well as presentations in international conferences too does not alter the discourse.

---

[34] Ibid, 166–167.

Furthermore, once Mill establishes firmly the connection between Hindus lacking any sense of civilization and barbarianism, he goes on to contend that the early Hindus were nomads and wanderers:

> If we suppose that India began to be inhabited at a very early stage in the peopling of the world, its first inhabitants must have been few, ignorant, and rude. Uncivilized and ignorant men, transported, in small numbers, into an uninhabited country of boundless extent, must wander for many ages before any great improvement can take place.... They wandered probably for ages in the immense plains and valleys of that productive region, living on fruits, and the produce of their flocks and herds, and not associated beyond the limits of a particular family.[35]

The above discourse solidified the description of ancient Hindus as wanderers, nomads, and cattle herders and paved the way for these "Aryans" to get onto the horseback as cattle-herding wandering nomads and invade India, perpetuating the Aryan Invasion Theory without the backing of any hard and conclusive evidence. This is also why when the cities of the Harappan Civilization were discovered, they were not linked to the Aryans (ancient Hindus), for in the European imagination (logic from their standpoint) it was not possible for a wandering nomadic people to build a massive civilization of such material scale as the Harappan civilization. It was, therefore, that the civilization (again without any hard and conclusive evidence) was linked to the "indigenous Dravidian" people whom the "invading Aryans" defeated. This is also despite that the same "cattle herding nomadic people" in abundance speak about cities in the Vedas.

Now when the AIT has been shot down, the description of the Aryan Migration Theory which is the officially stated or unstated stance of western academia, surprisingly as it may sound, is only a politically correct and sanitized version of how Mill described the ancient Hindus in the early ninetieth century. The *2016 California History and Social Science (HSS) Framework for Grade Six—World History and Geography: Ancient Civilization* which is an official guideline for publishers to put together books for Sixth grade students in the state of California states the following: People speaking Indic languages, which are part of the larger Indo-European family of languages, entered South Asia, probably by way of Iran.... The early Indic speakers were most likely animal herders. They may have arrived in India in scattered bands, later intermarrying with populations perhaps ancestral to those who

---

[35] Ibid, 173–175.

speak Dravidian languages, such as Tamil and Telugu, in southern India and Sri Lanka today.[36]

Why do we say that the above description by the *California HSS Framework* is a sanitized and politically correct version of the James Mill narrative? 1. Given that the Aryan is a much derided term because of the holocaust that the Nazis caused appropriating the term, the *California HSS Framework* does not use it but it basically means Aryans, substituting it with "people speaking Indic languages, which are part of larger Indo-European family of languages." And when it means Aryans, it does not suggest Aryans indigenous to India. It specifically means Aryans coming to India via Iran from Europe: White, fair-skinned, blond and blue-eyed Aryans. 2. The groups of "people speaking Indic languages" are essentially nomadic herders and wanderers just like how they were in the James Mill description. It is just that in the current 2016 *California HSS Framework* version they are not being called barbaric, uncivilized, ignorant and rude, and it does not describe the larger imperial context in which this narrative was framed to begin with. Needless to say, it is this very version that gets recycled in all History textbooks. In higher studies too, the narrative similar to the one mentioned in the *Framework* appears.

To sum up, the Aryan Invasion Theory or its politically correct sibling the Aryan Migration Theory is intimately tied with the colonial project. The invasion theory was tied directly to colonialism and the migration theory is entwined with the racial superiority of the European people. The invasion or the migration theory strips the Indians of their agency to conceive, foster, nurture, and perpetuate a civilization. It is about denying the indigenous Indian population the creative, intellectual, and rational capacity to engender a civilization. The direct colonial rule may have ended but the paradigm running the colonial enterprise that it is only the European people or people with European lineage who are capable of establishing civilizations is solidly intact when we take the AIT or AMT into consideration.

It is this "othering," this turning of the Indian civilization, its culture, its history, its contribution to humanity into the primitive "other" that the characteristics of the early Aryans as wandering and nomadic cattle herders was formulated, and James Mill is the architect-in-chief for this description. Max Müller arbitrarily ascribed the date of 1500 BCE to the coming of the Aryans, and since the day this issue became conflated with the stated and unstated aspirations of White and European

[36] (California Department of Education 2016:162–163).

supremacy, all reasoned evidence has been thrown to the wind. Scholars worldwide can keep providing evidence after evidence to show that neither the Aryan invasion nor the Aryan migration happened, the theory will remain intact. And it will remain intact until the time the scholars in the field with European ancestry consciously and unconsciously keep believing that it is they and they alone, who can build any civilization of any substance anywhere in the world.

References

1. Agarwal, D.P., and R.K. Sood. (1982) "Ecological Factors and Harappan Civilization," pp.223–31, in *Harappan Civilization: A Contemporary Perspective*, edited by Gregory L. Possehl. Delhi, India: Oxford and IBH Publishing Company.
2. Allchin, F.R. (1995) *The Archaeology of Early Historic South Asia: The Emergence of Cities and States.* Cambridge: Cambridge University Press.
3. Bryant, Edwin. (2001) *The Quest for the Origins of Vedic Culture: The Indo-Aryan Migration Debate.* New York: Oxford University Press.
4. Bryant, Edwin. F., and Laurie L. Patton, eds. (2005) *The Indo-Aryan Controversy: Evidence and Inference in Indian History.* New York: Routledge.
5. California Department of Education. (2016) *Chapter Ten: History Social Science Framework for California Public Schools: Kindergarten through Grade Twelve,* accessed May 15, 2019, https://www.cde.ca.gov/ci/hs/cf/documents/hssfwchapter10.pdf
6. Cavalli-Sforza, L., P. Menozzi, and A. Piazza. (1994) *The History and Geography of Human Genes.* Princeton, NJ: Princeton University Press.
7. Chakrabarti, D.K. (1976) "India and the Druids," in *Antiquity.* Vol.197:66–67.
8. Curzon, A. (1855)
9. Dales, G.F. (1964) "The Mythical Massacre at Mohenjo-daro." Expedition 6 (3), 36–43.
10. Filliozat, V., ed. (1997) *Vijayanagar as Seen by Dorningos Paes and Fernao Nuniz (16th Century Portuguese Chroniclers and Others).* New Delhi, India: National Book Trust.
11. Flam, L. (1981) *The Paleogeography and Prehistoric Settlement Patterns in Sindh, Pakistan* (ca. *4000–2000 BC*). PhD diss., South Asia Regional Studies, University of Pennsylvania.
12. Flam, L. (1993) "Fluvial Geomorphology of the Lower Indus Basin (Sindh, Pakistan) and the Indus Civilization," pp.265–326, in *Himalaya to the Sea*, edited by J.F. Schroder. New York: Routledge.
13. Flood, Gavin. (1996) *An Introduction to Hinduism.* Cambridge: Cambridge University Press.
14. Gamkrelidze, T., and V.V. Ivanov. (1985a) "The Ancient Near East and the Indo-European Question: Temporal and Territorial Characteristics of Proto-Indo-European Based on Linguistic and Historical-Cultural Data," in *Journal of Indo-European Studies.* Vol.13:3–48.

15. Gamkrelidze, T., and V.V. Ivanov. (1985b) "The Migration of Tribes Speaking the Indo-European Dialects from Their Original Homeland in the Near East to Their Historical Habitations in Eurasia," in *Journal of Indo-European Studies.* Vol.13:49–91.
16. Gimbutas, M. (1985) "Primary and Secondary Homeland of the Indo-Europeans" in *Journal of Indo-European Studies.* Vol.13:185–202.
17. Kautilya. (1992) *The Arthashastra.* Translated and edited by L.N. Rangarajan. New Delhi: Penguin Books.
18. Kelly, Robin D.G. (2000) "Poetics of Anticolonialism," pp.7–28, in *Discourse on Colonialism*, written by Aimé Césaire and translated by Joan Pinkham. New York: Monthly Review Press.
19. Kennedy, K.A.R. (1982) "Skulls, Aryans and Flowing Drains: The Interface of Archeology and Skeletal Biology in the Study of the Harappan Civilization," pp.289–295, in *Harappan Civilization: A Contemporary Perspective*, edited by Gregory L. Possehl. Delhi, India: Oxford and IBH Publishing Company.
20. Kennedy, K.A.R. (1984) "Trauma and Disease in Ancient Harappans," pp.425–36, in *Frontiers of the Indus Civilization*, edited by B.B. Lal and S.P. Gupta. Delhi, India: Books and Books.
21. Kennedy, K.A.R. (1994) "Identification of Sacrificial and Massacre Victims in Archeological Sites: The Skeletal Evidence," in *Man and Environment.* Vol.19, Nos.1–2: 247–51.
22. Kennedy, K.A.R. (2000) *God-Apes and Fossil Men: Paleoanthropology in South Asia.* Ann Arbor: University of Michigan Press.
23. Kennedy, V. (1828) *Researches into the Origin and Affinity of the Principal Languages of India.* London: Longman.
24. Kenoyer, J.M. (2005) "Culture Change During the Late Harappan Period at Harappa: New Insights on Vedic Aryan Issues," pp.21–49, in *The Indo-Aryan Controversy: Evidence and Inference in Indian History*, edited by Edwin F. Bryant and Laurie L. Patton. New York: Routledge.
25. Lal, B.B. (2005) "Aryan Invasion of India: Perpetuation of a Myth," pp.50–74, in *The Indo-Aryan Controversy: Evidence and Inference in Indian History,* edited by Edwin F. Bryant and Laurie L. Patton. New York: Routledge.
26. Lal, B.B. (2009) *How Deep are the Roots of Indian Civilization? Archaeology Answers.* New Delhi: Aryan Books International.
27. Lal, B.B. (2011) *Piecing Together: Memoirs of an Archaeologist.* New Delhi: Aryan International Books.
28. Lamberg-Karlovsky, C.C. (2002) "Archeology and Language: The Indo-Iranians" in *Current Anthropology.* Vol.43:63–88.
29. Mallory, J.P. (1989) *In Search of the Indo-Europeans: Language, Archeology, and Myth.* London: Thames and Hudson.
30. Mill, James. (2015) *The History of British India: Volume 1.* London: Forgotten Books.
31. Monboddo, J.B. (1774) *Of the Origins and Progress of Language.* Edinburgh, United Kingdom: Balfour.
32. Mughal, R.M. (1990) "Harappan Settlement Systems and Patterns in the Greater Indus Valley," in *Pakistan Archeology.* Vol.25:1–72.

33. Mughal, R.M. (1997) *Ancient Cholistan: Archaeology and Architecture.* Karachi, Pakistan: Ferozsons (Pvt.) Ltd.
34. Muir, J. (1860) *Original Sanskrit Texts.* London: Trüber.
35. Possehl, G.L. (2002) *The Indus Civilization: A Contemporary Perspective.* Boulder, CO: Alta Mira Press.
36. Renfrew, C. (1987) *Archeology and Language. The Puzzle of Indo-European Origin.* New York: Cambridge University Press.
37. Shaffer, J.G. (1981) "The Protohistoric Period in the Eastern Punjab: A Preliminary Assessment," pp.65–101, in *Indus Civilization: New Perspectives*, edited by A.H. Dani. Islamabad, Pakistan: Quaid-I-Azam University.
38. Shaffer, J.G. (1982) "Harappan Culture: A Reconsideration," pp.41–50, in *Harappan Civilization: A Contemporary Perspective*, edited by Gregory L. Possehl. Delhi, India: Oxford and IBH Publishing Company.
39. Shaffer, J.G. (1986) "Cultural Development in the Eastern Punjab," pp.74–90, in *Studies in the Archeology of India and Pakistan*, edited by J. Jacobson. Delhi, India: Oxford and IBH Publishing Company.
40. Shaffer, J.G. (1992) "Indus Valley, Baluchistan, and the Helmand Traditions: Neolithic through Bronze Age," pp.441–64 in Vol.1 and pp.425–46 in Vol.II, in *Chronologies in Old World Archaeology*: *Vols.I & II*, edited by R.W. Ehrich: Chicago: University of Chicago Press.
41. Shaffer, J.G. (1993) "Reurbanization: The Eastern Punjab and Beyond," pp.53–67, in *Meaning in South Asia: The Shaping of Cities from Prehistoric to Precolonial Times*, edited by H. Spodek and D.M. Srinivasan. Washington, DC: National Gallery of Art.
42. Shaffer, Jim. G., and Diane A. Lichtenstein. (1989) "Ethnicity and Change in the Indus Valley Cultural Tradition," pp.117–26, in *Old Problems and New Perspectives in the Archeology of South Asia*, edited by Jonathan M. Kenoyer. Madison: University of Wisconsin: Wisconsin Archeological Reports.
43. Shaffer, Jim. G., and Diane A. Lichtenstein. (1995) "The Concepts of Cultural Tradition and Paleoethnicity in South Asian Archaeology," pp.126–54, in *The Indo-Aryans of Ancient South Asia: Language, Material Culture and Ethnicity*, edited by G. Erdosy. Berlin, Germany: Walter de Gruyter.
44. Shaffer, Jim. G., and Diane A. Lichtenstein. (1999) "Migration, Philology and South Asian Archeology," pp.239–60, in *Aryan and Non-Aryan in South Asia: Evidence, Interpretation and Ideology*, edited by J. Bronkhurst and M.M. Deshpande. Cambridge, MA: Department of Sanskrit and Indian Studies, Harvard University.
45. Shaffer, Jim. G., and Diane A. Lichtenstein. (2005) "South Asian Archeology and the Myth of Indo-Aryan Invasions," pp.75–104, in *The Indo-Aryan Controversy: Evidence and Inference in Indian History,* edited by Edwin F. Bryant and Laurie L. Patton. New York: Routledge.
46. Singh, K. (2014) "Beyond Mind: The Future of Psychology as a Science," pp.40–52, in *Foundations and Applications of Indian Psychology*, edited by R.M.M. Cornellisen, G. Misra, and S. Varma. Delhi, India: Pearson.

47. Trautmann, T.R. (1982) "Elephants and the Mauryas," pp.245–81, in *India: History and Thought*, edited by S. Muckerjee. Calcutta, India: Subernarekha.
48. Wheeler, R.E.M. (1947) "Harappa 1946: The Defences and Cemetery R–37," in *Ancient India.* Vol.3:58–130.
49. Wheeler, M. (1959) *Early India and Pakistan: To Ashoka.* New York: Frederick A. Praeger.

Multi-Method Approach to Sources of Indian History and Culture

Choodamani Nandagopal

Abstract

Indian history is experienced within the time-tested ambit of Indian living culture. Here, history is not dead and gone but lived during the continuum of culture through several millennia. Indian sources of history to be understood, interpreted and passed on to generations not with one approach or method. Looking at the complexity of Indian history, a single window system is insufficient to approach the sources of Indian history and culture. This paper explores the various basic sources of Indian history and culture and offer certain methods and approaches for successive understanding and interpretation through illustrative examples.

The nature of Indian historical precedents and antecedents cover the time span of several millennia, development of multiple religious streams, language extensions, several literary movements, advent of chequered foreign invasions, creation of huge body of knowledge, functional scientific application, astounding astronomical analysis, changing life-style concerned with environment, philosophical and political systems, built environment, in-built belief system, vibrant traditions all have created uniqueness of tangible and intangible cultural heritage of pan-Asian nature. What is realised at this juncture is the need of multi-method approach consisting of handling the data culturally and historically situated, careful reanalysis of cultural data where historical understanding is a pre-requisite, successive re-reading of cultural texts are few of the approaches that help in enriching the potential of a source. There is no short-cut to a historian while dealing with a primary source with set of experiences, technique, understanding the precision of fact and time and above all certain traits and skills needed to interpret the historical source. Interpretation is an endless process when applied to history and culture. Potential interpretation is a serious concern of a historian and an analyst of culture. This paper explores the various basic sources of Indian history and culture and offer certain methods and approaches for successive understanding and interpretation through illustrative examples.

Introduction

Indian history is experienced within the time-tested ambit of Indian living culture. Here, history is not dead and gone but lived during the continuum of culture through several millennia. Indian sources of history to be understood, interpreted and passed on to generations not with one approach or method. Or any one ideal methodological process or a specific methodological implication is seldom thought in the context of interpreting Indian history. The nature of Indian historical precedents and antecedents cover the time span of several millennia, development of multiple religious streams, language extensions, several literary movements, advent of chequered foreign invasions, creation of huge body of knowledge, functional scientific application, astounding astronomical analysis, changing life-style concerned with environment, philosophical and political systems, built environment, in-built belief system, vibrant traditions all have created uniqueness of tangible and intangible cultural heritage of pan-Asian nature.

Looking at its magnanimity, a single window system is insufficient to approach the sources of Indian history and culture. What is realised at this juncture is the need of multi-method approach consisting of handling the data culturally and historically situated, careful reanalysis of cultural data where historical understanding is a pre-requisite, successive re-reading of cultural texts are few of the approaches that help in enriching the potential of a source. There is no short-cut to a historian while dealing with a primary source with set of experiences, technique, understanding the precision of fact and time and above all certain traits and skills needed to interpret the historical source. Interpretation is an endless process when applied to history and culture. Potential interpretation is a serious concern of a historian and an analyst of culture.

A researcher is familiar with a system and method followed to study Indian history, archaeology, art and culture. The sources of Indian history are brought under two major categories, namely Archaeological Sources, and Literary sources. Further archaeological excavations from pre-history to historical periods are of primary importance in knowing historical and cultural aspects. They are supported by the study of numismatics, epigraphy and monuments or built environment, that house artefacts, paintings and sculptures. All these are grouped under archaeological sources. Similarly equally significant are the literary sources in the form of textual and *Kavya*, poetic literature, and important accounts recorded by the natives of the specific culture and foreign visitors' accounts recorded. When these two major sources are examined with regard to the period or the time span selected for study, are to be carefully brought under the scanner of connecting more than one source. Such study brings interesting and factual data related to the history and culture of the specific period taken for interpretative analysis. Historical study is considered as authentic, only when strong evidences are drawn from these sources to analyse a fact. All of us know that fact finding analysis is the basic feature of historical study through exploring the historic background that underpins our understanding of the world, its challenges and opportunities.

In today's academia, there are more possibilities to interact with the most exciting and innovative approaches than before. As well as developing the traditional skills of classically-based degrees, such as language training and culture analysis that form an imaginative basis for the cutting-edge research. There is a need to combine the study of fascinating ancient civilizations with the intellectual challenges of studying language, literature, archaeology and history, as well as an in-depth exploration of the past and critical analysis of our contemporary world. Often interesting queries are raised to the sudden disappearance of Indus Civilization and one of the strong reasons put forth by Wheeler was that the Indus cities destroyed by the invaders and the rows of the houses are of the soldiers; hence Indus Civilization is of the nature of Military State. The argument is firmly refuted by Indian archaeologists like S.R. Rao[1] remarking, there is no archaeological evidence to suggest that the Indus Empire was a military state or priest ruled state, although existed a central authority. Contrary to Martin Wheeler's assumption it is regarded today, that the rows of houses near the granary outside the Citadel at Harappa were workers' quarters. The artificial mud packed terraces on which houses stood in almost all Indus cities and towns such as Harappa, Mohenjodaro, Kalibangan, Lothal, Rakhigarhi and Rangpur served as high plinths to save houses from recurring floods, and not from any invaders. Such path-breaking exploration of past in the context of contemporary critical analysis is possible by adopting multi methods drawn from social, economic, scientific and archaeological process.

[1] Nandagopal, 2006, p.3.

This brings a closer connection between three sets of knowledge sources namely, History, its organs such as archaeology and art history, Language and literature including folklore, non-written texts, chants oral narratives and Cultural studies, which covers a broad range of disciplines that are linked to the particular modes of cultural analysis. The methods of analysis encompass most of the disciplines of humanities and social sciences with interdisciplinary and cross-cultural approaches. The nature and scope of culture is so complex, because of the enormous possibilities of providing sources to historical studies. Let us try to understand culture from this perspective and try to explore the multi-methods and approaches it offers.

Can we understand the term 'culture' with the similar connotation like the terms, economy, society, technology, yoga, computer, printing, design, behaviour? These terms have specific connotations and understanding, a segment with a clear specific framework. But 'Culture', is complex, vague, deep rooted, all encompassing like a term 'God'. Each one of us have our own idea of god, may be strangely different from one another, so abstract too. Similarly we connect and understand culture in our own way. So the term culture has its own dynamics. Because of the nature of dynamism the words such as culture, spirituality, and creativity are used today in loose sense or sometimes used differently.

Vocabulary of Culture

Etymologically the term Culture is derived from Latin word, 'cultus', means care and the French 'colere' means 'to till' or cultivate—'to cultivate with care', that denotes a process. In the realm of arts, the term denotes 'cultivating taste' or 'aesthetic taste'. During middle ages in European countries the term culture caught the attention of population of sophisticated taste. Art, religion, literature were the frontal faces of elite society and were treated as basic components of culture. In the International Encyclopaedia of Social Sciences in 1968, there is one main entry on culture written by Milton Singer.[2] Later there were seven entries on the issues such as Cultural relativism, Cultural Adaptation, Cultural change, Culture and personality and Culture Area, covering different streams of social sciences, such as sociology, anthropology, psychology, Anthropology, and history. In the next edition of 2001, there were 34 entries covering much broader disciplines. Here

[2] Ed. Bennett and Frow, 2008:3.

Anthropology remains an important frame work while looking the range of these entries.

Cultural Studies as an independent discipline of its own has grown important and in higher education, this knowledge base is gaining increasing prominence and concerns within contemporary academic inquiry. But culture when used in common terminology, loses its gravity and used in vague sense. Thus Adam Kuper[3] remarks that 'It has proved impossible to define culture with any precision, it is also this flexibility and elasticity that has enabled the concept to be adapted to many different uses and purposes'. This nature made the concept of Culture as part of everyday discourse. In Indian understanding *Samskriti* is the term derived from the Sanskrit word, *Samskar* which means ritual performance, it is a process that internalises mind, heart and action through which refinement is sought for universal wellbeing. This understanding is manifested in Indian cultural understanding be it the thought, deed, social practices, literature, arts or value system. Again it's a complex phenomenon, which needs longer discourses. Thus the term 'culture' and cultural analysis in present day context have to be approached from two important methodologies namely, western—social sciences and eastern-philosophical perspectives.

Dynamics of Culture

The very nature of 'culture' is dynamic and never static. The way 'culture' defined, is changing from time to time, despite the core cultural value system remain strongly. As the nature of a river is flowing, similarly the nature of culture is changing. Whatever changes occur in the society, economic or political, it brings change in the culture. Social changes bring cultural changes and the changes that embedded as value system sustains as eternal values that manifests in cultural practices. Culture as the field of academic discipline is ever expanding. In early stage of development culture was used as synonym for arts, philosophy, sociology and human science. Then in the field of history Cultural History has drawn the attention followed with archaeological excavations: art, craft and utilitarian objects excavated demanded socio-cultural interpretations because they were the product of society that have served and existed because of their significance of social function.

In all these cases the culture of ordinary people, their attitudes, symbolism, literature and values began to receive attention and brought

[3] Kuper 1999:12.

under folk culture or popular culture. Folklore studies opened with great scope for oral narratives, art forms, indigenous literature, rituals, practices related to their life and professions. Culture is internal and integral element of social behaviour and a means of social change and social control. Classical, historical, rural, urban all these societies have culture one way or the other. Culture is a repository of social heritage, and helps in maintaining social order to certain extent and controls the behaviour of the people and establishes uniformity in the behaviour of people and makes them responsible towards the society. Culture brings people together to form a well knit socio-cultural system.

Culture as source

Culture is best realised through symbols, words, ideas, visual forms and communication. Some objects, although apparently similar have very different symbolic values and we understand their symbolic value because they are part of a system and such rich symbols have social sanction.

Language has its own set of rules and usages in forms of communication. A word is used in past, present and future. When and where do we use the word have specific connotations in culture. Ex: the word "*kalasha*", is formed by three syllables, but in its function it is symbolic, it is no longer a three syllable word. It has got the symbolic value. In India it has special significance in our system, whenever we want to create auspiciousness we use '*kalasha*'. The value we understand will be the part of the system. If the word *kalasha* was to be used elsewhere it doesn't have any meaning but of utilitarian value as container not related to auspiciousness. A foreigner will not understand any meaning of the *kalasha* unless explained. *Kalasha*, is a container made of terracotta, or any metal, filled with water, mango leaves and coconut symbolise the *Panchamahabhuta*, the primordial elements, earth, water, air, cosmic and energy. Each of the content has different usage and meaning. When they are all put together in the form of *kalash*a it will have a different meaning. That is how language is connected to symbols, values, structure, design, visual form and cultural significance.

Indigenous culture is connected to one's own history, family, historical incidents of own culture indigenous nature. In the indigenous culture you take pride and sometimes tend to ignore because it is your own culture. Sometimes we take it for granted and do not give the place that it deserves. Indian culture is basically endowed with *Shruthi* and *smrti* traditions, oral rendition, listening narratives retention through memory. Vedic, folk and indigenous knowledge systems are the foundations of Indian culture. *Upanishds*, *sutra* literature, *Pantha* literature, like Buddhist, *Jaina*, *Shaiva*, *Vaishnava*, *Shakta* literature, *Puranas*, *Agamas*, *Upavedas*, *Darshanas*, *Itihasas*, *Vedangas* and *Dharmashastras* evolved in oral and written form on one side. On the other each region is enriched with the local traditions, narratives, medicinal practices, food systems, poetics, songs, dance forms, architecture, painting traditions. All these provide knowledge streams and act as dynamic sources in academia.

William archer wrote an article on 'Distortions of Indian Culture', Sri Arurobindo was very much disturbed and published 'The Renaissance in India, A Defence of Indian Culture.[4] Though he was educated in western school of thought with scientific temperament, he was in true sense an Indian and a real rationalistic critique of Indian culture and so also Mahatma Gandhi. Their discussions on the concepts and practices such as *dharma*, inward looking thoughts, freedom of will, approach to truth and harmony are universally relevant and answer the curious minds of today sourced from the ethos of Indian culture. These concepts at crossroads are possibly put to discourses through emerging fields such as visual culture and material culture, which open greater scope for interdisciplinary studies. Literature, history, performing and visual arts, sociology, religious studies, archaeology, art history, philosophy, anthropology, political science, ethnography, economics, media studies, psychology, material science, environmental science and all such branches of academic disciplines owe greatly to culture because one could connect to the wider range of possibilities to choose the methods offered through interdisciplinary engagements.

Oral traditions

Earlier the study of oral tradition was not regarded as part of historical method. Realising its potential towards the time, space and narrative, Gilbert Garraghan in his book Guide to Historical Methods[5] considers oral tradition in two broad conditions. 1. The tradition should be supported by an unbroken series of witnesses 2. There should be several parallel and independent series of witnesses testifying to the fact. They should be again considered under six particular conditions. They are: 1. The tradition must report a public event of importance 2. The tradition must have been generally believed, at least for a definite period

[4] Aurobindo, (Fourth Impression 2013).

[5] Garraghan & Delanglez 1946:121.

3. During that definite period it must have gone without protest 4. The tradition must be one of relatively limited duration in cultures that excel in oral remembrance 5. Critical-minded persons who would surely have challenged the tradition. 6. Possibilities of Cross-checking, comparison with other material evidences.

Material Culture

Material Culture as a concept is connected with every walk of life, around which the civilizations, the cultures, the spirit of nationalism, the social life evolved and sustained and added new dimension whenever and wherever the relevance felt. This consists of human creation of objects by experimenting with different materials. It is a process driven and the way how the material acts and reacts on the basis of the power of creating for functional requirement. The need, method, proportions, process and material are the properties of material culture. Archaeological excavations have shown the different types of utensils, built structures, beads, jewellery, weapons, and such other materials through which the cultural understanding of life of the people, their taste, aspirations, customs, traditions, belief systems, food habits are known. If a large number of temple icons, ritual objects and exclusive pieces of jewellery are unearthed in a dilapidated temple premises, each of this object gives astounding cultural facts of the material they are made of. Also they reveal the condition in which the material was abandoned leading to speculations and finally to valuable research. Interpretation of objects collected in museums or artefacts excavated by archaeologists are receiving new dimensions of critical appraisal. In this scenario the potential approach of material culture now seems blindingly obvious and yet for many decades was neglected.[6] The collections and their display build the interactive relationship in understanding social functioning through the process of material culture.

Visual Culture

Visual Culture is one of the important methods heavily rely on historical and literary sources and pertains to 'seen world'. Visual practices, methods and analysis pay particular attention to visual aspects of culture. Similarly, this field of study, perhaps discipline, perhaps inter-discipline, has developed over the past decades, but took on its different names as rallying cries only in 1990s. Then journals such as the Journal of Visual Culture began to appear along with books and—academic programmes

[6] Bennett & Frow 2008:281.

defined and redefined the goals in terms of visual studies.[7] In today's world visual overpowering is taking place, in such scenario cultural interpretation of visuals is pragmatic. Visual culture initially evolved from Visual anthropology and is ever useful as illustrative resources. Early studies were mainly on ethnography and ethno-methodology was developed. Later Collier and Collier[8] brought out Photo Documentation of America. The digitisation of images and image sourcing techniques and methods have revolutionised the field of visual culture. History, archaeology, art history and museum studies, all heavily rely on visual evidences on the basis of documentation methods which are ever progressing. Ancient Indian historical and cultural sources pose many challenges and through visual culture and analysis several complexities can be simplified. For example, portraying the society visualised by Chanakya, in 3rd century BCE, with the available historical and archaeological and literary evidences are to be placed in the perspectives of visual culture to analyse the formal qualities (shapes and colour etc.), social values through performing arts and aesthetics etc.

Conclusion

The best example can be the way the two great epics of India, Ramayana and Mahabharata are immortalized in the form of oral tradition crossing the linguistic and geographical boundaries. These oral as well as written traditions give accounts of chariots in several episodes. Recently excavated chariot of Bronze Age, unearthed by archaeological Survey of India at Sinauli village in the state of Uttar Pradesh (UP) serves as material evidences to know the life of the people and the scientific knowledge of making of a chariot. In many cultures such as Greek, Mesopotamian and Egyptian chariots were used in war and later relegated to only pages of ancient history but in India Chariots are part of Hindu temple festivals and sustains as symbol of living culture of contemporaneous society.[9]

This is a brief overview of the possibilities of using multi-methods in handling the sources of ancient Indian history and culture. Knowing the magnanimity of sources of different kinds, running into several millennia, owing to sustenance of almost all world religious streams, heading towards rapid urban transformation, global technology and economy, positioning as an important nation in balance of global power, India has tremendous potential to revisit the sources of Indian History.

[7] Ibid:167.

[8] Collier, John Jr., and Malcolm Collier, 1986.

[9] Nandagopal & Iyengar 2002:7.

Through the methods and approaches discussed above, the Indian historical sources in the form of rich material, visual, literary and art resources, when interpreted and analysed, enriches the humanistic disciplines across the cultures of the world.

References

1. Aurobindo, *The Renaissance in India and other Essays on Indian Culture* (Fourth Impression 2013) Sri Aurobindo Ashram Pondichery.
2. Ed. Bennett Tony & Frow John (2008), *The Sage Handbook of Cultural Analysis*, Sage Los Angeles, London, New Delhi, Singapore.
3. Collier, John Jr., and Malcolm Collier. 1986. *Visual Anthropology: Photography as a Research Method.* Albuquerque: University of New Mexico Press.
4. Ed. Bennett Tony & Frow John *The Sage Handbook of Cultural Analysis,* (2008), Daniel Miller, *Material Culture* Sage Los Angeles, London, New Delhi, Singapore.
5. Garraghan Gilbert J and Delanglez Jean (1946) *A Guide to the Historical Method*, Fardhan University Press, New York.
6. Kuper Adam (1999) *Culture: The Anthropologist's Account,* Cambridge MA: Harvard University Press.
7. Ed. Bennett Tony & Frow *The Sage Handbook of Cultural Analysis* John (2008), Mieke Bal, *Visual Analysis,* Sage Los Angeles, London, New Delhi, Singapore.
8. Nandagopal Choodamani & Iyengar Vatsala (2002) *Temple Treasures Vol.III Temple Chariots*, Crafts Council of Karnataka Bangalore.
9. Nandagopal Choodamani, Introduction by S.R. Rao (2006), *Arts and Crafts of Indus Civilization,* Aryan Books International New Delhi.

AncientVoice: A Digital Portal to Veda-Ithihāsa-Purāṇas

Ravi Jijith

Abstract

AncientVoice is an online portal containing 23,000 plus wikified pages on Mahābhārata, Rāmāyaṇa, Ṛgveda, Yajurveda (both Kṛṣṇa and Sukla recensions), Sāmaveda, Atharvaveda and Vishnu Purāṇas. Currently in English, but the Samskṛt version is being developed. It uses a Wikipedia style format, with millions of hyperlinks forming a network of nouns, making the cross-referencing very easy. One may start out with the noun Ayodhya in the Mahābhārata to be lead to every other references to Ayodhya in the Mahābhārata, in the 18 Parvās and 2000 plus chapters. The search can be extended to Rāmāyaṇa, to find the references of Ayodhya in each of the 7 Kāndās and 600 plus chapters or into the Vedas or Purāṇas, leading to comparative analysis. It also aids in studying noun to noun relationship, such as starting with noun Arjuna leading to nouns of his wives or children. It has a database of nouns categorized into place-names (villages, cities, towns, kingdoms etc), names of kings, women, heroes, ascetics, Samskṛt non-translatables like Akṣauhini, Anīkini, Vyūha, Ṛta, Dharma, Manas, Chitta etc. The portal also hosts lineage trees of dynasties, analysis of the Yuga system, Kālachakra. It contains many art works and illustrations depicting heroes and heroines of Mahābhārata.

Introduction

I started reading the Indian epics from the age of ten. The Mahābhārata series of the Amar-Chitra Katha 1 books and the Mahābhārata of Krishna Dwaipāyana Vyāsa, in Samskṛt translated to Malayālam by Dr. P.S. Nair were my first books. This became a craze and I continued analyzing these books. I created maps of Bhāratavarsha by locating the kingdoms and cities mentioned in the Mahābhārata on A4 paper sheets. I painted the scenes from the Mahābhārata using water color and oil paints. All this was done during 1987 to 1995 period when I was 10 to 18 years of age.

My approach to reading the narratives in Veda, Itihāsa, Purāṇas is that mythology is nothing but a transformation of history. Absolute events transform into history after a few decades and history transforms into mythology after a few centuries. It is always possible to extract history from mythology and absolute events from history, but with a predictable loss of information. The Greek mythographer Euhemerus of the 4th century BCE of Macedonia held a similar view that many mythological tales can be attributed to historical persons and events, the accounts of which then get altered and exaggerated over time.

My view on Mahābhārata and Rāmāyaṇa is that they are the substitutes of history of the period they describe. Just like a candle-light is better than total darkness, these Itihāsās serve to tell us something about those periods. In the absence of a proper history to describing these periods, Mahābhārata and Rāmāyaṇa serve as something close to it. They are closer to historical documents than to mythological or imaginative works. It is very inappropriate to dismiss them as mere imaginations or as fables and legends or even as mythology. Careful readers can easily separate, fact and fiction from the narrations in the Mahābhārata and Rāmāyaṇa.

Mahābhārata contains more factual narratives than the Rāmāyaṇa where as the Purāṇas contain much more poetic exaggerations and embellishments than those are found in the Mahābhārata or in the Rāmāyaṇa. Mahābhārata narrates a very realistic and factual political conflict in the Kuru royal dynasty between its Kaurava and Pāṇḍava factions. This narrative is highly detailed so that it cannot be dismissed as a fictional narrative. No poet will labor to imagine up and render such huge amount of details at minute level such as the names of the obscure towns, villages, kingdoms and minor leaders of war. The main war-narrative is also huge and extensive like the eighteen-day war Kaurava-Pāṇḍava war at Kurukshetra is described in five out of its eighteen volumes or Parvās (viz. Bhīṣma, Droṇa, Karṇa, Śalya and Sauptika Parvās) running into more than twenty-three thousand verses, which again make it impossible to dismiss it as a mythological narrative or a poetic imagination.

Rāmāyaṇa too has huge and extensive war-narrative of the war between Rāma and Rāvaṇa, running into more than four thousand verses confined to one out of its 7 volumes or Kāndās viz. the Yuddha Kānda. Though this war-narrative is thus smaller than that of Mahābhārata, it is huge enough so that it is difficult to dismiss it as a fictional poetic imagination or a mythological narrative. However, the poet of Rāmāyaṇa viz. Vālmīki, unlike Vyāsa, the poet of Mahābhārata, chose to render many of the war heroes as apes, bears and birds. This increases the mythology quotient of Rāmāyaṇa in comparison with the Mahābhārata. The important point to note here is that, once we cross this outer layer of poetic imagination, the war-narrative in itself is factual and highly detailed.

Compared to the two Itihāsās, viz. Mahābhārata and Rāmāyaṇa, the Purāṇas contain much more poetic embellishment and imaginative narratives even though it is replete with factual data which is attested in historical records, such as the reign of the Nanda dynasty and Mourya dynasty in Magadha. Such references in the Purangs lead to the conclusion that a large portion of their content was authored during or after the reign of these historical dynasties.

Geographical and Historical content in Mahābhārata and Rāmāyaṇa

Below is a definition of Mahābhārata according to Kṛṣṇa Dvaipāyana Vyāsa is explained in its Ādi Parva first chapter itself:

Mahābhārata is the mystery of the Veda, and other subjects have been explained by me; the various rituals of the Upanishads with the Angas; the compilation of the Purāṇas and history formed by me and named after the three divisions of time, past, present, and future; the determination of the nature of decay, fear, disease, existence, and non-existence, a description of creeds and of the various modes of life; rule for the four castes, and the import of all the Purgnas; an account of asceticism and of the duties of a religious student; the dimensions of the sun and moon, the planets, constellations, and stars, together with the duration of the four ages; the Rik, Sama and Yajur Vedas; also the Adhyatma; the sciences called Nyaya, Orthoephy and Treatment of diseases; charity and Pasupatadharma; birth celestial and human, for particular purposes; also a description of places of pilgrimage and other holy places of rivers, mountains, forests, the ocean, of heavenly cities and the kalpas; the art of war; the different kinds of nations and languages: the nature of the manners of the people; and the all-pervading spirit;—all these have been represented (in this work).

The highest concentration of geographic information in Mahābhārata is found at the start of Bhiṣma Parva (Mahābhārata: Book 6 chapters 6 to 12), where he mentions more than 10000 geographic entities like rivers, lakes, place-names and names of kingdoms, regions, and sub-continents. Bhiṣma parva can be considered as the starting point of the core of Mahābhārata, authored by Vyāsa known as Jaya. The rest of the epic that precedes Bhiṣma Parva (book 6) and that succeed Sauptika Parva (book 10) is believed to be accumulated over this core called Jaya which grew to the work called Bhārata and later to Mahābhārata.

Thus, true to what Vyāsa says, his work Jaya starts with astronomy (contemporary to that period) and geography. In subsequent chapters he explains the major philosophies of the age, in the form of Bhagavat Gita. Some say Bhagavat Gita is a later addition, though Vyāsa seems to know much of this philosophy himself, since one of his major activity was to analyze Vedic knowledge and classify the Vedas. The Original Vyāsa along with his race of many other Vyāsas, probably spanning many generations engaged in this activity for centuries. The surname Vyas or Byas is still popular. Since Vyāsa divided or classified the Vedas he is known as Veda-Vyāsa (one who divided or classified the Vedas). The rest of Jaya is the Kurukshetra War narrative, where he describes the art of war, its strategies and finally its ill effects.

The Sabha Parva (Book 2), Chapter 14 contains passages that show glimpses of a political scenario, resulted due to the rising power of Magadha against the established Kuru rulers and how this threat is subdued by the combined policy of the Kurus (represented by the Pgndavgs) and Yādavas (represented by Krishna). In a later period, we see that the Magadhas re-emerged as the major political power overshadowing the Kurus. This phase is part of the well-established recorded history. Mahābhārata also gives a glimpse of other cultures like the Nāga. Most of the Kuru-Pancāla cities had an older name showing there Nāga origin, such as Hastinapura of the Kurus, which was formerly known as Nāga-pura. Here Nāga is taken as a synonym of Hasti viz. elephant. Yet it is interesting how the word Nāga came to mean both snake and elephant. The Maya Sabha of Indraprastha, the Pāṇḍava city, was built by clearing an earlier settlement of Nāgas at Khandava-prastha. The northern Pancāla city Ahichatra is named after name after Ahi (Nāga). It is tempting here to suggest a Kuru invasion into pre-existing Nāga territories. But many ancestors of the Kurus were Nāgas. We have the ancestral king Nahuṣa described as a Nāga. Pāṇḍava Bhīma's maternal ancestor was a Nāga. Thus, in close analysis, the Kurus and Nāgas turns out to be sharing kinships.

Rāmāyaṇa, as the name indicates is a narrative of travels (ayana) of Rāma, and thus is related to geography. At least, Vālmīkī when he named the epic as 'Rāmāyaṇa', which directly translates to the travels of Rāma, had this thought in his mind, and developed his epic to describe the extensive travels made by Rāma from Ayodhya to Lanka.

Divinity of Rāma and Kṛṣṇa

As Vaiṣnava Bhakti traditions spread, Rāma was counted as an Avatāra of Viṣṇu. This transformation is in agreement with the Dhārmic Vedāntic thought which states that divinity is inherent in every human and in every creature. It is up to any individual to express this divinity. Thus, the traditional Vaiṣnava view of seeing Rāma as a god, a divine being or an Avatāra of Viṣṇu, is actually not in conflict with the view of Rāma as a human hero. The true meaning of Avatāra is descendance, viz. the descend of higher consciousness into lower realms of consciousness, which can occur in the mind of any human being. Rāma can thus be seen as a human hero who, through the inner strength of his character brought forth the descend of the higher consciousness or Avatāra within himself, enabling him to be counted as an Avatgra of Viṣṇu. Hence the later generations revered him as a god. Same is the case of Kṛṣṇa, as revealed by Mahābhārata.

Hence, both the views about Rāma and Kṛṣṇa, viz. the view that they are human heroes of extraordinary capabilities, versus, the view that they were divine beings, gods or Avatāras—both can coexist without any mutual conflict. There is no conflict between the devotees who worship Rāma and Kṛṣṇa as gods and the historians who analyze the life of Rāma or Kṛṣṇa, based on the information available in our Itihāsās. The devotees (Bhaktās) and the traditionalists should accommodate the study of historicity of Rāma and Kṛṣṇa and the projects of dating Rāma and Kṛṣṇa in a linear historical time-line. This involves the historical analysis of the Rāmāyaṇa and Mahābhārata, focusing on the dating of events mentioned in them, including the birth and death of Rāma and Kṛṣṇa, using the data present in the narrative, which primarily contains the mention of the position of the planets, sun, moon, comets and stars in the sky. For this, the analysts and researchers use disciplines like archeoastronomy, archaeology, hydrology, climatology, bathymetry and so on.

Conversely, these analysts and researchers should be mindful of the sentiments of the traditionalists and the devotees. Mutual harmony between a researcher and a devotee is reinforced if both are able to subscribe to the higher philosophy of Vedanta which urges them to go beyond the imagery of Rāma or Kṛṣṇa to attain the ultimate divinity, which is within one's own self.

Aitihāsic literature and fossils

There are many similarities between the Aitihgsic literature and fossils. Just like fossils preserve signs of the existence of a creature that lived in the past, Aitihāsic literature preserve information about the people and their lives in the past, often distorted yet reconstruct-able. Just like fossils are deposited layer by layer, Aitihāsic literature is accumulated in layers after layers. By knowing in which fossil-layer a fossil belongs we are able to approximately know in which time the creature is fossilized. Same is more or less true with information crystallized inside layers of Aitihāsic literature. The Mahābhārata has several layers which were formed at different periods of time separated by centuries. Same is the case with the Rāmāyaṇa, the Purāṇas and the Vedas. Scholars are studying these layers of crystallized information to understand the life of people belonging to the period in which the layer was formed.

Every civilization had an obsession to become immortal. The Egyptians mummified the dead bodies of their kings and heroes to make them immortal. We find that even after thousands of years their bodies are preserved to today, achieving some sort of immortality. The Bhāratiyās on the other hand, created the Itihāsas, the Purāṇas and the Vedas. They added whatever they wanted to say into these literatures and preserved them through oral traditions, with great care, like the Egyptians preserved their mummies in the pyramids. Thus, the Indians gained immortality by constructing pyramids of literature like the Mahābhārata, the Rāmāyaṇa, the Vedas and the Purāṇas. Thus, we could see in Mahābhārata, the culture, the politics, the religion and the philosophy of the ancient people of Bhārata.

Aitihāsic personalities and distant light sources

Another analogy that comes into mind is the nature of Aitihgsic personalities and their similarities with distant light sources as explained by astronomy. In astronomy we know that some of the distant stars that we think as single are actually binary stars, multiple stars or sometimes even a galaxy of stars. Sometimes these stars that appear as one are never related and could be located at locations separated by light-years and appear as one as they happened to be on the same line of sight from us. This is true with some of the Aitihāsic personalities like Vyāsa and Vasistha. Due to their temporal-distance in the past they seem to us, when analyzing the Aitihāsic literature, to be a single person. But close study reveals them as a generation of people. Sometimes multiple personalities that lived at different ages and different places are fused together into one personality.

Transmission loss of information in Aitihgsic literature

Deep analysis of Itihāsas reveals that at their cores are actual events that occurred in some point of time in the distant past. Later, these turned into contemporary history. But unlike in our age, this historical information was transmitted from generation to generation through oral traditions. Information theory states that loss of information is inevitable due to the principle of entropy that maintains that any ordered system (coded-information being one example of an ordered system) is bound to lose its orderliness and tend to be chaotic. Ancient people who transmitted the epic history through oral traditions invented fables to fill the gaps that formed because of the missing information which was again due to information loss owing to the transmission loss. Thus, history turned into mythology.

A typical example is the lack of knowledge of actual number of people who participated in the Kurukshetra War. This was substituted by a table (a hymn) that explains the relations between various divisions of the army like Akṣauhini and Anīkini (MBH 1.2). If we follow this calculation we get an impossible figure (considering the human-population of that era) as the number of soldiers and animals who took part in the war. Some historians had used this impossibility to rule out the historicity of Kurukshetra War, dismissing it as a fable. By the same way, the lack of knowledge of exact duration of the war resulted in the myth that it took place in 18 days, making the war much more impossible to occur historically. This is the negative effect of adding fables to historical facts.

Sometimes the gaps in information is not due to transmission loss. The information required in a later stage is never transmitted initially but became a necessity subsequently. An example is the lack of information about the exact origin of the Kauravas and the Pāṇḍavas. This lead to the fable that Kauravas were all born out of a dead-fetus born by Gāṇḍhārī, which were divided into hundred pieces by Vyāsa and that the Pāṇḍavas were born of the five well known Devatās. The fables about the birth of Drona, Kripa, Dhristadyumna and Pāncālī are other such examples.

Sometimes absent information is never substituted by any fable but are approximated by other means. Examples are the names like Pāncālī and Gāṇḍhārī (and also Kaikeyi in Rāmāyaṇa). The original author (Vyāsa) seems to be ignorant about their actual maiden names. The name Pāncālī, Gāṇḍhārī and Kaikeyi were derived based on their mother-land viz the Pancala, Gāndhāra and Kekeya Kingdoms. Another name of Pāncālī, is Draupadi, which is derived from her father Drupada, the king of Pāncāla. Yet another name of Pāncālī is Kṛṣṇa, which could be the name by which she was called by her parents, but we can never be sure, since it can be a name derived from her physical appearance. She was darker in hue compared to other ladies and hence was called Krishna (the dark one). Same applies to Vasudeva Krishna and Krishna Dwaipāyana Vyāsa.

Steps taken to prevent the transmission loss

The ancient sages had devised a means to minimize the transmission loss by rendering the literature as poems and hymns, coded in a metric-system (Mātra:—guru and laghu sounds) so based on their phonetics. This is much like the check-sum used to ensure the integrity of transmitted information in digital transmission. Though this helped to reduce the distortions that occurred during oral transmission of epic literature, it could not eliminate the information-loss completely.

Similarly, one of the major occupation of the ancient sages and people who handled this epic literature though oral transmission was to assemble together at one place and render the whole epic committed in memory so that others can verify that they are having the same version and errors had not crept in. This tradition is still existing in India, in spite of the fact that the entire epic has already been written down and committed to text, and now into hypertext over Internet. The myth of Ganeúa writing down the Mahgbhgrata, as Vygsa rendered it from his memory is a glimpse of the stage at which the orally transmitted epic is written down into text for the first time, possibly by Gana-Patis (heads of the republics) of those ages.

Preservation effect of fables

There is a positive effect also in adding fables to historic facts. They serve to make the information more attractive and appealing which could encourage a society who were less inclined in preserving historical fact than in preserving stories that invoke a sense of wonder. The fiction part of the epic serves as an outer envelope that preserve the core historic information by continuous retelling over generations so that they reach us now (like a fruit is preserved by its outer covering, until it is ready to be consumed by its intended consumers). The ancient sages sometimes deliberately added these fables to the factual information to make the information long lived. This is a way of preserving information, which otherwise could have dissipated completely in course of a few centuries.

Comparing Illiad and Oddyssy to Mahābhārata and Rāmāyaṇa

Comparison of Illiad and Odyssey which are much less in size compared to Rāmāyaṇa and Mahābhārata, to the extent that the later ones are considered some-how to be a retelling of the former (Homeric) works, seems to be like comparing the stars like Sirius and Betelgeuse to the Sun. Due to proximity to Earth, the Sun is the most familiar star for people of Earth. But in absolute terms Sirius and Betelgeuse are obviously much larger and majestic than the Sun. Whoever says that Mahābhārata or Rāmāyaṇa are a retelling of Homeric works are doing this due to their greater familiarity with Homeric works and their lack of familiarity with the works of Vyāsa and Vālmīkī.

The Creation of AncientVoice

I was introduced to computers when I was in 9th standard in 1992. During 1993 to 1995 while doing pre-degree course I encounter unabridged versions of Mahabhgrata. Using that I created a database of place-names mentioned in Mahgbhgrata which contained more than 100 entries. During 1995 to 1999 while doing my graduation in Engineering College I used computer software to create digital maps of Bhāratavarsha to plot the newly analyzed place-names. From 2001 to 2006 I worked in ISRO. There I studied the journals containing the ISRO satellite imagery of the dried-up Sarasvati river basin. It is here where I first encountered the journals describing Dr. S.R. Rao's discovery of the submerged town of Dwarka. I expanded my maps with these new knowledge about Dwārakā and Sarasvatī.

While working in ISRO I explored internet to get more information about our Itihgsgs and it is when I realized that there is not much information available online on topics related to our culture while those about Greek epics were aplenty. I wanted to change this scenario. After many searches, in 2004 I encountered an online resource viz. Kisari Mohan Ganguli's English Translation of Mahābhārata, in the form of downloadable text files at the website named Sacred Texts made available by the tireless work of John Bruno Hare.[1] Using the full text of Mahābhārata available for free in this site, I created a Windows-Help-File system for Mahābhārata, enabling me to zero-in on any desired

[1] Sacred Texts—http://www.sacred-texts.com/hin/maha/index.htm

noun in Mahābhārata using the keyword search feature of help-file. Using this help-file as a tool I created articles focusing on each kingdom mentioned in the Mahābhārata, such as Kuru, Pāncāla, Kosala, Chedi, Matsya, Trigarta, Surasena and so on. I wanted to host it at some location in the internet so that internet will get filled with enough information about our Itihāsās. That is when I found Wikipedia where anyone can become editor and contribute articles. I uploaded my articles on Mahābhārata kingdoms to Wikipedia in a format understood by Wikipedia.[2] I authored 150 plus articles in Wikipedia describing each kingdom mentioned the Mahābhārata. This work continued in 2005 and 2006.

But since Wikipedia is not a place to publish original research, and because of the rampant vandalism quite common in the Wikipedia pages as it can be edited and modified by anyone, it became necessary for me to create a website of my own but with the same features offered by Wikipedia, such as, the interlinking thousands of nouns through hyperlinks with each noun expanding into an article of its own, where each such article connects with thousand other articles through noun to noun hyperlinks forming a connected network of articles expandable in the form of knowledge trees.

The website AncientVoice established in November 2009 was the result of this need. It was developed based on the approach outlined in the preceding sections. Initially I have created it to preserve my older works in Wikipedia. After creating a copy of all the articles, I wrote in Wikipedia, I concentrated my energy to create a Wiki for Mahābhārata. This involves creating a single-page article for each of the 2000 plus chapters of Mahābhārata, identifying the 7000 plus nouns in the Mahābhārata, connecting each occurrence of each of those 7000 plus nouns in any of the 2000 plus chapters of Mahābhārata through hyperlinks. I knew if I attempt to do it manually, it will take me many years. Hence, I automated the process by creating a software tool by coding in C++. I completed the development of software tool by January 2010. Using this tool, I generated the 2000 plus chapter-pages and 7000 plus noun-pages of Mahābhārata by parsing the full text of Ganguli's translation. These 9000 plus pages were then interconnected with an average of 100 hyperlink in each page. Each hyperlink represents a noun-occurrence. Thus, the entire Mahābhārata Wiki contains more than one million hyperlinks. The software tool dumped all this page as text files in Wiki format in a matter of four hours. All these files were then

---

[2] Wikipedia User Jijithnr—https://en.wikipedia.org/wiki/User:Jijithnr

systematically uploaded and the Wiki was completed in a matter of few weeks by around April 2010.

It still remains the only Mahābhārata Wiki available online.[3] Thus, a manual work of many years was reduced to a few hours. Wikipedia attempted to create a similar Mahābhārata Wiki as part of its Wikisource projects but it lacks the interconnecting hyperlinks and is still incomplete after 11 long years.[4] After the success of Mahābhārata Wiki in 2010 similar Wikis for Rāmāyaṇa, Ṛgveda, Yajurveda (both Kṛṣṇa and Sukla recensions), Sāmaveda, Atharvaveda and Vishnu Purāṇa were completed in 2011. There is no other site anywhere in the world with dedicated Wikis for any of these texts. Apart from these Wikis, analysis articles discussing the Veda, Itihāsa, Purāṇas, heroes like the five Pāṇḍavas, lineage trees of Ikshvākus, Ailās, Pūrus, Bharatās and Kurus, maps of Bhāratavarsha with its kingdoms, cities, towns, villages, rivers, forests, mountains etc and many paintings depicting various scenes from the Mahgbhgrata, all of these are hosted in the site. The total number of pages in the site now exceeds 23000.

Apart from AncientVoice, a similar website named Takshasila[5] was created for with Wikis for Iliad, Odyssey and Avestan texts like Vendidād, Visperad, Yasna, Yast and Siroza were created. Another site named Naalanda[6] with Wikis for the major Upanishads, Tamil text Tirukkural and Silappatikaram was created subsequently. My analysis of the Quantum Consciousness studies and other recent topics is published in yet another site named RecentVoice. A fourth website named Technospace containing my technical articles related to software is not updated now. AncientVoice Wiki Website is now the world's largest Wiki website dedicated for Veda Itihasa Puranas. The website has a structure similar to Wikipedia. But it is richer in information that Wikipedia in the area of Veda, Itihasa Puranas with highly detailed Bharatavarsha Maps containing the locations of kingdoms mentioned in the Veda-Itihasa-Puranas, illustrative paintings of personalities mentioned in it like Yudhisthira, Bhima, Arjuna and others. It contains comparative analysis of all major Puranas with respect to Mahabharata, Ramayana, the four Vedas and the Greek Text Iliad and Odyssey. It contains comparative analysis of all 18 Parvas of the Mahabharata. It contains lineage trees of dynasties like Ikshwakus of Ramayana and

[3] Mahābhārata Wiki of AncientVoice—http://ancientvoice.wikidot.com/source:mahabharata

[4] Incomplete Mahābhārata Wiki of Wikipedia Wiki-source—https://en.wikisource.org/wiki/The_Mahabharat

[5] Takshasila—http://takshasila.wikidot.com

[6] Naalanda—http://naalanda.wikidot.com

the Alia-Puru-Bharata-Kurus of the Mahabharata. It contains detailed analysis of the four Yugas of various lengths (4320000 years, 12000 years to 1 year).

The eight Wikis each dedicated for Mahabharata, Ramayana, Rgveda, Yajurveda (Krishna and Sukla Yajurvedas), Samaveda, Atharvaveda and Vishnu Purana resolve into sub sections like Parvas, Kandas, Mandalas, Adhyayas and Sargas. Each Adhyaya of Mahabharata or Sargas of Ramayana thus get one dedicated Wiki Page. Each unique noun in any of these texts also gets a dedicated page containing references to all occurrences of that noun in its respective text. Each of the unique occurrences of these nouns in the texts are hyperlinked back to the noun page. Around 7000 plus nouns of Mahabharata is analyzed and categorized and sub categorized into names of places, people, philosophical terms etc. Thus all the Wikis are well structured to form information networks to help deep research into these texts. It can also be read by readers as books sequentially without affecting the reading pleasure

The place names are plotted to create detailed the Bharatavarsha maps and names of kings are sequenced into the lineage trees. More than 100 individual research articles are also added to the site to provide a comprehensive analysis of Mahabharata, Ramayana, Vedas and

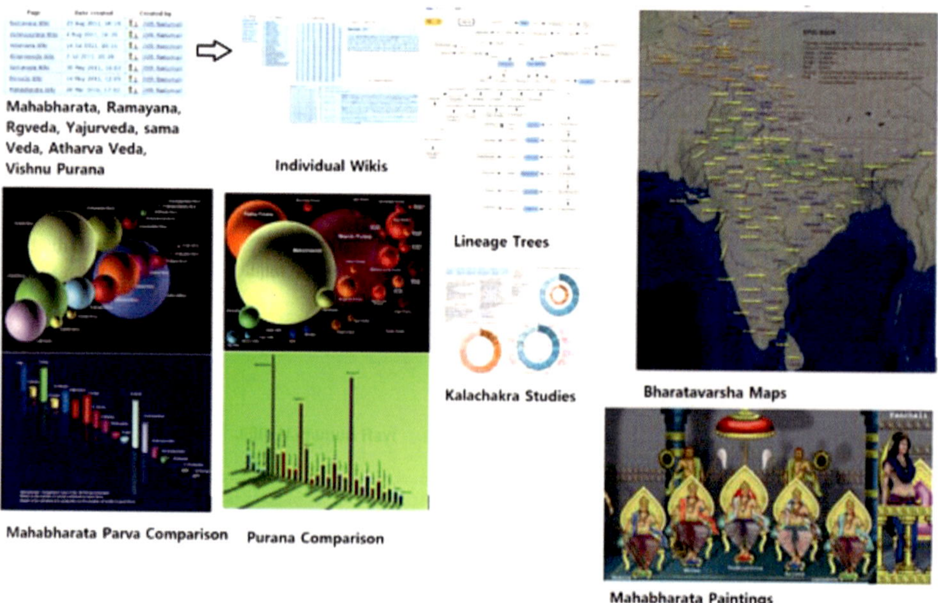

Figure illustrating the diversity of the AncientVoice Wiki Website.

Puranas. Thus this website is equivalent of 10 or more published books on Veda, Ithiāsa Purāṇas. Besides, unlike the case of printed books everything is cross-referenced and accessible online. Hence it is best described as a research platform which also simultaneously serves as a research tool, providing a solid foundations for researchers who are interested in studying Veda, Ithiāsa Purāṇas. It also helps novelists who wants to author novels on the topic of Veda, Ithiāsa, Purāṇas as it contains geographical references essential to set the plot and also good analysis of the events mentioned in them and the personalities mentioned inside them.

Conclusion

AncientVoice website is a well structured digital portal into the Veda Itihāsa Purāṇas with rich in data, analysis articles, diagrams, illustrations, comparison charts and digital maps of Bhāratavarsha. It is like a huge ocean of information. It is used as a reference site by researchers from different parts of the world. University research students, novelists writing novels based on Veda Ithiāsa Purāṇas and researchers in the academia are using the site for their research works. All the content in this site is published under Creative Commons Share Alike Attribution License. This allows any researchers to use data in this site without copyright related complications, by providing due credit to the website and its creator (myself). The site is made available for benefiting the entire research community and writers focusing on Bhāratiya Samskṛt literature, culture and tradition.

References

1. http://ancientvoice.wikidot.com/source:mahabharata

—×—

Examining Indian Culture and History on the Chessboard of Politics and Scholarship

Neera Misra

Abstract

It is disheartening to find that many Indians are ignorant of about the cultural history of their nation. As we travel through the past and present cultural status of our nation, correlating with its political journey, and the work of scholars, we get quite clear understanding of how invariably, and in most times, politics influenced scholarship and documentation. It is worthwhile to know how the creation and burial of historical facts and cultural identities has affected realistic understanding of national character and identity. This paper proposes to traverse through some historical periods of India, highlighting few significant political developments, to examine Indian Culture and History on the chessboard of politics and scholarship.'

One of the hottest debates among serious academicians today is the meaning of Bharata and 'Bharatriayata' that is India and 'Indian-ness'. What has led us to this state of affairs? This paper proposes to travel through some historical moments of India, to highlight few significant political developments. The matter gains importance due to the almost seventy years' propagation and promotion of misleading history of India, despite unshackling chains of suppression. Specific examples will draw our attention to the decades of distortions that show lopsided heritage legacies marring realistic knowledge. This paper pertains mostly to the developments of Post Independent India, through inference and activism in Education and Culture.

A nation's identity is reflected through its cultural and historical journey and related landmarks. Culture is the soul of any country, geography its backbone, philosophy the intellect and history its political legacy strength. To know one's country one has to know all these aspects factually, with correct perspectives. In this context, how does Bharat that is now India, fare? How many Indians know the real history, ancient geography or cultural journey of our country? This question is pertinent, as it is directly linked to politics and scholarship. Bharat is a land of heritage legacies and history spanning thousands of centuries. Yet, surprisingly our text books have almost five thousand years' history confined in a few pages whereas thousands of pages are devoted to a mere six hundred odd years of mediaeval invaders' rule at mostly north India ((1192–1857), and about ninety years of colonial rule (1857–1947) are covered in hundreds of pages. Almost three generations have been fed 'disinformation, half truths' and fallacious knowledge in the name of history and heritage. Politics of power, imported ideologies and vote bank politics have dented and agonized scholarship to immeasurable extent. 'Facts' of Itihasa have changed to 'myth', denigrating or deconstructing Bhartiya 'ancient wisdom' to promote 'limited cultural hegemony' of foreign rulers. At the geo-spatial level also the monuments aggressively promoted reflect only a few hundred years' history, whereas most ancient places lie in ruins for gradual decay and oblivion.

Controlling educational syllabi and dimensions of spatial cultural landscape changes many aspects of understanding of a nation's identity or even visible and widely known antiquity. Most affected is the individual's perception of his nation. Since the 'modern' concepts of democracy made inroads into established ancient pluralistic societies like that of Bharat, influencing an individual's or clan's 'thinking' became important for politicians to attain and retain power and rule by imposing their ideologies. Various methods have been used to change established norms or historical narratives in order to dominate the mind of people. Some of the prominent methods used have been to destroy and distort a society's established beliefs and systems by embedding deceptive narratives of history, and dwarfing, submerging, or even destroying geo-spatial spaces of their legacies of antiquity. 'Reading and seeing' creates perspectives, thus various means were used to camouflage, bury and obscure civilization and cultural identities. As we travel through the past, correlating with its political journey and the work of scholars, we get quite a clear understanding of how invariably, politicians have dominated and adversely influenced serious scholarship, including the documentation, preservation and conservation work in India.

Decisions and policies of political masters in power have a direct effect on the nation's centers of learning. Post partition, majority of the ruling politicians' perception of India was prejudiced by the trapping of invading foreigners' pressures and also based on 'colonial concepts', which clashed with Bhartiya civilization ethos. This led to disturbing the socio-cultural understanding of ground realities. Much misperception was injected into Indian education system, the cultural landscapes promotions, the bureaucracy and even the social engineering systems of independent India. Some landmark decisions taken by free India's political leaders like M.K. Gandhi, J.L. Nehru or even Indira Gandhi, has affected education system.. An examination of this from a purely scholastic point of view will reveal the political games and flaws that prevented dissemination of factual history of India to Indians. History records the players of this chess game, the grandmasters who checkmated 'Bharatiya scholarship'. A few examples reveal the maneuvers that led to massive structured historical deception about the oldest civilization.

Education shapes the mind and attitudes. It moulds the understanding of the national ethos too. Controlling dissemination of history is critical to any domineering ruler's policy, where tactics manipulate facts. The 'Latin rhetoricians called such a tactic *suppressio veri, suggestio falsi*.[1]

Politics in Penning History

Indian history is being viewed in official circles in the perspective of recent political developments. The official history of the freedom movement starts with the premises that India lost independence only in the eighteenth century and had thus an experience of subjection to a foreign power for only about a century. On the contrary, facts tell us that a large part of India lost independence about five centuries before, and merely changed masters in the eighteenth century. How this fact has materially affected the course of studying the freedom movement in India has been well documented in Prof. R.C. Mazumdar's History of Freedom Movement in India, Book I, Chapter III. We have two history books that elaborate the freedom movement of India, namely, the History of Freedom Movement in India by Prof. R.C. Mazumdar, and History of Freedom Movement in India by Dr. *Tara Chand.* These two books are a perfect example of this papers topic. Soon after independence, in 1948 Prof. Mazumdar put up a proposal to government of India to sponsor the writing of history of India through Indian perspective, with justification that free India should have history written by Indian scholars. On this request, in 1952 the government established a Board comprising of scholars and politicians as members. Prof. Mazumdar was appointed Director, with the task to draft the

---

[1] Bhyrappa, S.L., 2012, Article, 'What would be the Fate of Truth if a Historian takes Liberties like a Fiction Author?,' Folks Magazine.

proposed project. The first Education Minister, under Prime Minister Nehru, was a Maulana, Abdul Kalam Azad. Prof. Mazumdar's draft did not find favor with some of the Board members, as it mentioned historical facts unpalatable to many. The Board was dissolved and after some time a single person, Dr. Tara Chand, a bureaucrat with background of Mediaeval History and having close links with Nehru-Gandhi family, was assigned the task of writing the History of the Freedom Movement of India.

Prof. Mazumdar was shocked at the moves of the government. Dominance of politics paved the way for subjective history, to the detriment of scholarship, which essentially rests on honesty and truth. Political interference in academics started in free India, right from day one of 'freedom'. Rather than accept manipulated history, Prof. Mazumdar initiated his own project with likeminded colleagues and patrons, in full earnest and speed to write the factual History of the Freedom Movement in India, that covered three volumes. Moves of political ideologues to camouflage and submerge facts encountered the scholars' desire to ascertain, retain and reveal historical truths. Prof. Mazumdar's book had to be well in time to counter the official version of Dr. Tara Chand. We are fortunate that we have a source, in Prof. Mazumdar's books, published in 1962[2] to know the realities of our chequered history of India's long drawn freedom struggles, and many more aspects of our past.

At the stroke of midnight, on 14th August 1947, Indians thought they had left behind many hundreds of years' repression to finally be a free nation. The first Prime Minister Shri Jawahar Lal Nehru's, famous midnight speech reverberated with powerful phrases like, '... , India will awake to life and freedom ... when the soul of a nation, long suppressed, finds utterance ... At the dawn of history India started on her unending quest, and trackless centuries are filled with her striving and the grandeur of her success and her failures ... we cannot encourage communalism ...',[3] The source of *Bharat Ek Khoj*[4] could never really understand Bharat.

---

[2] Mazumdar, R.C., 1962, History of the Freedom Movement in India, Firma K.L. Mukhopadhyaya, Calcutta.

[3] Tryst with Destiny "was a speech delivered by Jawaharlal Nehru, the first Prime Minister of independent India, to the Indian Constituent Assembly in The Parliament, on the eve of India's Independence, towards midnight on 14 August 1947. It spoke on the aspects that transcend India's history. Wikipedia-.

[4] *Bharat Ek Khoj* is a 53–episode Indian historical drama based on the *book* The Discovery of India (1946) by Jawaharlal *Nehru—Wikipedia.*

This decisive turning point in focus of Indian education system had changed the course of teaching and understanding India's authentic past, its valid cultural journey. The tale of this incident has itself acquired such a historical status that details are worth reading, as recorded by Prof. R.C. Mazumdar himself.[5] This will explain the related moves that percolated to the newly established institutes of higher learning, layered with skewed outlook and 'socialist communal' patronage. Unfortunately the ideological bias seeped the roots of organizations national universities and the slanted approach in research gradually influenced the young towards misperceived notions of Indian civilization, culture and history.

One must also note here the critical role played by some European international entities, for example the likes of Schools of Divinity which were created primarily as a Seminary. In the name of clinical study of all religions these Schools also deconstruct other historical or religious texts. The Indian Epic Mahabharata has been reduced to a mere 'mythical' religious text, ignoring its narrative 'Itihasa' of ancient Bharat. The foundation of the academic discipline called Cultural Studies, camouflaged as ultra-modern academic theories of Humanities, have in reality been a powerful tool of Western Academics, to offer an anti-establishment, anarchist, rebellious, communist philosophy to the Indian aspirants of education. The discipline works towards the motto: "Cultural Studies does not study culture, it makes one.[6] Their fundamental commitment is of locating an intellectual and political space for the communist ideology. Their packaging attracted ultra modern rulers who were the fine tuned Indian disciples of systematized colonial mindset. An undercurrent of influence from the 'cultural hegemony' propagandist groups invaded the Indian psyche through mainstream education institutes. The ancient Indian social systems and beliefs, that had cemented its people for centuries, were attacked through targeted 'ideological invasions' into Bharat.

The Bhyrappa Case[7]

The target was not only the College and University level, but even the schools texts. A fate similar to Prof Mazumdar befell Prof. S.L. Bhyrappa, Reader of Philosophy of Education, at NCERT (National

---

[5] Introduction to his book, History of Freedom Movement in India Vol.1, Vidya Bhartiya Bhawan, 1862.

[6] Deshpande, Prassana A., 'Cultural Studies'—An Academic Discipline of Anti-India Politics, 2016.

[7] https://www.prekshaa.in/dr-s-l-bhyrappa-distorting-indian-history

Council for Education Research & Training), Ministry of Education of Government of India. He too was ousted out of a Committee on reforming school text curriculum of history, languages and social studies, planned under garb of national integration.

'During the year 1969–70 the Central Government under Mrs. Indira Gandhi established a committee under the Chairmanship of G. Parthasarathy, a diplomat close to Nehru-Gandhi family. Its task was to integrate the nation through education.'[8] At the first meeting of the committee its Chairman Mr. G. Parthasasthy explained that it is their duty to weed out the seeds of thorns from school texts of history, social studies, languages etc that act as barriers to national integration. The unstated objective was to remove specific historical facts from History text, like Aurangzeb destroyed temples or Muslims forcefully converted and tortured Hindus etc. Prof Bhyrappa argued that facts are sacrosanct to education, especially history and if texts have information of Aurangzeb's atrocities they also have narratives of Akbar's positive acts of outreach to Hindus, appreciation of Bhartiya culture and proactive administration that endeavored to take along all communities. Unconvinced by this, Shri Parathasastry again tried to influence Prof Bhyrappa to accept his proposal. When Prof Bhyrappa did not relent the meeting ended. Soon a new Committee was created and the eminent scholar of Education Philosophy was moved out, for standing firm on principles of truth. This is how another scholar was shunted out for upholding academic integrity and honesty by opposing political interference in matters of value based teaching.

The above examples show that the 1947 independence of India gave no significance to eminent Indian historians. It is equally true that it also did not give any freedom from oppression to Sanatan or Hindu sacred places that had for long been lying in oblivion and decay.[9] Beginning 1947 till date they are forced to lie in ruins or wither away. They are languishing and suffering pangs of deliberate neglect, as we learn from events of history.

The Politics of Somnath Temple restoration

Many of us are aware about the history of the destruction of the famous Somnath Temple, but very few however may know of the extreme opposition faced in rebuilding this sacred and once hallowed place of

---

[8] Bhyrappa, S.L., 2012, Article, 'What would be the Fate of Truth if a Historian takes Liberties like a Fiction Author?', Folks Magazine.

[9] **L.K. Advani** in **L.K. Advani's Blog** October 11, 2013, 4:42 PM IST India TOI.

worship and pride. Filled with obstructions at every stage, the tale of restoration of the Somnath Temple is painful and shocking as it involves supposedly 'learned and liberated' people who took charge of the nation. The intrigues reveal how the 1947 freedom at midnight rather saw a sad sunrise of intense political moves to further subjugate and bury ancient Bhartiya history and important historical places. In 1922 K.M. Munshi, a Minister in Nehru cabinet, had written an article on the painful site of demolished Somnath, narrating how the temple held on firmly standing out like "Desecrated, burnt and battered", ... "a monument to our humiliation, and ingratitude."[10] Munshi article brings out the pain of every Bhartiya.

Considering long raised public demands to restore the iconic holy spot where Lord Krishna left his mortal remains, soon after independence Sardar Patel and V.N. Gadgil went to Prabhas Patan and visited the ruins of Somanath Temple,. Here N.V. Gadgil requested Sardar for its restoration. Same evening at a public meeting, the Home Minister announced that '...we have decided that Somanath should be reconstructed...That the Government of India has decided to rebuild the temple and install the shrine."[11] The process for creation of a holistic development project was initiated immediately. Alas, the three stalwart initiators was unaware of the motivated political maneuvers that were waiting to sabotage this. The then Education Minister, Maulana, controlling Culture under his Education Ministry, insisted that the Somnath Temple remains be kept under Archaeological Survey of India (ASI) as 'ruins'. Thus he suggests 'subjugation' of Hindu sacred places, whereas no such idea for the Muslim shrines and mosques where ASI was spending large amounts in their renovation and maintenances. When the matter came up at Union Cabinet meeting, the so called liberal secular Prime Minister Nehru exposed his leanings as he backed Maulana's opinion, opposing the Home Minister Sardar Patel's project of reviving India's glorious landmark temple. After many heated exchanges the matter reached the eternal diplomat, M.K. Gandhi, who in his characteristic tactful style stated that temple should be re-built but not with government money. Patel and Munshi's renewed argument that government under same ASI was funding Muslim shrines and mosques across India, did not hold good for even the Nehru- Gandhi duo. Sardar

---

[10] Dr. Munshi's historic letter to Pandit Nehru: V.P. Menon calls it 'a masterpiece' October 11, 2013, 4:42 PM IST L.K. Advani in L.K. Advani's Blog India TOI Internet articles (through VIF).

[11] L.K. Advani in L.K. Advani's Blog October 11, 2013, 4:42 PM IST India TOI.

Patel remained resolute and sensitive to strong and widespread Hindu sentiments for rebuilding the sacred Shrine.

On 15 December, 1950 Sardar Patel passed away, and Nehru was now openly critical of the project, of K.M. Munshi and V.N. Gadgil, terming their initiatives as '*Hindu revivalism*'.[12] This sting was too much for Munshi who responded to Nehru with a terse long letter. This is how we have the famous Munshi papers, telling us the tale of the games politicians play with history and culture of a civilization that was once again trying to breathe in its 'free' land. This long letter of 24 April, 1951 addressed to Prime Minister Nehru detailed events leading to decisions on reconstruction of the sacred symbol of national pride. But for this letter, few would have known the realities of historical decisions that change the course of nations. Munshi candidly details the issues, hitting the nail on the head with—"... that the Government gave subsidies and grants to thousands of mosques and tombs and there could be nothing objectionable if it spent a little money in restoring a Hindu temple. I understood secularism to mean the equality of all religions..."[13]

However the success of the determined tri-stalwarts in revival of Somnath Temple had deeper unfortunate implications for Bharat. It saw the beginning of the end of any further restoration or rebuilding of ancient places of India. Hibernation in ruinous state for landmarks of Bhartiya 'Itihasa' became the norm. Even the few significant ones at ASI's Nationally Protected historical cities of the Epic 'itihasa' still suffer grave neglect. The chessboard of truth and politics saw a game of nerves that exposes the pseudo-secularism roots in India. The repercussions of this episode, immortalized in the Munshi papers, had far reaching implications. They still reverberate in ASI's policies and actions. The long term impact was that Ministry of Culture, Ministry of Education, Archaeological Survey of India all worked extra hard to keep ancient India in ruins and shifted focus to promote mediaeval India in books, and also at the geo-spatial landscape of archaeological sites.

The policy that Maulana Azad had propounded for keeping Somnath Temple in ruins was adopted at all India level for all ancient Indian historical sacred places, keeping them under wraps under ASI so no one can even privately renovate them. However the renovation of Muslim places, again with government has continued till date. Thus little wonder that today we cannot recognize the Indraprastha of Pandavas, or Dilllika

---

[12] Wikipedia.

[13] Dr. Munshi's historic letter to Pandit Nehru, dated 24 April, 1951. .... Also reproduced in Makkhan Lal, 2008, *Secular Politics Communal Agenda*, pp.150–154.

or Dillipuri of Tomars. Rather Purana Pandav Qila has not only been transformed into a purely Mughal monument, but also fallaciously promoted merely as 'Dinpanah' of Humayun, subverting its ancient identity as Indrapath Pandav Qila, that invader Humayun took over, as documented by Akbar's historian Abul Fazal. Strangely, the Afghan ruler Sher Shah Suri is also overlooked, even though the existing structures at Purana Qila are from Sher Shah Suri regime. Purana Qila has no museum to show and list the hundreds of rulers who exercised power from this most ancient fort of our capital city. In fact the DPR of AKTC for the so called Humayun's Tomb interpretation starts Delhi's history from Sultanate period, thereby creating misperceptions about antiquity of 'Indrapath' that Humayun occupied.

As Education ministry wiped out great historical personalities that fought invasions for thousands of years, ASI further blurred Indraprastha and other significant ancient sites. While text books glorified invaders as the great Mughals, small citadels and cantonments of invaders became cities of 'so called great rulers'. It is no surprise to that ruins linked to Khilji, Humayun, Shahjahan etc became favorites for ASI preservation, renovation and recreation, highlighting India's limited subjectively scripted past. Tourism focused on mediaeval structures, while pre-Sultanat ancient forts like Lal Kot or Rai Pithora and ancient temples of marvelous art and architecture hidden in brazen neglect. Qutub Minar submerged Ganesha and beautifully carved temple pillars. Of the hundreds of sacred places left in ruins how many have survived, how many succumbed to natural calamities or destroyed due human encroachments or occupation is difficult to fathom. The pathetic state of Hastinapura, Kampilya, Indraprastha gives an idea of the policy of continued subjugation of Bharatiya legacies.

Generally Indians take pride in speaking of a five thousand year old civilization, but the visible is contrary to reality. Today a visitor to India's capital Delhi, sees many small and big decorated, lit up monuments, that create an impression that Delhi is just a few hundred years' years old mediaeval city, as there is not a single ASI sponsored place in Delhi that prominently promotes its real history of over about five thousand years, when Pandavs established Indraprastha, as recorded in our texts? The Maulana set in motion the idea to play differently with historical places of antiquity once again, after the onslaughts of the Gazni and Aurangzeb. All invaders after 1192, whether from Muslim world or European world came with strong sectarian ideas of religion which they wished to impose on Bharat. Then free India promoted fallacious history, created built heritage to match that, continuously throttling any attempt to revive glorious past of the world's oldest civilization. In n effect for centuries India checkmated Bharat. This is the time for corrective historical action to rectify the blunders and faulty policies that let to them, Nourishing and preserving roots of History, Civilization and Culture are intrinsic to identity of a nation and its peoples. As said by Winston Churchill, 'A nation that forgets its past has no future'.

References

1. Advani, L.K., 2013, Dr. Munshi's historic letter to Pandit Nehru: V.P. Menon calls it 'a masterpiece' October 11, 2013, 4:42 PM IST L.K. Advani in L.K. Advani's Blog | India | TOI, Internet article (through VIF), Wikipedia.
2. Chand, Tara, 1961, *History of the Freedom Movement in India*, Ministry of Information and Broadcasting, Government of India.
3. K.M. Munshi, 1922, in East and West. As quoted in 'Somanath: Fulfilment of a Collegian's Dream', *Bhawan's Journal*, January 1, 1967.
4. K.M. Munshi, 1967, *Pilgrimage to Freedom,* Appendix 105, p.560, Ibid.
5. K.M. Munshi, 1951, *Pilgrimage to Freedom,* pp.560–64.
6. K.M. Munshi's letter to Jawaharlal Nehru dated 24 April 1951. In K.M. Munshi, above. Also reproduced in Makkhan Lal, 2008, *Secular Politics Communal Agenda,* pp.150–154.
7. Mazumdar, R.C., 1962, History of the Freedom Movement in India, Firma K.L. Mukhopadhyaya, Calcutta
   Internet—https://www.prekshaa.in/dr-s-l-bhyrappa-distorting-indian-history
8. N.V. Gadgil, 1968, *Government From Inside*, Meerut, pp.185–86; (Views expressed are of the author and do not necessarily reflect the views of the VIF) Ain-e-Akbari, Abul Fazal.
9. Oak, Milind, 2016, Jaagtik Vichar Prabhavo Ke Sandharbha Mein Hindu Vichardhara, Bharat Ki Bhartiya Avadharna, Vimarsh Prakashan,
10. Prassana, Deshpande,A., 2016, 'Cultural Studies'—An Academic Discipline of Anti-India Politics, Bharat Ki Bhartiya Avadharna, Vimarsh Prakashan, S.L. Byrappa on Distorting History—'What would be the Fate of Truth if a Historian takes Liberties like a Fiction Author?' This is an abridged translation of the original; it first appeared in *Folks Magazine* on 20 May 2012. Also direct from discussions with Dr. S.L. Byrappa in 2018 at New Delhi.
11. Thakur, Narendra, 2016, Bharat Ki Bhartiya Avadharna, Vimarsh Prakashan, Article
12. Vaidya, Manmohan 2016, Preface, Bharat Ki Bhartiya Avadharna, Vimarsh Prakashan.

—×—

Biographies of Authors

Banerji, Debashish

Debashish Banerji is the Haridas Chaudhuri Professor of Indian Philosophy and Culture and Doshi Professor of Asian Art at the California Institute of Integral Studies. He is also the program chair in the East-West Psychology department. He obtained his PhD in Art History from the University of California, Los Angeles. He has edited a book on the Indian poet Rabindranath Tagore and is the author of two books: *The Alternate Nation of Abanindranath Tagore* (Sage, 2010) and *Seven Quartets of Becoming: A Transformational Yoga Psychology Based on the Diaries of Sri Debashish* (DK Printworld and Nalanda International, 2012). debbanerji@yahoo.com

Bhatt, Purnima Mehta

Purnima Mehta Bhatt is Professor Emerita of History of history, anthropology and interdisciplinary studies at Hood College, USA, where she has taught since 1977. Dr. Bhatt is the author of numerous peer reviewed papers and five books: *Scholar's Guide to Washington D.C.: African Studies; 'Reminiscences'*, Zubaan Publications; '*Sharadabehn Mehta: Una Mujer Exceptional en al India de su Tiempo', Her Space, Her Story: Exploring the Stepwells of Gujarat*, 2014, *Womens' Leadership in Chaotic Environments*, 2016 *The African Diaspora in India: Assimilation, Cultural Change and Survivals* (Routledge), 2017. kbhatt@mindspring.com

Das, Sonia

Sonia Das is Junior Research Fellow at the National Institute of Advanced Studies (NIAS) in a project titled "Advancing Landscape Archaeology Using High-resolution Digital Elevation Models" (funded by SERB-DST) studying topography of Bodhgaya, Vikramashila, Vaishali, Patna and their environs and pursuing a PhD in Trans-Disciplinary University. sonia.civil@gmail.com

Dutta, Shatarupa

Shatarupa Dutta has recently completed her post-graduation from in Historical Studies from Nalanda University, Rajgir, Bihar. Her areas of interest include Archaeology, Asian Cultural Trends and Networks, Comparative Religion Studies, and Anthropology. She has worked as an intern in the Archaeological Survey of India. Her master's research was focused on the Buddhist archaeology in Bengal region which she wishes to expand further in the future. shatarupa.dutta@nalandauniv.edu.in

Gaur, A.S.

A.S. Gaur is a research scholar at CSIR-National Institute of Oceanography, Goa asgaur@nio.org

Jairam, Rajani

Rajani Jairam is currently working as the Professor of Sanskrit and Dean (Student Welfare) of Jain University. With a doctorate on the topic, "Mahabharata—A Transcultural Study from Bangalore University, she has to her credit 72 paper presentations and 61 publications."
Email: rajanijairam@gmail.com

Janatkal, Gautam

Gautam Janatkal has a MA in Numismatics & Archaeology, University of Mumbai. He is a regular Contributor to Numismatic bulletins of South Indian Numismatic Society, Karnataka Numismatic Society and IIRNS Nashik. He has delivered many talks in theDepartment of History in various colleges in Bengaluru. As a Numismatic Consultant for major auction house in India. gautamjr@gmail.com

Jijith, Nadamuri Ravi

Nadamuri Ravi Jijith is a former scientist of ISRO who worked as part of the Chandrayan1 study phase. Currently engaged in the geographical analysis of Mahābhārata. He owns the web-portal Ancient Voice. As an artist he has visualized many scenes from the Mahābhārata exhibited in different conference venues. Combining the art and software expertise he is engaged in creating Virtual Avataras of Itihgsa personalities in Virtual Reality. Currently he works for Wipro as a Creative Director focusing on creative expression through the fusion of Virtual Reality and Artificial Intelligence. Jijith.nr@gmail.com

Lakkana, Muralidhar

Muralidhar Lakkanna (b.1973) holds Doctor of Philosophy from National Institute of Technology Karnataka, Master of Philosophy from Alagappa University, Master of Technology Vesweshwaraiah Technological University and Master of Management from Pondicherry University. Presently he is Advanced Manufacturing Research fellow at National Institute of Advanced Studies, Bengaluru. lmurali.research@yahoo.com

Lamb, Ramdas

Ramdas Lamb is a Professor of Religion at the University of Hawai'i. From 1969 through 1978, he was a sadhu in the Ramananda Sampraday in northern India, and he remains a householder member of the order. After earning his PhD (University of California, Santa Barbara, 1991), he began teaching at UH. Some of his publications include, Imagining Hagiographies in Chhattisgarh, in *Hagiography in Abrahamic and Dharmic Traditions: Manifesting Sanctity and Truth*. Academic Publications, 2016, Symbols: Rām.in Brill's Encyclopedia of Hinduism. Vol.5. Brill Academic Publishers, 2013, Yoga and Higher Education: Adding Concentration, Clarity, and Compassion to Learning.
Ramdas214@gmail.com

Mahanta, Namrata Rathore

Namrata Rathore Mahanta teaches at Mahila Mahavidyalaya, Banaras Hindu University, Varanasi. She is the author of V.S. Naipaul Indian Trilogy (2004). For the last few years she has been working on women and Hinduism She has worked on two UGC Major Research Projects: on women's vratas (2007) and on the iconography of Indian nationalism (2009). Her recent work includes entries for The Encyclopedia of Indian Religions ed. Arvind Sharma (2018).

Misra, Neera

Neera Misra is an Independent Research Scholar, with a focus on the Vedic and epic periods and its socio-cultural impacts. She is the Founder Trustee and Chairperson of Draupadi Dream Trust Edited books are Papers on How Deep Are Roots of Indian Civilization, Indraprastha Revisited in 2017, Draupadi and Her Panchala: Reasserting their place in History, Mahabharata Manthan; A Critical Revisit to Tangible and Intangible Heritage, Felicitating an Archaeologist, B.B. Lal and The Mahabharata: Antiquity. Neera dt@draupaditrust.org

Nagarkar, Sneha

Sneha Nagarkar is a Mumbai based freelance lecturer of Ancient Indian Culture and Archaeology and an independent researcher. She has done her Masters in Ancient Indian History, Culture and Archaeology from Deccan College Post Graduate and Research Institute, Pune in 2010. sneha.itihaas@gmail.com

Nandagopal, Choodamani

Choodamani Nandagopal is an Art Historian with 22 publications on ancient Indian arts. She is the first Nehru Fellow at Victoria and Albert Museum London, UNESCO Fellow for Art History, UNSW (Sidney) Fellow, University of Exeter Fellow for her research on the study of suburban culture. She set departments of Art History and Cultural Studies and engaged in teaching assignments in Indian and universities abroad. She is the general secretary of Dr. S.R. Rao Memorial Foundation. choodamani.nandagopal@gmail.com

Phuong, Tran Ky

Tran Ky Phuong is a former curator of the Museum of Cham Sculpture in Da Nang, Vietnam (1978–98); currently he is a researcher of the Center for Cultural Relationship Studies in Mainland Southeast Asia (CRMA Center) of Chulachomklao Royal Military Academic, Thailand and at the APSARA Authority, Siem Reap. His books include *Champa Iseki/Champa Ruins* (co-authored) *Vestiges of Champa Civilization*, *Vibrancy in Stone: Masterpieces of the Danang Museum of Cham Sculpture* (co-edited).
Trankyphuong.cham@gmail.com

Potdar, Vithal. D

Vithal. D Potdar holds an MA and PhD in Ancient Indian History & Epigraphy, Karnatak University, Dharwad. Presently, he is working as Senior Research Associate in The Mythic Society, Bengaluru. Vital.potdar@gmail.com

Rajani, M.B.

M.B. Rajani is an Assistant Professor at NIAS, Bangalore, a Homi Bhabha Fellow and member of Indian National Young Academy of Science. Rajani's research interests are in the area of Landscape Archaeology. She uses space based remote sensing images to interpreting earth's surface and subsurface features in order to extract information that enhances our understanding of the archaeology of an area. mbrajani.nias@gmail.com

Rao, Nalini

Nalini Rao, PhD in Art History (UCLA) and PhD in Ancient History and Archaeology (University of Mysore), is Prof. of World Art in Soka University of America, Ca, USA, Her publications include *Boundaries and Transformations, Sangama, Contours of Modernity (co-authored), Royal Imagery and Networks of Power at Vijayanagara*: and (ed.) *Sindhu-Sarasvati Civlilization: New Perspectives, The Hindu Monastery in South India*, Rowman and Littlefield, NY, 2020. nrao@soka.edu

Sanket, Purnanand

Purnanand Sanket has an MA Numismatics & Archaeology, University of Mumbai. He received the Nicholas Lowick Fellowship by Royal Numismatic Society in 2014. He is a Guest Speaker in various History colleges in Bengaluru and is a regular Contributor to Numismatic bulletins of South Indian Numismatic Society and IIRNS Nashik. Purnanand's current research focus is on the coinage of Hyder Ali and Tipu Sultan. purnanands@gmail.com

Sastry, B.V.K.

B.V.K. Sastry is a senior 'researcher' in several disciplines related to Sanskrit and Yoga studies. Traditionally trained in 'shaastra- sampradaya' system, he holds a PhD in Sanskrit. Significant amongst his contributions are (i) Inputs to 'Vedic Unicode proposal'—at Brown University (ii) Development of Fully online Sanskrit education courses for Florida International University, Miami. Dr. Sastry holds a US patent related to 'Sanskrit applications in Computers'. He serves as CEO of Yoga-Samskrutham University, Florida, USA. Sastry.bvk@gmail.com

Sharma, Preetee

Preetee Sharma teaches in the Department of history Cotton University, Guwahati, Assam as an assistant professor. She received her doctorate degree from the Center for Historical Studies, Jawaharlal Nehru University (JNU), New Delhi, on the Brahmaputra Valley of Assam with particular emphasis on the pottery (5th–17th century CE). Preetee.chs@gmail.com

Shastri, Yajneshwar Sadashiv

Yajneshwar Sadashiv Shastri is internationally known scholar of Indian Philosophy, Religion and Sanskrit. Dr. Shastri (former Vice Chancellor of Sanchi University of Buddhist-Indic Studies). Dr. Shastri was the former Director of University School of Psychology, Education and Philosophy, Gujarat University, Ahmedabad, India. He has more than 17 books such as

'Foundation of Hinduism', *'Traverses on Less Trodden Path of Indian Philosophy and Religion'*, *Mahayansutralankara of Asanga—A study in Vijnanavada Buddhism*, *Selient Features of Hindu Culture*, *Prashamaratiprakarana of Umaswati Vacaka* etc. He is the chief Editor of Ishavasya Upnishad with 51 Sanskrit Commentaries and Chief Editor of Shri Lalitatrishati—Shankarabhashya. Yajnashstri48@yahoo.com

Singh, Kundan

Dr. Kundan Singh is faculty at Sofia University, Palo Alto. He has authored The *Evolution of Integral Yoga: Sri Aurobindo, Sri Ramakrishna, and Swami Vivekananda* and book chapters in "Beyond Mind: The Future of Psychology as Science," "Beyond Postmodernism: Towards a Future Psychology," "Beyond Postmodernism: Towards a Future Psychology" and "Sri Aurobindo's Invalidation of the Aryan Invasion Theory and Contemporary Western Archaeological Evidence" (forthcoming). forkundan@hotmail.com

Sivasubramanian, Sivaram

Sivaram Sivasubramanian is a PhD student on Cosmological aspects in Ancient Indian Scriptures limited to Vedas and Upanishads, Puranas and Yoga Vasista at Jain University. Sivaram has a MSC degree in Chemistry, from IIT, Chennai, 1997. He is Founder of Satyachetana. He has worked as Sr. Mentor-Cyber Security, Accenture as Sr. Manager-GRC and is one of the inventors for a patent issued by USPTO (US Patent No: 7,865,382) and recipient of Accenture Inventor Award in 2011. sivr.sss30@gmail.com

Suchiang, Evelinda

Evelinda Suchiang is in the Department of Philosophy, Kiang Nangbah Government College, Assam and has studied the history of Indian philosophy and is particularly interested in the social history of Meghalaya. The relation between anthropology, women and ritual is a neglected area of study that Evelinda attempts to explore. suchiangevelinda@gmail.com

Suganya, Kulli

Kulli Suganya is a Conservation Architect and currently a PhD scholar at NIAS, Bangalore. Her heritage conservation career involved documentation and condition assessment of ancient temples. Her research interest is in understanding ancient water features and built forms in archaeological landscape using geo-spatial tools. kuilisuganya@gmail.com

Varasani, Vinay

Vinay Varasani is a writer,an architect. He has co-translated 'The Eternal Elixir' from Telugu to English, along with senior journalist and translator, Smt. Ambika Ananth. They are currently working on translating 'Manidveepa Varnana' to English under 'Rishi Peetham' banner. Vinay is a Vainika—Veena player, a lyricist and has written pallavis in Carnatic music, that have been tuned and sung by the eminent musicians: Ranjani and Gayatri. He has founded a start-up, 'Unbind', which aims to bridge the gap between academics and practice in design. Vinay313@gmail.com

Vungsonching, Tombing

Tombing Ms. Vungsonching is finishing her first year at St. Joseph's College, Bangalore where she is doing her Masters in MA (Economics). She completed her Bachelor's degree with a triple major in History, Economics and Political Science at Kristu Jayanti College, Bangalore. She is currently doing her internship at NIAS. chiching.tombing@gmail.com